FUTURE ADVANCED

Second Edition

Series Consultants
Sarah Lynn
Ronna Magy
Federico Salas-Isnardi

Learning Expert
Lia Olson

Authors
Christine Drieling
Katherine Edwards
Hilary Hodge
Tamara Jones
Kristine Kelly
Lia Olson
Geneva Tesh

Future Advanced
English for Work, Life, and Academic Success
Copyright © 2020 by Pearson Education, Inc.
All rights reserved. No part of this publication may be reproduced, stored in a retrieval system, or transmitted in any form or by any means, electronic, mechanical, photocopying, recording, or otherwise, without the prior permission of the publisher.

Pearson Education, 221 River Street, Hoboken, NJ 07030 USA

Staff credits: The people who made up the *Future* team, representing content development, design, manufacturing, marketing, multimedia, project management, publishing, rights management, and testing, are Jennifer Castro, Dave Dickey, Gina DiLillo, Warren Fischbach, Pamela Fishman, Gosia Jaros-White, Joanna Konieczna, Michael Mone, Mary Perrotta Rich, Katarzyna Starzyńska-Kościuszko, and Joseph Vella.

Text composition: ElectraGraphics, Inc.
Cover Design: EMC Design Ltd
Illustration credits: ElectraGraphics, Inc.
Photo credits: See Credits page 296.
Audio: CityVox
Development: Publishing Solutions LLC

Library of Congress Cataloging-in-Publication Data
A catalog record for the print edition is available from the Library of Congress.

ISBN-13: 9780135278352 (Student Book with App and MyEnglishLab)
ISBN-10: 013527835X (Student Book with App and MyEnglishLab)

ISBN-13: 9780134537894 (Student Book with App)
ISBN-10: 0134537890 (Student Book with App)

1 2020

Contents

To the Teacher iv

About the Series Consultants and Learning Expert vii

Unit Tour viii

Scope and Sequence xvi

Correlations xxii

Acknowledgments xxiv

UNIT 1   The Power of Goals 1

UNIT 2   Getting a Job 21

UNIT 3   The Thoughtful Consumer 41

UNIT 4   At Peak Performance 61

UNIT 5   Affordable Housing 81

UNIT 6   When Nature Is in Charge 101

UNIT 7   Protecting the Planet 121

UNIT 8   The Digital Age 141

UNIT 9   Health in the Balance 161

UNIT 10   Navigating Healthcare 181

UNIT 11   Citizenship 201

UNIT 12   Rights and Responsibilities 221

My Soft Skills Log 241

Writing Models and Templates 243

Grammar Review 273

Audioscript 281

Index 292

Credits 296

To the Teacher

Welcome to *Future: English for Work, Life, and Academic Success*

Future is a six-level, standards-based English language course for adult and young-adult students. The 21st-century curriculum in *Future*'s second edition provides students with the contextualized academic language, strategies, and critical-thinking skills needed for success in workplace, life, and academic settings. *Future* is aligned with the requirements of the Workforce Innovation and Opportunity Act (WIOA), the English Language Proficiency (ELP) and College and Career Readiness (CCR) standards, and the National Reporting System (NRS) level descriptors. Competency- and skill-based standards are incorporated in the curriculum at every level of *Future*'s second edition, providing a foundation for academic rigor, research-based teaching strategies, corpus-informed language, and the best of digital tools.

In revising the course, we listened to hundreds of *Future* teachers and learners and studied the standards for guidance. *Future* continues to be the most comprehensive English communication course for adults, with its signature scaffolded lessons and multiple practice activities throughout. *Future*'s second edition provides enhanced content, rigorous academic language practice, and cooperative learning through individual and collaborative practice. Every lesson teaches the interpretive, interactive, and productive skills highlighted in the standards.

Future Advanced is the highest level of the *Future* program. *Future Advanced* builds upon the language, competencies, strategies, and skills developed in the previous levels of *Future*. The rigorous and relevant curriculum prepares students to transition to higher levels of civic engagement, successful employment, and high-school equivalency and college and career preparation coursework.

Future's Instructional Design

Learner Centered and Outcome Oriented

The student is at the center of *Future*. Lessons start by connecting to student experience and knowledge, and then present targeted skills in meaningful contexts. Varied and dynamic skill practice progresses from controlled to independent in a meticulously scaffolded sequence.

Headers highlighting Depth of Knowledge (DOK) terms are used throughout *Future* to illuminate the skills being practiced. Every lesson culminates in an activity in which students apply their learning, demonstrate their knowledge, and express themselves orally or in writing. A DOK glossary for teachers includes specific suggestions on how to help students activate these cognitive skills.

Future Advanced utilizes current relevant topics to engage students in rigorous learning tasks that develop the resilience students need to build knowledge from complex oral and written texts. Opportunities for research, academic discussions, and formal presentations provide authentic demonstration of student learning outcomes.

Varied Practice

Cognitive science has proven what *Future* always knew: Students learn new skills through varied practice over time. *Future Advanced* provides content-rich units that contextualize academic and employability skills and strategically recycle and reinforce complex concepts, language, and targeted skills. Lessons support both individual self-mastery and student collaboration through practice activities that engage learners, develop independent-learning and interpersonal skills, and lead to authentic products that provide lasting outcomes. Students develop the interpretative, productive, and interactive skills identified in the NRS guidelines, while using the four language skills of reading, writing, listening, and speaking.

Goal Setting and Learning Assessment

For optimal learning to take place, students need to be involved in setting goals and in monitoring their own progress. *Future* addresses goal setting in numerous ways. In the Student Book, Unit Goals are identified on the unit opener page. Checkboxes at the end of lessons invite students to evaluate their mastery of the material, and suggest additional online practice. In addition to these methods, *Future Advanced* provides checklists to guide development and self/peer evaluation of presentations and writing tasks.

High-quality assessment aligned to the standards checks student progress and helps students prepare to take standardized tests. The course-based assessment program is available in print and digital formats and includes a bank of customizable test items. Digital tests are assigned by the teacher and reported back in the LMS online gradebook. All levels include a midterm and final test. Test items are aligned with unit learning objectives and standards. The course Placement Test is available in print and digital formats. Test-prep materials are also provided for specific standardized tests.

One Integrated Program

Future provides everything adult English-language learners need in one integrated program using the latest digital tools and time-tested print resources.

Integrated Skills Contextualized with Rich Content

Future contextualizes grammar, listening, speaking, pronunciation, reading, writing, and vocabulary in meaningful activities that simulate real workplace, educational, and community settings. A special lesson at the end of each unit highlights soft skills at work. While providing relevant content, *Future* helps build learner knowledge and equips adults for their many roles. *Future Advanced* takes this preparation to the next level, developing the skills students need to transition into higher-skilled jobs and college and career preparation courses.

Meeting Work, Life, and Education Goals

Future recognizes that every adult learner brings a unique set of work, life, and academic experiences, as well as a distinct skill set. With its diverse array of print and digital resources, *Future* provides learners with multiple opportunities to practice with contextualized materials to build skill mastery. Specialized lessons for academic and workplace skill development are part of *Future*'s broad array of print and digital resources.

Future Advanced includes three employment-based units. In addition, it contains two employment-based lessons in each of the 12 units: Lesson 3 Workplace, Life, & Community Skills and Lesson 10 Workplace Soft Skills.

Workplace, Life, & Community Skills Lessons

In the second edition, the Life Skills lesson has been revised to focus on workplace, life, and community skills and to develop the real-life language, document literacy, and civic skills required today. Lessons integrate and contextualize workplace content. In addition, every lesson includes practice with digital skills on a mobile device.

Workplace Soft Skills Lessons

Future has further enhanced its development of workplace skills by adding a soft skills–focused lesson to each unit of *Future* at each level. Soft skills are the critical interpersonal communication skills needed to succeed in any workplace. In *Future Advanced,* each Workplace Soft Skills lesson begins with a problematic work-related interaction. Students work collaboratively to identify the problematic behavior and its consequence. Then, students apply the lesson-focused soft skill to the situation and role-play a "do over" with a successful outcome. In addition, the log at the back of the Student Book encourages students to track their own application of the soft skill, which they can use in job interviews and workplace performance reviews.

Academic Rigor

Rigor and respect for the ability and experiences of the adult learner have always been central to *Future.* The standards provide the foundation for academic rigor. The reading, writing, listening, and speaking practice require learners to analyze, use context clues, interpret, cite evidence, build knowledge, support a claim, and summarize from a variety of text formats. Regular practice with complex and content-rich materials develops academic language and builds knowledge. Interactive activities allow for collaboration and exchange of ideas in workplace and in academic contexts.

Future Advanced is the gateway to college and career preparation, and as such, provides meticulously sequenced, scaffolded, and reinforced rigorous practice of the essential CCR standards. Students and teachers alike are provided scaffolds every step of the way in the form of graphic organizers, targeted signal words and academic language, sentence frames, language models, note-taking templates, and checklists for guidance and evaluation.

Writing Lessons

In addition to the increased focus on writing in many end-of-lesson activities, *Future* has added a cumulative writing lesson to every unit, a lesson that requires students to synthesize and apply their learning in a written outcome. Using a highly scaffolded approach students begin by analyzing writing models before planning and finally producing written work of their own In addition to these features, *Future Advanced* includes a Writing Workshop lesson that focuses on an academic writing skill needed for the cumulative writing task. The Writing lesson requires students to incorporate research into their writing. The rigorous demands of the lesson are supported by writing models, note-taking and writing templates, and self/peer evaluation checklists.

Reading Lessons

All reading lessons have new, information-rich texts and a revised pedagogical approach in line with the CCR and ELP standards as well as the NRS descriptors. *Future Advanced* uses strategically designed and sequenced reading activities to develop the critical academic reading skills students need to engage with level-appropriate complex texts. Each reading lesson—two per unit—moves from pre-reading activities that activate prior knowledge and introduce critical topic-specific and corpus-informed academic vocabulary for deep analysis of the text through lesson-focused academic reading skills. The readings build students' knowledge and develop their higher-order reading skills by teaching citation of evidence, summarizing, interpretation of complex information from a variety of text formats, analysis of relationships presented in text, inference, and evaluation of arguments. In addition, the second reading lesson includes an academic reading, with activities that require students to conduct their own research on the topic and incorporate that research into an academic conversation or formal presentation. Students are supported in this work by note-taking and presentation templates.

Future Grows with Your Student

Future takes learners from absolute beginner level through low-advanced English proficiency, addressing students' abilities and learning priorities at each level. As the levels progress, the curricular content and unit structure change accordingly, incorporating more advanced academic language and skills in order to ensure student success and growth.

Future Intro	Future Level 1	Future Level 2	Future Level 3	Future Level 4	Future Advanced
NRS Beginning ESL Literacy	NRS Low Beginning ESL	NRS High Beginning ESL	NRS Low Intermediate ESL	NRS High Intermediate ESL	NRS Advanced ESL
ELPS Level 1	**ELPS** Level 1	**ELPS** Level 2	**ELPS** Level 3	**ELPS** Level 4	**ELPS** Level 5
CCRS Level A	**CCRS** Level A	**CCRS** Level A	**CCRS** Level B	**CCRS** Level C	**CCRS** Level D
CASAS 180 and below	**CASAS** 181–190	**CASAS** 191–200	**CASAS** 201–210	**CASAS** 211–220	**CASAS** 221–235

To the Teacher

To the Teacher

The **Pearson Practice English App** provides easy mobile access to all of the audio files, plus Grammar Coach videos and activities. Listen and study on the go—anywhere, any time!

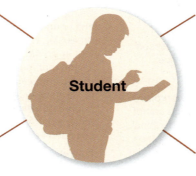

Abundant Opportunities for Student Practice

Student

MyEnglishLab allows online independent self-study and interactive practice in vocabulary, reading, writing, listening, and grammar. The MEL includes the popular Grammar Coach videos and activities.

Student Book is a complete student resource, including lessons in listening and speaking, reading, writing, vocabulary, grammar, and Workplace Life Skills and Soft Skills, taught and practiced in contextual activities.

Workbook—with audio—provides additional practice for each lesson in the Student Book, with new readings and practice in writing, grammar, and listening and speaking, plus activities for new Workplace Soft Skills lessons.

Teacher's Edition includes culture notes, teaching tips, and numerous optional and extension activities, with lesson-by-lesson correlations to CCR and ELP standards. Rubrics are provided for evaluation of students' written and oral communication.

Outstanding Teacher Resources

Teacher

College and Career Readiness Lessons supplement the Student Book with challenging reading and writing lessons for every level above Intro.

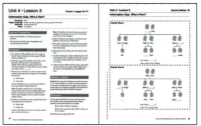

ActiveTeach for front-of-classroom projection of the Student Book includes audio at point of use and pop-up activities, including grammar examples, academic conversation stems, and reader's anticipation guides.

The **Assessment Program**, accessed online with interactive and printable tests and rubrics, includes a Placement Test; unit, midterm, and final exams; and computer-based ExamView with additional ready-to-use and customizable tests. In addition, sample high-stakes test practice is included with CASAS test prep for listening and reading.

Multilevel Communicative Activities provide an array of reproducible communication activities and games that engage students through different modalities. Teachers' notes provide multilevel options for pre-level and above-level students, as well as extension activities for additional speaking and writing practice.

Go to the Teacher website for easy reference, correlations to federal and state standards, and course updates.
www.pearsonelt.com/future2e

About the Series Consultants and Learning Expert

SERIES CONSULTANTS

Sarah Lynn is an ESOL teacher trainer, author, and curriculum design specialist. She has taught adult learners in the United States and abroad for decades, most recently at Harvard University's Center for Workforce Development. As a teacher-trainer and frequent conference presenter throughout the United States and Latin America, Ms. Lynn has led sessions and workshops on topics such as fostering student agency and resilience, brain-based teaching techniques, literacy and learning, and teaching in a multilevel classroom. Collaborating with program leaders, teachers, and students, she has developed numerous curricula for college and career readiness, reading and writing skill development, and contextualized content for adult English language learners. Ms. Lynn has co-authored several Pearson ELT publications, including *Business Across Cultures, Future, Future U.S. Citizens,* and *Project Success.* She holds a master's degree in TESOL from Teachers College, Columbia University.

Ronna Magy has worked as an ESOL classroom teacher, author, teacher-trainer, and curriculum development specialist. She served as the ESL Teacher Adviser in charge of professional development for the Division of Adult and Career Education of the Los Angeles Unified School District. She is a frequent conference presenter on the College and Career Readiness Standards (CCRS), the English Language Proficiency Standards (ELPS), and the language, literacy, and soft skills needed for academic and workplace success. Ms. Magy has authored/co-authored and trained teachers on modules for CALPRO, the California Adult Literacy Professional Development Project, including modules on integrating and contextualizing workforce skills in the ESOL classroom and evidence-based writing instruction. She is the author of adult ESL publications on English for the workplace, reading and writing, citizenship, and life skills and test preparation. Ms. Magy holds a master's degree in social welfare from the University of California at Berkeley.

Federico Salas-Isnardi has worked in adult education as a teacher, administrator, professional developer, materials writer, and consultant. He contributed to a number of state projects in Texas, including the adoption of adult education content standards and the design of state-wide professional development and accountability systems.

Over nearly 30 years he has conducted professional development seminars for thousands of teachers, law enforcement officers, social workers, and business people in the United States and abroad. His areas of concentration have been educational leadership, communicative competence, literacy, intercultural communication, citizenship, and diversity education. He has taught customized workplace ESOL and Spanish programs as well as high-school equivalence classes, citizenship and civics, labor market information seminars, and middle-school mathematics. Mr. Salas-Isnardi has been a contributing writer or series consultant for a number of ESL publications, and he has co-authored curriculum for site-based workforce ESL and Spanish classes.

Mr. Salas-Isnardi is a certified diversity trainer. He has a master's degree in applied linguistics and doctoral-level coursework in adult education.

LEARNING EXPERT

Lia Olson, PhD, has served as an ESOL classroom teacher, professional developer, curriculum design specialist, author, and consultant. She has taught adult learners for more than 20 years at St. Paul Public Schools Adult Education. In addition, she is an adjunct professor for the Teaching English as a Foreign Language program and Adult Basic Education licensure program at Hamline University. As a curriculum design expert, Dr. Olson has developed curricula and teaching materials for ESOL students at all levels that integrate English language acquisition with numeracy, technology, and work-readiness skills. More recently, she has designed College and Career Readiness (CCR)–aligned curriculum for pre-GED and GED-level students. Dr. Olson is a frequent conference presenter on CCR and English Language Proficiency (ELP) standards, multi-level instruction, contextualized phonics, supporting rigorous instruction for ESOL students, and curriculum development. She currently works as a coach on two national projects sponsored by the U.S. Department of Education's Office of Career, Technical, and Adult Education. Dr. Olson is the author of a phonics-based reading series for beginning-level ESOL adults and a set of teacher's guides that bridge ESOL students to GED preparation. Dr. Olson holds a PhD in Post-Secondary and Adult Education from Capella University.

Unit Tour

Preview questions activate student background knowledge and help the teacher assess how much students know about the unit theme.

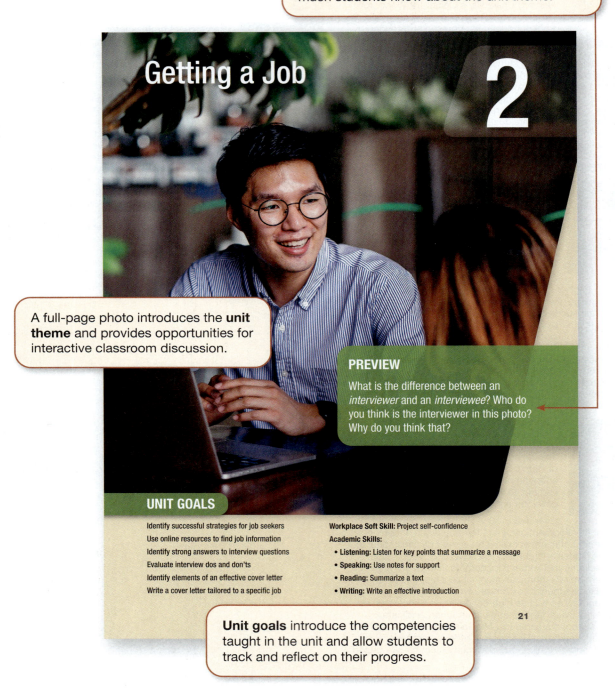

Getting a Job 2

A full-page photo introduces the **unit theme** and provides opportunities for interactive classroom discussion.

PREVIEW

What is the difference between an *interviewer* and an *interviewee*? Who do you think is the interviewer in this photo? Why do you think that?

UNIT GOALS

Identify successful strategies for job seekers
Use online resources to find job information
Identify strong answers to interview questions
Evaluate interview dos and don'ts
Identify elements of an effective cover letter
Write a cover letter tailored to a specific job

Workplace Soft Skill: Project self-confidence
Academic Skills:
- **Listening:** Listen for key points that summarize a message
- **Speaking:** Use notes for support
- **Reading:** Summarize a text
- **Writing:** Write an effective introduction

21

Unit goals introduce the competencies taught in the unit and allow students to track and reflect on their progress.

Two **Listening and Speaking** lessons provide students opportunities to build knowledge from authentic listening formats, such as podcasts, interviews, and realistic workplace conversations. Carefully sequenced Academic Listening Skills are targeted to help students extract meaning from these conversations.

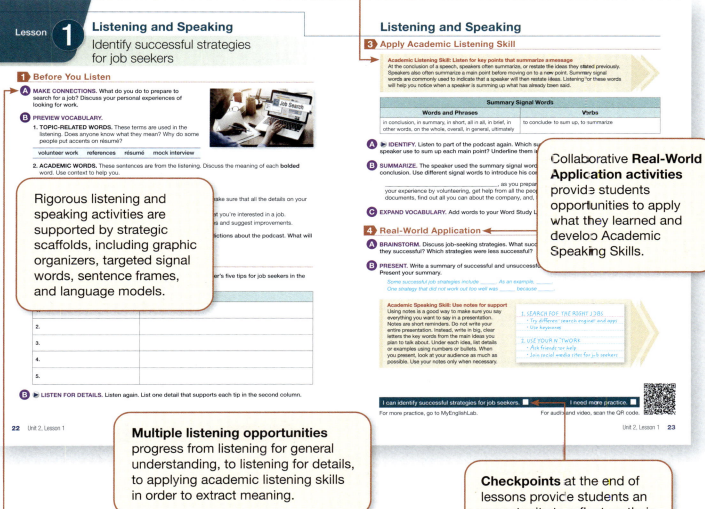

Rigorous listening and speaking activities are supported by strategic scaffolds, including graphic organizers, targeted signal words, sentence frames, and language models.

Collaborative Real-World Application activities provide students opportunities to apply what they learned and develop Academic Speaking Skills.

Multiple listening opportunities progress from listening for general understanding, to listening for details, to applying academic listening skills in order to extract meaning.

Checkpoints at the end of lessons provide students an opportunity to reflect on their progress and identify further resources for more practice.

Before You Listen activities let students make connections between the topic and their own experience and develop vocabulary-building strategies to interpret the specific topic-related and academic words used in the lesson.

Unit Tour   ix

Unit Tour

Each unit presents two **Grammar** lessons in a systematic grammar progression. Every Grammar lesson begins with a focus on the usage of the language introduced in the preceding Listening and Speaking lesson and, through an inductive approach, proceeds to a focus on language structure. Additional grammar practice is available in the Grammar Review and online.

Real-life examples provide context for meaningful grammar practice.

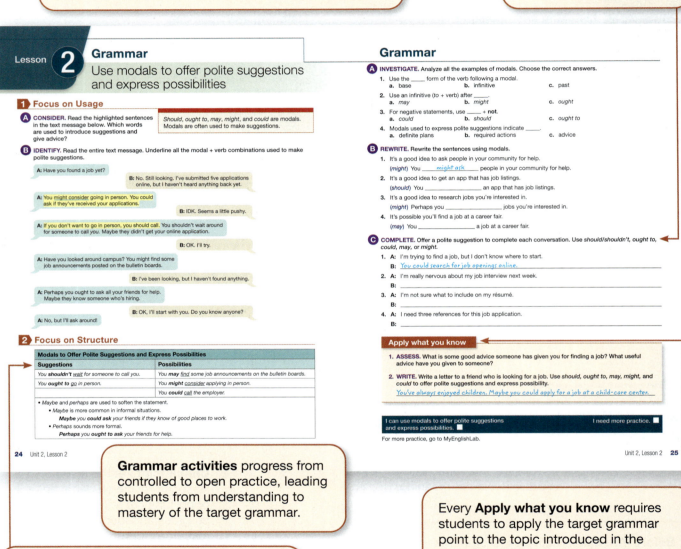

Grammar activities progress from controlled to open practice, leading students from understanding to mastery of the target grammar.

Grammar charts present the target grammar point in a clear and simple format. Grammar activities that follow provide students with opportunities to analyze these grammar points and determine language patterns.

Every **Apply what you know** requires students to apply the target grammar point to the topic introduced in the preceding Listening and Speaking lesson. Students participate in an interactive exchange and a writing task to demonstrate mastery of the target grammar point.

Workplace, Life, & Community Skills lessons develop real-life language and civic literacy, prepare students for the workplace, and encourage community participation.

In **Go Online activities,** students use their devices to practice concrete online tasks, such as researching information or inputting data.

Each lesson provides students the opportunity to reflect on an **authentic** workplace, life, or community problem and problem-solve by consulting authentic document and/or digital resources.

Apply what you know allows students to apply their online practice in Go Online to their own situations. Students share their research with one another in speaking or writing, and thus develop real-life communication skills.

Unit Tour   xi

Unit Tour

All-new informational **Reading** lessons develop academic language and build content knowledge to meet the rigorous requirements of the CCRS.

There are two informational reading lessons per unit—a 2-page lesson focused on practical topics and a 4-page lesson focused on more academic topics. Each contains level-appropriate complex text, close reading to extract meaning from the text, and tasks to demonstrate understanding.

Each 4-page reading lesson concludes with an opportunity for students to extend their knowledge through research and share that research in academic conversations or formal presentations. Note-taking and presentation templates support students in every step of these academic endeavors.

Close-reading activities require that students return to the reading to find textual evidence of detail, to summarize for general understanding, to make inferences, and to evaluate arguments.

In each 4-page reading lesson, students participate in **rigorous** close reading tasks that target carefully sequenced Academic Reading Skills. Scaffolds such as annotation strategies, graphic organizers, and strategic questions help students dig deeply into the text to extract meaning.

---

3 Close Reading

A LOCATE DETAILS. Are the statements true or false? Write the line numbers of your evidence.

	T/F	Lines
1. Look on the *Home* page of the company's website to find the company's mission.	____	____
2. A T-chart is a helpful way to match your goals with the company's goals.	____	____
3. Prospective employers usually want a cover letter with a very formal tone.	____	____
4. It is important to describe how your skills and experience will contribute to the company.	____	____

B APPLY ACADEMIC READING SKILL.

Academic Reading Skill: Summarize a text
A **summary** of a text reports the most important points. When summarizing, provide information about the text in a brief, or shortened, way. Try to include each main idea, but rewrite it in your own words. This rewriting is called **paraphrasing**.

First, use summary signal words below to introduce your summary. Then use sequence signal words like *first, next,* and *then* to introduce each of the restated main ideas. These sequence signal words help give structure to your summary and create smooth transitions.

Summary Signal Words and Phrases	Sequence Signal Words
in conclusion, in summary, in short, all in all, in brief, in other words, on the whole, overall, in general, ultimately, to conclude, to sum up, to summarize	first, second, next, then, finally

1. These sentences are from the concluding summary of an article on how to research a cover letter. Write 1–4 to put the steps in order.
   _____ Research the company so that your cover letter can show what you know about it.
   _____ In summary, writing a great cover letter is worth the effort.
   _____ Follow five important steps to combine your research into your cover letter.
   _____ Learn about the position you are applying for.

2. Restate each of the steps above for researching a cover letter, following the order you listed them in. Paraphrase each step by writing it in your own words to create a summary.
   1. _____
   2. _____
   3. _____
   4. _____

3. Now look back at the five criteria of a dynamic cover letter given at the end of the article. Restate those five criteria. Paraphrase each criteria by writing it in your own words.
   1. _____
   2. _____
   3. _____
   4. _____
   5. _____

C SUMMARIZE. Use your answers to Exercise 3 above to write a paragraph summarizing the five criteria for writing a cover letter. Remember to use sequence words for transitions.

36 Unit 2, Lesson 7

---

4 Prepare for an Academic Conversation

A GO ONLINE. Read about *Using Search Engines*. Then try out a few different search engines in YOUR TURN.

✓ Search	✓ Choose Sources	✓ Evaluate Sources

Using Search Engines

A search engine is an online tool that helps you locate information. The three most popular search engines in the U.S. are Google, Bing, and Yahoo, in that order. All three provide access to excellent resources, so choosing one is a matter of preference. Try each one to see which one you like best.

Online users enter in keywords to describe what they are looking for. Search engines match those words to any content published online. This content can be texts, images, or even videos. The list of content that the search engine produces is called the **search engine results page**, or SERP.

Search engines follow a complex set of problem-solving operations, called algorithms, to determine the order of the results. That doesn't mean, however, that the first result on the list or the first page of results is where you will find the best information. Always check results on later pages before you stop your search.

Make sure you choose the keywords that best describe what you are looking for. Enter the topic you want with specific information to narrow the search. For example, to search for cover letter templates, you can add the word *free* to eliminate the ones that cost money. If you want one that you can download, add *downloadable*.

YOUR TURN...
Try out different search engines. Enter the same keywords into each one. What different results do you get?

B CHOOSE A SOURCE. Use one search engine to find a source for cover letter templates. Choose one cover letter template to help you write your own cover letter.

Search Terms: cover letter templates   free   downloadable

Apply what you know   Academic Conversation

1. **PREPARE NOTES.** You will share the cover letter template you choose. Remember to take notes to help you remember everything you want to say.

2. **REPORT.** Share your cover letter template. Describe the search engine and keywords you used to find it. Explain why you chose it.

3. **USE NOTES FOR SUPPORT.** As you present, remember to look at your audience as much as possible. Only glance at your notes when necessary.

I can identify elements of an effective cover letter. ☐   I need more practice. ☐
For more practice, go to MyEnglishLab.   For audio and video, scan the QR code.

Unit 2, Lesson 7 **37**

Graphs and charts in many Reading lessons introduce students to information in a variety of formats, developing their visual literacy. Students develop **numeracy** skills by interpreting numeric information in text and in charts and graphs.

Flexibility in the style of information delivery is promoted. In half of the units, the 4-page reading lessons conclude with an informal Academic Conversation. The other units conclude with a formal Academic Presentation. Students present to a partner with the option for teachers to choose students to present to the class.

Unit Tour   **xiii**

Unit Tour

Writing Workshops introduce targeted Academic Writing Skills through an inductive approach. Students compare two writing examples, determine which is stronger, and analyze what makes it stronger.

Writing lessons follow a robust and scaffolded writing-process approach, engaging students in analyzing writing models, planning, and producing a final product.

A cumulative writing task requires students to complete online research and incorporate it into the task.

The rigorous demands of the writing task are supported by writing models, note-taking and writing-model templates.

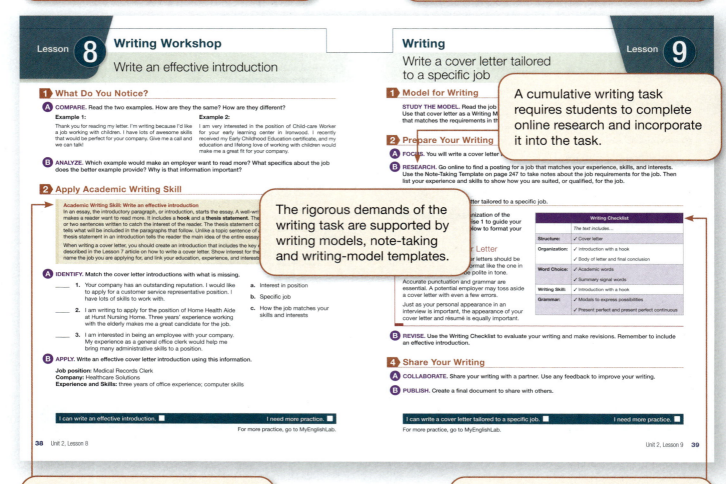

The **Academic Writing Skill** explains and models the target skill. Students then practice the skill to prepare for using it in the cumulative writing task in the Writing Lesson.

The **Writing Checklist** provides students with a helpful rubric for the writing task. It outlines the key unit objectives that should be incorporated. It also provides a concrete checklist for self/peer evaluation.

New **Workplace Soft Skills** lessons engage students in real-life situations that develop the personal, social, and cultural skills critical for career success and help students meet the WIOA requirements.

A brief audio scenario introduces a problematic workplace interaction that can be solved using **critical thinking** and **soft skills**.

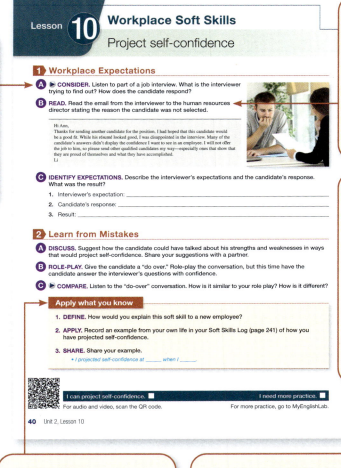

Problem-solving activities build student collaboration and strategic critical thinking about effective workplace behavior.

Students apply the targeted soft skill to the situation and role-play a "do over" with a successful outcome. Students compare their role play with a provided "do over" to develop deeper understanding of the soft skill.

Apply what you know invites students to share examples of how they have applied the target soft skill in their own lives and workplaces.

The **My Soft Skills Log** in the back of the student book is a personal resource for students as they apply for jobs or undergo performance reviews.

Unit Tour   **xv**

Scope and Sequence

Unit	Listening & Speaking	Grammar	Workplace, Life, & Community Skills
1 **The Power of Goals** *page 1*	**Unit Goals:** • Identify factors to consider when choosing a career • Evaluate and set SMART goals **Academic Listening skill:** • Listen for main ideas and supporting details **Academic Speaking skill:** • Collaborate with others as a team	**Unit Goals:** • Use gerunds and infinitives to share interests and preferences • Use gerunds and infinitives to describe career goals and action steps	**Unit Goal:** • Use career assessment tools to identify interests and skills **Digital skill:** • Use an online interest and skills assessment
2 **Getting a Job** *page 21*	**Unit Goals:** • Identify successful strategies for job seekers • Evaluate interview dos and don'ts **Academic Listening skill:** • Listen for key points that summarize a message **Academic Speaking skill:** • Use notes for support	**Unit Goals:** • Use modals to offer polite suggestions and express possibilities • Use present perfect and present perfect continuous	**Unit Goal:** • Use online resources to find job information **Digital skill:** • Consult online job sites
3 **The Thoughtful Consumer** *page 41*	**Unit Goals:** • Explain the steps of financial management • Evaluate strategies for making a big purchase **Academic Listening skill:** • Listen for information that compares and contrasts **Academic Speaking skill:** • Encourage others to participate	**Unit Goals:** • Use comparative adjectives and adverbs • Use superlative adjectives and adverbs	**Unit Goal:** • Create a budget using budgeting tools **Digital skill:** • Use an online budget calculator
4 **At Peak Performance** *page 61*	**Unit Goals:** • Rank factors that influence job promotion • Evaluate conversations for effective conflict resolution **Academic Listening skill:** • Listen for evidence that supports a speaker's message **Academic Speaking skill:** • Ask for clarification	**Unit Goals:** • Express purpose, reason, or contrast • Make polite requests with *Would you mind*	**Unit Goal:** • Use training resources to identify growth opportunities **Digital skill:** • Consult online training opportunities

Document Literacy & Numeracy	Reading	Writing	Workplace Soft Skills
• Interpret and complete career assessment tools • Rank personal interests • Complete a flowchart with details • Complete a SMART goals chart	**Unit Goals:** • Identify the criteria of a SMART goal • Identify main ideas and details in a biography about César Cruz **Academic Reading skill:** • Identify main ideas and supporting details **Presentation focus:** • Use main ideas and supporting details to structure a presentation on a famous person	**Unit Goal:** • Write about interests, skills, and career goals **Academic Writing skill:** • Write effective topic sentences **Writing focus:** • Give examples to support writing	**Unit Goal:** • Demonstrate a willingness to learn
• Interpret online job information • Calculate wages and hours • Complete a chart to compare information	**Unit Goals:** • Identify strong answers to interview questions • Identify elements of an effective cover letter **Academic Reading skill:** • Summarize a text **Go Online focus:** • Use search engines	**Unit Goal:** • Write a cover letter tailored to a specific job **Academic Writing skill:** • Write an effective introduction **Writing focus:** • Format a cover letter	**Unit Goal:** • Project self-confidence
• Interpret budget information • Use a budget calculator to create a budget and answer questions • Calculate housing cost percentage • Use evidence from bar graphs to complete a chart • Create a Venn diagram to identify similarities and differences • Calculate income differences using bar graph statistics	**Unit Goals:** • Identify the steps for planning a big purchase • Use compare-and-contrast signal words effectively • Compare and contrast earning potential of educational levels **Academic Reading skill:** • Mark text to highlight compare-and-contrast relationships **Presentation focus:** • Monitor presentation delivery in a presentation comparing two jobs	**Unit Goal:** • Write a compare-and-contrast essay about two jobs of interest **Academic Writing skill:** • Use compare-and-contrast signal words to highlight similarities and differences **Writing focus:** • Write a compare-and-contrast essay	**Unit Goal:** • Respond effectively to customer needs
• Rate work performance • Complete a chart using dilemmas and suggestions • Use infographics as support • Interpret course catalog information • Read a graphic organizer for information • Read a chart and a timeline about worker rights to answer questions • Use domain names • Use a chart to identify tone and audience	**Unit Goals:** • Identify solutions to workplace dilemmas • Describe how to protect workers' rights **Academic Reading skill:** • Recognize how infographics provide evidence to support a text **Go Online focus:** • Use top level domains	**Unit Goal:** • Write a workplace incident report **Academic Writing skill:** • Match tone to audience and purpose **Writing focus:** • Write objectively	**Unit Goal:** • Negotiate to resolve conflict

Text in purple refers to workplace and employability topics.

Scope and Sequence **xvii**

Scope and Sequence

Unit	Listening & Speaking	Grammar	Workplace, Life, & Community Skills
5 **Affordable Housing** *page 81*	**Unit Goals:** • Describe the homeless problem in the U.S. • Describe the requirements for getting a home loan **Academic Listening skill:** • Identify problem-and-solution relationships **Academic Speaking skill:** • Present evidence to support points	**Unit Goals:** • Use adjective clauses • Reduce adjective clauses to adjective phrases	**Unit Goal:** • Use resources to explore housing options **Digital skill:** • Use search filters on a housing website
6 **When Nature Is in Charge** *page 101*	**Unit Goals:** • Use weather reports to inform decisions • Describe the effects of natural disasters **Academic Listening skill:** • Listen for cause-and-effect relationships **Academic Speaking skill:** • Extend the contributions of others	**Unit Goals:** • Use real conditionals • Use present and future unreal conditionals	**Unit Goal:** • Use a GPS app to choose routes **Digital skill:** • Consult GPS maps
7 **Protecting the Planet** *page 121*	**Unit Goals:** • Describe climate change • Discuss ways to limit our carbon footprint **Academic Listening skill:** • Identify components in a causal chain **Academic Speaking skill:** • Acknowledge the contributions of others	**Unit Goals:** • Use expressions to state conditions • Use past unreal conditionals	**Unit Goal:** • Promote responsible waste disposal practices **Digital skill:** • Consult local online recycling information
8 **The Digital Age** *page 141*	**Unit Goals:** • Identify the pros and cons of the digital age • Describe the dangers of texting and driving **Academic Listening skill:** • Identify evidence used to support a claim **Academic Speaking skill:** • Disagree politely	**Unit Goals:** • Use the simple future and future continuous to make predictions • Use the simple past, past continuous, and past perfect	**Unit Goal:** • Evaluate social media for reliability **Digital skill:** • Use online fact-checking resources

Document Literacy & Numeracy	Reading	Writing	Workplace Soft Skills
• Interpret housing graphics and financial service resources • Rank categories in order of importance • Organize information from a reading into a chart • Estimate percentage of income • Scan an affordable housing graph for details • Calculate statistics from infographics	**Unit Goals:** • Explain the causes and results of the housing crash • Describe the problem of affordable housing and offer a solution **Academic Reading skill:** • Evaluate the problem and solution presented in an argument **Presentation focus:** • Use statistics to support your points	**Unit Goal:** • Write a problem-solution essay **Academic Writing skill:** • Write an effective conclusion **Writing focus:** • Write problem-solution essay	**Unit Goal:** • Demonstrate responsibility
• Interpret and follow GPS routes • Read graphics to inform decisions • Complete a chart with cause-and-effect relationships • Interpret a graphic organizer • Interpret information on a GPS map • Complete a natural disaster chart • Use keyboard commands to find web results	**Unit Goals:** • Identify safety measures for severe weather events • Explain the science of tornadoes **Academic Reading skill:** • Mark text to highlight cause-and-effect relationships **Go Online focus:** • Narrow online searches	**Unit Goal:** • Write about the process of a severe weather event **Academic Writing skill:** • Use complex sentences to create writing that flows **Writing focus:** • Write with a process	**Unit Goal:** • Exercise leadership
• Interpret community resources that promote environmental practices • Identify components in a causal chain using a graphic organizer • Scan and interpret infographics • Identify a causal chain about carbon footprints • Complete causal chains about climate change	**Unit Goals:** • Describe green jobs • Provide examples of the effects of climate change **Academic Reading skill:** • Use a graphic organizer to identify components in a causal chain **Presentation goal:** • Share a presentation explaining an effect of climate change **Presentation focus:** • Keep the audience's attention through poise and gestures	**Unit Goal:** • Write an argument that makes a claim about an effect of climate change **Academic Writing skill:** • Identify components of a valid argument **Writing focus:** • State a clear, concise claim	**Unit Goal:** • Work effectively with a team
• Record survey responses in a chart • Scan and interpret infographics	**Unit Goals:** • Describe cyberbullying and recommend responses to it • Discuss the impact of excessive screen time on brain and social development **Academic Reading skill:** • Evaluate evidence for relevance and sufficiency. **Go Online focus:** • Evaluate the reliability of a source	**Unit Goal:** • Write an argument for or against limiting children's screen time **Academic Writing skill:** • Use relevant and sufficient evidence to support an argument **Writing focus:** • Incorporate evidence	**Unit Goal:** • Exercise self-discipline with digital devices

Text in purple refers to workplace and employability topics.

Scope and Sequence **xix**

Scope and Sequence

Unit	Listening & Speaking	Grammar	Workplace, Life, & Community Skills
9 **Health in the Balance** *page 161*	**Unit Goals:** • Identify tips for promoting well-being • Identify ways to manage mental health **Academic Listening skill:** • Differentiate between fact and opinion **Academic Speaking skill:** • Paraphrase the contributions of the group	**Unit Goal:** • Use active and passive voice strategically	**Unit Goal:** • Identify benefits of preventive healthcare **Digital skill:** • Access and navigate online preventive care resources
10 **Navigating Healthcare** *page 181*	**Unit Goals:** • Contact the right specialist for specific health needs • Describe the factors that increase the cost of healthcare • Discuss logical fallacies **Academic Listening skill:** • Evaluate soundness of reasoning **Academic Speaking skill:** • Provide direction for the group	**Unit Goals:** • Use embedded *W*-questions • Use embedded *yes/no* questions	**Unit Goal:** • Follow medication instructions **Digital skill:** • Interpret medication information
11 **Citizenship** *page 201*	**Unit Goals:** • Describe the process and benefits of becoming a citizen • Describe how a bill becomes law **Academic Listening skill:** • Identify steps in a process **Academic Speaking skill:** • Keep collaboration guidelines in mind	**Unit Goals:** • Use nouns and possessive nouns as adjectives • Use participial adjectives	**Unit Goal:** • Interpret time zone maps **Digital skill:** • Access and navigate time zone maps
12 **Rights and Responsibilities** *page 221*	**Unit Goals:** • Identify civic responsibilities • Identify the rights of people accused of crimes **Academic Listening skill:** • Make inferences and support with evidence **Academic Speaking skill:** • End collaborative tasks on a positive note	**Unit Goals:** • Use modals of deduction • Punctuate adjective clauses	**Unit Goal:** • Interpret citations and law enforcement resources **Digital skill:** • Access and navigate online citation information

Document Literacy & Numeracy	Reading	Writing	Workplace Soft Skills
• Scan and interpret informational brochures • Rate personal well-being • Chart goals and initiatives • Use infographics to support points	**Unit Goals:** • Describe community practices that support public health • Describe the causes of obesity and its impact **Academic Reading skill:** • Differentiate between fact and opinion **Presentation Goal:** • Share a presentation describing one possible solution to the obesity problem **Presentation focus:** • Use infographics to support your points	**Unit Goal:** • Write a problem-solution essay about obesity in the United States **Academic Writing skill:** • Use passive voice to create an academic tone **Writing focus:** • Use passive voice effectively	**Unit Goal:** • Display a positive attitude
• Interpret medication labels • Read a line graph for details • Evaluate advantages and disadvantages • Interpret infographics	**Unit Goals:** • Interpret healthcare plans • Evaluate a strategy for making healthcare accessible **Academic Reading skill:** • Evaluate the soundness of reasoning in a text **Go Online focus:** • Evaluate a source for sound reasoning	**Unit Goal:** • Write an argument to support accessible healthcare **Academic Writing skill:** • Revise fragments and run-on sentences **Writing focus:** • Use logical reasoning	**Unit Goal:** • Demonstrate professionalism
• Calculate time zone map information • Scan and interpret infographics • Complete a diagram about passing a bill	**Unit Goals:** • Identify workers' rights and the laws that protect them • Describe the organization of the U.S. government **Academic Reading skill:** • Identify steps in a process **Presentation goal:** • Share a presentation describing one branch of the U.S. government **Presentation focus:** • Use quotations for support	**Unit Goal:** • Write a formal email to an elected official to request a specific action **Academic Writing skill:** • Use clear and concise language **Writing focus:** • Use formal email structure and tone	**Unit Goal:** • Respect individual differences
• Scan and interpret citations and law enforcement resources • Summarize amendments into a chart • Follow flowcharts to make inferences	**Unit Goals:** • Identify the rights described in the Bill of Rights • Evaluate campaign propaganda **Academic Reading skill:** • Make inferences **Go Online focus:** • Use wide and deep research	**Unit Goal:** • Write an argument to evaluate the reliability of a news article **Academic Writing skill:** • Use qualifiers to avoid hasty generalizations **Writing focus:** • Evaluate a news article	**Unit Goal:** • Take initiative

Text in purple refers to workplace and employability topics.

Scope and Sequence **xxi**

Correlations

Unit	CASAS Reading Standards (correlated to CASAS Reading Standards 2016)	CASAS Listening Standards (correlated to CASAS Listening Basic Skills Content Standards)	CASAS Competencies (correlated to CASAS Competencies: Essential Life and Work skills for Youth and Adults)
1	L1: RDG 2.4, 2.8; L2: RDG 2.6, 2.9; L3: RDG 3.4; L4: RDG 2.3, 2.8, 3.2, 3.9, 3.11, 3.12; L5: RDG 2.4, 2.8; L6: RDG 2.6, 2.9; L7: RDG 2.3, 2.8, 3.8, 3.11, 3.12, 4.2, 4.3; L8: RDG 3.16; L10: RDG 3.15	L1: 2.3, 2.4, 2.9, 3.11, 4.6, 5.8, 6.1, 6.8; L2: 2.4, 2.9, 3.13; L3: 4.6; L4: 4.2; L5: 2.8, 2.9, 4.6, 5.8, 6.1, 6.8; L6: 2.4, 2.9, 3.13; L7: 4.2; L9: 4.6; L10: 4.6, 5.6, 6.6	L1: 0.1.2, 0.1.5, 0.2.1, 4.1.9; L2: 0.1.2, 0.1.5, 0.2.1, 4.1.9; L3: 0.1.2, 0.1.5, 0.2.1, 4.1.3, 4.1.9, 6.6.5, 7.7.3; L4: 0.1.2, 0.1.5, 0.2.1, 7.1.1, 7.1.2; L5: 0.1.2, 0.1.5, 0.2.1, 7.1.1, 7.1.2; L6: 0.1.2, 0.1.5, 0.2.1, 4.1.9; L7: 0.1.2, 0.1.5, 0.2.1, 7.1.2, 7.4.2, 7.7.3; L8: 0.1.2; L9: 0.1.2, 0.1.5, 4.1.9, 7.1.2, 7.4.2, 7.7.3; L10: 0.1.2, 0.1.5, 4.1.5
2	L2: RDG 2.6, 2.9; L3: RDG 3.4; L4: RDG 2.3, 2.8, 3.8, 3.11, 3.12, 4.5; L6: RDG 2.6, 2.9; L7: RDG 2.3, 2.4, 2.8, 3.8, 3.11, 3.12, 4.2, 4.3; L8: RDG 3.16; L10: RDG 3.15	L1: 2.4, 2.7, 2.9, 3.11, 4.6, 5.8; L2: 3.13; L3: 4.6; L4: 4.2; L5: 2.8, 2.9, 4.6, 5.8, 6.1, 6.8; L6: 2.4, 2.9, 3.13; L7: 4.2; L9: 4.6; L10: 4.6, 5.6, 6.6	L1: 0.1.2, 0.1.5, 4.1.9, 7.2.6; L2: 0.1.2, 0.1.3, 0.1.5, 4.1.9; L3: 0.1.2, 0.1.5, 4.1.3, 4.1.9, 6.6.5, 7.7.3, 7.4.4; L4: 0.1.2, 0.1.5, 0.2.1, 4.1.5, 7.2.6; L5: 0.1.2, 0.1.5, 0.2.1, 4.1.5; L6: 0.1.2, 0.1.5, 0.2.1, 4.1.2, 4.1.9; L7: 0.1.2, 0.1.5, 0.2.1, 4.1.2, 7.1.2, 7.4.2, 7.4.4, 7.7.3; L8: 0.1.2, 4.1.2; L9: 0.1.2, 0.1.5, 4.1.2, 7.1.2, 7.4.2, 7.4.4, 7.7.3; L10: 0.1.2, 0.1.5, 4.1.5
3	L1: 2.4, 2.7, 2.9, 3.11, 4.6, 5.8, 6.1, 6.2; L2: 3.10, 3.12; L3: 4.6; L4: 4.6; L5: 2.9, 4.6, 6.1, 6.8; L6: 2.4, 2.9, 3.13; L7: 4.6, 5.9; L9: 4.6; L10: 4.6, 5.6, 6.6	L1: 2.1, 2.3, 4.1, 4.2, 6.1; L2: 2.1, 3.9, 4.1, 4.2; L3: 2.1, 2.3; L4: 2.1, 2.3, 4.1, 4.2, 4.6; L5: 2.3, 3.9, 4.1, 4.2; L6: 2.3, 4.1, 4.2, 6.1, 6.3; L7: 2.1, 2.3, 4.2, 4.6, 6.1, 6.3; L8: 3.9; L10: 2.1, 4.6, 5.9	L1: 0.1.2, 0.1.5, 1.5.1; L2: 0.1.2, 0.1.5, 1.8.1, 1.8.6; L3: 0.1.2, 0.1.5, 1.5.1, 6.6.5, 7.2.6, 7.4.4, 7.4.8, 7.7.3; L4: 0.1.2, 0.1.5, 1.4.6, 1.5.2, 7.2.6; L5: 0.1.2, 0.1.5, 1.5.2, 1.8.6, 1.9.5; L6: 0.1.2, 0.1.5, 1.5.2, 1.9.5; L7: 0.1.2, 0.1.5, 0.2.1, 6.6.5, 7.4.2, 7.4.4, 7.7.3; L8: 0.1.2, 2.8.1; L9: 0.1.2, 0.1.5, 4.1.8, 7.1.2, 7.4.2, 7.4.4, 7.7.3; L10: 0.1.2, 0.1.5, 4.8.3, 4.8.4
4	L2: RDG 2.4, 2.9, 3.15; L3: RDG 2.3, 3.10, 4.3; L4: RDG 2.3, 2.8, 3.8, 3.11, 3.12, 4.2, 4.5; L5: RDG 3.4; L6: RDG 2.6, 2.9; L7: RDG 2.3, 2.4, 2.8, 3.4, 3.8, 3.11, 3.12, 4.3; L8: RDG 3.16, 4.6; L10: RDG 3.15	L1: 2.4, 2.7, 2.9, 3.11, 4.6, 6.1, 6.7, 6.9; L2: 3.11; L3: 4.6; L4: 4.6; L5: 2.8, 2.9, 4.6, 6.1, 6.8, 6.9; L6: 3.13; L7: 4.6, 5.9; L9: 4.6; L10: 4.6, 5.6, 6.6	L1: 0.1.2, 0.1.5, 4.4.2; L2: 0.1.2, 0.1.5, 4.1.2; L3: 0.1.2, 0.1.5, 4.1.4, 4.4.5, 4.4.6, 7.2.6, 7.3.1, 7.3.2, 7.4.4, 7.7.3; L4: 0.1.2, 0.1.5, 7.3.1, 7.3.2; L5: 0.1.2, 0.1.5, 4.8.6, 6.6.5, 7.3.1, 7.3.2; L6: 0.1.2, 0.1.5, 0.1.7; L7: 0.1.2, 0.1.5, 0.2.1, 4.2.6, 6.6.5, 7.4.4, 7.7.3; L8: 0.1.2, 4.3.4; L9: 0.1.2, 0.1.5, 4.3.4, 7.1.2, 7.3.4, 7.4.2, 7.4.4, 7.7.3; L10: 0.1.2, 0.1.5, 4.8.3, 4.8.5, 7.4.4, 7.7.3
5	L1: RDG 3.2; L2: RDG 2.6, 2.9; L3: RDG 2.3, 3.10, 4.3; L4: RDG 2.3, 2.8, 3.8, 3.11, 3.12, 4.2, 4.5; L5: RDG 3.4; L6: RDG 2.6, 2.9; L7: RDG 2.3, 2.8, 3.4, 3.8, 3.11, 3.12, 4.3; L8: RDG 3.16	L1: 2.4, 2.7, 2.9, 3.11, 4.6, 6.1, 6.9; L2: 4.6; L3: 4.6; L4: 4.6; L5: 2.8, 2.9, 4.6, 6.1, 6.8, 6.9; L6: 3.13; L7: 4.6, 5.9; L9: 4.6; L10: 4.6, 5.6, 6.6	L1: 0.1.2, 0.1.5, 7.3.2, 7.4.4, 7.7.3; L2: 0.1.2, 0.1.5, 7.3.2; L3: 0.1.2, 0.1.5, 1.4.1, 1.4.2, 7.4.4, 7.7.3; L4: 0.1.2, 0.1.5, 7.2.6; L5: 0.1.2, 0.1.5, 1.4.6, 7.3.1, 7.3.2; L6: 0.1.2, 0.1.5, 1.4.6; L7: 0.1.2, 0.1.5, 0.2.1, 5.8.1, 5.8.2, 6.6.5, 7.3.1, 7.3.2, 7.4.4, 7.7.3; L8: 0.1.2, 5.8.2; L9: 0.1.2, 0.1.5, 5.8.2, 7.1.2, 7.3.4, 7.4.2, 7.4.4, 7.7.3; L10: 0.1.2, 0.1.5
6	L1: RDG 3.2, 3.4; L2: RDG 2.6, 2.9; L3: RDG 2.3, 3.4, 3.10, 4.3; L4: RDG 2.3, 2.8, 3.8, 3.11, 3.12, 4.5; L6: RDG 2.6, 2.9; L7: RDG 2.3, 2.8, 3.4, 3.8. 3.11, 3.12, 4.2, 4.3; L8: RDG 3.16	L1: 2.4, 2.7, 2.9, 3.11, 4.6, 6.1, 6.9; L2: 4.6; L3: 4.6; L4: 4.6; L5: 2.8, 2.9, 4.6, 5.8, 6.1, 6.5, 6.8, 6.9; L6: 3.13; L7: 4.6; L9: 4.6; L10: 4.6, 6.6	L1: 0.1.2, 0.1.5, 2.3.3, 6.6.5, 7.4.2; L2: 0.1.2, 0.1.5, 2.3.3; L3: 0.1.2, 0.1.5, 2.2.5, 6.6.5, 7.4.4, 7.7.3; L4: 0.1.2, 0.1.5, 2.3.3; L5: 0.1.2, 0.1.5, 2.3.3; L6: 0.1.2, 0.1.5, 2.3.3; L7: 0.1.2, 0.1.5, 2.3.3, 6.6.5, 7.4.4, 7.7.3; L8: 0.1.2, 2.3.3; L9: 0.1.2, 0.1.5, 2.3.3, 7.4.2, 7.4.4, 7.7.3; L10: 0.1.2, 0.1.5, 4.8.5
7	L1: RDG 3.2; L2: RDG 2.6, 2.9; L3: RDG 2.3, 3.4, 4.10, 4.3; L4: RDG 2.3, 2.8, 3.4, 3.8, 3.11, 3.12, 4.5; L6: RDG 2.6, 2.9; L7: RDG 2.3, 2.8, 3.8, 3.11, 3.12, 4.2, 4.3; L8: RDG 3.15, 3.16;	L1: 2.4, 2.7, 2.9, 3.11, 4.6, 6.1, 6.9; L2: 4.6; L3: 4.6; L4: 4.6; L5: 2.8, 2.9, 4.6, 5.8, 6.1, 6.5, 6.8, 6.9; L6: 3.13; L7: 4.6; L9: 4.6; L10: 4.6, 6.6;	L1: 0.1.2, 0.1.5, 5.7.1; L2: 0.1.2, 0.1.5, 5.7.1; L3: 0.1.2, 0.1.5, 5.6.4, 6.6.5, 7.4.4, 7.7.3; L4: 0.1.2, 0.1.5, 5.6.4, 6.6.5; L5: 0.1.2, 0.1.5, 5.7.1; L6: 0.1.2, 0.1.5, 5.7.1, 7.4.4, 7.7.3; L7: 0.1.2, 0.1.5, 5.7.1, 7.4.4, 7.7.3; L8: 0.1.2, 5.7.1; L9: 0.1.2, 0.1.5, 5.7.1, 7.4.2, 7.4.4, 7.7.3; L10: 0.1.2, 0.1.5, 4.8.1;
8	L1: RDG 2.4, 3.2, 3.15; L2: RDG 2.6, 2.9; L3: RDG 2.3, 3.4, 3.10, 4.3; L4: RDG 2.3, 2.8, 3.4, 3.8, 3.11, 3.12, 4.5; L6: RDG 2.6, 2.9; L7: RDG 2.3, 2.8, 3.4, 3.8, 3.11, 3.12, 4.3; L8: RDG 3.15, 3.16;	L1: 2.4, 2.7, 2.9, 3.11, 4.6, 4.9, 6.1, 6.9; L2: 4.6; L3: 4.6; L4: 4.6; L5: 2.8, 2.9, 4.6, 5.8, 6.1, 6.5, 6.8, 6.9; L6: 3.13; L7: 4.6; L9: 4.6; L10: 4.6, 6.6;	L1: 0.1.2, 0.1.5, 7.7.1; L2: 0.1.2, 0.1.5, 7.7.1; L3: 0.1.2, 0.1.5, 6.6.5, 7.4.4, 7.7.1, 7.7.3, 7.7.5; L4: 0.1.2, 0.1.5, 6.6.5, 7.7.5; L5: 0.1.2, 0.1.5, 7.7.5; L6: 0.1.2, 0.1.5, 7.7.5; L7: 0.1.2, 0.1.5, 6.6.5, 7.4.4, 7.7.3, 7.7.5; L8: 0.1.2, 7.4.4; L9: 0.1.2, 0.1.5, 7.4.2, 7.4.4, 7.7.3; L10: 0.1.2, 0.1.5, 4.3.3
9	L1: RDG 2.4, 3.2, 4.7; L2: RDG 2.6, 2.9 L3: RDG 2.3, 3.4, 3.10, 4.3; L4: RDG 2.3, 2.8, 3.4, 3.8, 3.11, 3.12, 4.5; L5: RDG 2.3, 2.8; L6: RDG 2.6, 2.9; L7: RDG 2.3, 2.8, 3.4, 3.8, 3.11, 3.12, 4.3; L8: RDG 3.16;	L1: 2.4, 2.7, 2.9, 3.11, 4.6, 4.9, 6.1, 6.9, 6.11; L2: 4.6; L3: 4.6; L4: 4.6; L5: 2.8, 2.9, 4.6, 5.8, 6.1, 6.5, 6.8, 6.11; L6: 3.13; L7: 4.6; L9: 4.6; L10: 4.6, 6.6	L1: 0.1.2, 0.1.5, 3.5.9, 7.6.3; L2: 0.1.2, 0.1.5, 3.5.9; L3: 0.1.2, 0.1.5, 3.5.9, 6.6.5, 7.3.4, 7.4.4, 7.7.3; L4: 0.1.2, 0.1.5, 3.5.9, 6.6.5; L5: 0.1.2, 0.1.5, 3.5.9, 7.6.3; L6: 0.1.2, 0.1.5, 3.5.9; L7: 0.1.2, 0.1.5, 3.5.9, 6.6.5, 7.4.4, 7.7.3; L8: 0.1.2; L9: 0.1.2, 0.1.5, 7.4.2, 7.4.4, 7.7.3; L10: 0.1.2, 0.1.5, 4.8.3
10	L1: RDG 2.4, 3.2, 3.15, 4.7; L2: RDG 2.6, 2.9; L3: RDG 2.3, 3.4, 3.10, 4.3; L4: RDG 2.3, 2.8, 3.8, 3.11, 3.12, 4.5; L5: RDG 2.3, 2.8, 3.15; L6: RDG 2.6, 2.9; L7: RDG 2.3, 2.8, 3.4, 3.6, 3.8, 3.11, 3.12, 3.15, 4.3; L8: RDG 3.16	L1: RDG 2.4, 2.7, 2.9, 3.11, 4.6, 6.1, 6.9, 6.11; L2: 4.6; L3: 4.6; L4: 4.6; L5: 2.8, 2.9, 4.6, 5.8, 6.1, 6.5, 6.8, 6.11; L6: 3.13; L7: 4.6; L9: 4.6; L10: 4.6, 6.6	L1: 0.1.2, 0.1.5, 3.1.4, 3.6.2, 3.6.3; L2: 0.1.2, 0.1.5, 3.6.3, 3.6.4; L3: 0.1.2, 0.1.5, 3.3.1, 3.3.2, 3.3.4, 6.6.5, 7.4.4, 7.7.3; L4: 0.1.2, 0.1.5, 3.1.6; L5: 0.1.2, 0.1.5, 3.6.2, 7.2.6; L6: 0.1.2, 0.1.5, 3.1.6; L7: 0.1.2, 0.1.5, 3.1.2, 6.6.5, 7.4.2, 7.4.4, 7.7.3; L8: 0.1.2; L9: 0.1.2, 0.1.5, 7.4.2, 7.4.4, 7.7.3; L10: 0.1.2, 0.1.5, 4.8.1, 4.8.3
11	L1: RDG 2.4, 3.2, 4.4; L2: RDG 2.6, 2.9; L3: RDG 2.3, 3.4, 3.10, 4.3; L4: RDG 2.3, 2.8, 3.8, 3.11, 3.12, 4.5; L5: 2.3, 2.8; L6: 2.6, 2.9; L7: 2.3, 2.8, 3.4, 3.8, 3.11, 3.12, 4.3; L8: 3.16	L1: 2.4, 2.7, 2.9, 3.11, 4.6, 6.1; L2: 4.6; L3: 4.6; L4: 4.6; L5: 2.8, 2.9, 4.6, 5.8, 6.1, 6.5, 6.8; L6: 3.13; L7: 4.6; L9: 4.6; L10: 4.6, 6.6	L1: 0.1.2, 0.1.5, 5.3.6; L2: 0.1.2, 0.1.5, 5.2.1, 7.4.4, 7.7.3; L3: 0.1.2, 0.1.5, 2.3.5, 6.6.5, 7.3.2, 7.4.4, 7.7.3; L4: 0.1.2, 0.1.5, 4.2.6, 7.2.6; L5: 0.1.2, 0.1.5, 5.3.1; L6: 0.1.2, 0.1.5, 7.2.6; L7: 0.1.2, 0.1.5, 5.5.2, 5.5.3, 5.5.4, 6.6.5, 7.4.2, 7.4.4, 7.7.3; L8: 0.1.2; L9: 0.1.2, 0.1.5, 7.4.2, 7.4.4, 7.7.3, 7.7.4; L10: 0.1.2, 0.1.5, 4.8.1, 4.8.3
12	L1: RDG 2.4, 3.2; L2: RDG 2.6, 2.9; L3: RDG 2.3, 3.4, 3.10, 4.3; L4: RDG 2.3, 2.8, 3.8, 3.11, 3.12, 4.5; L5: RDG 2.3, 2.8; L6: RDG 2.6, 2.9; L7: RDG 2.3, 2.8, 3.8, 3.11, 3.12, 4.2, 4.3; L8: RDG 3.16; L9: RDG 4.9	L1: 2.4, ,2.7, 2.9, 3.11, 4.6, 6.1, 6.3; L2: 4.6; L3: 4.6; L4: 4.6; L5: 2.8, 2.9, 4.6, 6.1, 6.3, 6.5, 6.8; L6: 3.13; L7: 4.6; L9: 4.6; L10: 4.6, 6.6	L1: 0.1.2, 0.1.5, 5.6.3; L2: 0.1.2, 0.1.5; L3: 0.1.2, 0.1.5, 5.3.1, 6.6.5, 7.4.4, 7.7.3; L4: 0.1.2, 0.1.5, 5.2.2; L5: 0.1.2, 0.1.5, 5.3.2; L6: 0.1.2, 0.1.5, 5.2.1, 5.5.3, 7.4.4, 7.7.3; L7: 0.1.2, 0.1.5, 5.5.2, 5.5.3, 5.5.4, 7.4.4, 7.7.3; L8: 0.1.2; L9: 0.1.2, 0.1.5, 7.4.4, 7.7.3; L10: 0.1.2, 0.1.5, 4.8.3

CASAS: Comprehensive Adult Student Assessment System
CCRS: College and Career Readiness Standards (R=Reading; W=Writing; SL=Speaking/Listening; L=Language)
ELPS: English Language Proficiency Standards

CCRS Correlations, Level D	ELPS Correlations, Level 5
L1: SL.8.1, SL.8.2, L.6.4a, L.6.4d, L.8.6; **L2:** L.6.1/L.8.1f; **L3:** RI.6.7, RST.6-8.7, W.7.7; **L4:** RI/RL.7.1, RI/RL.6-8.1, RST.6-8.1, RI/RL.6.2, RST.6-3.2, RI/RL.6.4, RI.8.6, RH.8.6, W/WHST.6-8.9a, L.6.4a, L.6.4d, L.8.6; **L5:** SL.8.1, SL.8.2, L.6.4a, L.6.4d; **L6:** L.6.1/L.8.1f; **L7:** RI/RL.7.1, RI/RL.6-8.1, RST.6-8.1, RI/RL.6.2, RST.6-8.2, RI/RL.6.4, RI.8.6, RH.8.6, W.7.7, W/WHST.6-8.9a, SL.8.4, SL.8.6, L.6.4a, L.6.4d, L.8.6; **L8:** RI.8.9, W/WHST.6-8.4; **L9:** W/WHST.6-8.2, W/WHST.6-8.4, W/WHST.6-8.5, W.7.6, W.7.7, L.6.3/L.7.3a, L.6.3/L.7.3b, L.6.3/L.7.3c; **L10:** RI/RL.7.1, RI/RL.6-8.1, RST.6-8.1, SL.8.1	ELPS 1–5, 7–10
L1: W/WHST.6-8.4, SL.8.1, SL.8.2, SL.8.4, SL.8.6, L.6.4a, L.6.4d, L.8.6; **L3:** RI.6.7, RST.6-8.7, W.7.7, W/WHST.6-8.8; **L4:** RI/RL.7.1, RI/RL.6-8.1, RST.6-8.1, RI/RL.6.2, RST.6-8.2, RI.8.3, RH.6-8.3, RI/RL.6.4, RI.8.6, RH.8.6, W/WHST.6-8.9a, W/WHST.6-8.9b, L.6.4a, L.6.4d, L.8.6; **L5:** SL.8.1, SL.8.2, L.6.4a, L.6.4d; **L7:** RI/RL.7.1, RI/RL.6-8.1, RST.6-8.1, RI.8.3, RH.6-8.3, RI/RL.6.4, RI.8.6, RH.8.6, W/WHST.6-8.4, W.7.7, W/WHST.6-8.9a, W/WHST.6-8.9b, L.6.4a, L.6.4d, L.8.6; **L8:** RI.8.9, W/WHST.6-8.4; **L9:** W/WHST.6-8.2, W/WHST.6-8.4, W/WHST.6-8.5, W.7.6, W.7.7, L.6.3/L.7.3a, L.6.3/L.7.3b, L.6.3/L.7.3c; **L10:** RI/RL.7.1, RI/RL.6-8.1, RST.6-8.1, SL.8.1	ELPS 1–5, 7–10
L1: SL.8.1, SL.8.2, L.6.4a, L.6.4d, L.8.6; **L2:** W/WHST.6-8.4; **L3:** RI/RL.7.1, RI/RL.6-8.1, RST.6-8.1, RI.6.7, RST.6-8.7, W.7.7; **L4:** RI/RL.7.1, RI/RL.6-8.1, RST.6-8.1, RI/RL.6.2, RST.6-8.2, RI/RL.6.4, RI.8.6, RH.8.6, W/WHST.6-8.9a, L.6.4a, L.6.4d, L.8.6; **L6:** W/WHST.6-8.4; **L7:** RI/RL.7.1, RI/RL.6-8.1, RST.6-8.1, RI/RL.6.2, RST.6-8.2, RI/RL.6.4, RI.6.5, RI.7.5, RI.8.6, RH.8.6, RI.6.7, RST.6-8.7, W.7.7, W/WHST.6-8.9a, SL.8.4, SL.8.6, L.6.4a, L.6.4d, L.8.6; **L8:** RI.8.9, W/WHST.6-8.4; **L9:** W/WHST.6-8.2, W/WHST.6-8.4, W/WHST.6-8.5, W.7.6, L.6.3/L.7.3a, L.6.3/L.7.3b, L.6.3/L.7.3c; **L10:** SL.8.1	ELPS 1–5, 7–10
L1: SL.8.1, SL.8.2, L.6.4a, L.6.4d, L.8.6; **L2:** W/WHST.6-8.4, L.6.1/L.8.1j, L.6.1/L.8.1l; **L3:** W.7.7, W/WHST.6-8.8; **L4:** RI/RL.7.1, RI/RL.6-8.1, RST.6-8.1, RI/RL.6.2, RST.6-8.2, RI/RL.6.4, RI.7.5, RI.8.6, RH.8.6, W.7.7, W/WHST.6-8.9a, L.6.4a, L.6.4d, L.8.6; **L5:** W/WHST.6-8.4, SL.8.1, SL.8.2, L.6.4a, L.6.4d; **L6:** RI/RL.6.4, L.8.6; **L7:** RI/RL.6.2, RST.6-8.2, RI/RL.6.4, RI.8.6, RH.8.6, RI.6.7, RST.6-8.7, W/WHST.6-8.8, W/WHST.6-8.9a, SL.8.1, L.6.4a, L.6.4d, L.8.6; **L8:** RI.8.9, W/WHST.6-8.4; **L9:** W/WHST.6-8.2, W/WHST.6-8.4, W/WHST.6-8.5, W.7.6, L.6.3/L.7.3a, L.6.3/L.7.3b, L.6.3/L.7.3c; **L10:** RI/RL.7.1, RI/RL.6-8.1, RST.6-8.1, SL.8.1	ELPS 1–2, 4–5, 7–10
L1: W.7.7, SL.8.1, SL.8.2, SL.8.3, L.6.1/L.8.1j, L.6.1/L.8.1l, L.6.4a, L.6.4d, L.8.6; **L2:** W/WHST.6-8.4; **L3:** RI/RL.7.1, RI/RL.6-8.1, RST.6-8.1, RI.6.7, RST.6-8.7, W.7.7; **L4:** RI/RL.7.1, RI/RL.6-8.1, RST.6-8.1, RI/RL.6.2, RST.6-8.2, RI/RL.6.4, RI.8.6, RH.8.6, W/WHST.6-8.9a, L.6.4a, L.6.4d, L.8.6; **L5:** SL.8.1, SL.8.2, L.6.4a, L.6.4d; **L6:** W/WHST.6-8.4, L.6.1/L.8.1j, L.6.1/L.8.1l; **L7:** RI/RL.7.1, RI/RL.6-8.1, RST.6-8.1, RI/RL.6.2, RST.6-8.2, RI/RL.6.4, RI.7.5, RI.8.6, RH.8.6, RI.6.7, RST.6-8.7, RI.8.8, W.7.7, W/WHST.6-8.9a, SL.8.4, SL.8.6, L.6.4a, L.6.4d, L.8.6; **L8:** RI.8.9, W/WHST.6-8.4; **L9:** W/WHST.6-8.2, W/WHST.6-8.4, W/WHST.6-8.5, W.7.6, W.7.7, L.6.3/L.7.3a, L.6.3/L.7.3b, L.6.3/L.7.3c; **L10:** SL.8.1	ELPS 1–10
L1: SL.8.1, SL.8.2, L.6.4a, L.6.4d, L.8.6; **L2:** W/WHST.6-8.4, L.6.1/L.8.1h; **L3:** RI.6.7, RST.6-8.7, W.7.7, L.8.6; **L4:** RI/RL.7.1, RI/RL.6-8.1, RST.6-8.1, RI/RL.6.2, RST.6-8.2, RI/RL.6.4, RI.6.5, RI.7.5, RI.8.6, RH.8.6, W/WHST.6-8.9a, L.6.4a, L.6.4d, L.8.6; **L5:** SL.8.1, SL.8.2, L.6.4a, L.6.4d, L.8.6; **L6:** W/WHST.6-8.4, L.6.1/L.8.1h; **L7:** RI/RL.7.1, RI/RL.6-8.1, RST.6-8.1, RI/RL.6.2, RST.6-8.2, RI.8.3, RH.6-8.3, RI/RL.6.4, RI.8.6, RH.8.6, RI.6.7, RST.6-8.7, W/WHST.6-8.4, W.7.7, W/WHST.6-8.9a, W/WHST.6-8.9b, L.6.4a, L.6.4d, L.8.6; **L8:** RI.8.9, L.6.1/L.8.1k; **L9:** W/WHST.6-8.2, W/WHST.6-8.5, W.7.6, W.7.7, L.6.3/L.7.3a, L.6.3/L.7.3b, L.6.3/L.7.3c; **L10:** SL.8.1	ELPS 1–5, 7–10
L1: SL.8.1, SL.8.2, SL.8.4, SL.8.6, L.6.4a, L.6.4d, L.8.6; **L2:** L.6.1/L.8.1h; **L3:** RI.6.7, RST.6-8.7, W.7.7, SL.8.1, L.8.6; **L4:** RI/RL.7.1, RI/RL.6-8.1, RST.6-8.1, RI/RL.6.2, RST.6-8.2, RI/RL.6.4, RI.8.6, RH.8.6, RI.6.7, RST.6-8.7, W.7.7, W/WHST.6-8.9a, L.6.4a, L.6.4d, L.8.6; **L5:** SL.8.1, SL.8.2, SL.8.4, SL.8.6, L.6.4a, L.6.4d, L.8.6; **L6:** W/WHST.6-8.4, W.7.7, L.6.1/L.8.1h; **L7:** RI/RL.7.1, RI/RL.6-8.1, RST.6-8.1, RI/RL.6.2, RST.6-8.2, RI/RL.6.4, RI.8.6, RH.8.6, W.7.7, W/WHST.6-8.9a, SL.8.4, SL.8.6, L.6.4a, L.6.4d, L.8.6; **L8:** RI.8.8, RI.8.9, W/WHST.6-8.4; **L9:** W.7.1, W/WHST.6-8.4, W/WHST.6-8.5, W.7.6, W.7.7, W/WHST.6-8.8, L.6.3/L.7.3a, L.6.3/L.7.3b, L.6.3/L.7.3c; **L10:** SL.8.1	ELPS 1–10
L1: SL.8.1, SL.8.2, SL.8.3, L.6.4a, L.6.4d, L.8.6; **L2:** W/WHST.6-8.4; **L3:** W.7.7, W/WHST.6-8.8, SL.8.1, L.8.6; **L4:** RI/RL.7.1, RI/RL.6-8.1, RST.6-8.1, RI/RL.6.2, RST.6-8.2, RI/RL.6.4, RI.8.6, RH.8.6, W/WHST.6-8.9a, L.6.4a, L.6.4d, L.8.6; **L5:** SL.8.1, SL.8.2, SL.8.3, L.6.4a, L.6.4d, L.8.6; **L6:** W/WHST.6-8.4; **L7:** RI/RL.7.1, RI/RL.6-8.1, RST.6-8.1, RI/RL.6.2, RST.6-8.2, RI/RL.6.4, RI.8.6, RH.8.6, RI.6.7, RST.6-8.7, RI.8.8, W.7.7, W/WHST.6-8.8, W/WHST.6-8.9a, L.6.4a, L.6.4d, L.8.6; **L8:** RI.8.9, W/WHST.6-8.4, W.7.7; **L9:** W.7.1, W/WHST.6-8.4, W/WHST.6-8.5, W.7.6, L.6.3/L.7.3a, L.6.3/L.7.3b, L.6.3/L.7.3c; **L10:** SL.8.1	ELPS 1–2, 4–10
L1: SL.8.1, SL.8.2, SL.8.3, L.6.4a, L.6.4d, L.8.6; **L2:** W/WHST.6-8.4, L.6.1/L.8.1g; **L3:** RI/RL.7.1, RI/RL.6-8.1, RST.6-8.1, W.7.7, L.8.6; **L4:** RI/RL.7.1, RI/RL.6-8.1, RST.6-8.1, RI/RL.6.2, RST.6-8.2, RI/RL.6.4, RI.8.6, RH.8.6, W/WHST.6-8.9a, L.6.4a, L.6.4d, L.8.6; **L5:** SL.8.1, SL.8.2, L.6.4a, L.6.4d, L.8.6; **L6:** W/WHST.6-8.4, W.7.7, L.6.1/L.8.1g; **L7:** RI/RL.7.1, RI/RL.6-8.1, RST.6-8.1, RI/RL.6.2, RST.6-8.2, RI/RL.6.4, RI.8.6, RH.8.6, W.7.7, W/WHST.6-8.9a, SL.8.4, SL.8.5, SL.8.6, L.6.4a, L.6.4d, L.8.6; **L8:** RI.8.9, W/WHST.6-8.4; **L9:** W/WHST.6-8.2, W/WHST.6-8.4, W/WHST.6-8.5, W.7.6, W.7.7, L.6.3/L.7.3a, L.6.3/L.7.3b, L.6.3/L.7.3c; **L10:** SL.8.1	ELPS 1–10
L1: SL.8.1, SL.8.2, SL.8.3, L.6.4a, L.6.4d, L.8.6; **L3:** RI/RL.7.1, RI/RL.6-8.1, RST.6-8.1, W.7.7, L.8.6; **L4:** RI/RL.7.1, RI/RL.6-8.1, RST.6-8.1, RI/RL.6.2, RST.6-8.2, RI/RL.6.4, RI.8.6, RH.8.6, W/WHST.6-8.9a, L.6.4a, L.6.4d, L.8.6; **L5:** SL.8.1, SL.8.2, SL.8.3, L.6.4a, L.6.4d, L.8.6; **L6:** W/WHST.6-8.4; **L7:** RI/RL.7.1, RI/RL.6-8.1, RST.6-8.1, RI/RL.6.2, RST.6-8.2, RI/RL.6.4, RI.8.6, RH.8.6, RI.6.7, RST.6-8.7, W.7.7, W/WHST.6-8.8, W/WHST.6-8.9a, SL.8.4, SL.8.6, L.6.4a, L.6.4d, L.8.6; **L8:** RI.8.9, W/WHST.6-8.4; **L9:** W.7.1, W/WHST.6-8.4, W/WHST.6-8.5, W.7.6, W.7.7, L.6.3/L.7.3a, L.6.3/L.7.3b, L.6.3/L.7.3c; **L10:** RI/RL.7.1, RI/RL.6-8.1, RST.6-8.1, SL.8.1;	ELPS 1–10
L1: SL.8.1, SL.8.2, SL.8.3, L.6.4a, L.6.4d, L.8.6; **L2:** W/WHST.6-8.4, W.7.7; **L3:** RI/RL.7.1, RI/RL.6-8.1, RST.6-8.1, RI.6.7, W.7.7, L.8.6; **L4:** RI/RL.7.1, RI/RL.6-8.1, RST.6-8.1, RI/RL.6.2, RST.6-8.2, RI/RL.6.4, RI.8.6, RH.8.6, W/WHST.6-8.9a, L.6.4a, L.6.4d, L.8.6; **L5:** RI.8.3, RH.6-8.3, W.7.7, W/WHST.6-8.9b, SL.8.1, SL.8.2, SL.8.4, SL.8.6, L.6.4a, L.6.4d, L.8.6; **L6:** L.6.1/L.8.1f; **L7:** RI/RL.7.1, RI/RL.6-8.1, RST.6-8.1, RI/RL.6.2, RI/RL.6.4, RI.8.6, RH.8.6, RST.6-8.2, RI.8.3, RH.6-8.3, W/WHST.6-8.4, W.7.7, W/WHST.6-8.8, W/WHST.6-8.9a, SL.8.4, SL.8.6, L.6.4a, L.6.4d, L.8.6; **L8:** RI.8.9, W/WHST.6-8.4; **L9:** W.7.1, W/WHST.6-8.4, W/WHST.6-8.5, W.7.6, W.7.7, L.6.3/L.7.3a, L.6.3/L.7.3b, L.6.3/L.7.3c; **L10:** SL.8.1	ELPS 1–10
L1: SL.8.1, SL.8.2, L.6.4a, L.6.4d, L.8.6; **L3:** RI/RL.7.1, RI/RL.6-8.1, RST.6-8.1, W.7.7, L.8.6; **L4:** RI/RL.7.1, RI/RL.6-8.1, RST.6-8.1, RI/RL.6.2, RST.6-8.2, RI/RL.6.4, RI.8.6, RH.8.6, W/WHST.6-8.9a, L.6.4a, L.6.4d, L.8.6; **L5:** SL.8.1, SL.8.2, L.6.4a, L.6.4d; **L6:** W.7.7, L.6.1/L.8.1l; **L7:** RI/RL.7.1, RI/RL.6-8.1, RST.6-8.1, RI/RL.6.2, RST.6-8.2, RI/RL.6.4, RI.8.6, RH.8.6, W.7.7, W/WHST.6-8.9a, SL.8.4, SL.8.6, L.6.4a, L.6.4d, L.8.6; **L8:** RI.8.9, W/WHST.6-8.4; **L9:** W.7.1, W/WHST.6-8.4, W/WHST.6-8.5, W.7.6, W.7.7, L.6.3/L.7.3a, L.6.3/L.7.3b, L.6.3/L.7.3c; **L10:** SL.8.1	ELPS 1–10

All units of *Future* meet most of the **EFF Content Standards**. For details, as well as for correlations to other state standards, go to www.pearsoneltusa.com/future 2e.

Acknowledgments

The Publisher would like to acknowledge the teachers, students, and survey and focus-group participants for their valuable input. Thank you to the following reviewers and consultants who made suggestions, contributed to this *Future* revision, and helped make *Future: English for Work, Life, and Academic Success* even better in this second edition. There are many more who also shared their comments and experiences using *Future*—a big thank you to all.

Fuad Al-Daraweesh The University of Toledo, Toledo, OH

Denise Alexander Bucks County Community College, Newtown, PA

Isabel Alonso Bergen Community College, Hackensack, NJ

Veronica Avitia LeBarron Park, El Paso, TX

Maria Bazan-Myrick Houston Community College, Houston, TX

Sara M. Bulnes Miami Dade College, Miami, FL

Alexander Chakshiri Santa Maria High School, Santa Maria, CA

Scott C. Cohen, M.A.Ed. Bergen Community College, Paramus, NJ

Judit Criado Fiuza Mercy Center, Bronx, NY

Megan Ernst Glendale Community College, Glendale, CA

Rebecca Feit-Klein Essex County College Adult Learning Center, West Caldwell, NJ

Caitlin Floyd Nationalities Service Center, Philadelphia, PA

Becky Gould International Community High School, Bronx, NY

Ingrid Greenberg San Diego Continuing Education, San Diego Community College District, San Diego, CA

Steve Gwynne San Diego Continuing Education, San Diego, CA

Robin Hatfield, M.Ed. Learning Institute of Texas, Houston,TX

Coral Horton Miami Dade College, Kendall Campus, Miami, FL

Lori Howard ESOL Teacher Education Specialist

Roxana Hurtado Miami-Dade County Public Schools, Miami, FL

Lisa Johnson City College of San Francisco, San Francisco, CA

Kristine R. Kelly ATLAS @ Hamline University, St. Paul, MN

Jennifer King Austin Community College, Austin, TX

Lia Lerner, Ed.D. Burbank Adult School, Burbank, CA

Ting Li The University of Toledo, Ottawa Hills, OH

Nichole M. Lucas University of Dayton, Dayton, OH

Ruth Luman Modesto Junior College, Modesto, CA

Josephine Majul El Monte-Rosemead Adult School, El Monte, CA

Dr. June Ohrnberger Suffolk County Community College, Selden, NY

Sue Park The Learning Institute of Texas, Houston, TX

Dr. Sergei Paromchik Adult Education Department, Hillsborough County Public Schools, Tampa, FL

Patricia Patton Uniontown ESL, Uniontown, PA

Matthew Piech Amarillo College, Amarillo, TX

Guillermo Rocha Essex County College, NJ

Audrene Rowe Essex County Schools, Newark, NJ

Naomi Sato Glendale Community College, Glendale, CA

Alejandra Solis Lone Star College, Houston, TX

Geneva Tesh Houston Community College, Houston, TX

Karyna Tytar Lake Washington Institute of Technology, Kirkland, WA

Miguel Veloso Miami Springs Adult, Miami, FL

Minah Woo Howard Community College, Columbia, MD

The Power of Goals

1

PREVIEW
What methods do you use to organize your thoughts or tasks? What do you think this woman is doing?

UNIT GOALS

Identify factors to consider when choosing a career

Use career assessment tools to identify interests and skills

Identify the criteria of a SMART goal

Evaluate and set SMART goals

Give a presentation to describe a person you admire

Write about your interests, skills, and career goals

Workplace Soft Skill: Demonstrate a willingness to learn

Academic Skills:
- **Listening:** Listen for main ideas and supporting details
- **Speaking:** Collaborate with others as a team
- **Reading:** Identify main ideas and supporting details
- **Writing:** Write effective topic sentences

1

Lesson 1  Listening and Speaking

Identify factors to consider when choosing a career

1 Before You Listen

A BRAINSTORM. With thousands of career options available, what are some strategies for choosing the right one for you?

B PREVIEW VOCABULARY.

1. **TOPIC-RELATED WORDS.** These terms are used in the listening. Does anyone know what they mean? Look for root words to help you.

career counselor	assessment	aspirations
internship	advancement	

2. **ACADEMIC WORDS.** These sentences are from the listening. Discuss the meaning of each **bolded** word. Use context to help you.

   1. In order to maintain a satisfying work-life balance, it's important to **pursue** a career that's right for you.
   2. The key is to figure out what you're **inherently** good at.
   3. I **consulted** with a career counselor at my college.
   4. These tests helped me **clarify** what type of work I would be good at.
   5. An internship allows you to build **expertise** as you begin your career.

C PREDICT. Use the lesson title, vocabulary, and image to make predictions about the podcast. What will its purpose be? What information do you expect?

2 Listen

A ▶ LISTEN FOR IMPORTANT IDEAS. Listen to the podcast. What strategy did each person use to find a suitable career? Complete the chart.

Speaker	Strategy
Henry	Find your passion.
Jessica	Career counselor. Take a test.
Emma	Taken internship

B ▶ LISTEN FOR DETAILS. Listen again to Henry. What reasons does he give for liking his career?
He helps his clients gain extra confidence.

Listening and Speaking

3 Apply Academic Listening Skill

Academic Listening Skill: Listen for main ideas and supporting details
In an interview, speakers will clearly state their main points or main ideas. Speakers also give examples to help the listener better understand the main ideas. Read the list of example signal words. Listening for these words will help you notice when a speaker is providing examples to support a main idea.

Example Signal Words	
Words and Phrases	**Verbs**
for example, another example, for instance, such as, much like, similar to, specifically, in the same way as, including	to illustrate, to exemplify, to demonstrate

A ▶ **IDENTIFY MAIN IDEA.** Listen to Jessica again. What is the main idea of this part of the podcast?
The main idea is that Jessica consulted a career counselor to help her find a career

B ▶ **IDENTIFY SIGNAL WORDS.** Listen again. Which signal words or phrases does Jessica use to introduce her examples? Underline them in the chart above.

C ▶ **GIVE EXAMPLES.** Listen to Jessica's answer to the second question. What kinds of assessments did Jessica take, and what were they used for? List each assessment and its use.
Personality test & career test. The personality test provides information about herself, such as communication style, interests, abilities and values.

D **EXPAND VOCABULARY.** Add words to your Word Study Log to show structure and meaning.

4 Real-World Application

A **SURVEY.** Ask questions to find out about your classmates' interests and skills.

Name	Interests	Skills
Helena	teach ... Stitches	Stitches
Reynaldo		

B **COLLABORATE.** Work as a group to decide which interests and which skills are common among your classmates. Summarize your group's results and report them to the class.

Academic Speaking Skill: Collaborate with others as a team
At school or at work, when collaborating with others, it's important to give each person an opportunity to share and contribute. Listening carefully to others will help ensure that others listen carefully to you.

- *Remember, everyone should have an opportunity to participate.*
- *Let's make sure each of us has time to share.*

I can identify factors to consider when choosing a career. ☐   I need more practice. ☐

For more practice, go to MyEnglishLab.   For audio and video, scan the QR code.

Unit 1, Lesson 1   **3**

Lesson 2 Grammar

Use gerunds and infinitives to share interests and preferences

1 Focus on Usage

A **CONSIDER.** Read the highlighted sentences in the career center advertisement below. Which words express interests and preferences?

> A gerund is the *-ing* form of the verb. An infinitive is **to** + the base form of the verb. Both gerunds and infinitives are often used as nouns to express preferences.

B **IDENTIFY.** Read the entire advertisement. Identify the verbs that are followed by a gerund or an infinitive. Underline all examples of verb + gerund. Circle all examples of verb + infinitive.

🏆 Taylor College Career Center Helping you find your calling

Choosing a career path may be one of the most difficult decisions you ever make. You should consider your competencies, 能力. interests, values, and personal characteristics. For example, do you like being in an office? Or do you love to work outdoors? Do you prefer to work alone or on a team? Are you a morning person, or do you hate waking up early? Do you enjoy helping other people? What do you like to do in your free time?

At the Taylor Career Center, we help you take real steps towards your career goals. If you are unsure about what you would want to do and where you hope to be in five years, we offer a full career assessment. When you finish taking the assessment, we provide a list of career options best suited for you. If you decide to switch careers, we can help you choose a suitable major. We can also help you practice interviewing for jobs. Plan to visit the Career Center today!

2 Focus on Structure

Gerunds	Infinitives
I enjoy **helping** other people.	
	I want **to work** in an office.
I like **being** part of a team.	I like **to be** part of a team.

- Some verbs can only be followed by a gerund, and others can only be followed by an infinitive.
- Some verbs can be followed by either a gerund or an infinitive.

For a list of which verbs are used with gerunds or infinitives, search online for: verbs with gerunds and infinitives.

A **INVESTIGATE.** Analyze all the examples of gerunds and infinitives. Which verbs are followed by gerunds? Which verbs are followed by infinitives? If the verb is followed by either a gerund or an infinitive, check both columns.

	Gerund	Infinitive
like, love, hate, prefer	√	√
agree, decide, plan		√
enjoy, practice, finish	√	
need, want, hope, would like		√

4 Unit 1, Lesson 2

Grammar

B **COMPLETE.** Complete the sentences with a gerund or an infinitive. Some sentences have two possible correct answers.

1. (*listen*) I enjoy _____listening_____ to music while I work.

2. (*learn*) I plan _to learn_ about medical technology.

3. (*write*) Angela doesn't like _to write_ *or writing* in her second language because it's too difficult.

4. (*speak*) How often do you practice _speaking_ English?

5. (*work*) Do you want _to work_ in an office?

6. (*negotiate*) I don't have good communication skills, so I hate _negotiating_. *to negotiate*

C **REWRITE.** Combine the sentences using a gerund or an infinitive.

1. Sara bakes wedding cakes. She enjoys it.
   Sarah enjoys baking wedding cakes.

2. Rick spends time in his garden every evening. He loves it.
   He loves to spend time in his garden every evening. *spending time*

3. Emma doesn't use social media. She hates it.
   She hates to use social media, or she hates using social media

4. Mike will take five classes next semester. That's what he needs.
   Mike needs to take five classes next semester.

5. I usually study in the morning. That's what I prefer.
   I prefer to study in the morning.

6. Katy will look for a job at the hospital. That's what she decided.
   Katy decided to look for a job at the hospital.

Apply what you know

1. **DESCRIBE.** Discuss your job-related interests and skills. Use gerunds and infinitives.

   1. What do you like to do?
   2. What kind of job do you hope to find?

2. **WRITE.** Write several sentences about your career plans or aspirations. Use gerunds and infinitives.
   I want to pursue a career in portrait and wedding photography. I enjoy taking pictures.
   I need to take some classes to improve my camera skills.

I can use gerunds and infinitives to share interests and preferences. ☐   I need more practice. ☐

For more practice, go to MyEnglishLab.

Unit 1, Lesson 2   **5**

Workplace, Life, & Community Skills

Lesson **3**

Use career assessment tools to identify interests and skills

1 Identify Personal Interests and Goals

A **REFLECT.** Share your personal interests. What type of person are you? Why?

I like to ___I to 5___

1. work with my hands and enjoy being outdoors
2. watch and learn and enjoy solving problems
3. use my imagination and create new ideas
4. inspire and help people
5. lead people and achieve goals
6. work with information and carry out detailed tasks

B **PROBLEM-SOLVE.** Why is it important to have a career goal based on your personal interests?

2 Consult Resources

Interest and Skills Assessments

There are two different tools to help you identify a career that suits you: an interest assessment and a skills assessment. An interest assessment helps match a person to careers that align with the specific interests the person has. A skills assessment looks at a person's skills or abilities and finds careers that use those particular skills.

A **SCAN.** A young woman was taking classes to help get a job at a law firm. But she wasn't enjoying the classes, so she took an interest assessment. Look at her assessment results.

1. Which of the occupations listed in the assessment is the highest paying? _Elementary music teacher_

2. What symbol is used to show the most favorable choices or prospects? _Choices_

3. What does the letter "R" stand for in the bar graph? _Stand for Realistic_

Interest Assessment Results

We found **26** occupations that match your interests.

	OCCUPATION	PROSPECT	HOURLY WAGE	PREPARATION
☆	nanny	great	$10.90	
★	preschool childcare worker	best	$11.17	high school diploma and certificate of training
	actor	good	$17.54	
	choreographer	good	$22.98	high school diploma and advanced dance training
	human resources representative	good	$23.55	Bachelor's degree
★	elementary music teacher	best	$25.70	Master's degree

- ■ **R** – **Realistic** (doers)
- ■ **I** – **Investigative** (thinkers)
- ■ **A** – **Artistic** (creators)
- ■ **S** – **Social** (helpers)
- ■ **E** – **Enterprising** (resourceful self-starters)
- ■ **C** – **Conventional** (traditional rule-followers)

Your Interests

R	■	3
I	■	3
A	■	38
S	■	25
E	■	13
C		0

0 5 10 15 20 25 30 35 40

---

6 Unit 1, Lesson 3

Workplace, Life, & Community Skills

B **DEFINE KEY WORDS.** Find these words on the interest assessment. Match each word to its definition.

_e_ **1.** (adj) conventional   **a.** money earned, usually on a regular basis

_d_ **2.** (adj) enterprising   **b.** job or profession

_b_ **3.** (n) occupation   **c.** tending to take on untried plans

_c_ **4.** (n) prospect   **d.** likelihood of success

_a_ **5.** (n) wage   **e.** tending to follow established guidelines

C **INTERPRET.** Locate information on the interest assessment.

1. Which occupation has the lowest pay but is a great match? _Perschool childcare worker_

2. Which occupations require no high school diploma? _Perschool childcare worker & choreographer_

3. Which occupation would be a poor choice since it's just a "good" prospect with a low wage? _actor_

D **RANK.** Six interest categories are used in the results bar graph. Rank the categories from the best fit (1) to the poorest fit (6) to show your personal interests. What does your ranking tell you about yourself?

_3_ **(R) Realistic** – have athletic interests; prefers to work with objects, machines, tools, plants, or animals; often likes to be outdoors

_1_ **(I) Investigative** – likes to observe, learn, analyze, and solve problems

_6_ **(A) Artistic** – likes to work in unstructured situations using their imagination and creativity

_3_ **(S) Social** – likes to work with people to inspire, inform, help, train, or cure them

_2_ **(E) Enterprising** – likes to work with people to influence, persuade, and lead them; likes to achieve new goals

_3_ **(C) Conventional** – likes to work with set information, carry out detailed tasks, and have clerical or numerical interests; likes to achieve fixed goals

E **GO ONLINE.** Use the Search Terms to find an interest assessment *or* a skills assessment. Take that assessment.

Search Terms: interest assessment   skills assessment

F **TAKE NOTES.** What are the best-matching occupations from your assessment? Which of those occupations sound most interesting to you and use the skills you have?

G **SHARE.** Tell a partner why you chose an interest assessment or a skills assessment. Share your results. Describe something you learned about your occupation goals.

Apply what you know

1. **APPLY.** Use the interest or skills assessment you found online to get more information. Sort your results in other categories—for example, outlook, wages, or education needed.

2. **SHARE.** Explain your assessment results to a partner. Discuss whether or not you feel the results are accurate.
   - *The results say _____, (but/and) I (dis)agree because _____.*

I can use career assessment tools to identify interests and skills. ☐   I need more practice. ☐

For more practice, go to MyEnglishLab.

Unit 1, Lesson 3   **7**

Lesson 4 Reading

Identify the criteria of a SMART goal

1 Before You Read

A REFLECT. What are your goals for next year? List one goal in each column.

Health	Career	Money
Be health	Find a better job	$22

B PREVIEW VOCABULARY.

1. **TOPIC-RELATED WORDS.** These terms are used in the article. Does anyone know what they mean? You can look for clues in the article.

   techniques   deadline   short-term   long-term   vision

2. **ACADEMIC WORDS.** Discuss the meaning of the **bolded** words in the article. Use context to help you. After reading the article, add any words you learned to your Word Study Log.

C PREDICT. Preview the article title and image. What is the purpose of the article? What information do you expect?

2 Read for Gist

A READ. What do the letters in SMART stand for?

Setting SMART Goals for Success

1 A 2015 study showed that people who write down their goals are 33% more likely to achieve them. One of the most well-known techniques for setting personal and professional goals is the SMART method. A SMART goal is a goal that is Specific, Measurable, Achievable,
5 Relevant, and Time-bound:
   • To make a goal Specific, say exactly what you want to achieve.
   • To make it Measurable, attach a number or amount to the goal.
   • To make it Achievable, be sure you can realistically achieve the goal.
   • To make it Relevant, make sure the goal is important to you.
10 • To make it Time-bound, set a deadline for completing the goal.
   Let's look at an example of SMART goals in action. Women for Women International is an organization that helps women in countries devastated by war. The organization has helped more than 500,000 women. Many of these women have lost their husbands and families. They have to work and earn money, often for the first time in their lives.
15   The first step is for the women to enroll in a free Women for Women International program. The women learn how to find and keep a job. Then they learn how to set up a bank account and save money. Many of the women start small businesses. Finally, the women find business loans through the Women for Women International community.
    One of the skills the women learn is how to set goals. They set both short-term and long-term goals. A short-term goal is something they want to accomplish soon. An example of a short-term goal is opening a bank account. A
20 long-term goal is something they hope to achieve in the next year. An example of a long-term goal is for the women to save four–five times more money by the end of the year than they had at the beginning.

8 Unit 1, Lesson 4

Reading

The Women for Women International program participants could set a goal to simply "save more money." However, by **specifying** how much they want to save and by when, they make it more likely that they will achieve their goal. And this kind of **explicit** goal-setting works. For example, in Rwanda, participants begin the year with an average of $24.20
25 in savings. They end the year with an average of $117.67 in savings.

How could you set short-term and long-term SMART goals in your own life? Think about your <u>vision</u> for the next year of your life. What do you want to achieve? Get a promotion? Find a new job? Earn a certificate or degree? Setting SMART goals gives you the direction you need to **transform** your goals into reality.

B IDENTIFY MAIN IDEAS. Choose the main idea of the article. Where is it stated? Lines _____

a. Women for Women International used SMART goals.
b. You are more likely to achieve your goals when you make them SMART.
c. It is important to set both short-term and long-term SMART goals.

3 Close Reading

A RECOGNIZE STRUCTURE. What topic, or major subject, is covered in each of these paragraphs:

Paragraph 2 _____
Paragraph 3 _____
Paragraph 4 _____

B LOCATE DETAILS. Label each step as: *Specific, Measurable, Achievable, Relevant,* or *Time-bound.*

1. I want to achieve this goal by next summer. _____
2. I need English at work so I can speak at meetings. _____
3. I'm going to take two more English classes a week. _____
4. Two classes a week take three hours, which fits into my schedule. _____
5. I want to become more fluent and articulate in English. _____

C EXPAND UNDERSTANDING. Are the statements true or false? Write the line numbers of your evidence.

	T/F	Lines
1. People who told a friend about their goals are 33% more likely to achieve them.	____	____
2. To make a goal specific, set a deadline for completing it.	____	____
3. Something you hope to accomplish in the next year is an example of a long-term goal.	____	____
4. Women for Women International participants set SMART goals around saving money.	____	____

Apply what you know

1. **APPLY.** Choose a goal from Exercise 1A. Create a T-Chart as shown. State each goal as a SMART goal.

2. **SHARE.** Share your goals with a partner.

   • *My (short-term/long-term) goal is to* _____ *by* _____.
                                           (goal)   (date)

Short-term	Long-term

I can identify the criteria of a SMART goal. ☐   I need more practice. ☐

For more practice, go to MyEnglishLab.   For audio and video, scan the QR code.

Unit 1, Lesson 4   9

Lesson 5 Listening and Speaking

Evaluate and set SMART goals

1 Before You Listen

A **REFLECT.** What long-term career goal did you list in Lesson 4 *Apply what you know*? What specific steps will you take to reach your goal?

B **PREVIEW VOCABULARY.**

1. **TOPIC-RELATED WORDS.** These terms are used in the listening. Does anyone know what they mean? For compound words, it often helps to think about the meaning of each word separately.

| upper management | small-business loan | academic advisor |

2. **ACADEMIC WORDS.** These sentences are from the listening. Discuss the meaning of each **bolded** word. Use context to help you.
    1. A goal that is specific is very clear. To **demonstrate**, it's not enough to say you're going to take *some* classes.
    2. I need to **acquire** some cooking techniques, so I'll take some culinary arts classes.
    3. That step has two parts, and those two parts need to be **coordinated**.
    4. **Initially**, I want to start out working part-time so that I have time to study.
    5. For now, **shift** your energy to finding a catering job and choosing your college classes.

food catering

C **PREDICT.** Use the lesson title, vocabulary, and images to make predictions about the listening. Who will participate in the conversation? What will the purpose of the conversation be?

2 Listen

A ▶ **LISTEN FOR MAIN IDEAS.** Listen to the conversation between Ruben and his counselor. What is Ruben's long-term goal?

_____

B ▶ **LISTEN FOR DETAILS.** Listen again. Complete the flowchart as you listen.

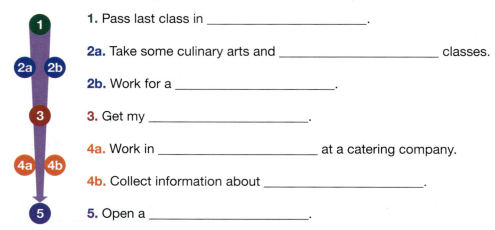

1. Pass last class in _____.

2a. Take some culinary arts and _____ classes.

2b. Work for a _____.

3. Get my _____.

4a. Work in _____ at a catering company.

4b. Collect information about _____.

5. Open a _____.

10 Unit 1, Lesson 5

Listening and Speaking

3 Apply Academic Listening Skill

A ▶ **IDENTIFY MAIN IDEAS.** Listen to part of the conversation again. What is the main idea?

B ▶ **IDENTIFY DETAILS.** Listen to part of the conversation again. What examples does the career counselor give to demonstrate SMART goals?

Specific	
Measurable	
Achievable	
Relevant	
Time-bound	

C **EXPAND VOCABULARY.** Add words to your Word Study Log to show structure and meaning.

4 Real-World Application

A **EVALUATE.** Which statement expresses a SMART goal? Explain why.
   a. I'll have a good job in the future.
   b. I'll take some classes at the community college.
   c. I'll have a job as an X-ray technician, with an income over $50,000 a year, within three years.
   d. I'll make enough money to support my family and send my children to college.

B **SHARE.** Discuss your five-year or ten-year SMART career goal. Create a flowchart for your career path. Use the flowchart for Ruben's career path in Exercise 2B as a model.
   - *My first goal is to _____ and then _____.*
   - *In five years I hope to _____.*
   - *By the time I graduate, I plan on _____.*

culinary arts class

I can evaluate and set SMART goals. ☐   I need more practice. ☐

For more practice, go to MyEnglishLab.   For audio and video, scan the QR code.

Lesson 6 Grammar
Use gerunds and infinitives to describe career goals and action steps

1 Focus on Usage

A CONSIDER. Read the highlighted sentences about setting goals in the blog below. Notice where the gerunds and infinitives are used.

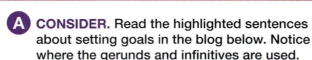

Gerunds and infinitives can occur in different places in a sentence and be used in many different ways. Gerunds and infinitives often function as nouns.

B IDENTIFY. Read the entire blog. Underline all the gerunds. Circle all the infinitives.

Achieving a goal can be difficult. You can make the path clearer and easier by setting SMART goals. First, it is important to be specific when you create goals. Your goals need to be as well defined as possible. Ask yourself what you want to accomplish, why you want it, and how you plan to achieve it. The next step is to make your goal measurable. This will allow you to track your progress. Measuring your progress will help you stay focused and motivated. Third, make sure your goal is attainable. An attainable goal is one that is possible to accomplish. Next, ask yourself if the goal is relevant. This is the time to decide what is most important to you. Will the goal help you move closer to accomplishing a bigger goal? Finally, your goal needs to be time-bound. Set a realistic time frame by giving yourself enough time to complete the goal. It's always a good idea to give yourself a little more time than you need. These five steps will increase your chances of reaching a goal.

2 Focus on Structure

	Gerund	Infinitive
Subject	*Achieving* a goal can be difficult.	
Object of <u>verb</u>	You should <u>consider</u> **setting** SMART goals.	Your goal <u>needs</u> **to be** specific.
Following a <u>preposition</u>	It will move you closer <u>to</u> **accomplishing** your goal.	
Following an <u>adjective</u>		Choose goals that are <u>possible</u> **to achieve**.
Following a <u>noun</u>		Give yourself <u>time</u> **to accomplish** the goal.
Following a <u>pronoun</u>		It allows <u>you</u> **to track** your progress.

- It is possible to use an infinitive as the subject of a sentence, but it is not as common.
- Gerunds can also follow *have* + noun expressions:
  - She has trouble **setting** goals.
  - He had a hard time **meeting** the deadline.

12 Unit 1, Lesson 6

Grammar

A **INVESTIGATE.** Analyze all the examples of gerunds and infinitives. Choose the correct answers.

1. A preposition may be followed by _____.
   a. only a gerund *(circled)* b. only an infinitive c. either a gerund or an infinitive

2. Use *It is* + adjective + _____.
   a. gerund b. infinitive *(circled)* c. gerund or infinitive

3. Use _____ after a noun or pronoun.
   a. only a gerund b. only an infinitive *(circled)* c. either a gerund or an infinitive

B **COMPLETE.** Complete the sentences. Use gerunds or infinitives.

1. (*discuss*) I'm meeting with my counselor _to discuss_ my goals.

2. (*study*) Jackie passed her exams by _studying_ for hours every night.

3. (*find*) Sam's counselor advised him _to find_ an internship.

4. (*achieve*) Gavin set too many big goals. I'm not sure it's possible _achieving_ that many goals in only a month.

5. (*Choose*) _Choosing_ a specific goal is the first step.

6. (*solve*) Andrea's career assessment showed that she is good at _solving_ problems.

7. (*go*) James is afraid of _going_ on job interviews.

8. (*help*) Martin thanked his career counselor for _helping_ him.

Apply what you know

1. **EXPLAIN.** Describe one of your SMART goals to a partner. Then complete the sentences with a gerund or an infinitive and information about that goal.

   1. I would like to _graduate from college_

   2. I want to be better at _____.

   3. I can improve by _learning_.

   4. It's important _to have a college degree_

2. **WRITE.** Write a paragraph about your SMART goal. Use gerunds and infinitives.

   My goal is to become a dental hygienist in two years. First, I plan on meeting an academic advisor next week. It's important to have a specific degree plan.

I can use gerunds and infinitives to describe career goals and action steps. ☐   I need more practice. ☐

For more practice, go to MyEnglishLab.

Unit 1, Lesson 6   **13**

Lesson 7 Reading

Identify main ideas and details in a biography about César Cruz

1 Before You Read

A DISCUSS. Who is someone you admire? What qualities does this person have that you admire? What admirable qualities do you have?

B PREVIEW VOCABULARY.

1. **TOPIC-RELATED WORDS.** These terms are used in the article. Does anyone know what they mean? For compound words, think about the meaning of each word separately. You can also look for clues in the article.

| undocumented immigrant | deportation | civil rights |
| social justice | hunger strike | |

2. **ACADEMIC WORDS.** Discuss the meaning of the **bolded** words in the article. Use context to help you. After reading the article, add any words you learned to your Word Study Log.

C PREDICT. Preview the article title and image. What is the purpose of the article? What information do you expect?

2 Read for Gist

A READ. Think about the important ideas as you read.

Dr. César Cruz: Modern-Day Unsung Hero

1   There is a poem by the African-American poet Paul Dunbar titled "Unsung Heroes." It honors the slaves who became free men and sacrificed their lives in the Civil War. These men died leaving no name to mark their graves, no song to remember their sacrifice. So when we speak of unsung heroes, we do not speak of them lightly. It is
5   a title that is earned from hardship and sacrifice. Unsung heroes work, fight, and inspire behind the scenes. They may never appear upon the pages of history. Dr. César Cruz is one such *unsung hero*.

César Cruz was born in Guadalajara, Jalisco, Mexico, in 1974. He learned early on that his life would not be easy. His father **abandoned** him at the age of two. Three years later, his mother left him to
10 work in the U.S. At the age of nine, young Cruz joined his mother in the U.S. He lived in poverty as an undocumented immigrant. He felt the **constant** threat of deportation. In fact, his mother was deported three times while Cruz was a boy. Cruz felt lost and angry. By middle school, he was struggling in school and getting into trouble.

Then one day Cruz read a biography that changed his life. It was the biography of Reies López Tijerina, a friend of Dr. Martin Luther King, Jr. Like King, Tijerina fought for civil rights. The biography opened Cruz's eyes to the history
15 of Latino people. It inspired him to a new purpose in life: the fight for social justice. For Cruz, education became the key to **achieve** that purpose. Cruz completed high school and graduated from the University of California, Berkley.

Cruz became a teacher in a poor school district in California. When he saw how much poorer his district was than others, he decided to do something about it. In 2004, Cruz led students, their families, and community members on a 70-mile march to the state capitol. Their goal was to talk to Governor Arnold Schwarzenegger about unequal school
20 **funding**. When they got there, however, the governor refused to see them. So Cruz and several other adults began a hunger strike to get the governor's attention. They went 26 days without food. Finally, the governor agreed to return $600,000 a year of interest payments on the school district's loans over a period of 15 years.

14 Unit 1, Lesson 7

Reading

In 2009, César's own experience with gang violence led him to start the Homies Empowerment Program. The program, which is still active, offers education and hope to gang members. Rival gang members sit next to each other in classes
25 where they learn about their cultural history. They also prepare and eat monthly dinners together. Currently, Cruz is **expanding** the program to include a community high school.

make bigger

In 2016, Cruz became the first Mexican-American male to earn a doctorate from the Harvard Graduate School of Education. But Cruz is most proud of his role as husband and father. Perhaps it is his humanness that is most inspiring. If he is like us, then we, too, can make this world a better, kinder place.

30 Cruz's story may remain unsung on the pages of history. However, his song will be sung from the lips of those he has touched and the thousands who have learned from the sacrifices of this unsung hero.

B **IDENTIFY MAIN IDEAS.** Read the Academic Reading Skill. Then choose the main idea of the article and of Paragraphs 2–5.

Academic Reading Skill: Identify main ideas

Main Idea of a Text - An academic text, such as this biography, has a main idea for the complete text. The main idea gives the topic of the text or the general idea of what the text is about. Usually, this main idea is stated in the first paragraph as part of the introduction.

Main Idea of a Paragraph - An academic text will have many paragraphs. The main idea of each paragraph describes the topic of the paragraph or the general idea of what the paragraph is about. The main ideas of the paragraphs work together to support the main idea of the complete text.

Article Main Idea	Lines
a. Paul Dunbar wrote the poem "Unsung Heroes."	
b. César Cruz is an unsung hero.	7
c. Unsung heroes were former slaves who fought and died in the Civil War.	
Paragraph Main Ideas	
2 a. Cruz's life was difficult as a boy.	
b. Cruz's mother was deported three times.	9–12
c. Cruz began to get into trouble.	
3 a. Cruz read the biography of Reies López Tijerina.	
b. Education became the key to Cruz's discovery of a purpose in life.	13
c. The Reies López Tijerina biography inspired Cruz to change his life.	
4 a. Cruz went on a hunger strike for 26 days.	
b. Cruz was a teacher in a poor school district in California.	22
c. Cruz led the fight to get more money for his school district.	
5 a. Cruz started the Homies Empowerment Program.	
b. Rival gangs participate in activities together.	23
c. Cruz had experience with gang violence.	

C **APPLY ACADEMIC SKILL.** Now that you have identified the main ideas, find the evidence in the article that supports each paragraph's main idea. Write the line numbers in the last column.

Unit 1, Lesson 7 **15**

3 ▶ Close Reading

A **LOCATE DETAILS.** Read the Academic Reading Skill. Then read the statements and decide if they are true or false. Write the line numbers of your evidence.

> **Academic Reading Skill: Identify supporting details**
> After identifying the main idea of a paragraph, look at the other information in the paragraph. This information supports the main idea by giving examples, facts, and explanations. These specifics are called **supporting details**. A paragraph typically has several supporting details.

	T/F	Lines
1. Unsung heroes are often written about in history books.	F	6
2. Cruz's mother was removed from the United States three times.	T	11
3. The governor met with Cruz right after the 70-mile march.	F	
4. According to Cruz, his degree from Harvard is his most important accomplishment.	F	28

B **EXPAND UNDERSTANDING.**

1. **INFER.** What qualities does Cruz have that the author most admires?

_____

2. **SUMMARIZE.** Summarize the important events in Cruz's life.

1. He Started the Homies Empowerment program.
2. He fought with the goverment for unequal school.

_____

4 ▶ Prepare for an Academic Presentation

A **FOCUS.** You will give a formal presentation to describe a famous person you admire.

B **RESEARCH.** Find a source that gives biographical information about that person. Use the Note-Taking Template on page 243 to take notes from that source.

C **ORGANIZE.** It's important to choose your main ideas carefully. Read the instructions on the next page about *Main Ideas and Supporting Details.* Use those suggestions to help you choose the main ideas that you want to focus on. Then use the Presentation Template on page 244 to organize your information.

Main Ideas and Supporting Details

Always choose three or four main ideas to focus on. Choose main ideas that have a few specific supporting details. Here is an example of main ideas and supporting details that could be used in a presentation about César Cruz.

Introduction	
Main Ideas of Presentation	César Cruz is a famous person I admire.
Section 1	César Cruz had a difficult childhood.
Section 2	There were many key events in Cruz's life that led to his major accomplishments.
Section 3	Cruz has many personal qualities that I admire.
Section 1	
Main Idea	César Cruz had a difficult childhood.
Basic information	Cruz was born in Guadalajara, Mexico, in 1974. He moved to the United States when he was nine.
Reason for fame	Despite his difficult childhood, Cruz is known for fighting for social justice.

D **REVISE AND PRACTICE.** Use the Presentation Checklist to assess your presentation and make revisions. Then practice your presentation until you feel confident.

Presentation Checklist	
	The presentation includes...
Organization:	✓ Introduction
	✓ Three main points or sections
Support:	✓ Main ideas
	✓ Supporting details
Word Choice:	✓ Academic words
	✓ Example signal words
Delivery:	✓ Speech at appropriate volume and rate
	✓ Speech that is clear and easy to understand
	✓ Eye contact

Apply what you know — Academic Presentation

1. **PRESENT.** Share your presentation with a partner. Your teacher may also choose you to present to the class.

2. **EVALUATE.** Have your partner evaluate your presentation using the Presentation Checklist.

3. **COLLABORATE WITH OTHERS.** Listen carefully to your partner's suggestions. Ask questions to make sure you understand his or her comments.

I can identify main ideas and details in a biography. ☐   I need more practice. ☐

For more practice, go to MyEnglishLab.   For audio and video, scan the QR code.

Unit 1, Lesson 7   17

Lesson 8

Writing Workshop

Write effective topic sentences

1 What Do You Notice?

A COMPARE. Read the two examples. Which is more clearly organized and interesting to read?

Example 1:

Cruz became a teacher in a poor school district in California. When he saw how much poorer his district was than others, he decided to do something about it. In 2004, Cruz led students, their families, and community members on a 70-mile march to the state capitol. Their goal was to talk to Governor Arnold Schwarzenegger about unequal school funding. When they got there, however, the governor refused to see them. So Cruz and several other adults began a hunger strike to get the governor's attention. They went 26 days without food. Finally, the governor agreed to return $600,000 a year of interest payments on the school district's loans over a period of 15 years.

Example 2:

Arnold Schwarzenegger was governor of California. Cruz was teaching in a poor school district. Cruz led many people to protest unequal funding of schools. He convinced the governor to agree to return money to California schools. He also went on a hunger strike. The governor gave the people what they wanted.

B ANALYZE. Which highlighted sentence more clearly explains what the paragraph is about? Underline the information in that sentence that makes it more interesting to read.

2 Apply Academic Writing Skill

Academic Writing Skill: Write effective topic sentences
Remember that effective paragraphs include a sentence that states the main idea of the paragraph. It is called the **topic sentence**. The topic sentence should be general enough to tell your reader what the paragraph will be about. An effective topic sentence includes both the **topic** of the paragraph and a **controlling idea**, or the point you want to make about the topic.

A topic sentence is usually at the beginning of a paragraph, but not always. The remaining sentences in a paragraph give **supporting details**, which explain more about the topic sentence.

A IDENTIFY. Read these topic sentences. Underline the topic once and the controlling idea twice.

In 2009, Cruz started the Homies Empowerment Program.

He learned early on that his life would not be easy.

Then one day Cruz read a biography that changed his life.

B APPLY. Rewrite each topic sentence. Make sure the sentence is not too narrow or too general and could introduce a paragraph with several supporting details.

1. Heroes are amazing. _because they sacrific they lives to defend human right_

2. Education helped César Cruz. _became a teacher to change his life._

| I can write an effective topic sentence. ▢ | I need more practice. ▢ |

For more practice, go to MyEnglishLab.

18 Unit 1, Lesson 8

Writing

Write about your interests, skills, and career goals

Lesson 9

1 ▶ Model for Writing

STUDY THE MODEL. Read the Writing Model that describes a person's interests, skills, and goals on page 245. Analyze that model. Underline the topic sentence in each paragraph. Double underline the example signal words the writer uses to introduce the examples.

2 ▶ Prepare Your Writing

A **FOCUS.** You will write several paragraphs about your interests, skills, and career goals.

B **RESEARCH.** Choose a career goal that matches the results of your interest or skills assessment in Lesson 3. Record your interests and skills that match that goal.

3 ▶ Write Write about your interests, skills, and goals.

A **ORGANIZE.** Use the organization of the Writing Model from Exercise 1 to guide your writing. Be sure to give several examples in each paragraph as suggested below.

⎡ Giving Examples

When you want to describe or explain something, remember to use examples to help the reader understand what you mean. Include specific examples to describe your interests and skills, and use example signal words to introduce your examples.

Writing Checklist	
	The text includes…
Structure:	✓ Paragraphs with examples
Organization:	✓ Topic sentences with supporting details
Word Choice:	✓ Academic words
	✓ Example signal words
Writing Skill:	✓ Effective topic sentences
Grammar:	✓ Gerunds and infinitives to state interests and describe career goals

I would like a career in nursing. As a nurse, I could combine my interest in helping others with my personal skills, such as patience and the ability to communicate well.

B **REVISE.** Use the Writing Checklist to evaluate your writing and make revisions. Remember to include effective topic sentences.

4 ▶ Share Your Writing

A **COLLABORATE.** Share your writing with a partner. Use any feedback to improve your writing.

B **PUBLISH.** Create a final document to share with others.

I can write about my interests, skills, and career goals. ■   I need more practice. ■

For more practice, go to MyEnglishLab.

Unit 1, Lesson 9   **19**

Lesson 10: Workplace Soft Skills

Demonstrate a willingness to learn

1 Workplace Expectations

A ▶ **CONSIDER.** Listen to part of a job interview for a position at Fresh 'n Fast. What is the interviewer trying to find out? How does the candidate respond?

B **READ.** Read the email from the interviewer to the human resources director stating the reason the candidate was not selected.

> **Subject:** Today's candidate
>
> Yuki,
> Thanks for sending another candidate for the entry-level position. I'm looking for someone who demonstrates a strong desire to grow with our company. Today's candidate did not communicate a willingness to learn in the interview.
> Jan

C **IDENTIFY EXPECTATIONS.** Describe the interviewer's expectation and the candidate's response. What was the result?
1. Interviewer's expectation: _____
2. Candidate's response: _____
3. Result: _____

2 Learn from Mistakes

A **DISCUSS.** How could the candidate have responded better to the interviewer's questions? Suggest specific things the candidate could have done differently. Share your suggestions with a partner.

B **ROLE-PLAY.** Give the candidate a "do-over." Role-play the conversation, but this time have the candidate meet the interviewer's expectations.

C ▶ **COMPARE.** Listen to the "do-over" conversation. How is it similar to your role play? How is it different?

Apply what you know

1. **DEFINE.** How would you explain this soft skill to a new employee?

2. **APPLY.** Record an example from your own life in your Soft Skills Log (page 241) of how you have demonstrated a willingness to learn.

3. **SHARE.** Share your example.
    - I demonstrated a willingness to learn at _____ when I _____.

I can demonstrate a willingness to learn. ☐   I need more practice. ☐

For audio and video, scan the QR code.   For more practice, go to MyEnglishLab.

Getting a Job

2

PREVIEW

What is the difference between an *interviewer* and an *interviewee*? Who do you think is the interviewer in this photo? Why do you think that?

UNIT GOALS

Identify successful strategies for job seekers
Use online resources to find job information
Identify strong answers to interview questions
Evaluate interview dos and don'ts
Identify elements of an effective cover letter
Write a cover letter tailored to a specific job

Workplace Soft Skill: Project self-confidence
Academic Skills:
- **Listening:** Listen for key points that summarize a message
- **Speaking:** Use notes for support
- **Reading:** Summarize a text
- **Writing:** Write an effective introduction

21

Lesson 1 — Listening and Speaking
Identify successful strategies for job seekers

1 Before You Listen

A MAKE CONNECTIONS. What do you do to prepare to search for a job? Discuss your personal experiences of looking for work.

B PREVIEW VOCABULARY.

1. **TOPIC-RELATED WORDS.** These terms are used in the listening. Does anyone know what they mean? Why do some people put accents on résumé?

volunteer work   references   résumé   mock interview

2. **ACADEMIC WORDS.** These sentences are from the listening. Discuss the meaning of each **bolded** word. Use context to help you.
   1. The more experience you can **accumulate**, the better.
   2. **Compile** a list of names of all the people who might help you.
   3. **Ultimately**, it is these important documents that will help you make sure that all the details on your résumé are accurate.
   4. If possible, **approach** that person directly and tell him or her that you're interested in a job.
   5. The career counselor can **comment** on your interview responses and suggest improvements.

C PREDICT. Use the lesson title, vocabulary, and image to make predictions about the podcast. What will its purpose be? What information do you expect?

2 Listen

A ▶ LISTEN FOR MAIN IDEAS. Listen to the podcast. List the speaker's five tips for job seekers in the first column. Then compare your tips with a partner.

Tips	Details
1.	
2.	
3.	
4.	
5.	

B ▶ LISTEN FOR DETAILS. Listen again. List one detail that supports each tip in the second column.

Listening and Speaking

3 Apply Academic Listening Skill

Academic Listening Skill: Listen for key points that summarize a message
At the conclusion of a speech, speakers often summarize, or restate the ideas they stated previously. Speakers also often summarize a main point before moving on to a new point. Summary signal words are commonly used to indicate that a speaker will then restate ideas. Listening for these words will help you notice when a speaker is summing up what has already been said.

Summary Signal Words	
Words and Phrases	**Verbs**
in conclusion, in summary, in short, all in all, in brief, in other words, on the whole, overall, in general, ultimately	to conclude, to sum up, to summarize

A ▶ **IDENTIFY.** Listen to part of the podcast again. Which summary signal words or phrases does the speaker use to sum up each main point? Underline them in the chart above.

B **SUMMARIZE.** The speaker used the summary signal words *to conclude* and *to sum up* to introduce his conclusion. Use different signal words to introduce his conclusion.

_____, as you prepare for your job search, you should increase your experience by volunteering, get help from all the people you know, collect your important documents, find out all you can about the company, and, lastly, practice your interview.

C **EXPAND VOCABULARY.** Add words to your Word Study Log to show structure and meaning.

4 Real-World Application

A **BRAINSTORM.** Discuss job-seeking strategies. What successful strategies have you used? Why were they successful? Which strategies were less successful?

B **PRESENT.** Write a summary of successful and unsuccessful job strategies. Give specific examples. Present your summary.

Some successful job strategies include _____. As an example, _____.
One strategy that did not work out too well was _____ because _____.

Academic Speaking Skill: Use notes for support
Using notes is a good way to make sure you say everything you want to say in a presentation. Notes are short reminders. Do not write your entire presentation. Instead, write in big, clear letters the key words from the main ideas you plan to talk about. Under each idea, list details or examples using numbers or bullets. When you present, look at your audience as much as possible. Use your notes only when necessary.

> 1. SEARCH FOR THE RIGHT JOBS
>   • Try different search engines and apps
>   • Use keywords
>
> 2. USE YOUR NETWORK
>   • Ask friends for help
>   • Join social media sites for job seekers

I can identify successful strategies for job seekers. ☐   I need more practice. ☐

For more practice, go to MyEnglishLab.   For audio and video, scan the QR code.

Unit 2, Lesson 1   23

Lesson 2 Grammar
Use modals to offer polite suggestions and express possibilities

1 Focus on Usage

A **CONSIDER.** Read the highlighted sentences in the text message below. Which words are used to introduce suggestions and give advice?

> *Should*, *ought to*, *may*, *might*, and *could* are modals. Modals are often used to make suggestions.

B **IDENTIFY.** Read the entire text message. Underline all the modal + verb combinations used to make polite suggestions.

A: Have you found a job yet?

B: No. Still looking. I've submitted five applications online, but I haven't heard anything back yet.

A: You might consider going in person. You could ask if they've received your applications.

I don't know
B: IDK. Seems a little pushy.

A: If you don't want to go in person, you should call. You shouldn't wait around for someone to call *you*. Maybe they didn't get your online application.

B: OK. I'll try.

A: Have you looked around campus? You might find some job announcements posted on the bulletin boards.

B: I've been looking, but I haven't found anything.

A: Perhaps you ought to ask all your friends for help. Maybe they know someone who's hiring.

B: OK, I'll start with you. Do you know anyone?

A: No, but I'll ask around!

2 Focus on Structure

Modals to Offer Polite Suggestions and Express Possibilities	
Suggestions	**Possibilities**
You **shouldn't** wait for someone to call you.	You **may** find some job announcements on the bulletin boards.
You **ought to** go in person.	You **might** consider applying in person.
	You **could** call the employer.

- *Maybe* and *perhaps* are used to soften the statement.
  - *Maybe* is more common in informal situations.
    Maybe you **could ask** your friends if they know of good places to work.
  - *Perhaps* sounds more formal.
    Perhaps you **ought to ask** your friends for help.

24 Unit 2, Lesson 2

Grammar

A INVESTIGATE. Analyze all the examples of modals. Choose the correct answers.

1. Use the _____ form of the verb following a modal.
   - (a) base
   - **b.** infinitive
   - **c.** past

2. Use an infinitive (*to* + verb) after __C__.
   - **a.** *may*
   - **b.** *might*
   - **c.** *ought*

3. For negative statements, use __C__ + **not**.
   - **a.** *could*
   - **b.** *should* 可表明
   - **c.** *ought to*

4. Modals used to express polite suggestions indicate __B C__
   - **a.** definite plans
   - **b.** required actions
   - **c.** advice

B REWRITE. Rewrite the sentences using modals.

1. It's a good idea to ask people in your community for help.

   (*might*) You _____*might ask*_____ people in your community for help.

2. It's a good idea to get an app that has job listings.

   (*should*) You ___*should get*___ an app that has job listings.

3. It's a good idea to research jobs you're interested in.

   (*might*) Perhaps you __*might research*__ jobs you're interested in.

4. It's possible you'll find a job at a career fair.

   (*may*) You ____*may find*____ a job at a career fair.

C COMPLETE. Offer a polite suggestion to complete each conversation. Use *should/shouldn't, ought to, could, may,* or *might.*

1. **A:** I'm trying to find a job, but I don't know where to start.
   B: You could search for job openings online.

2. **A:** I'm really nervous about my job interview next week.
   B: You should be prepare your job interview, and you may have some confidence

3. **A:** I'm not sure what to include on my résumé.
   B: You should search for an example online, or you could find someone to help you

4. **A:** I need three references for this job application.
   B: You could ask your teacher, your manager and your friends for references application.

Apply what you know

1. **ASSESS.** What is some good advice someone has given you for finding a job? What useful advice have you given to someone?

2. **WRITE.** Write a letter to a friend who is looking for a job. Use *should, ought to, may, might,* and *could* to offer polite suggestions and express possibility.

   You've always enjoyed children. Maybe you could apply for a job at a child-care center.

I can use modals to offer polite suggestions and express possibilities. ■	I need more practice. ■

For more practice, go to MyEnglishLab.

Unit 2, Lesson 2   **25**

Lesson 3

Workplace, Life, & Community Skills
Use online resources to find job information

1 Find Job Information

A **REFLECT.** Describe a time when you wanted to do something new—for example, move, go back to school, or find a new job—but didn't know how to get started. How did you feel at the time?

B **PROBLEM-SOLVE.** Where do you go to look for a job? What suggestions do you have for others looking for a job?

2 Consult Resources

Online Job Sites

When you are looking for a job, you can use a job-search website. These sites will allow you to specify certain aspects of the job. For example:

- Job title—the type of work you want
- Location—the general area where you would like to work
- Shift—the time of day you are available
- Salary—the amount of money you would like to earn
- Skills needed—your abilities or experience

After determining which job qualities you want, you can set filters to show just the jobs that match those qualities. Then, only those jobs will show in your job search results.

A **SCAN.** A young man was looking for a new job. Look at his online job search results.

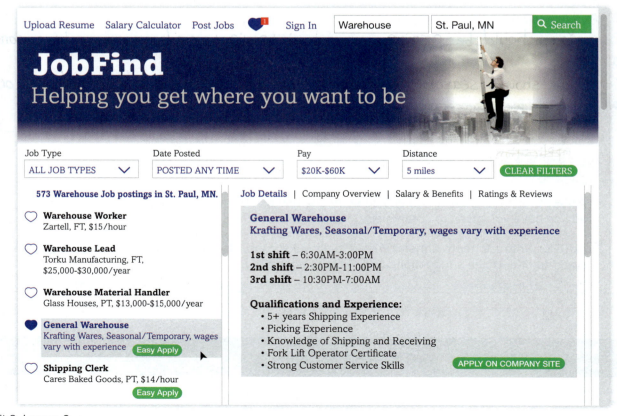

26 Unit 2, Lesson 3

Workplace, Life, & Community Skills

Use the job search results to answer the questions.

1. How many jobs were found using the keywords "warehouse" and "Saint Paul, MN"? _____

2. What type of information was chosen and shown for the highlighted job? _____

3. Can you apply for the highlighted job directly on the website? If so, how? _____

B **DEFINE KEY WORDS.** Find these words on the online job site. Match each word to its definition.

_____ **1.** (n) date posted

_____ **2.** (n) filter

_____ **3.** (n) qualification

_____ **4.** (adj) seasonal

_____ **5.** (n) shift

_____ **6.** (v) upload

a. move a document from your computer to a website so others can see it

b. regular time scheduled to work

c. when something was published online

d. happening during a certain time of year

e. accomplishment that makes one suitable for a job

f. something that removes unwanted information or choices

C **INTERPRET.** Locate information on the online job site.

1. How can you filter your search by location? _____

2. Which menu tab tells you what qualifications and experience are needed? _____

3. Are there any jobs that need workers only part of the year? _____

4. Which shift begins on one day and ends on the next? _____

D **CALCULATE.**

1. At full-time hours, which income is higher, $14/hour or $14,000/year? _____

2. How many hours is the shift from 6:30 a.m. to 3:00 p.m.? _____

E **GO ONLINE.** Use the Search Terms to find two job search sites. Share the two sites with a partner. How are the sites similar? How are they different?

Search Terms: job search sites

Apply what you know

1. **APPLY.** Use one job search site. Choose a job field and a location that interests you. Look at any qualities that are important to you.

2. **SHARE.** Explain your job search results to a partner. Which job interests you and why? Evaluate how helpful the results were to you.
    - *According to the results, _____. I think I would choose _____ because _____.*
    - *The information says _____, (but/and) it is (un)helpful because _____.*

I can use online resources to find job information. ■   I need more practice. ■

For more practice, go to MyEnglishLab.

Unit 2, Lesson 3   **27**

Lesson 4 Reading
Identify strong answers to interview questions

1 Before You Read

A BRAINSTORM. What are some questions frequently asked in a job interview?

B PREVIEW VOCABULARY.

1. **TOPIC-RELATED WORDS.** These terms are used in the article. Does anyone know what they mean? Use roots and affixes to help you. You can also look for clues in the article.

| unnatural | accomplishments | candidates | profitable |

2. **ACADEMIC WORDS.** Discuss the meaning of the **bolded** words in the article. Use context to help you. After reading the article, add any words you learned to your Word Study Log.

C PREDICT. Preview the article title and image. What is the purpose of the article?

2 Read for Gist

A READ. What important question does the interviewer ask both women?

How to Identify Strong Answers to Interview Questions

1 What was your last job interview like? Did you answer all the questions clearly and **coherently**? Or did you stumble a few times? It's **normal** for a job interview to feel unnatural. You have to talk about yourself and your accomplishments. These are things we aren't used to doing every day.

5 Fortunately, there are techniques you can **utilize** to help in job interviews. The STAR technique is a great example. You can use the STAR technique to answer questions about how you solve problems. Let's take a look at these two job candidates and how one of them uses the STAR technique.

Lydia is a hiring manager at Southwest Community Hospital. Last week she interviewed two candidates. Lydia's first
10 interview was with Angela. Lydia asked, "Describe a time when you faced a challenge at work. How did you handle it?" Angela replied, "When I first started my job, the lines at the pharmacy were long on the weekends. I talked to my manager. We made some changes to the schedule. We also reorganized the pharmacy. We put popular medicines closer to the cashier. We noticed that the lines got shorter."

Lydia's second interview was with a candidate named Carmen. Lydia asked Carmen the same question, "Describe a
15 time when you faced a challenge at work. How did you handle it?" Carmen replied, "When I first started working at the pharmacy, I noticed we had the wrong inventory. We ran out of popular medicines. We had too much of medicines no one needed. I decided to adopt inventory-tracking software. I reviewed three types of software. Then I chose MedQuick. It's the most popular software on the market. It costs only $89 a month. MedQuick automatically orders medicine when we run low. Now we have the right inventory. The software has worked so well that three other branches
20 of our pharmacy adopted it, too."

Both candidates gave good answers. However, Carmen's answer was stronger because she used the STAR technique. Follow these steps to use the STAR technique.

28 Unit 2, Lesson 4

Reading

Interview question: *Describe a time when you faced a challenge at work. How did you handle it?*	
Situation	Describe the event or situation you were in.
Task	Explain the task you had to do.
Action	Describe the actions you took to finish the task.
Result	Share the positive results of your actions.

Angela's example of how she tackled long lines at the pharmacy was good. However, her answer was unclear. Did she make the changes to the schedule? Or did her manager? What were the changes? Which change shortened the lines:
25 the changes to the schedule or the decision to move popular medicines near the cashier? And by shortening the lines, what was the result? Were the customers happier? Was the pharmacy more profitable?

In contrast, Carmen's answer using the STAR technique was much clearer. She described the situation (wrong inventory). She explained the task she had to do (find a way to improve inventory management). She described her actions (adopt MedQuick software). Then she shared the results (the right inventory, other branches of the pharmacy
30 adopted the software, too).

Lydia was impressed by Carmen's answer. She could tell Carmen was good at solving problems. Lydia offered the job to Carmen. You can **adapt** the STAR technique to a number of interview questions. Use it at your next job interview and be prepared to shine.

B **IDENTIFY MAIN IDEAS.** Choose the main idea of the article. Where is it stated? Lines _____
   a. Carmen was a better candidate because she used the STAR technique.
   b. It is normal for a job interview to feel unnatural.
   c. The STAR technique helps job candidates structure their answers in job interviews.

3 Close Reading

A **RECOGNIZE STRUCTURE.** Complete the chart to compare Angela's and Carmen's answers.

	Angela	**Carmen**
Situation		
Task		
Action		
Result		

B **LOCATE DETAILS.** Match each action to a step in the STAR technique.

_____ 1. Focus on the consequences of the steps you took.   a. situation
_____ 2. Explain the job you had to do.   b. task
_____ 3. Describe the event or problem you faced.   c. action
_____ 4. Describe the steps you took to complete the job.   d. result

Apply what you know

1. **APPLY.** How did you handle a challenge at work? Create a chart like the one above.
2. **SHARE.** Share your answers. Describe the situation, task, action, and result.

I can identify strong answers to interview questions. ☐   I need more practice. ☐

For more practice, go to MyEnglishLab.   For audio and video, scan the QR code.

Unit 2, Lesson 4 **29**

Lesson 5

Listening and Speaking

Evaluate interview dos and don'ts

1 Before You Listen

A **GIVE EXAMPLES.** Someone you know is going for a job interview. What advice would you give him or her?

B **PREVIEW VOCABULARY.**

1. **TOPIC-RELATED WORDS.** These terms are used in the listening. Does anyone know what they mean? For compound words, think about the meaning of each word separately.

| employment agency | body language |
| first impression | eye contact |

2. **ACADEMIC WORDS.** These sentences are from the listening. Discuss the meaning of each **bolded** word. Use context to help you.
   1. There are several other **aspects**, or key elements, that can **affect** your performance in a job interview.
   2. First impressions are very important, so be sure to dress **appropriately** for the job you want.
   3. Your body language should **indicate** that you are interested but relaxed.
   4. Although pay is **obviously** important, don't ask about **compensation** right away.

C **PREDICT.** Use the lesson title, vocabulary, and images to make predictions about the podcast. What will its purpose be? What information do you expect?

2 Listen

A ▶ **LISTEN FOR MAIN IDEAS.** Listen to an employment counselor talk about job interviews. List the four important aspects of a job interview in the first column. Then compare your list with a partner.

Important Aspects	Details

B ▶ **LISTEN FOR DETAILS.** Listen again. List at least one detail that supports each important aspect of a job interview.

30 Unit 2, Lesson 5

Listening and Speaking

3 Apply Academic Listening Skill

A ▶ **SUMMARIZE.** Listen to four job applicants answer interview questions. After the interviews, the interviewer wrote a summary of the mistake each person made. Complete her summary.

To sum up, the candidates today had the following issues:

Beatriz: _____

Sam: _____

Bruno: _____

Jin: _____

B **EXPAND VOCABULARY.** Add words to your Word Study Log to show structure and meaning.

4 Real-World Application

A **APPLY.** Create a list of typical interview questions.

B **ASK AND ANSWER.** Interview a partner using your questions. Then switch roles and answer his or her questions.

C **DISCUSS.** Discuss your concerns about interviews. What makes you nervous? What mistakes have you made in past interviews? What will you do differently next time?

- *I made a mistake at an interview when _____.*
- *I'm worried about _____ in future interviews.*
- *I can avoid _____ by _____.*

I can evaluate interview dos and don'ts. ☐   I need more practice. ☐

For more practice, go to MyEnglishLab.   For audio and video, scan the QR code.

Unit 2, Lesson 5   31

Lesson 6

Grammar
Use present perfect and present perfect continuous

1 Focus on Usage

A **CONSIDER.** Read the highlighted sentences in the cover letter below. Which statements describe actions that are finished and had specific results? Which statements describe actions that are still happening and are still in progress?

> The present perfect can be used to focus on the completion of an action. It describes an action that is finished.
> The present perfect continuous emphasizes the continuation of an action into the present and possibly into the future. It focuses on an action in progress.

B **IDENTIFY.** Read the entire cover letter. Underline all the present perfect verbs. Circle all the present perfect continuous verbs.

Dear Ms. Jones,

Please consider my application for the office manager position at your company.

I have been working in a medical office for over five years. In this position, I have gained extensive experience and developed many skills. I have proven to be a reliable, professional, and efficient office worker. I have filled in for my manager whenever she has needed to take a leave of absence.

For the past two years, I have been taking classes at the community college. I've been striving to improve my business and communication skills. I have already received a certificate in office management. I plan to continue my studies and pursue a degree.

I would love to meet with you in person to learn more about your job opening. Please call me at 713-555-2123 or email me at toriwatson@officemanager.com. Thank you for your time and consideration.

Sincerely,
Tori Watson

---

2 Focus on Structure

Present Perfect	Present Perfect Continuous
Iris **has done** a lot of research.	Iris **has been doing** a lot of research.
I'**ve taken** courses at the community college.	I'**ve been taking** classes at the community college <u>since</u> last year.
Jane **has** <u>already</u> **served** as an assistant manager.	Jane **has been working** as an assistant manager <u>for</u> months.
I **have** recently **made** an effort to greet everyone at the beginning of my shift.	I **have** recently **been making** an effort to greet everyone at the beginning of my shift.
I **haven't studied** for my certification exam <u>yet</u>.	I **haven't been studying** for my certification exam.
Tom **has** <u>never</u> **worked** in a hotel.	
• The present perfect is often used with *already, yet, ever,* and *never.* • The present perfect continuous is often used with *for* + an amount of time, or *since* + a point in time. • Many verbs have irregular past forms, such as *do, did, done.* For a list of irregular past participles, search online for: irregular verbs.	

32 Unit 2, Lesson 6

Grammar

A INVESTIGATE. Analyze all the examples of present perfect. Are the rules true or false? Correct the false rules.

	T/F
1. Use *have/has* + past participle to form the present perfect.	_____
2. Use *have/has* + *been* + past participle to form the present perfect continuous.	_____
3. Place adverbs such as *already* and *recently* before *have/has*.	_____
4. Use *haven't/hasn't* or *have never/has never* to make a negative statement.	_____
5. Use the present perfect continuous to show the action is complete.	_____

B ▶ COMPLETE. Listen and complete the sentences. Then check whether the action is completed or continuing.

	Completed	Continuing
1. I _____ my résumé.	☐	☐
2. I _____ night classes.	☐	☐
3. My friend _____ my résumé.	☐	☐
4. I _____ for full-time jobs.	☐	☐
5. Miriam _____ classes in landscape design.	☐	☐
6. Shelly _____ all her classes for her degree.	☐	☐
7. We _____ all day for our math exam.	☐	☐
8. She _____ her applications for college.	☐	☐

Apply what you know

1. **WRITE.** Use the ideas below to create questions about someone's work experience. Write the questions using either the present perfect or the present perfect continuous.

   Have you…
   1. learn new work skills this year
   2. write a résumé
   3. use English outside of class as much as possible
   4. look for a new job
   5. practice interview skills

2. **ASK AND ANSWER.** Interview a partner using your questions. Then switch roles and answer your partner's questions.

I can use present perfect and present perfect continuous. ☐   I need more practice. ☐

For more practice, go to MyEnglishLab.   For audio and video, scan the QR code.

Unit 2, Lesson 6   33

Lesson 7 Reading
Identify elements of an effective cover letter

1 Before You Read

A **DISCUSS.** What is the purpose of a cover letter? Have you ever written one? Why did you write it?

B **PREVIEW VOCABULARY.**

1. **TOPIC-RELATED WORDS.** These terms are used in the article. Does anyone know what they mean? Use roots and affixes to help you. You can also look for clues in the article.

| prospective employer | mission | job description | personal qualities |

2. **ACADEMIC WORDS.** Discuss the meaning of the **bolded** words in the article. Use context to help you. After reading the article, add any words you learned to your Word Study Log.

C **PREDICT.** Preview the article title and images. What is the purpose of the text? What information do you expect?

2 Read for Gist

A **READ.** Think about the main ideas as you read. Underline any sentences that help you identify main ideas.

Creating a Dynamic Cover Letter

1   You may have heard the phrase "Finding a job is a full-time job." Although that is a bit of an exaggeration, a job search can be a lot of work. Your cover letter serves as a way to introduce yourself and your skills to a company. An effective cover letter can help convince a prospective employer that you are
5   the best person for the job. It can move your résumé to the short stack instead of the recycling bin.

The cover letter is an opportunity to show your knowledge of the company. An employer wants to see that you are not just looking for *any* job but a job with *that* company. Take time to research the company's website. Look in the About Us or Careers section of the website. Be sure to take notes on your research. A T-chart can be especially useful for showing
10 how the company's interests match your own interests. In the left column, note information about the company, especially the company's mission or goal. In the right column, note how those goals match your own employment goals.

HealingHands
Healing Begins at Home

Home | About Us | Services | Resources | Contact | 🔍 Search

Company and Mission	Experience and Skills
- Provide a personal touch to customer service	- 4 yrs customer service experience
- Solve problems for our clients	- Called customers by name
	- Worked at customer service desk to help people w/ returns and problems

34   Unit 2, Lesson 7

Reading

Next, learn everything you can about the position. Carefully read the job description to be sure you know the requirements. Add those notes to the left column of the T-chart. Take detailed notes on the education and experience
15 that are required. Pay attention to both the skills and personal qualities that are desired. In the right column, match the job requirements and skills with your own education, training, and experience.

Now, it's time to put your research to use in your cover letter. Follow these five **criteria** to write a **dynamic** cover letter that gets you noticed.

1. Choose a tone that matches the culture of the company. Most employers **appreciate** a cover letter that is
20 more conversational than formal. Be professional, but also show your personality.

2. Write a catchy introduction. If you want the employer to read more than the first line of your cover letter, include these three things in your introduction:
- Explain how your goals match the goals of the company.
- Show enthusiasm for the specific position.
25 - State how the job description matches your skill set and experience.

3. Describe how you will contribute to the company. Focus on one or two areas where your skills and experience match the job description. Describe how you will **contribute** to the company in each of these areas.

4. Summarize the points you have made in the cover letter. In two or three sentences, **summarize** the important aspects of your cover letter, such as why the company is a good fit for you and how your skills and experience are a
30 good match for the position.

5. Write a closing that indicates your desire to meet in person. Express your desire for an interview but in a polite, non-pushy way. State your enthusiasm for the opportunity to discuss how you can contribute to the company.

Taking the time to create a cover letter that follows these criteria is truly worth its weight in gold. Create that dynamic cover letter and get the job of job search done!

B **IDENTIFY MAIN IDEAS. Choose the main idea of the article and of Paragraphs 2–4. Find the sentences that best support each main idea. Write the line numbers.**

Article Main Idea	Lines
a. A job search can be a lot of work.	
b. Writing an effective cover letter is worth the effort.	
c. An effective cover letter shows your knowledge of the company.	
Paragraph Main Ideas	
2 a. Research the company's website.	
b. Use a T-chart to take notes.	
c. A cover letter should show your knowledge of the company.	
3 a. Learn all about the position.	
b. Take notes in a T-chart.	
c. Match your skills to the job requirements.	
4 a. Write a catchy introduction.	
b. Describe your contribution to the company.	
c. Follow the criteria to write a good cover letter.	

Unit 2, Lesson 7   35

3 Close Reading

A LOCATE DETAILS. Are the statements true or false? Write the line numbers of your evidence.

	T/F	Lines
1. Look on the *Home* page of the company's website to find the company's mission.	_____	_____
2. A T-chart is a helpful way to match your goals with the company's goals.	_____	_____
3. Prospective employers usually want a cover letter with a very formal tone.	_____	_____
4. It is important to describe how your skills and experience will contribute to the company.	_____	_____

B APPLY ACADEMIC READING SKILL.

Academic Reading Skill: Summarize a text

A **summary** of a text reports the most important points. When summarizing, provide information about the text in a brief, or shortened, way. Try to include each main idea, but rewrite it in your own words. This rewriting is called **paraphrasing**.

First, use summary signal words below to introduce your summary. Then use sequence signal words like *first, next,* and *then* to introduce each of the restated main ideas. These sequence signal words help give structure to your summary and create smooth transitions.

Summary Signal Words and Phrases	Sequence Signal Words
in conclusion, in summary, in short, all in all, in brief, in other words, on the whole, overall, in general, ultimately, to conclude, to sum up, to summarize	first, second, next, then, finally

1. These sentences are from the concluding summary of an article on how to research a cover letter. Write 1–4 to put the steps in order.

_____ Research the company so that your cover letter can show what you know about it.

_____ In summary, writing a great cover letter is worth the effort.

_____ Follow five important steps to combine your research into your cover letter.

_____ Learn about the position you are applying for.

2. Restate each of the steps above for researching a cover letter, following the order you listed them in. Paraphrase each step by writing it in your own words to create a summary.

1. _____

2. _____

3. _____

4. _____

3. Now look back at the five criteria of a dynamic cover letter given at the end of the article. Restate those five criteria. Paraphrase each criteria by writing it in your own words.

1. _____

2. _____

3. _____

4. _____

5. _____

C SUMMARIZE. Use your answers to Exercise 3 above to write a paragraph summarizing the five criteria for writing a cover letter. Remember to use sequence words for transitions.

36 Unit 2, Lesson 7

4 Prepare for an Academic Conversation

A **GO ONLINE.** Read about *Using Search Engines.* Then try out a few different search engines in **YOUR TURN**.

✓ **Search**	✓ **Choose Sources**	✓ **Evaluate Sources**

Using Search Engines

A search engine is an online tool that helps you locate information. The three most popular search engines in the U.S. are Google, Bing, and Yahoo, in that order. All three provide access to excellent resources, so choosing one is a matter of preference. Try each one to see which one you like best.

Online users enter in keywords to describe what they are looking for. Search engines match those words to any content published online. This content can be texts, images, or even videos. The list of content that the search engine produces is called the **search engine results page**, or SERP.

Search engines follow a complex set of problem-solving operations, called algorithms to determine the order of the results. That doesn't mean, however, that the first result on the list or the first page of results is where you will find the best information. Always check results on later pages before you stop your search.

Make sure you choose the keywords that best describe what you are looking for. Enter the topic you want with specific information to narrow the search. For example, to search for cover letter templates, you can add the word *free* to eliminate the ones that cost money. If you want one that you can download, add *downloadable*.

YOUR TURN...
Try out different search engines. Enter the same keywords into each one. What different results do you get?

B **CHOOSE A SOURCE.** Use one search engine to find a source for cover letter templates. Choose one cover letter template to help you write your own cover letter.

Search Terms: cover letter templates   free   downloadable

Apply what you know	**Academic Conversation**

1. **PREPARE NOTES.** You will share the cover letter template you choose. Remember to take notes to help you remember everything you want to say.

2. **REPORT.** Share your cover letter template. Describe the search engine and keywords you used to find it. Explain why you chose it.

3. **USE NOTES FOR SUPPORT.** As you present, remember to look at your audience as much as possible. Only glance at your notes when necessary.

I can identify elements of an effective cover letter. ▢	I need more practice. ▢

For more practice, go to MyEnglishLab.

For audio and video, scan the QR code.

Unit 2, Lesson 7   **37**

Lesson 8 Writing Workshop

Write an effective introduction

1 What Do You Notice?

A COMPARE. Read the two examples. How are they the same? How are they different?

Example 1:

Thank you for reading my letter. I'm writing because I'd like a job working with children. I have lots of awesome skills that would be perfect for your company. Give me a call and we can talk!

Example 2:

I am very interested in the position of Child-care Worker for your early learning center in Ironwood. I recently received my Early Childhood Education certificate, and my education and lifelong love of working with children would make me a great fit for your company.

B ANALYZE. Which example would make an employer want to read more? What specifics about the job does the better example provide? Why is that information important?

2 Apply Academic Writing Skill

Academic Writing Skill: Write an effective introduction
In an essay, the introductory paragraph, or introduction, starts the essay. A well-written introduction makes a reader want to read more. It includes a **hook** and a **thesis statement**. The hook is one or two sentences written to catch the interest of the reader. The thesis statement comes next and tells what will be included in the paragraphs that follow. Unlike a topic sentence of a paragraph, the thesis statement in an introduction tells the reader the main idea of the entire essay.

When writing a cover letter, you should create an introduction that includes the key elements described in the Lesson 7 article on how to write a cover letter. Show interest for the job, specifically name the job you are applying for, and link your education, experience, and interests to that job.

A IDENTIFY. Match the cover letter introductions with what is missing.

_____ 1. Your company has an outstanding reputation. I would like to apply for a customer service representative position. I have lots of skills to work with.

_____ 2. I am writing to apply for the position of Home Health Aide at Hurst Nursing Home. Three years' experience working with the elderly makes me a great candidate for the job.

_____ 3. I am interested in being an employee with your company. My experience as a general office clerk would help me bring many administrative skills to a position.

a. Interest in position
b. Specific job
c. How the job matches your skills and interests

B APPLY. Write an effective cover letter introduction using this information.

Job position: Medical Records Clerk
Company: Healthcare Solutions
Experience and Skills: three years of office experience; computer skills

I can write an effective introduction. ☐   I need more practice. ☐

For more practice, go to MyEnglishLab.

Writing

Write a cover letter tailored to a specific job

Lesson 9

1 Model for Writing

STUDY THE MODEL. Read the job posting and the cover letter responding to that posting on page 246. Use that cover letter as a Writing Model. Analyze the model. Underline the language in the cover letter that matches the requirements in the job posting.

2 Prepare Your Writing

A **FOCUS.** You will write a cover letter targeted to a specific job.

B **RESEARCH.** Go online to find a posting for a job that matches your experience, skills, and interests. Use the Note-Taking Template on page 247 to take notes about the job requirements for the job. Then list your experience and skills to show how you are suited, or qualified, for the job.

3 Write Write a cover letter tailored to a specific job.

A **ORGANIZE.** Use the organization of the Writing Model from Exercise 1 to guide your writing. Follow the tips below to format your cover letter correctly.

Formatting a Cover Letter

Like all formal letters, cover letters should be typed, follow a standard format like the one in the Writing Model, and be polite in tone.

Accurate punctuation and grammar are essential. A potential employer may toss aside a cover letter with even a few errors.

Just as your personal appearance in an interview is important, the appearance of your cover letter and résumé is equally important.

Writing Checklist	
The text includes…	
Structure:	✓ Cover letter
Organization:	✓ Introduction with a hook
	✓ Body of letter and final conclusion
Word Choice:	✓ Academic words
	✓ Summary signal words
Writing Skill:	✓ Introduction with a hook
Grammar:	✓ Modals to express possibilities
	✓ Present perfect and present perfect continuous

B **REVISE.** Use the Writing Checklist to evaluate your writing and make revisions. Remember to include an effective introduction.

4 Share Your Writing

A **COLLABORATE.** Share your writing with a partner. Use any feedback to improve your writing.

B **PUBLISH.** Create a final document to share with others.

I can write a cover letter tailored to a specific job. ☐   I need more practice. ☐

For more practice, go to MyEnglishLab.

Unit 2, Lesson 9   **39**

Lesson 10 Workplace Soft Skills

Project self-confidence

1 Workplace Expectations

A ▶ **CONSIDER.** Listen to part of a job interview. What is the interviewer trying to find out? How does the candidate respond?

B **READ.** Read the email from the interviewer to the human resources director stating the reason the candidate was not selected.

> Hi Ann,
> Thanks for sending another candidate for the position. I had hoped that this candidate would be a good fit. While his résumé looked good, I was disappointed in the interview. Many of the candidate's answers didn't display the confidence I want to see in an employee. I will not offer the job to him, so please send other qualified candidates my way—especially ones that show that they are proud of themselves and what they have accomplished.
> Li

C **IDENTIFY EXPECTATIONS.** Describe the interviewer's expectations and the candidate's response. What was the result?

1. Interviewer's expectation: _____
2. Candidate's response: _____
3. Result: _____

2 Learn from Mistakes

A **DISCUSS.** Suggest how the candidate could have talked about his strengths and weaknesses in ways that would project self-confidence. Share your suggestions with a partner.

B **ROLE-PLAY.** Give the candidate a "do over." Role-play the conversation, but this time have the candidate answer the interviewer's questions with confidence.

C ▶ **COMPARE.** Listen to the "do-over" conversation. How is it similar to your role play? How is it different?

Apply what you know

1. **DEFINE.** How would you explain this soft skill to a new employee?

2. **APPLY.** Record an example from your own life in your Soft Skills Log (page 241) of how you have projected self-confidence.

3. **SHARE.** Share your example.
   - *I projected self-confidence at _____ when I _____.*

I can project self-confidence. ☐   I need more practice. ☐

For audio and video, scan the QR code.   For more practice, go to MyEnglishLab.

The Thoughtful Consumer

3

PREVIEW

What does the word *finances* mean? Which types of occupations help people with their finances? Who do you think is working with this couple?

UNIT GOALS

Explain the steps of financial management

Create a budget using budgeting tools

Identify the steps for planning a big purchase

Evaluate strategies for making a big purchase

Give a presentation comparing two jobs that interest you

Write a compare-and-contrast essay about two jobs of interest

Workplace Soft Skill: Respond effectively to customer needs

Academic Skills:

- **Listening:** Listen for information that compares and contrasts
- **Speaking:** Encourage others to participate
- **Reading:** Mark text to highlight compare-and-contrast relationships
- **Writing:** Use compare-and-contrast signal words to highlight similarities and differences

Lesson 1

Listening and Speaking

Explain the steps of financial management

1 Before You Listen

A DISCUSS. How do you manage your finances to meet your financial responsibilities and goals?

B PREVIEW VOCABULARY.

1. **TOPIC-RELATED WORDS.** These terms are used in the listening. Does anyone know what they mean? For compound words, think about the meaning of each word separately. Also use roots and affixes to help you.

| financial consultant | budget | trial and error |
| money management | cutback | |

2. **ACADEMIC WORDS.** These sentences are from the listening. Discuss the meaning of each **bolded** word. Use context to help you.
   1. In order to manage your **finances** successfully, you need to start with a budget.
   2. Are there any expenses you can reduce or **eliminate**?
   3. If your budget is very tight and **restrictive**, it may be impossible for you to stick to it.
   4. Make **adjustments** to your budget each month.
   5. Remember that your utility bills will vary depending on the season. The cost of gasoline and groceries can also **fluctuate**.
   6. Those who **anticipate** emergency situations recognize the need to set money aside for emergencies.

C PREDICT. Use the lesson title, vocabulary, and image to make predictions about the podcast. What will its purpose be? What information do you expect?

2 Listen

A ▶ LISTEN FOR MAIN IDEAS. Listen to the podcast. List the speaker's five strategies for money management in the first column. Then compare your strategies with a partner.

Strategies	Tip for Using Each Strategy

B ▶ LISTEN FOR DETAILS. Listen again. List one tip for using each strategy.

42 Unit 3, Lesson 1

Listening and Speaking

3 Apply Academic Listening Skill

Academic Listening Skill: Listen for information that compares and contrasts
Speakers use comparison words to point out a **similarity** between two subjects. Contrast words are used to point out **differences**. Read this list of compare-and-contrast signal words. Listening for these words will help you notice when a new idea is similar to or different from the previous idea.

Compare-Contrast Signal Words	
Compare	**Contrast**
like, as, just as, just like, likewise, in like manner, much as, equally, similarly, similar to, in a similar fashion, the same as, in the same way	unlike, less than, more than, different from, but, however, although, in contrast, instead, conversely, nevertheless, even though, despite, on the other hand, on the contrary

A ▶ **IDENTIFY.** Listen to part of the podcast again. Which compare-and-contrast signal words or phrases does the speaker use? Underline them in the chart above.

B ▶ **COMPARE AND CONTRAST.** Listen to these parts of the podcast. Check to show whether the speaker is highlighting a similarity or difference. Then describe the similarity or difference.

1. ☐ similarity ☐ difference _____

2. ☐ similarity ☐ difference _____

3. ☐ similarity ☐ difference _____

C **EXPAND VOCABULARY.** Add words to your Word Study Log to show structure and meaning.

4 Real-World Application

A **APPLY.** List any successful money management strategies you follow. What other strategies would you add? Why?

B **EXPLAIN.** Share your current and future money management strategies and describe the steps you take. Include examples and explanations.

- *I manage my money by _____. For example, I _____.*
- *I need to add _____ because _____.*

Academic Speaking Skill: Encourage others to participate
In any group, some people are more likely to give their opinions than others. You should always try to encourage the quieter individuals to share their ideas. When more people contribute, the discussion is more interesting.

- *Do you have anything to add?*   • *We haven't heard from _____.*
- *What do you think?*

I can explain the steps of financial management. ☐	I need more practice. ☐

For more practice, go to MyEnglishLab.   For audio and video, scan the QR code.

Unit 3, Lesson 1 **43**

Lesson 2 Grammar

Comparative adjectives and adverbs

1 Focus on Usage

A **CONSIDER.** Read the highlighted sentences in the conversation below. Which adjectives and adverbs show a comparison? What two things are being compared?

> The comparative form is used to compare two things. The things being compared can be a noun or a verb. Comparative adjectives are used to compare nouns. Comparative adverbs are used to compare verbs.

B **IDENTIFY.** Read the entire conversation between two brothers. Underline all the comparative adjectives and adverbs.

A: I have a higher salary than you, but you save money faster than I do. What's your secret?
B: I spend my money more carefully than you do.
A: How so? Can you give me an example?
B: Sure. You paid $75 for those headphones at the store, but I found them online for a much lower price.
A: But I wanted them right away. It takes longer to order something online and wait for it to ship. Besides, it was just a pair of headphones. I usually compare prices when I'm making bigger purchases.
B: You should compare prices for all purchases, big or small. And you need to record your expenses to keep track of your spending.
A: I do! Well, I guess I can keep track of my spending more accurately.
B: And you need a savings account.
A: But I have a checking account. It's easier to keep all my money in one account.
B: A checking account is good, but when it comes to setting money aside, a savings account is better.
A: OK, thanks. Those are all good suggestions.
B: Right. Now you just need to follow them!

2 Focus on Structure

Adjectives	Comparative Adjectives
I compare prices when I make **big** purchases.	I save money for **bigger** purchases.
It takes a **long** time to save money.	It takes a **longer** time without a budget.
Money management is not **easy**.	It's **easier** to set money aside in a savings account.
A checking account is **good**.	A savings account is **better**.
Adverbs	**Comparative Adverbs**
You saved a lot of money **fast**.	You save money **faster** than I do.
I spend money **carefully**.	I spend money **more carefully** than you do.

- *Good* and *bad* have irregular comparative forms: *good—better*   *bad—worse*.
- Most 2-syllable comparatives use either *-er* or *more*. But some 2-syllable comparatives can only use either *-er* or *more*.
      friendlier or *more friendly*   only *earlier*   only *more modern*
- Longer comparatives tend to use *more*.
      more beautiful   *more* affordable   *more* carefully

For a complete list of rules, search online for: comparative and superlative spelling rules.

Grammar

A **INVESTIGATE.** Analyze all the examples of comparatives. Match to complete the rules.

_____ 1. For most one-syllable adjectives and adverbs, _____.

_____ 2. For adjectives ending in **-y**, delete the **-y** and _____.

_____ 3. For most long adjectives and adverbs, _____.

_____ 4. For one-syllable adjectives ending in one vowel + one consonant, _____.

a. use **more**

b. add **-er**

c. double the consonant and add **-er**

d. add **-ier**

B **COMPLETE.** Complete the sentences with the comparative form.

1. (*fast*) You can save money _____*faster*_____ if you follow a few simple steps.

2. (*carefully*) I downloaded a new app so that I can plan my budget _____.

3. (*easy*) It is _____ to keep track of your expenses if you write them down.

4. (*difficult*) I prefer using a debit card instead of cash. It is _____ to keep track of expenses when I use cash.

5. (*tight*) I'm on a _____ budget now that I'm trying to save money to buy a car.

6. (*good*) I'm trying to find a _____ way to manage my money.

C **WRITE.** Use the adjective or adverb to make comparisons.

1. (*expensive*) a car / a bicycle
   A car is more expensive than a bicycle.

2. (*quick*) using an ATM / going inside a bank
   _____

3. (*cheap*) a sandwich / a steak dinner
   _____

4. (*heavy*) coins / paper money
   _____

5. (*thin*) a dime / a nickel
   _____

6. (*important*) paying rent / buying a movie ticket
   _____

Apply what you know

1. **EVALUATE.** Share what money management strategies you use. Which do you think are better or worse? Why?

2. **WRITE.** Write a paragraph comparing different money management strategies. Use comparative adjectives and adverbs.

   I think using cash is a better strategy than using credit cards. Credit cards may be more expensive than cash because they usually have extra fees or interest charges. Plus, I spend more carefully when I use cash.

I can use comparative adjectives and adverbs. ☐	I need more practice. ☐

For more practice, go to MyEnglishLab.

Unit 3, Lesson 2   **45**

Lesson 3: Workplace, Life, & Community Skills

Create a budget using budgeting tools

1 Use a Budget

A BRAINSTORM. What experiences with budgets have you had? Was keeping a budget helpful or unhelpful? Why?

B PROBLEM-SOLVE. What information about your earnings and spending do you track? What suggestions do you have to help others stick to a budget?

2 Consult Resources

Budget Calculator

A budget calculator helps individuals better understand their **income** (earnings) and **expenses** (spending) in order to manage their finances. Track money going in and out of a household to avoid overspending. The money you save can then be used to pay down student loans or credit card debt. You can also save it for a future expense, such as making a big purchase or dealing with an emergency.

A SCAN. A young man wanted to pay down his student loan, so he used a budget calculator.

1. List two personal items tracked in the budget. _____
2. The Personal Items total of $860 is listed twice. Why? _____
3. How much of his student loan was the young man currently paying off each month? _____

Finances First!

Home | Contact Us | Site Map

Personal Budget Calculator – Free

Personal Budget | Parents' Education Budget

Monthly Income
- Biweekly Paycheck: $2,355
- Biweekly Paycheck: $2,355
- TOTAL Income: $4,710

Monthly Expenses
- Housing (Mortgage, Rent): $1,400
- Food: $575
- Utilities: (Electricity, Water, Phone): $250
- Transportation: $220
- Health: (Insurance, Prescriptions): $190
- Personal Items: $860
- Student Loan Repayment: $375
- TOTAL Monthly Expenses: $3,870

Personal Items-Itemized
- Clothing: $180
- Entertainment: $50
- Eating Out: $300
- Childcare: $250
- Gym Membership: $30
- Pet Supplies: $50
- TOTAL: $860

Annual Expenses (*Divide by 12 for month*):
- Homeowner's or Renter's Insurance: $1,200
- City lights, sewer, cleaning, street maintenance: $150
- Car registration: $90
- TOTAL Annual Expenses: $1,440 Divided by 12 = $120 per month

Semiannual Expenses (*Divide by 6 for month*):
- Car Insurance: $300
- TOTAL Semiannual Expenses: $300 Divided by 6 = $50 per month

TOTAL EXPENSES by Month: $4,040 Additional Remaining for Savings or further Debt Reduction: **$670**

Our Advice: You have a surplus of $670. This is 14% of your budget. Consider setting up an Emergency Fund or begin Investing!

Unit 3, Lesson 3

Workplace, Life, & Community Skills

B **DEFINE KEY WORDS.** Find these words on the budget calculator. Match each word to its definition.

_____ 1. (adj) semiannual

_____ 2. (n) debt reduction

_____ 3. (adj) itemized

_____ 4. (n) finances

_____ 5. (n) utilities

a. things like electricity, water, and phone

b. listed as separate elements

c. act of paying off money owed

d. twice a year

e. the management of a person's money

C **INTERPRET.** Locate information on the budget calculator.

1. On which monthly expense does he spend the most? What is that total? _____

2. What is his total income for each month? _____

3. How much of his student loan could he afford to pay back each month? _____

4. What do **biweekly** and **semiannual** mean? How can you tell? _____

_____

D **CALCULATE.** According to Lendkey.com, a household should spend no more than 30% of its income on housing.

1. What percentage of his total income did he spend on housing? _____

2. Did he follow the 30% recommended percentage for housing/income? Or did he go over? _____

3. What percentage of his monthly income does the budget show he could use for savings or for additional debt reduction? _____

4. How much does he budget for car registration each month? _____

E **RELATE.** If this were your budget, what other expenses would you need to add to the budget? To increase your savings, which of your expenses would you try to reduce?

F **GO ONLINE.** Use the Search Terms to find two budget calculators. Share your budget calculators with a partner. Which one seems easier to use? Why?

Search Terms: budget   calculator

Apply what you know

1. **APPLY.** Enter your data into a budget calculator.

2. **SHARE.** If you feel comfortable, share your results with a partner. What aspect of your finances did the budget calculator help you learn more about? Why was that information helpful?

   • *The budget helped me see _____. That was helpful because _____.*
   • *I was surprised to see _____. In the future, I will _____.*

I can create a budget using budgeting tools. ☐   I need more practice. ☐

For more practice, go to MyEnglishLab.

Unit 3, Lesson 3   **47**

Lesson 4 Reading

Identify the steps for planning a big purchase

1 Before You Read

A **DESCRIBE.** What is the next big purchase you are planning to make? Why is that purchase important?

B **PREVIEW VOCABULARY.**

1. **TOPIC-RELATED WORDS.** These terms are used in the article. Does anyone know what they mean? Use roots and affixes to help you. You can also look for clues in the article.

| prequalified | preapproved | mortgage | inspection |

2. **ACADEMIC WORDS.** Discuss the meaning of the **bolded** words in the article. Use context to help you. After reading the article, add any words you learned to your Word Study Log.

C **PREDICT.** Preview the article title and image. What is the purpose of the article? What information do you expect?

2 Read for Gist

A **READ.** What steps should you follow when buying a new home?

Ready to Buy a House? Be Sure to Follow These Eight Steps

1 Buying a home is likely to be one of the most exciting moments of your life—and one of the most stressful! Fortunately, there are steps you can take to make the process more manageable.

   1. First, you need to figure out how much you can afford to spend. Experts
5 recommend you spend no more than 3–5 times your yearly household income on a home. Once you know what you can afford, you can decide what you are looking for. Do you want an apartment or a house? What neighborhood do you want to live in? How many bedrooms do you need? Do you want to be close to public transportation? Schools? A grocery store? Restaurants?

   2. Then step two is to do your research. Look at listings for apartments or houses that meet your criteria. Pay attention
10 to how long they are on the market and whether there are any changes to the price. This will help you **predict** how quickly you need to make an offer if you become interested in a home.

   3. Next, get <u>prequalified</u> and <u>preapproved</u> for a <u>mortgage</u>. You can go to the bank where you have your checking and savings accounts and find a mortgage banker. This person will look at your income, savings, and **credit** score and give you an **estimate** of how big of a mortgage you can afford to take out.

15 **4.** Now you're ready for step 4 — find a real estate agent. Look for an agent with plenty of experience and good negotiating skills. Choose a person who knows a lot about the neighborhood you're interested in.

   5. Once you have an agent, you can start looking at apartments or houses. When you visit, check that everything is working. Turn on the water in the showers and sinks. Turn all the lights on and off. Check the heating and air conditioner. Open and close windows and doors. Look for any signs of damage to the walls or floors.

48   Unit 3, Lesson 4

Reading

20 **6.** When you find the right home, you are ready to make an offer. If the seller accepts your offer, schedule a home <u>inspection</u>. An inspector will come to the house and look for any structural problems. Then you and the seller can negotiate what the seller needs to fix before you move in. If the inspector **detects** serious or expensive problems, you may be able to withdraw your offer.

7. The next to last step is to work with the mortgage banker to choose and take out a loan to pay for your mortgage.

25 **8.** Once you have your loan in place, you are finally ready to close the sale. This step can take anywhere from one to three months — so be patient!

The home-buying process can be nerve-racking, especially for first-time buyers. If you follow the steps above, you'll find yourself moving into the apartment or house of your dreams in no time!

B **IDENTIFY MAIN IDEAS.** Choose the main idea of the article. Where is it stated? Lines _____

a. The home-buying process is always stressful for first-time buyers.
b. Buying a home is much easier if you follow a series of steps.
c. Once you figure out how much you can spend, the home-buying process gets easier.

3 Close Reading

A **RESTATE.** Create a list to restate each step in your own words.

B **LOCATE DETAILS.** Are the statements true or false? Write the line numbers of your evidence.

	T/F	Lines
1. When you are thinking about buying a home, the first thing you should do is get prequalified for a loan.	_____	_____
2. You can make an offer on a home before you find a real estate agent.	_____	_____
3. You need to do a home inspection before you close the sale.	_____	_____
4. You should wait to do research on apartment or house listings until after you have taken out a loan.	_____	_____

C **EXPAND UNDERSTANDING.**

1. SUMMARIZE. Summarize how you get preapproved for a mortgage as described in Step 3.
2. BRAINSTORM. Imagine you are looking at an apartment or house. In addition to what is described in Step 5, what would you check?

Apply what you know

1. LIST. Think about the big purchase you described in Exercise 1A. List the steps you need to take before you make the purchase.

2. SHARE. Share your list with a partner.

The next big purchase I'm going to make is _____. The first thing I need to do is _____. The second thing I need to do is _____.

I can identify the steps for planning a big purchase. ☐   I need more practice. ☐

For more practice, go to MyEnglishLab.   For audio and video, scan the QR code.

Unit 3, Lesson 4   **49**

Lesson 5 Listening and Speaking
Evaluate strategies for making a big purchase

1 Before You Listen

A   **MAKE CONNECTIONS.** How do you make a big purchase? Do you use a credit card, take out a loan, or save money for the purchase?

B   **PREVIEW VOCABULARY.**

1. **TOPIC-RELATED WORDS.** These terms are used in the listening. Does anyone know what they mean? For compound words, think about the meaning of each word separately. Also use roots and affixes to help you.

trade-in	lease	short-term loan	long-term loan	dealership

2. **ACADEMIC WORDS.** These sentences are from the listening. Discuss the meaning of each **bolded** word. Use context to help you.
   1. Our car is very old, so it will **inevitably** break down soon.
   2. Perhaps the smartest **option** is to invest in a new car, even if we have to take out a loan.
   3. We should have our car **inspected** to see which repairs are the most important.
   4. Should we **purchase** a new car or a used one?
   5. We can start saving for a new **vehicle**. If we save carefully, we can buy a new car in a year or two.
   6. A lot of dealerships offer special **incentives** for purchasing new cars, such as free oil changes.

C   **PREDICT.** Use the lesson title, vocabulary, and image to make predictions about the listening. Who will participate in the conversation? What will the purpose of the conversation be?

2 Listen

A   ▶ **LISTEN FOR MAIN IDEAS.** Listen to the two conversations. What strategy does each couple decide to use to buy a car?

Couple 1: _____

Couple 2: _____

Listening and Speaking

B ▶ **LISTEN FOR DETAILS.** Listen to parts of the two conversations again. What advantages or disadvantages do the speakers mention? Complete the chart.

	Advantage	Disadvantage
Long-term loan		
Short-term loan		
New car		
Used car		

3 Apply Academic Listening Skill

A ▶ **COMPARE AND CONTRAST.** Listen to part of the conversation again. Describe the similarities and differences between leasing a car and taking out a loan. Then write a paragraph to contrast leasing a car to taking out a loan for a car.

_____
_____
_____
_____
_____

B **EXPAND VOCABULARY.** Add words to your Word Study Log to show structure and meaning.

4 Real-World Application

A **EVALUATE.** Which couple do you think thought about their decision more thoroughly? Explain why.

B **SHARE.** What decisions have you made when purchasing a car or making another big purchase? If you plan to purchase a car in the future, which strategy will you use? Explain your decision to a partner.
   • *When I purchased a car, I decided to _____ because _____.*

| I can evaluate strategies for making a big purchase. ☐ | I need more practice. ☐ |

For more practice, go to MyEnglishLab.   For audio and video, scan the QR code.

Unit 3, Lesson 5   **51**

Lesson 6 Grammar

Superlative adjectives and adverbs

1 Focus on Usage

A CONSIDER. Read the highlighted sentences in the website below. What is the superlative adjective or adverb comparing?

B IDENTIFY. Read the entire website. Underline all the superlative adjectives and adverbs.

> The superlative form is used to express the highest or most extreme degree of an adjective or adverb. A superlative adjective or adverb is also used to compare three or more people or things.

Buying vs. Leasing:
What is the best option for you?

Buying Benefits

- Buying the most reasonably priced vehicle and keeping it a few years after you buy it may be the most affordable choice.
- If you plan to take a lot of road trips or put a lot of wear and tear on your car, buying is the smartest choice. Owning a vehicle means you may drive it as many miles as you like.
- Buying a vehicle is also the most flexible option. You can customize or upgrade your vehicle as you want.

Leasing Benefits

- Leasing allows you to drive a new vehicle every two or three years. This may be the wisest choice if you want the newest technology and the latest features in a car.
- A lease may provide the most comprehensive warranty. Your vehicle will be covered by the manufacturer warranty for the full term of the lease.
- When you go to pay for the car, leasing a vehicle is usually the least expensive option because it requires no down payment and offers the lowest monthly payments.

2 Focus on Structure

Superlative Adjectives
What is **the most affordable** choice?
I'm looking for **the least expensive** option.
We want **the newest** technology and **the latest** features in a car.
Superlative Adverbs
We should shop for **the most reasonably** priced car.
Buying a car allows us to invest our money **the most effectively**.

- The words *good* and *bad* have irregular superlative forms:
    good — the best   bad — the worst

Grammar

A **INVESTIGATE.** Analyze all the examples of superlatives. Choose the correct words to complete the rules.

1. For most one-syllable adjectives, add _____ to form the superlative.
   a. -er   **b.** -est

2. A superlative usually begins with _____.
   a. a   **b.** the

3. For most long adjectives and adverbs, use _____ to form the superlative.
   a. most   **b.** more

4. The superlative form of **bad** is _____.
   a. the worse   **b.** the worst

B **COMPLETE.** Complete the sentences. Use the superlative form.

1. (*difficult*) What is _____ financial decision you have ever made?

2. (*good*) What do you think is _____ strategy for making a big purchase?

3. (*bad*) Buying a car I couldn't afford was _____ mistake I've ever made.

4. (*large*) My car payment is my _____ expense.

5. (*smart*) _____ way to manage money is to save more than you spend.

6. (*carefully*) Of everyone in my family, my sister Emma manages money _____.

7. (*actively*) Of all of us, Emma is _____ involved in her budgeting.

C **CONSIDER.** Answer the questions with complete sentences. Use superlative forms in your response.

1. What is the largest purchase you have ever made? _____

2. What is your biggest priority this year? _____

3. What is the most difficult school subject for you? _____

4. What do you think are the best and worst strategies for saving money? _____

Apply what you know

1. **DESCRIBE.** People use different strategies when they want to make a big purchase. Some buy items and pay them off in time. Others save the needed cash first. What was the last big purchase you made? What strategies did you use? Use superlative adjectives and adverbs.

2. **WRITE.** Write a paragraph about the strategy you discussed in Step 1.
   My last big purchase was a new computer. I used what I think of as the safest strategy —I saved enough money before I went to buy it.

I can use superlative adjectives and adverbs. ■   I need more practice. ■

For more practice, go to MyEnglishLab.

Unit 3, Lesson 6   **53**

Lesson 7 Reading
Compare and contrast earning potential of educational levels

1 Before You Read

A **DISCUSS.** What is your educational goal? Does the cost of higher education worry you? Why or why not?

B **PREVIEW VOCABULARY.**

1. **TOPIC-RELATED WORDS.** There is a progression of degrees for students continuing education after high school: *associate's, bachelor's, master's,* and *doctoral.* Those terms are used in the article.
The terms below are also used. Does anyone know what they mean? For compound words, think of the meaning of each word separately. You can also look for clues in the article.

| return on investment | earning potential | median |

2. **ACADEMIC WORDS.** Discuss the meaning of the **bolded** words in the article. Use context to help you. After reading the article, add any words you learned to your Word Study Log.

C **PREDICT.** Preview the article title and the two bar graphs. What is the purpose of the article? What information do you expect?

2 Read for Gist

A **READ.** Think about the main ideas as you read. Underline any sentences that help you identify main ideas.

Is Higher Education Still a Good Return on Investment?

The rising cost of higher education may make you pause before pursuing any degree. But before you put off your educational pursuits, consider the <u>return on investment</u> that education can provide. Education is still the best ticket out there for increasing your <u>earning potential</u>.

The average cost of college has risen on average 2.3% each year over the past ten years. In 2018, in-state
5   public college tuition averaged $9,970 a year. Meanwhile, the average out-of-state public college tuition was $25,620. Private colleges were the most expensive at $34,740. Room and board added **approximately** $10,000 to $12,000 to the bill. Given these costs, most students end up with thousands of dollars in student loans.
10   No wonder some people question whether higher education is worth it.

As it turns out, it is indeed—at least that's what the numbers say. According to the Bureau of Labor
15   Statistics (BLS), higher education *does* pay off. In 2017, people with a bachelor's degree earned $461 more per week than people with only a high school diploma. That figure
20   increases to $650 when comparing those same college graduates to students without a high school

Median weekly earnings by educational level, 2017

Degree	Approx. weekly earnings
Doctoral degree	~$1,750
Master's degree	~$1,400
Bachelor's degree	~$1,175
Associate's degree	~$825
Some college, no degree	~$750
High school diploma, no college	~$700
Less than a high school diploma	~$500

---

54   Unit 3, Lesson 7

Reading

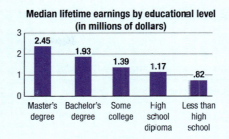

Median lifetime earnings by educational level (in millions of dollars)

diploma. As you go up the educational ladder, the difference continues to increase. Master's degree holders earn $689 more per week than high school graduates. Doctoral degree holders earn $1,031 more. It is clear from these **statistics** that education does make a difference.

When we consider this increase in earnings over a lifetime, the numbers are even more **convincing**. This second graph looks at the <u>median</u>, or middle number in the range, of lifetime earnings for people with different education levels. It shows that lifetime earnings increase with more education. People with a bachelor's degree earn $760,000 more in a lifetime than people with only a high school diploma. Individuals with a master's degree make almost $1.3 million more in a lifetime. Of course, these differences are even greater when comparing graduates to people without a high school diploma: $1.11 million more for a bachelor's degree and $1.63 million more for a master's degree.

There is one surprising statistic that is not captured in the BLS research above. A recent study of five states (Arkansas, Colorado, Tennessee, Texas, and Virginia) reports that graduates completing an associate's degree in a **technical** field earned more on average in their first year than college graduates with bachelor's degrees. Depending on the state, these graduates earned $2,000 to $11,000 more. Similarly, individuals with one- or two-year certificates in the industrial, construction, and healthcare fields earned more than graduates with bachelor's degrees. In fact, some certificates—radiology, hospital facilities management, and aircraft mechanics and maintenance—outearned bachelor degree holders by more than $20,000.

What does this mean for you? Only *you* can make that decision. But two important **trends** are clear. First, education does offer a valuable return on investment. Second, if you choose a career in a growing technical field, you may get even more bang for your buck. Making smart choices in education is clearly an important part of long-range career planning.

B IDENTIFY MAIN IDEAS. Choose the main idea of the article and of Paragraphs 2–4. Find the sentences that best support each main idea. Write the line numbers.

Article Main Idea	Lines
a. Higher education increases your earning potential. b. The cost of higher education is rising. c. Higher education costs may make you choose not to pursue a postsecondary degree.	
Paragraph Main Ideas	

2   a. In-state public college tuition in 2018 was $9,970 on average.
       b. Many students have thousands of dollars in student loans.
       c. The average cost of college has risen each year.	

3   a. The Bureau of Labor Statistics reports that higher education is worth it.
       b. Bachelor's degree holders earn $461 more per week than individuals with only a high school diploma.
       c. The difference in earnings increases as you move up the educational ladder.	

4   a. Individuals with a bachelor's degree make $760 more in a lifetime than those with only a high school diploma.
       b. Statistics on lifetime earnings clearly show the increased earning potential of individuals with higher levels of education.
       c. Differences in lifetime earnings are even higher when comparing college graduates to individuals without a high school diploma.	

3 Close Reading

A LOCATE DETAILS. Use evidence from the article and the bar graphs to complete the chart.

Difference in Earnings as Compared to ...	Bachelor's	Master's	Doctorate
With high school diploma only (weekly)			
Without high school diploma (weekly)			
With high school diploma only (lifetime)			NA
Without high school diploma (lifetime)			NA

B APPLY ACADEMIC READING SKILL.

> **Academic Reading Skill: Mark text to highlight compare-and-contrast relationships**
> Remember, when people compare and contrast different items, they describe the similarities and differences between those items. Look for common compare-and-contrast signal words and phrases. Then mark the text to highlight them. This skill will improve your reading comprehension for texts that compare and contrast items.

1. Reread Paragraph 3. Circle compare-and-contrast signal words and phrases. Underline the two items being compared and draw an arrow from the first item to the second item.

   > In 2017, <u>individuals with a bachelor's degree</u> earned $461 (more) per week (than) <u>individuals with only a high school diploma</u>.

2. Reread Paragraph 5. Create a Venn diagram to compare students who earned a technical associate's degree with those who earned a one- or two-year technical certificate.

   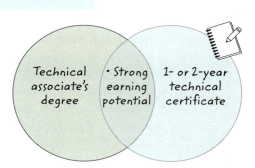

3. Create a Venn diagram to compare two other degree levels.

   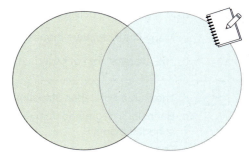

C CALCULATE. Use the statistics from the bar graphs to calculate differences in income.

1. What is the approximate difference in weekly earnings between individuals with an associate's degree and those without a high school diploma? _____

2. What is the difference between the lifetime earnings of individuals with some college and individuals without a high school diploma? _____

56   Unit 3, Lesson 7

4 Prepare for an Academic Presentation

A FOCUS. You will give a formal presentation to compare two different careers or two types of jobs that interest you.

B RESEARCH. Go online to research information about the two jobs. Use the Note-Taking Template on page 248 to take notes on the two jobs. You can also create a Venn Diagram to help you visualize your data.

C ORGANIZE. Use the Presentation Template on page 249 to organize your information. Use the suggestions below to improve your presentation delivery.

Presentation Checklist	
	The presentation includes...
Organization:	✓ Introduction with 3 main points, or sections
Support:	✓ Venn diagram to show similarities/differences
Word Choice:	✓ Academic words
	✓ Compare-contrast signal words
Delivery:	✓ Speech at appropriate volume and rate
	✓ Speech that is clear and easy to understand
	✓ Eye contact

Presentation Delivery

The content and organization of a presentation are very important. Delivery, however, is equally important. Delivery is the use of **speech** and **body language** when you present.

Three important components of speech are **volume**, **rate**, and **clarity**.
- **Volume** is how loudly or softly you speak. Speak loudly enough for your audience to hear but not too loudly. Check your volume before your presentation. Ask, "Can everyone hear me all right?"
- **Rate** is how quickly or slowly you speak. Speak quickly enough so your audience won't get frustrated but slowly enough so they can follow. Remember that people often speak too quickly when they're nervous.
- **Clarity** refers to how clearly you speak and how well your audience can understand you. Try to pronounce your words carefully.

Body language includes **good eye contact** and **gestures**.
- To have **good eye contact** means to look directly at *all* your audience *often*. Know your information well so that you can look more at your audience than at your notes.
- **Gestures** include all the ways you use your body when you speak. Use gestures to emphasize what you say but not so many that your gestures distract your audience.

D REVISE AND PRACTICE. Use the Presentation Checklist to evaluate your presentation and make revisions. Then practice your presentation until you feel confident.

Apply what you know — Academic Presentation

1. **PRESENT.** Share your presentation with a partner. Your teacher may also choose you to present to the class.

2. **EVALUATE.** Have your partner evaluate your presentation using the Presentation Checklist.

3. **ENCOURAGE OTHERS.** If your partner is hesitant to give feedback, remember to ask questions to draw out any comments.

I can compare and contrast earning potential of educational levels. ☐   I need more practice. ☐

For more practice, go to MyEnglishLab.   For audio and video, scan the QR code.

Lesson 8

Writing Workshop
Use compare-and-contrast signal words effectively

1 What Do You Notice?

A COMPARE. Read the two examples. Which is more clearly organized and easier to read? Why?

Example 1:

Higher education takes time and money but will likely pay off in the long run. True, college can be expensive. And it is also true that people without college degrees can still make a decent living. In fact, some say that a bachelor's degree isn't worth what it once was. On the other hand, people who have college degrees will likely make more money each month than those who don't. Similarly, they will likely make more money over a lifetime compared to those without higher education. However, a four-year degree may not be needed for all careers; for example, many one- and two-year degrees can be very profitable.

Example 2:

Higher education takes time and money but will likely pay off in the long run. College can be expensive. People without college degrees can still make a decent living. Some say that a bachelor's degree isn't worth what it once was. People who have college degrees will likely make more money each week than those who don't. They will likely make more money over a lifetime compared to those without higher education. A four-year degree may not be needed for all careers. Many one- and two-year degrees can be very profitable.

B ANALYZE. Read the highlighted sentences in each example. Which makes a clearer comparison? Underline the information that makes the comparison clearer.

2 Apply Academic Writing Skill

Academic Writing Skill: Use compare-and-contrast signal words to highlight similarities and differences
You will often be asked to compare and contrast two people, places, or things. Remember that when you compare, you show how two items are similar; when you contrast, you show how they are different. Remember to use the signal words that let readers know you are comparing or contrasting. Use comparison signal words to highlight any similarities. Use contrast signal words to highlight any differences.

A IDENTIFY. Underline any compare-and-contrast signal words.

1. Individuals with a bachelor's degree can make $650 more per week than someone with no high school diploma.

2. Putting off college is less expensive than continuing your education, but it may be similar to putting off going to see the doctor.

B APPLY. Use a comparison or a contrast signal word to compare the two ideas stated. Rewrite the sentences using those signal words.

1. Individuals with two-year postsecondary certificates in healthcare careers earned more than those with bachelor's degrees. Individuals with construction certificates earned more as well.

2. Some people question whether or not a college degree is worth the money. The numbers say higher education is worth it.

I can use compare-and-contrast signal words effectively. ☐   I need more practice. ☐

For more practice, go to MyEnglishLab.

58   Unit 3, Lesson 8

Writing

Write a compare-and-contrast essay about two jobs of interest

Lesson 9

1 ▶ Model for Writing

STUDY THE MODEL. Read the Writing Model that compares and contrasts two jobs on page 250. Analyze that model. Which two jobs does the writer compare and contrast? Circle the compare-and-contrast signal words. Then underline the two key sentences that indicate how the model is organized.

2 ▶ Prepare Your Writing

A **FOCUS.** You will write a compare-and-contrast essay about two jobs that interest you.

B **RESEARCH.** Go online and choose two jobs that interest you. You can choose the same two jobs you researched in Lesson 7 or you can choose other jobs. Use a Venn diagram to compare and contrast the two jobs.

3 ▶ Write Write a compare-and-contrast essay about two jobs.

A **ORGANIZE.** Use the organization of the Writing Model from Exercise 1 to guide your writing. Follow the tips below to explain the similarities and differences between the two jobs.

Compare-and-Contrast Essay

To write an essay that compares and contrasts, choose two topics that have both similarities and differences. Choose three to four criteria to compare and contrast. For example, when comparing jobs, you may want to focus on similarities and differences in these areas:

- education and training required
- Experience and skills needed; job duties
- Income – including both salary and job outlook

Writing Checklist	
	The text includes...
Structure:	✓ Compare-contrast essay
Organization:	✓ Introduction
	✓ Body of essay
	✓ Final conclusion
Word Choice:	✓ Academic words
	✓ Compare-contrast signal words
Writing Skill:	✓ Signal words to highlight similarities and differences
Grammar:	✓ Comparative and superlative adjectives and adverbs

An easy way to organize the essay is to discuss all the similarities in one paragraph and all the differences in another. Don't forget to include an introduction and a conclusion.

B **REVISE.** Use the Writing Checklist to evaluate your writing and make revisions. Remember to use compare and contrast signal words.

4 ▶ Share Your Writing

A **COLLABORATE.** Share your writing with a partner. Use any feedback to improve your writing.

B **PUBLISH.** Create a final document to share with others.

I can write a compare-and-contrast essay about two jobs of interest. ☐   I need more practice. ☐

For more practice, go to MyEnglishLab.

Unit 3, Lesson 9   **59**

Lesson 10

Workplace Soft Skills
Respond effectively to customer needs

1 Workplace Expectations

A ▶ **ANALYZE.** Listen to part of a conversation between a customer, a customer service representative, and a manager. What is the problem? How does the customer service representative try to resolve it? Why does the manager step in?

B **IDENTIFY EXPECTATIONS.** Describe the customer's expectation and the customer service representative's response. Why was the customer upset? What was the result?

1. Customer's expectation: _____

2. Customer service representative's response: _____

3. Result: _____

2 Learn from Mistakes

A **DISCUSS.** How could the customer service representative respect the company policy and still respond effectively to the customer's needs? Suggest specific things he could have done differently. Share your suggestions with a partner.

B **ROLE-PLAY.** Give the customer service representative a "do over." Role-play the conversation, but this time have the customer service representative respond effectively to the customer's complaint.

C ▶ **COMPARE.** Listen to the "do over" conversation. How is it similar to your role play? How is it different?

Apply what you know

1. **DEFINE.** How would you explain this soft skill to a new employee?
2. **APPLY.** Record an example from your own life in your Soft Skills Log (page 241) of how you have responded to customer needs or have had your needs responded to effectively.
3. **SHARE.** Share your example.
   - *I responded effectively to customer needs at _____ when I _____.*

I can respond effectively to customer needs. ☐   I need more practice. ☐

For audio and video, scan the QR code.   For more practice, go to MyEnglishLab.

At Peak Performance

4

PREVIEW
Read the unit title. What might be happening in this picture? Why do you think that?

UNIT GOALS

Rank factors that influence job promotion
Use training resources to identify growth opportunities
Identify solutions to workplace dilemmas
Evaluate conversations for effective conflict resolution
Describe how to protect workers' rights
Write a workplace incident report

Workplace Soft Skill: Negotiate to resolve conflict

Academic Skills:
- **Listening:** Listen for evidence that supports a speaker's message
- **Speaking:** Ask for clarification
- **Reading:** Recognize how infographics provide evidence to support a text
- **Writing:** Match tone to audience and purpose

Lesson 1

Listening and Speaking
Rank factors that influence job promotion

1 Before You Listen

A **DISCUSS.** What factors influence job promotion?

B **PREVIEW VOCABULARY.**

1. **TOPIC-RELATED WORDS.** These terms are used in the listening. Does anyone know what they mean? For compound words, think about the meaning of each word separately.

| career ladder | human resources | above and beyond |
| mentor | team player | |

2. **ACADEMIC WORDS.** These sentences are from the listening. Discuss the meaning of each **bolded** word. Use context to help you.
   1. Are you **seeking** a promotion or trying to work your way up the career ladder at your company?
   2. If you stay with a company long enough, will you **eventually** be promoted? Not necessarily.
   3. There are several **dimensions**, such as arriving to work on time, doing a good job, and staying out of trouble.
   4. Employers want to promote people who are **flexible** and will adapt to new responsibilities easily.
   5. One more important factor is taking the **initiative** in solving problems.

C **PREDICT.** Use the lesson title, the vocabulary, and image to make predictions about the podcast. What will its purpose be? What information do you expect?

2 Listen

A ▶ **LISTEN FOR MAIN IDEAS.** Listen to the podcast. Write 1–5 to order the factors that influence getting a promotion as they are presented in the podcast. Then compare your order with a partner.

Order	Factors That Influence Promotion	Details
	Flexibility	
	Initiative	
	Communication Skills	
	Teamwork	
	Length of time	

B ▶ **LISTEN FOR DETAILS.** Listen again. List one detail that supports each factor.

62 Unit 4, Lesson 1

Listening and Speaking

3 Apply Academic Listening Skill

Academic Listening Skill: Listen for evidence that supports a speaker's message
Speakers often give evidence to support what they are saying or to provide proof for an argument. This evidence may be given in the form of statistics. It may also be provided as specific information from other sources. Speakers often introduce this evidence with evidence signal words. Listening for these words will help you recognize when an argument is justified or supported by evidence.

Evidence Signal Words	
Signal Phrases	**Verbs**
according to, as stated by, based on	state, say, show, suggest, explain, describe, claim, indicate

A ▶ **IDENTIFY.** Listen to part of the podcast again. Which evidence signal words or phrases does the speaker use? Underline them.

B ▶ **RECOGNIZE EVIDENCE.** Listen again. What evidence from other sources does the speaker give to support his main point? List at least two examples.

C **EXPAND VOCABULARY.** Add words to your Word Study Log to show structure and meaning.

4 Real-World Application

A **EVALUATE.** How successful are you at meeting the factors that influence promotion? Rate your performance for each factor (1 = poor; 5 = excellent). If you do not have a job, skip number 1 and rate yourself in the other areas.

1. Length of time with your employer   1   2   3   4   5
2. Relationship with other employees (or students)   1   2   3   4   5
3. Flexibility and willingness to learn new things   1   2   3   4   5
4. Communication skills   1   2   3   4   5
5. Initiative in solving problems   1   2   3   4   5

B **COLLABORATE.** Share your ratings with a partner. Support your ratings with examples.

- *My rating for length of time with my employer is _____ because I have worked at my job for _____.*
- *I gave myself a rating of _____ for flexibility because _____.*

Academic Speaking Skill: Ask for clarification
When other people make statements, ask questions to help you better understand what they are saying. This type of questioning will improve your understanding of what others mean.

- *Could you explain what you mean by _____?*
- *I'm not sure I understand what you're saying. Could you explain that further?*

I can rank factors that influence job promotion. ☐   I need more practice. ☐

For more practice, go to MyEnglishLab.   For audio and video, scan the QR code.

Unit 4, Lesson 1   63

Lesson **(2)** **Grammar**

Express purpose, reason, or contrast

1 Focus on Usage

A **CONSIDER.** Read the highlighted sentences in the letter below. Which words express purpose, reason, and contrast?

B **IDENTIFY.** Read the entire letter. Underline all words that express purpose, reason, or contrast.

> Use words such as *in order to* to express a purpose, or *because* to state a reason. Use words like *although* to express an exception or a contrast. These words can be used with a clause, a phrase, or an infinitive.

Dear Ms. Gordon,

I am writing in order to express my interest in the recently posted management position. I feel I am qualified for this position because of my strong collaboration and communication skills. I understand management positions normally require a college degree. Although I do not have a degree yet, I will finish my bachelor's degree in business in December. Because my supervisor identified my leadership potential, I have been invited to participate in several leadership training opportunities. Despite my busy school and work schedules, I have taken advantage of every training opportunity. I want to learn as much as possible so that I can develop my skills and grow professionally. I hope to have the opportunity to use my skills to contribute to your company's success. Thank you for your consideration.

2 Focus on Structure

Purpose
I am writing **(in order) to express** my interest in the management position.
I want to learn as much as possible **so that** I can develop my skills.
Reason
I participated in leadership training **because** my supervisor recommended it.
I feel I am qualified for the position **because of** my background and education.
Contrast
Although I don't have a degree yet, I expect to graduate soon.
Despite my busy schedule, I have attended every training opportunity.

- *In order to* can be shortened to just the infinitive (*to* + verb).
- These words have the same meaning:
  - *because* and *since*   • *because of* and *due to*   • *although, even though,* and *though*
- *In order to, because, because of, due to, although, even though,* and *though* can go at the beginning or in the middle of the sentence. *So that* can only go in the middle of the sentence.

A **INVESTIGATE.** Analyze all the examples that express purpose, reason, or contrast. Match to complete.

_____ **1.** *even though / although / because / so that* + _____   **a.** phrase

_____ **2.** *despite / because of / due to* + _____   **b.** infinitive

_____ **3.** *in order* + _____   **c.** clause

64   Unit 4, Lesson 2

Grammar

B **COMPLETE. Read the first sentence. Check the sentence that has the same meaning.**

1. I didn't get a promotion although I was qualified for it.
   - ☐ I didn't get the promotion because I was qualified for it.
   - ☐ I was qualified for the promotion, but I didn't get it.

2. Due to her strong collaboration skills, Jessie was promoted to team leader.
   - ☐ She was promoted because she has good collaboration skills.
   - ☐ Despite her strong collaboration skills, she was promoted.

3. In order to be considered for a promotion, you need to submit a letter and an application
   - ☐ You need to submit an application so that you will be considered for a promotion.
   - ☐ You will be considered for a promotion even though you submitted an application.

4. Harold was not promoted to manager because of his poor communication skills.
   - ☐ Even though he has poor communication skills, Harold was not promoted.
   - ☐ Since he has poor communication skills, Harold was not promoted.

C **WRITE. Combine the sentences.**

1. Alex works hard. He is not a good team player.

   (although) Although Alex works hard, he is not a good team player.

2. Amy encourages her co-workers. She is well-liked at the company.

   (because) _____

3. I need to update my résumé. I want to apply for the management position.

   (in order to) _____

4. Tom has a negative attitude. He doesn't work well with others.

   (because of) _____

5. Kelly is taking some classes. She wants to improve her writing skills.

   (so that) _____

Apply what you know

1. **SHARE.** Use an *expression of purpose* to share an improvement you have made.
   Use an *expression of reason* to describe your expected outcome.
   Use an *expression of contrast* to share a possible unexpected outcome.

Purpose	• *I took nursing classes in order to get a job at the hospital.*
Reason	• *Because I kept trying, I finally found a great job at a clinic.*
Contrast	• *Even though I was certified, I couldn't find a job.*

2. **WRITE.** Write a paragraph about the improvement you described above.

I can express purpose, reason, or contrast. ☐   I need more practice. ☐

For more practice, go to MyEnglishLab.

Unit 4, Lesson 2   **65**

Lesson 3

Workplace, Life, & Community Skills
Use training resources to identify growth opportunities

1 Find Ways to Improve Skills

A **BRAINSTORM.** How can you gain experience before getting a job? What are some ways to improve your current skills or get more training? Support your suggestions with evidence from your life.

B **PROBLEM-SOLVE.** When you don't know how to solve a problem or do a particular task, where do you go to find help? What suggestions do you have for helping others gain knowledge in their careers?

2 Consult Resources

Online Training Opportunities

There are training courses in almost every field to help you gain knowledge and skills. Face-to-face courses are helpful for learners who like to interact directly with the teacher, while online courses are more convenient because you can do them on your own schedule. There are many different types of training: one course for a specific job or a series of courses that focus on a particular area. Gaining specific training in your field can help you become more desirable to current and future employers.

A **SCAN.** A young woman is working as a salesclerk at a large store. She wants to gain skills to get promoted, so she looked at an online course catalog. Use the course catalog to answer the questions.

1. What are the three different levels of training? _____

2. How many different courses are available? _____

3. How are the courses organized? _____

Train4Advancement.org

Retail Curriculum
"We have over **150** courses with **3** levels of training related to retail selling and buying. This curriculum is organized into **4** areas of specialty or tracks. All our educators are specialists in their area and will provide you with the skills and competencies needed for advancement. Certificates of course completion are provided for each course.

4 Retail Tracks
Customer Service - Sales Track
Purchasing & Merchandising – Buyer Track
Overall Process (including Technology & Safety) – Operations Track
Leadership & Advancement – Management Track

3 Different Levels of Training
Entry | Intermediate | Advanced

Courses Offered

Intro to Retail
Level: Entry   Track: Sales   Prerequisite: none
After learning general information about retail history, students will learn about retail job responsibilities and career opportunities.
Register NOW

Inventory Basics
Level: Entry   Track: Buyer   Prerequisite: None
Students will learn the basic steps for keeping track of inventory using multiple forms of technology. They will learn the latest methods for organization, labeling, counting, and keeping track of products. Register NOW

---

66 Unit 4, Lesson 3

Workplace, Life, & Community Skills

Ladder Safety
Level: Entry   **Track:** Operations   **Prerequisite:** None
Students will learn how to safely use stepladders. Techniques learned will help students create a safe work environment. They will learn about the care of ladders and how to select the appropriate ladder for the job. Register NOW

Suggestive Selling
Level: Intermediate   **Track:** Sales   **Prerequisite:** Customer Relations
Students will learn how to sell suggestively in a friendly manner. Techniques learned will assist students in providing great customer service as well as increase store sales. Register NOW

Web and Mobile Sales, Part I
Level: Intermediate   **Track:** Operations   **Prerequisite:** Expanding Markets
Students will learn effective methods for selling on digital devices. This course will help students create digital content. It will show how to analyze customers' digital usage. Upon completion of this course, students may enroll in Web and Mobile Sales, Part II. Register NOW

B DEFINE KEY WORDS. Find these words in the online course catalog. Match each word to its definition.

_____ **1.** (n) advancement

_____ **2.** (n) curriculum

_____ **3.** (n) certificate

_____ **4.** (n) competencies

_____ **5.** (n) prerequisite

a. a course that needs to be completed beforehand

b. document showing a person has completed a course

c. required knowledge and abilities to do a task

d. complete list of courses

e. increase of level or status

C INTERPRET. Locate information in the online course catalog.

1. What is the prerequisite for the Suggestive Selling course? _____

2. What is the prerequisite for Web and Mobile Sales, Part II? _____

3. If your track is Operations, which two courses listed would you mostly likely take? _____

D INFER. Why might a person in retail sales need to know about ladder safety? Why would a company be glad to see that an employee has taken a safety course?

E GO ONLINE. Use the Search Terms to find two online training sites that offer courses that interest you. Share the sites with a partner. How are the sites similar? How are they different?

Search Terms: *online   training* _____ (For the third search term, choose an occupation or training that interests you.)

Apply what you know

1. APPLY. Choose one of the online training sites. It will give you an idea of the type of training available for your specific field. Choose two courses that sound interesting.

2. SHARE. Explain your choices to a partner. Explain why you would like to take those courses.
- *According to the online course catalog, _____. So, I would like to take _____.*
- *One course is _____, but / and I would(n't) take it because _____.*

I can use training resources to identify growth opportunities. ■   I need more practice. ■

For more practice, go to MyEnglishLab.

Unit 4, Lesson 3   **67**

Lesson 4 Reading
Identify solutions to workplace dilemmas

1 Before You Read

A **REFLECT.** Think of a time you faced a dilemma at work. What was the dilemma? How did you try to solve it?

B **PREVIEW VOCABULARY.**

1. **TOPIC-RELATED WORDS.** These terms are used in the article. Does anyone know what they mean? Use roots and affixes to help you. You can also look for clues in the article.

| responsibilities | overwhelmed | confronting | feedback |

2. **ACADEMIC WORDS.** Discuss the meaning of the **bolded** words in the article. Use context to help you. After reading the article, add any words you learned to your Word Study Log.

C **PREDICT.** Preview the website. What is the purpose of the site? What information do you expect?

2 Read for Gist

A **READ.** What two workplace dilemmas are discussed?

What to Do at Work
Real-life workplace questions and answers

Dear Wanda,

1   One of my co-workers recently left his job. My manager is not planning to fill his role. I've taken on many of his former responsibilities. I am struggling to keep up with my work. I have worked late into the night many times these past few weeks. I want to talk to my manager. I want to tell her that I am overwhelmed, but I don't want her to think I'm complaining. What should I do?

5   Daniel

Dear Daniel,

My first suggestion for you is don't beat yourself up! It's common for workers to struggle with this problem, and you're not complaining. Your concerns are **valid**. It sounds like you have too much on your plate, and that's OK. However, you need to let your manager know what's going on immediately. She won't know how busy you are until you tell her! Find
10 time on her calendar as soon you can.

When you go to the meeting, make sure to follow one of my **fundamental** rules for the workplace. Don't come to your manager with a dilemma if you haven't identified a possible solution. Could your manager give some of your old colleague's responsibilities to your other teammates? Could she help you prioritize your projects?

A few tips for the meeting:

15 • Be relaxed, confident, and professional. Your manager won't think you're complaining if you come to the meeting with a positive attitude.

• Bring a list of your responsibilities so that you can go over it together.

• Follow up on anything you decide in the meeting as quickly as possible. This will show your manager you are eager to find a solution that works.

20 In the future, when you are overwhelmed, speak up as early as possible. Your manager is not a mind reader and may not notice you are too busy or working late unless you tell her.

68   Unit 4, Lesson 4

Reading

Dear Wanda,

One of my co-workers is always late, and it's driving me crazy! He gets to work 20 minutes later than the rest of us every morning. He takes longer lunches than the rest of us, too. He's also often late to meetings. I don't know him very well, so
25 I don't feel comfortable <u>confronting</u> him. What should I do?

Tina

Dear Tina,

This is a very common issue in the workplace. Everyone manages time differently, and some people simply don't manage their time well. It doesn't make them bad people. However, it does mean they need <u>feedback</u> or their **conduct**
30 so they can improve. Talk to your manager about your co-worker. See what your manager says. Be sure to respect the office **hierarchy**. It's always best to involve your manager at the start. That way your manager can handle the situation, and you don't have to get involved.

Now about the meetings—if your co-worker is late, start without him. He'll feel awkward coming into a meeting that is already in progress. If his presence is crucial to the meeting, and he is more than ten minutes late, cancel the meeting.
35 When he shows up to an empty room and realizes everyone left because of his tardiness, maybe he'll take the hint.

B IDENTIFY MAIN IDEAS. Choose the main idea of the article. Find the two sentences that support the main idea. Write the line numbers. _____

a. When you have a dilemma at work, notify your manager as quickly as possible.
b. When you have a problem with a co-worker, confront him or her immediately.
c. Experiencing problems with a co-worker is very common, so don't feel like it's your fault.

3 Close Reading

A RECOGNIZE STRUCTURE. Create a chart like the one shown to describe both dilemmas and Wanda's suggestions.

Person and Dilemma	Wanda's Suggestions

B LOCATE DETAILS. Are the statements true or false? Write the line numbers of your evidence.

	T/F	Lines
1. Daniel feels overwhelmed because he has taken on a former co-worker's responsibilities.	___	___
2. Wanda tells Daniel to set up a meeting with his manager after finishing his projects.	___	___
3. Tina is frustrated because her co-worker never invites her to meetings.	___	___
4. Wanda tells Tina that it is normal to have co-workers who don't manage time well.	___	___

C EVALUATE. What do you think of Wanda's advice? What additional advice would you give?

Apply what you know

1. **APPLY.** Record the details of the workplace dilemma you described in Exercise 1A.
2. **SHARE.** Share your experience.
   • *One time at work, I had a dilemma. I _____. I tried to solve the dilemma by _____.*

I can identify solutions to workplace dilemmas. ☐   I need more practice. ☐

For more practice, go to MyEnglishLab.   For audio and video, scan the QR code.

Unit 4, Lesson 4   69

Lesson 5

Listening and Speaking
Evaluate conversations for effective conflict resolution

1 Before You Listen

A REFLECT. What types of conflicts have you encountered with a specific co-worker? How did you try to resolve the conflict?

B PREVIEW VOCABULARY.

1. **TOPIC-RELATED WORDS.** These terms are used in the listening. Does anyone know what they mean? Use roots and affixes to help you.

| distracting | productive | personal calls |
| inconsiderate | defensive | |

2. **ACADEMIC WORDS.** These sentences are from the listening. Discuss the meaning of each **bolded** word. Use context to help you.
   1. I had to attend an **orientation** for new employees.
   2. I really appreciate your **cooperation**!
   3. According to our company **policy**, we each get only 30 minutes for lunch.
   4. Why don't we come up with a **consistent** break **schedule**, and then we can all stick to it?

C PREDICT. Use the lesson title, vocabulary, and image to make predictions about the listening. Who will participate in the conversation? What will the purpose of the conversation be?

2 Listen

A ▶ LISTEN FOR MAIN IDEAS. Listen to the conversations. What is the conflict about in each conversation? Compare your answers with a partner.

Conversation 1 _____

Conversation 2 _____

Conversation 3 _____

Conversation 4 _____

B ▶ LISTEN FOR DETAILS. Listen again. In each conversation, how do the speakers agree to resolve the situation? Check all that apply.

	Use headphones	Eat in the break room	Take personal calls outside	Follow a schedule
Conversation 1				
Conversation 2				
Conversation 3				
Conversation 4				

Listening and Speaking

3 Apply Academic Listening Skill

A ▶ **USE INFOGRAPHICS AS SUPPORT.** Speakers often give evidence to support their message by providing statistics or by referring to other sources. Speakers also often use visuals to support their message. Listen to the four conversations again. Which symbols could a speaker giving a talk on resolving conflict use to support his or her message? List the appropriate symbol numbers for each conversation.

Conversation 1 _____   Conversation 3 _____

Conversation 2 _____   Conversation 4 _____

B **EXPAND VOCABULARY.** Add words to your Word Study Log to show structure and meaning.

4 Real-World Application

A **REFLECT.** Write about a workplace conflict you are having or have had with another co-worker.

B **ROLE-PLAY.** Share the conflict with a partner. Then role-play resolving the conflict.

I can evaluate conversations for effective conflict resolution. ☐   I need more practice. ☐

For more practice, go to MyEnglishLab.   For audio and video, scan the QR code.

Lesson 6

Grammar
Make polite requests with *Would you mind*

1 Focus on Usage

A **CONSIDER.** Read the highlighted sentences in the text message below. How do the writers make polite requests?

B **IDENTIFY.** Read the entire text message. Underline all the polite requests. Circle all the responses.

> *Would you mind if I…?* means the person speaking wants to do something.
> *Would you mind* + verb + *-ing…?* means the person speaking wants you to do something.

A: Would you mind if I left early tomorrow?

B: No, not at all.

A: Great! I was supposed to close the office. Would you mind closing for me?

B: That's not going to work. I can't work late tomorrow because I have class. I've already covered for you twice this month. Would you mind not asking me to cover your shift every week?

A: I'm really sorry. I have a meeting at my son's school tomorrow. I don't know what to do.

B: Why don't you ask Jim? He wants to work more hours this week. He can probably cover your shift.

A: I don't know him very well. Would you mind asking him for me?

B: No, that's fine. I'll text him right now. I'll make it a group text and include you.

A: Thanks! I really appreciate your help.

2 Focus on Structure

Polite Requests	Typical Responses
*Would you mind **if I left** early?*	*No, not at all. / No, that would be fine. / No problem.*
*Would you mind **if we changed** the schedule?*	
*Would you mind **if I didn't attend** the meeting today?*	
*Would you mind **closing** the office?*	*Sure. / OK.*
*Would you mind **not eating** at your desk?*	

- *Would you mind* means, "Would it bother you?"
- If the listener agrees to a request that starts with *Would you mind,* the response is often negative. That negative response means, "No, it wouldn't bother me."
- In informal situations, the listener can also express agreement by simply saying, "Sure" or "OK."
- In informal English, sometimes the simple present instead of the simple past is used in *Would you mind if…?*. Sometimes the expression is even shortened to *Mind if…?*
  - **Formal:** *Would you mind if I <u>sat</u> here?*
  - **Informal:** *Would you mind if I <u>sit</u> here? / Mind if I <u>sit</u> here?*

72 Unit 4, Lesson 6

Grammar

A **INVESTIGATE.** Analyze all the examples of polite requests and responses. Choose the correct answers.

1. The subject of *Would you mind* + verb + *-ing* is _____.
   a. *I* or *we*   b. *you*   c. *he* or *she*

2. The subject of *Would you mind if* is usually _____.
   a. *I* or *we*   b. *you*   c. *he* or *she*

3. For negative requests, use *Would you mind if I* _____ + verb.
   a. *doesn't*   b. *didn't*   c. *not*

4. For negative requests when the subject is *you*, use _____ + verb + *-ing*.
   a. *don't*   b. *didn't*   c. *not*

B **COMPLETE.** Complete the sentences with *if I* + the past tense or the *-ing* form of the verb.

1. (*throw*) The refrigerator in the staff room is full of old food and starting to smell bad. Would you mind
   _____ out any food that you don't want anymore?

2. (*borrow*) I can't find my stapler. Would you mind _____ yours?

3. (*remove*) I've gotten a dozen emails about the sales meeting, but I don't work in sales. Would you mind
   _____ my name from the email list?

4. (*give*) I'm applying for a new job, and they've asked me for three references. Would you mind
   _____ them your name and phone number as a reference?

5. (*not work*) I need to go to my niece's graduation next Saturday, and I'm moving to a new apartment on
   Sunday. Would you mind _____ next weekend?

C **WRITE.** Read the situations. Write a polite request using *Would you mind.*

1. Your office mate borrowed your pen without asking. You want her to return it.
   Would you mind returning my pen?

2. The office is very warm. You want to adjust the thermostat.
   _____

3. You don't know how to use the copy machine. You want a co-worker to help you.
   _____

4. You need to make a personal call from your office. You share the office with five people.
   _____

Apply what you know

1. **SHARE.** Create a chart to describe typical problems caused by other people. Then state the solutions as requests. Share your chart with a partner.

What does the person do?	Polite request

2. **WRITE.** Write a brief letter to one of the people to express your concern. Express your request politely using *would you mind.*

   Dear Robin, I noticed you often use my coffee mug in the morning. That mug was a special gift from my niece. Would you mind using a different mug?

I can make polite requests with *Would you mind.* ☐   I need more practice. ☐

For more practice, go to MyEnglishLab.

Unit 4, Lesson 6   73

Lesson 7 Reading

Describe how to protect workers' rights

1 Before You Read

A DISCUSS. What rights do workers have? Have you ever felt unfairly treated at work, or that your workplace was unsafe? Explain.

B PREVIEW VOCABULARY.

1. **TOPIC-RELATED WORDS.** These terms are used in the article. Does anyone know what they mean? Use roots and affixes to help you. You can also look for clues in the article.

| minimum wage | complaint | whistleblower | retaliation | chain of command |

2. **ACADEMIC WORDS.** Discuss the meaning of the **bolded** words in the article. Use context to help you. After reading the article, add any words you learned to your Word Study Log.

C PREDICT. Preview the website, time line, and bar graph. What is the purpose of the article? What information do you expect?

2 Read for Gist

A READ. Think about the main ideas as you read. Underline any sentences that help you identify main ideas.

Worker Advocate
Know your rights!

Home | About Us | Services | Resources | Contact | SEARCH

Protecting Workers' Rights

1 The fight for fair wages and treatment for workers has been part of U.S. history from the country's beginning. The wealth of this country was first built upon the inhumane practice of slave labor. It was further built through the mistreatment of workers over the next 100 years. Lucky for us, these workers' sacrifices created the laws that now protect us. However, even with these laws, workers still face unfair practices. It is important for all
5 workers to know their rights and what to do if those rights are **violated**.

   Workers across the U.S. are **guaranteed** basic workers' rights. These include a <u>minimum wage</u>, a safe workplace, and protection from **discrimination**. The Fair
10 Labor Standards Act requires a federal minimum wage and time-and-a-half pay for overtime. The Occupational Safety and Health Act protects workers from dangers in the workplace. The Civil Rights Act makes it illegal to discriminate on the basis of race, religion, sex, or
15 ethnicity. The Age Discrimination and Employment Act protects workers over 40. The Americans with Disabilities Act protects workers with disabilities. Finally, the Fair Pay Act provides protection against wage discrimination.

Important Legislative Acts Protecting Workers' Rights

1938	Fair Labor Standards Act
1964	Civil Rights Act
1967	Age Discrimination and Employment Act
1970	Occupational Safety and Health Act
1989	Whistleblower Protection Act
1990	Americans with Disabilities Act
2009	Fair Pay Act

74   Unit 4, Lesson 7

Reading

These Acts protect workers' rights, but they do not guarantee that employers will follow them. Workers also
20 have the right to **file** a <u>complaint</u> when their rights are violated. The <u>Whistleblower</u> Protection Act (WPA) guarantees workers this right. A whistleblower is a worker who reports an employer's illegal activity. WPA protects whistleblowers from <u>retaliation</u>. It is illegal for an employer to take any action against the whistleblower.

Workers need to know what to do if their rights are violated. It is important to file a complaint within the company first. It is also important to follow the <u>chain of command</u>. Report complaints about safety or
25 co-workers to lower management. If the complaint is not handled well, take the complaint to the human resources department or higher management. For complaints about higher management, file the complaint directly with human resources.

Sometimes, the employer ignores the complaint or retaliates against the whistleblower. In this case, the worker can file a complaint with the appropriate government agency. **Contact** the U.S. Department of Labor to
30 determine which agency would handle your complaint. Your complaint should include a detailed account of the situation. It should also include the steps you took to solve it and the company's responses. The government agency will then help you through the complaint process. You can also contact a
35 "whistleblower attorney" to help you with your complaint.

Not all companies mistreat their employees, and workers' safety has improved over time. However, history has shown how greed can lead to the inhuman
40 treatment of others. We all have an obligation to protect the safety and well-being of ourselves and others. Know that the law is on your side to help improve the workplace for you, your co-workers, and all workers to come.

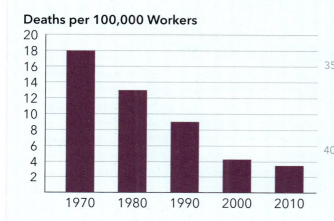

Deaths per 100,000 Workers

B **IDENTIFY MAIN IDEAS.** Choose the main idea of the article and of Paragraphs 2–4. Find the sentences that best support each main idea. Write the line numbers.

Article Main Idea	Lines
a. Important rights for workers in the United States b. What to do if your workers' rights are violated c. Important workers' rights and how to protect them	
Paragraph Main Ideas	

2   a. Workers are guaranteed basic workers' rights.
    b. The Fair Labor Standards Act provides a federal minimum wage.
    c. The Civil Rights Act protects workers from discrimination.	

3   a. A whistleblower is a worker who reports the illegal activity of an employer.
    b. The Whistleblower Act was created in 1989.
    c. Workers can file complaints if their rights are violated.	

4   a. Report complaints about co-workers to lower management.
    b. Follow the chain of command to file a complaint.
    c. File complaints directly with human resources for complaints about higher management.	

Unit 4, Lesson 7   **75**

3 Close Reading

A **LOCATE DETAILS.** Are the statements true or false? Write the line numbers of your evidence.

	T/F	Lines

1. The Civil Rights Act makes it illegal to discriminate on the basis of age. _____ _____

2. The Whistleblower Protection Act protects a worker's right to report an employer's illegal activity. _____ _____

3. Report complaints about safety issues and co-workers to higher management first. _____ _____

4. Contact the U.S. Department of Labor to find out which agency to file your complaint with. _____ _____

B **APPLY ACADEMIC READING SKILL.**

Academic Reading Skill: Recognize how infographics provide evidence to support a text
The word **infographic** combines the words *information* and *graphics*. It refers to any information presented in a graphic, or visual way such as in a graph, table, symbol, or time line. An infographic provides evidence to support a text by showing the information in a simpler way. For example, the time line in the article "Protecting Workers' Rights" allows you to easily see the chronological order of all the laws.

An infographic can also add new information to the text. For example, the bar graph shows the decrease in worker deaths since the passage of the Occupational Safety and Health Act in 1970. In this way, it supports the text's claim that laws help protect workers.

Answer the questions.

1. Which act was the first important legislation passed to protect workers' rights?

   _____

2. How many years are between the passage of the Fair Labor Standards Act and the Fair Pay Act? _____

3. How many worker deaths were there in 1970?
   a. a total of 18 deaths
   b. about 18 deaths for every 100,000 workers
   c. about 13 deaths for every 100,000 workers

4. Approximately how many more worker deaths were there in 1970 than in 2010?
   a. approximately 14 more deaths
   b. approximately 15 more deaths for every 100,000 workers
   c. approximately 14 more deaths for every 100,000 workers

C **CONCLUDE.** Answer the questions based on the infographics.

1. What conclusion can you draw from the time line?
   a. It took workers 50 years to get sufficient laws to protect their rights.
   b. Employers continued to mistreat different groups of workers even after the passage of the Civil Rights Act.
   c. The Civil Rights Act protected all workers from discrimination.

2. What conclusion can you draw from the graph?
   a. The number of worker deaths stayed the same after the passage of OSHA.
   b. The number of worker deaths increased after the passage of OSHA.
   c. The number of worker deaths decreased after the passage of OSHA.

76 Unit 4, Lesson 7

4 Prepare for an Academic Conversation

A **GO ONLINE.** Read the information about *Top Level Domains.* Then try it out in **YOUR TURN**.

| ✓ Search | ✓ Choose Sources | ✓ Evaluate Sources |

Top Level Domains

When you go online, you want to make sure that you can trust the information you find. Is it true? Is it accurate? How can you be sure? Although there are many steps to evaluating an internet source, a good place to start is by checking its **Top Level Domain**, or TLD.

A TLD refers to the letters after the final period of an internet address. There are hundreds of TLDs out there, but knowing the purpose of the most common TLDs can help you find trustworthy sources.
- **.com:** Commercial sites—The content is trying to promote the sales of a particular company.
- **.edu:** Educational sites—The content is carefully examined by educators and teachers at that particular school or organization.
- **.gov:** Government sites—The information is usually well researched and considered accurate. It provides public information to support all citizens.
- **.org:** Nonprofit organization sites—Information can be well researched but may promote a specific view.
- **.net:** Any kind of site—Content varies from site to site.

Depending on their purpose, the most trustworthy TLDs tend to be *.edu* and *.gov.* However, an *.org* site can have excellent information, as long as you recognize the organization's point of view. Similarly, a *.com* site can contain trustworthy information, if you remember the commercial reason the company is providing the information.

YOUR TURN...

1. Enter *workers' rights* into a search engine. List the different TLDs you see on the first results page.
   _____

2. Open one result with a *.gov* TLD. What is the internet address? What is the title?
   URL: _____
   Title: _____

B **CHOOSE A SOURCE.** Find a trustworthy source that describes one or more workers' rights. Use the information on TLDs to help you evaluate the source.

Apply what you know | **Academic Conversation**

1. **ASK FOR CLARIFICATION.** When listeners make comments or ask questions about what you say, remember to take the time to try to understand their meaning.
   - *I'm not sure I understood what you meant when you said _____.*
   - *Could you help me understand what you mean by _____?*

2. **REPORT.** Share the source you found. Identify the TLD it contains and why you think it is trustworthy. Describe one of the workers' rights described in the source.

I can describe how to protect workers' rights. ☐   I need more practice. ☐

For more practice, go to MyEnglishLab.   For audio and video, scan the QR code.

Unit 4, Lesson 7   77

Lesson 8

Writing Workshop

Match tone to audience and purpose

1 What Do You Notice?

A COMPARE. Read the two examples. How are they the same? How are they different?

Example 1:

So I was lifting a large box n I hurt my back. Unlucky! Those boxes of paper r heavy. You'd think a co-worker would have helped a guy out. Now I'll need smthing 4 the pain because my back hurts really bad. No more boxes of paper 4 me. Other ppl can do it. Anyway, that's all.

Example 2:

On 10/13 at 11:15 a.m., I hurt my back when I attempted to move a box of paper from the supply room to the copy machine in the second floor accounting office. I immediately reported my injury to my supervisor, Lela Martin.

B ANALYZE. Which example is clearer and more professional? Underline the words or phrases in the other example that are not appropriate for workplace writing.

2 Apply Academic Writing Skill

Academic Writing Skill: Match tone to audience and purpose

The way you communicate with friends and family is different from the way you communicate with co-workers or classmates. You use a different **tone**. Your tone should reflect your relationship with your audience. Ask yourself, "What is the purpose of what I am writing? Who am I writing for?" Then match your tone.

Always use a formal tone in a workplace setting.

- **Purpose:** to report something that happened at work
- **Audience:** supervisor, human resources, other employees
- **Tone:** formal, objective, professional

A IDENTIFY. Is the tone of each sentence formal or informal? Who is the audience?

	Tone		Audience	
	Formal	**Informal**	**Co-worker**	**Manager**
1. How's it going? I wanna come to work but can't. Sorry!				
2. I would like to request a meeting regarding my current position.				
3. This company is awesome!! I'm learning tons of new things!!				

B APPLY. Rewrite each sentence using a workplace tone.

1. Your excuse for missing work yesterday is dumb.

   _____

2. Our staff has gotta get this project done or else!

   _____

I can match tone to audience and purpose. ☐   I need more practice. ☐

For more practice, go to MyEnglishLab.

78 Unit 4, Lesson 8

Writing

Lesson 9

Write a workplace incident report

1 Model for Writing

STUDY THE MODEL. Read the Writing Model for an incident report on page 251. Analyze that model. Underline the action that led to the employee's injury. Double underline the solution offered by the supervisor to prevent future incidents.

2 Prepare Your Writing

A **FOCUS.** You will write a workplace incident report as an employee. Later, you will take the role of the supervisor and give a recommendation to prevent future incidents.

B **RESEARCH.** Go online and choose a common workplace injury to use for your incident report. Use the search term: *most common workplace injuries*. Record how the injury usually occurs and ways to prevent it.

3 Write Write an incident report about a common workplace injury.

A **ORGANIZE.** Use the blank Writing-Model Template for an incident report on page 252. Complete the Employee Report section. Follow these tips to write in an objective tone.

Objective Writing

Objective writing includes statements of fact and not personal feelings or opinions. In the workplace, when you write incident reports, evaluations, or observations, be as clear and as truthful as possible.

- Use statements of fact, not feelings or opinions.
- Be as specific as you can by including details.
- Use actual names rather than personal pronouns.
- Use a serious, professional tone.

Writing Checklist		
	The text includes...	
Structure:	✓ Workplace incident report	
Organization:	✓ Employee's report	
	✓ Supervisor's recommendation	
Word Choice:	✓ Academic words	
	✓ Objective language	
Writing Skill:	✓ Tone to match audience and purpose	
Grammar:	✓ Language to express purpose and reason	

B **REVISE.** Use the Writing Checklist to evaluate your writing and make revisions. Remember to match your tone to your audience and purpose.

4 Share Your Writing

A **COLLABORATE.** Trade your completed Employee Report with a partner's Employee Report.

B **SOLVE THE PROBLEM.** Think of a solution to prevent a future incident like your partner's. Complete the Supervisor Recommendation section on your partner's incident report.

I can write a workplace incident report. ■	I need more practice. ■

For more practice, go to MyEnglishLab.

Unit 4, Lesson 9 **79**

Lesson 10: Workplace Soft Skills

Negotiate to resolve conflict

1 Workplace Expectations

A CONSIDER. Read the email from a manager to a jobsite supervisor. What was the original issue? Why did the employee file a complaint with OSHA? What does the manager have the supervisor do?

Subject: OSHA complaint

Manny,
I recently heard from our regional OSHA office regarding a complaint filed against us. I was very upset to hear this. You should know that we are required to provide personal protective equipment for our employees. When an employee talks to you about the need for hearing protection, you should not tell him or her that the noise "isn't too bad" and that they are "endangering the company's bottom line."

You need to learn to negotiate to resolve conflict, so it doesn't escalate to OSHA. Please order hearing protection for all employees and make a formal apology ASAP.
Carlos

B IDENTIFY EXPECTATIONS. Describe the manager's expectation and what the jobsite supervisor actually did. Why was the manager upset? What was the result?

1. Manager's expectation: _____
2. Jobsite supervisor's action: _____
3. Result: _____

2 Learn from Mistakes

A REFLECT. What did the supervisor originally say to the employee who complained about the noise level? What **should** the supervisor have said? Suggest specific actions he could have taken. Share your suggestions with a partner.

B ROLE-PLAY. Give the supervisor a "do over" with the employee at the jobsite. Role-play the conversation, but this time have the supervisor respond favorably to the employee's complaint.

C ▶ COMPARE. Listen to the "do-over" conversation. How is it similar to your role play? How is it different?

Apply what you know

1. **DEFINE.** How would you explain this soft skill to a new employee?
2. **APPLY.** Record an example from your own life in your Soft Skills Log (page 241) of how you have negotiated to resolve conflict.
3. **SHARE.** Share your example.
    - *I negotiated to resolve conflict at _____ when I _____.*

I can negotiate to resolve conflict. ☐   I need more practice. ☐

For audio and video, scan the QR code.   For more practice, go to MyEnglishLab.

Affordable Housing 5

PREVIEW

What type of event is happening in this photo? Why is that type of event beneficial? What do the people in the photo hope to accomplish?

UNIT GOALS

Describe the homeless problem in the U.S.

Use resources to explore housing options

Explain the causes and results of the housing crash

Describe the requirements for getting a home loan

Give a presentation on affordable housing

Write a problem-solution essay

Workplace Soft Skill: Demonstrate responsibility

Academic Skills:

- **Listening:** Identify problem-and-solution relationships
- **Speaking:** Present evidence to support points
- **Reading:** Evaluate the problem and solution presented in an argument
- **Writing:** Write an effective conclusion

Lesson 1 Listening and Speaking
Describe the homeless problem in the U.S.

1 Before You Listen

A **DISCUSS.** Is homelessness a major problem in your town or city? Give evidence to support your belief.

B **PREVIEW VOCABULARY.**

1. **TOPIC-RELATED WORDS.** These terms are used in the listening. Does anyone know what they mean? Use roots and affixes to help you.

nonprofit organization	shelter
affordable housing	evicted

2. **ACADEMIC WORDS.** These sentences are from the listening. Discuss the meaning of each **bolded** word. Use context to help you.
   1. What does homelessness look like in our community? It's actually not as **apparent** as you might expect.
   2. Many people don't realize just how large the homeless population is because the homeless are often not **visible**.
   3. Two concerns that are largely responsible for the rise in homelessness over the past two **decades** are **insufficient income** and lack of affordable housing.
   4. Government **subsidy** houses are built by the government and given to low-income families.

C **PREDICT.** Use the lesson title, vocabulary, and image to make predictions about the podcast. What will its purpose be? What information do you expect?

2 Listen

A ▶ **LISTEN FOR MAIN IDEAS.** Listen to the podcast. Who are the homeless, and where do they live?

_____

B ▶ **LISTEN FOR DETAILS.** Listen again and complete the statistics.

1. More than _____ people experience homelessness on a single night.
2. _____% are people with children.
3. Veterans make up another _____ %.
4. About _____% of the homeless population are chronically homeless.
5. In our city, _____% of the homeless were evicted from their residence because they couldn't pay rent or house payments.
6. Other challenges include domestic violence, substance abuse, and mental illness. This group makes up about _____% of the homeless population here in our city.

C **CONCLUDE.** What does the speaker mean when he says homeless people are trapped in a vicious cycle?

_____

82 Unit 5, Lesson 1

Listening and Speaking

3 Apply Academic Listening Skill

Academic Listening Skill: Identify problem-and-solution relationships
A common organization that is used in speech or in text is to focus on problems and solutions. There may be one problem with several solutions proposed, or there may be several problems, each with their own possible solutions. Speakers and writers often use problem-and-solution signal words to highlight the problems and solutions. Listening for these words will help you recognize problems and proposed solutions.

Problem-and-Solution Signal Words	
Problem	**Solution**

the, one, a...
     problem, issue, dilemma, question, challenge, concern
 	
 this leads to...
	the, one, a...
	     solution, answer, remedy, resolution, cure
	
	 to answer/solve the problem
	 to address the problem

A ▶ **IDENTIFY.** Listen to part of the podcast again. Which problem-and-solution signal words or phrases does the speaker use? Underline them in the chart above.

B ▶ **ANALYZE PROBLEMS AND SOLUTIONS.** Listen to that part of the podcast again.

1. Make a list of the problems the speaker mentions. For which problems does the speaker offer possible solutions? List the solutions.

2. Which problems does the speaker present without offering a solution?

C **INFER.** Why do you think the speaker chooses **not** to present a solution to some problems?

D **EXPAND VOCABULARY.** Add words to your Word Study Log to show structure and meaning.

4 Real-World Application

A **RESEARCH.** Research statistics on homelessness in your town or city.

B **COLLABORATE.** Work in small groups and compare your research.

Academic Speaking Skill: Present evidence to support points
When you present information, it's important to give your listeners evidence or proof that what you are saying is true. This support for your points can come in many forms. You can refer to the original research that provided the information. You can also give examples that make your points more believable. This evidence will help convince your listeners.

- *According to the text/author/researcher, _____.*
- *The website _____ stated that _____.*
- *An example of this is _____.*
- *_____ provides an illustration of _____.*

I can describe the homeless problem in the U.S. ☐	I need more practice. ☐

For more practice, go to MyEnglishLab.

For audio and video, scan the QR code.

Unit 5, Lesson 1   **83**

Lesson 2  Grammar

Use adjective clauses

1 Focus on Usage

A CONSIDER. Read the highlighted clauses in the home-warranty ad below. Which adjective clauses help describe a particular person or thing?

> An adjective clause modifies a noun. It comes immediately after the noun it modifies and usually begins with a relative pronoun—*that, which, who, whom* or *whose*. Sometimes, the relative pronoun can be omitted.

B IDENTIFY. Read the entire advertisement. Underline all adjective clauses. Circle what the clause describes.

For many people, home ownership is a dream come true, but it also comes with some headaches. A home repair can be a huge (problem) that breaks your budget. Do you have a leaky faucet you don't know how to fix? Are you frustrated with an appliance that isn't working properly? Are you having a hard time finding a repairperson whom you can trust?

The solution is simple. Let us do the work for you! We offer a yearly service contract that covers the cost of home repairs. If they can't be repaired, we'll replace any important household appliances that break down over time. We're the only home warranty company whose services are 100% guaranteed.

2 Focus on Structure

Adjective Clauses	
Object	**Subject**
We know a great <u>repairperson</u> **who / whom / that / Ø** we trust.	We should use a <u>repairperson</u> **who / that** has experience.
I like the <u>plumber</u> **who / whom / that / Ø** I've used before.	I need to find a <u>plumber</u> **who / that** can fix this shower.
I'm not happy with the home warranty <u>contract</u> **which / that** we have.	A home warranty is a <u>contract</u> **which / that** covers the cost of home repairs.

- When the relative pronoun is the **object** of the adjective clause, you can use *who* or *whom* for people. You can use *that* for people or things or omit the pronoun altogether (Ø).
- When the relative pronoun is the **subject** of the adjective clause, use *who* or *that* for people, but never use *whom*. Use *which* or *that* for things. Never omit the relative pronoun when it is the subject. Do not use *whom* and do not omit the relative pronoun.
- Use *whose* when the relative pronoun helps clarify ownership.
  *I'm looking for a home warranty company **whose** customer ratings are consistently high.*

A INVESTIGATE. Analyze all the examples of adjective clauses. Choose **all** the correct answers.

1. Use _____ for adjective clauses that refer to people.
   a. that   b. which   c. who   d. whom

2. Use _____ for adjective clauses that refer to things.
   a. that   b. which   c. who   d. whose

3. Use _____ for adjective clauses that show possession.
   a. that   b. who   c. whom   d. whose

84 Unit 5, Lesson 2

Grammar

B **COMPLETE. Choose all the correct relative pronouns. Ø stands for no pronoun.**

1. **A:** Hi. Sorry to call you at work, but the living room lights won't turn on.
   B: Could you go check the fuse box? It's that gray metal box _____ we have in the garage.
      a. that   **b.** which   **c.** who   **d.** whom   **e.** whose   **f.** Ø

2. **A:** Do you know where our rental agreement is?
   B: Yes. It's in the desk in the folder _____ is labeled "Lease."
      a. that   **b.** which   **c.** who   **d.** whom   **e.** whose   **f.** Ø

3. **A:** The key broke off in the lock. I'm not sure what to do.
   B: We need to call a locksmith. That's a person _____ makes and repairs locks.
      a. that   **b.** which   **c.** who   **d.** whom   **e.** whose   **f.** Ø

4. **A:** It's raining really hard, and now we have some water on the ceiling. We need someone to look at the roof.
   B: We have a neighbor _____ father is a roofer. Let's ask him for advice.
      a. that   **b.** which   **c.** who   **d.** whom   **e.** whose   **f.** Ø

5. **A:** Could you give me the name and number of the painter _____ you recommended?
   B: Sure! I'll text you her information right now. She does very good work.
      a. that   **b.** which   **c.** who   **d.** whom   **e.** whose   **f.** Ø

C **REWRITE. Combine the sentences. Make the second sentence an adjective clause. If possible, omit the relative pronoun.**

1. We have some wood damage. The damage might be from termites.
   We have some wood damage that might be from termites.

2. Termites are insects. They feed on wood.
   _____

3. We need to find a pest control company. They can get rid of termites.
   _____

4. The damage might be wood rot. Wood rot can be caused by water.
   _____

5. We should call the repair person. Our neighbor recommended him.
   _____

Apply what you know

1. **DISCUSS. Describe a problem that you have had in your home.**
   1. What was the problem?
   2. What did you do to fix it?

2. **WRITE. Write a paragraph about a household problem you dealt with. Use adjective clauses.**
   My refrigerator stopped working. First, I threw out all the food that had gone bad. Then I called someone who could fix it.

I can use adjective clauses. ■   I need more practice. ■

For more practice, go to MyEnglishLab.

Unit 5, Lesson 2   **85**

Lesson 3

Workplace, Life, & Community Skills
Use resources to explore housing options

1 Search for Housing

A **REFLECT.** When you were looking for a place to live, what features were important to you? Which features were unimportant?

B **PROBLEM-SOLVE.** What problems did you encounter when you were searching for a place to live? What suggestions do you have to help others search for housing?

2 Consult Resources

Housing-Search Filters

There are many choices when looking for a new place to live. It's important to decide which features—such as price, location, and number of bedrooms and bathrooms—are essential. You can then filter your housing search to find the right place. **Filters** let you narrow your search by removing unwanted choices. You can also **sort** your choices based on what is most important to you. A real estate agent can help you make these decisions.

A **SCAN.** A young man was transferred to a new city. He went online to find possible apartments.

1. What city was he transferred to? _____
2. How are the results sorted? _____
3. How many results did he find that matched his search? _____

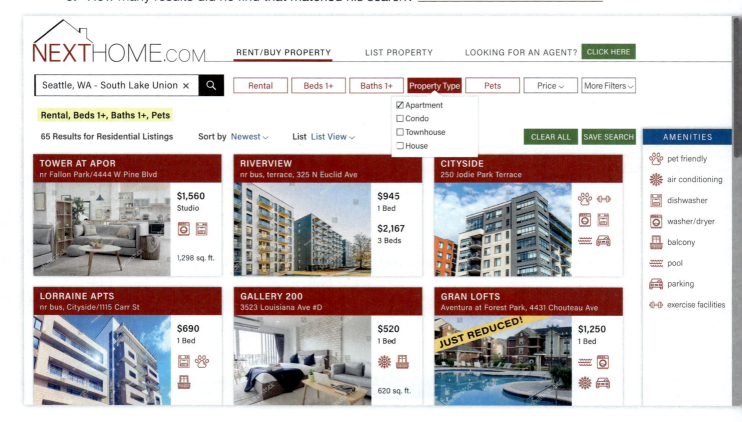

86 Unit 5, Lesson 3

Workplace, Life, & Community Skills

B **INTERPRET GRAPHICS.** Locate these symbols on the housing search. Match each symbol to its meaning.

_____ **1.** ❄

_____ **2.** ▥

_____ **3.** | Beds 1+ |

_____ **4.** | Price ⌄ |

_____ **5.** | ⌄ |

_____ **6.** | × | 🔍 |

    a. search box

    b. filter to choose number of bedrooms

    c. drop-down arrow

    d. air-conditioning

    e. filter to set range for cost

    f. balcony

C **DRAW CONCLUSIONS.** Discuss the answers to the questions.

1. Would you expect the result with no price to be expensive or inexpensive?

2. Do you think a three-bedroom version of the Cityside apartment would cost more than $1,000 per month, or less? Why?

3. "List view" is chosen in the search. What is another type of view? When would you use that other view?

D **RANK.** These six filters were used in the search. First, state your choice for each filter in the space following the question mark. Then rank the categories from most important (1) to least important (6) to show which specific features are most important to you.

_____ Location? _____

_____ Rent or Own? _____

_____ Number of bedrooms? _____

_____ Number of bathrooms? _____

_____ Apartment, Condo, Townhouse, or House? _____

_____ Price? _____

E **GO ONLINE.** Use the Search Terms to find two real estate websites. Which of the sites is easier to use? Explain to a partner why you like that site.

🔍 **Search Terms:** apartments rent _____ *(For the third search term, enter the name of a city or neighborhood.)*

Apply what you know

1. **APPLY.** Use the real estate site you liked to find homes. Use the filters you ranked in Exercise 2D to narrow your search. After filtering, don't forget to look at all the pages listed and sort using the category that is most important to you.

2. **SHARE.** Share your search results with a partner. How did using filters and sorting help you find appropriate choices?

   • *I used a filter for _____ because _____.*
   • *When I sorted the results according to _____, it was easier to see appropriate listings because _____.*

| I can use resources to explore housing options. ◼ | I need more practice. ◼ |

For more practice, go to MyEnglishLab.

Unit 5, Lesson 3   **87**

Lesson 4

Reading
Explain the causes and results of the housing crash

1 Before You Read

A **BRAINSTORM.** What do you know about the housing crash? What caused it? What were the consequences?

B **PREVIEW VOCABULARY.**

1. **TOPIC-RELATED WORDS.** These terms are used in the article. Does anyone know what they mean? Use roots and affixes to help you. You can also look for clues in the article.

| credit score | defaulted | foreclose | assets |

2. **ACADEMIC WORDS.** Discuss the meaning of the **bolded** words in the article. Use context to help you. After reading the article, add any words you learned to your Word Study Log.

C **PREDICT.** Preview the article title and image. What is the purpose of the article?

2 Read for Gist

A **READ.** What were the causes of the 2008 housing crash?

The Housing Crash:
The Causes and Aftermath

1 In the early 2000s, it was a great time to buy a house. There was a housing boom. Construction companies built hundreds of thousands of new houses across the United States. The value of houses skyrocketed. During that same **period**, mortgage
5 companies loosened their requirements. Many more people were able to get a mortgage. A lot of those people had low credit scores and unstable employment. The mortgages these people got were called "subprime." People who took out subprime mortgages often had low, affordable payments for the first few years.

The problem was that, as time went on, the monthly payments on these subprime mortgages increased greatly. At
10 that point, the **bulk** of people with subprime mortgages couldn't afford their payments. Many of them defaulted on their mortgages. When people defaulted on their mortgages, the banks had to foreclose on their houses.

As banks foreclosed on more and more houses, the value of houses across the country started to drop. There were more houses available than people who wanted to buy them. Many homeowners were shocked to discover they owed more on their mortgages than their houses were worth. Those people tried to sell their houses but couldn't. As millions
15 of people defaulted on their mortgages, banks began to lose vast amounts of money.

Subprime mortgages turned out to be a disaster for the economy of the entire country. Those mortgages triggered the biggest economic crisis since the Great Depression of the 1930s. Banks around the world had invested in assets backed by mortgages in the U.S. These banks lost billions of dollars. In 2008, the U.S. government **intervened** in the crisis. It loaned $700 billion to banks and other businesses. The government took over the country's two biggest
20 mortgage companies, Fannie Mae and Freddie Mac.

88   Unit 5, Lesson 4

Reading

As the economy struggled, unemployment soared. The construction, real estate, and banking industries were particularly hurt. In October 2007, the unemployment rate was only 4.7%. By October 2009, the unemployment rate was over 10%. Many unemployed people struggled to keep up with their mortgages. These individuals then defaulted on their loans, further worsening the housing crisis.

25 In addition to high unemployment, there were many other consequences of the economic crash. It is estimated that the global economy suffered $15 trillion in losses, and banks foreclosed on nearly 10 million houses. Many Americans became anxious about **buying** a home, so rental rates shot up, especially in the 35–44 age range. That is the age at which people typically buy their first home. In 2006, only 31% of people in that age range were renters. A decade later, over 41% of people in that age range were renters.

30 One of the biggest lessons of the economic crash was that big businesses like large banks and mortgage companies are **integral** to the economy. If these big companies face financial difficulties, they will drag the economy down with them. As a result, government sponsored mortgage companies, such as Fannie Mae and Freddie Mac now manage 90% of the country's mortgages. The U.S. government is hoping to prevent such a crisis from happening again. In 2010, Congress passed the Dodd-Frank Act. This law prohibited banks from issuing subprime mortgages. Yet, experts worry that another 35 crash could be on the horizon. To prevent that, we must keep a close eye on the companies that are too big to fail.

B **IDENTIFY MAIN IDEAS.** Choose the main idea of the article. Where is it stated? Lines _____

a. The housing crash was caused by construction companies that built too many houses.
b. Banks foreclosed on 10 million homes during the crash, which caused an economic crisis.
c. The housing crash, which caused a major crisis, was caused by banks giving subprime mortgages.

3 Close Reading

A **RECOGNIZE STRUCTURE.** In which paragraph is each cause first discussed?

Causes of the Housing Crash	Paragraph	Details
subprime mortgages		
banks foreclosed	2	
value of houses fell		
unemployment soared		

B **LOCATE DETAILS.** Add one detail that tells more about each cause of the housing crash.

C **SUMMARIZE.** Summarize the consequences of the housing crash as described in Paragraph 6.

Apply what you know

1. **APPLY.** Think back to your answers in Exercise 1A. What did you learn about the housing crash?

2. **SHARE.** Share your answers.
   - *The housing crash was caused by _____.*
   - *The consequences of the housing crash were _____.*

I can explain the causes and results of the housing crash. ☐   I need more practice. ☐

For more practice, go to MyEnglishLab.   For audio and video, scan the QF code.

Unit 5, Lesson 4   **89**

Lesson 5

Listening and Speaking
Describe the requirements for getting a home loan

1 Before You Listen

A REFLECT. How do you get a home loan? What are the requirements?

B PREVIEW VOCABULARY.

1. **TOPIC-RELATED WORDS.** These terms are used in the listening. Does anyone know what they mean? For compound words, think about the meaning of each word separately.

| net worth | gross income | assets vs. liabilities |

2. **ACADEMIC WORDS.** These sentences are from the listening. Discuss the meaning of each **bolded** word. Use context to help you.
   1. We want to make sure we can **secure** a loan before we make an offer on a house.
   2. We're worried our loan application will be **rejected**.
   3. The down payment is the amount of money that you pay as a lump **sum**.
   4. Your credit score is a number **ranging** from 300 to 850.
   5. A pre-approval is a written letter **confirming** the price of the home you can purchase.

C PREDICT. Use the lesson title, vocabulary, and image to make predictions about the listening. Who will participate in the conversation? What will the purpose of the conversation be?

2 Listen

A ▶ LISTEN FOR MAIN IDEAS. Listen to the conversation between a couple and a loan officer. Why are they meeting with a loan officer? Check all that apply.
- ☐ They are interested in applying for a home loan.
- ☐ They are checking on the status of a loan that they have already applied for.
- ☐ They want to find out how much they can spend on a home.
- ☐ They will start shopping for a new home soon.

B ▶ LISTEN FOR DETAILS. Listen again. Write 1 to 5 to put the steps in order.

	Get a pre-approval letter.
	Find out if you pre-qualify for a loan.
	Calculate your assets and liabilities to determine your net worth.
	Determine how much your down payment will be.
	Provide tax returns, pay stubs, and bank statements.

90 Unit 5, Lesson 5

Listening and Speaking

3 Apply Academic Listening Skill

A ▶ **EVALUATE PROBLEMS AND SOLUTIONS.** Listen to the conversation the couple had after they got back from talking to the loan officer. They would like to get a loan for 15 years at a fixed percentage rate. Look at the loan options and requirements.

1. Which option would they prefer to use? Why? _____
2. Why don't they qualify for that option? _____
3. What other choices for buying a home do they discuss? _____

	Option #1	Option #2	Option #3	Option #4
Term	15 years	15 years	20 years	30 years
Fixed Interest rate	3.5%	4%	4.25%	4.6%
Minimum down payment	20%	5%	20%	10%
Minimum credit score	720	680	660	680
Mortgage insurance	No	Yes	No	Yes

B **EXPAND VOCABULARY.** Add words to your Word Study Log to show structure and meaning.

4 Real-World Application

A **CONCLUDE.** Would you be eligible for a home loan? Why or why not? Determine which requirements you meet and draw a conclusion.

☐ Good credit score
☐ History of paying rent on time
☐ Steady employment
☐ Down payment amount
☐ Documents: tax returns, pay stubs, bank statements, references

B **ROLE-PLAY.** Role-play a loan application interview with a partner.

A: What type of loan are you interested in?
B: I want to apply for a home loan.
A: I can help you with that. Let's go over a few requirements.

I can describe the requirements for getting a home loan. ☐   I need more practice. ☐

For more practice, go to MyEnglishLab.   For audio and video, scan the QR code.

Unit 5, Lesson 5   91

Lesson 6 — Grammar
Reduce adjective clauses to adjective phrases

1 Focus on Usage

A CONSIDER. Read the highlighted sentences in the housing brochure below. Notice the adjective phrases. How have they been reduced from adjective clauses?

> Remember, a **clause** is a group of words that contains a subject and a verb. A **phrase** is a group of words that does not contain a subject and a verb. Some adjective clauses can be reduced to an adjective phrase. The adjective phrase will be missing the relative pronoun.

B IDENTIFY. Read the entire brochure. Underline all the adjective phrases.

Home-Now Apartments are for individuals and families living on limited incomes. To be eligible for our apartments, you must be within the income limit set for the size of your family. For specific requirements, please refer to the income limits listed in the property description for every apartment on our website. If your income is the same as or lower than the income limit shown for that apartment, then you are eligible to rent it. In addition to meeting the income requirements, you will need to provide references from your current landlord confirming you have paid your rent for at least three years. For more information about our eligibility requirements, contact us at the number provided on our website.

2 Focus on Structure

Adjective Clause	Adjective Phrase
Contact the number **that is provided** on our website.	Contact the number **provided** on our website.
Please give this information to anyone **who is looking** for affordable housing.	Please give this information to anyone **looking** for affordable housing.
Here is a list of apartments **which are still available**.	Here is a list of apartments **still available**.
You will need a pay stub **that confirms** your income.	You will need a pay stub **confirming** your income.
These apartments are for people **who live** on limited incomes.	These apartments are for people **living** on limited incomes.

- Only adjective clauses that have a subject pronoun (*who, that, which*) can be reduced to adjective phrases.
- When an adjective clause contains the verb *be* and a single adjective, the adjective can be moved to the normal position in front of the noun it modifies:
    - Here is a list of apartments which **are available**.
    - Here is a list of **available** apartments.

Grammar

A **INVESTIGATE.** Analyze all the examples of adjective phrases. Match to complete the rules.

_____ 1. When reducing an adjective clause to an adjective phrase, always _____.

_____ 2. If the adjective clause contains a form of the verb *be*, _____.

_____ 3. If the adjective clause does not contain the verb *be*, _____.

a. delete the relative pronoun and the verb *be,* but do not change anything else

b. delete the relative pronoun and change the verb to *-ing*

c. delete the relative pronoun

B **REWRITE.** Rewrite the sentences. Reduce the adjective clauses to adjective phrases.

1. This scholarship is for students who are entering their first year of college.
   This scholarship is for students entering their first year of college.

2. We provide health insurance to anyone who is employed here full-time.
   _____

3. Senior housing may be an option for those who are 62 and older.
   _____

4. Students who attend the university may live in a dormitory.
   _____

C **COMBINE.** Combine the sentences. Change the second sentence to an adjective phrase.

1. These apartments are for students. The students must be enrolled in at least 12 academic hours.
   These apartments are for students enrolled in at least 12 academic hours.

2. A discount is available for tenants. The tenants must renew their lease.
   _____

3. Employees are eligible for medical leave. Medical leave is known as sick leave benefits
   _____

4. School buses are provided for children. The children must live over a mile from school.
   _____

Apply what you know

1. **ANALYZE.** Describe the requirements students must meet by December 15.

   The business school offers scholarships for current students who meet certain eligibility requirements. The scholarships are for students who are currently enrolled in the university and have declared a business major. Qualified applicants must have a GPA of 3.5 or higher. These scholarships are only for students who do not receive other outside scholarships. Applications are due by December 15.

2. **WRITE.** Write a paragraph to describe the requirements. Use adjective clauses or phrases.
   The business school scholarships are for students currently attending the university...

I can reduce adjective clauses to adjective phrases. ■   I need more practice. ■

For more practice, go to MyEnglishLab.

Unit 5, Lesson 6   **93**

Lesson 7

Reading
Describe the problem of affordable housing and offer a solution

1 Before You Read

A **ESTIMATE.** What percentage of your income do you spend on housing? Do you think that is reasonable? Why or why not? Which groups of people struggle to pay for housing? Explain.

B **PREVIEW VOCABULARY.**

1. **TOPIC-RELATED WORDS.** These terms are used in the article. Does anyone know what they mean? For compound words, think about the meaning of each word separately. You can also look for clues in the article.

housing subsidies	extremely low-income	household

2. **ACADEMIC WORDS.** Discuss the meaning of the **bolded** words in the article. Use context to help you. After reading the article, add any words you learned to your Word Study Log.

C **PREDICT.** Look at the format of the article. What kind of article is it? What is its purpose? Preview the two infographics. What information do you expect?

2 Read for Gist

A **READ.** Think about the main ideas as you read. Underline any sentences that help you identify main ideas.

January 25, 2020   **Weekly Herald**   K3

Editorial
Affordable Housing for All

1 Food, water, and shelter are the three most basic needs of all human beings. Yet, every night in the U.S., just more than half a million people go without shelter. Renters across the country cannot afford the high rent
5 charged in many places. Renters at the lowest income levels face eviction and homelessness. How can we make sure that all Americans have an affordable home? Americans must all come together to support housing subsidies to provide **assistance** for renters in need.

10 Finding affordable housing is the most difficult for extremely low-income renters. These renters have household incomes of less than 30% of the national average. In 2019, that meant a yearly income of less than $19,000. To be affordable, housing costs should
15 not **exceed** 32% of household income. However, 71% of extremely low-income renters spend more than 50% of their income on housing. Because those renters spend such a large percentage on housing, they often have a very hard time meeting their other needs.

20 Why are extremely low-income renters paying so much for housing? Simply put, there are not enough affordable housing units. For every 100 of these households, there are only 35 units available. That means 65% of this group does not have affordable
25 housing. Many try to pay rents they cannot afford. Others become homeless.

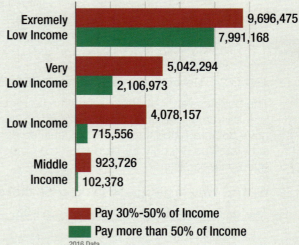

Number of Households Paying More Than 30% of Income on Housing

- Exremely Low Income: 9,696,475 / 7,991,168
- Very Low Income: 5,042,294 / 2,106,973
- Low Income: 4,078,157 / 715,556
- Middle Income: 923,726 / 102,378

■ Pay 30%-50% of Income
■ Pay more than 50% of Income
2016 Data

---

94 Unit 5, Lesson 7

Reading

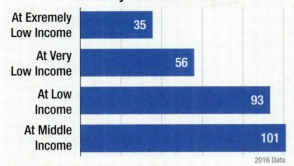

Number of Affordable and Available Rental Units for Every 100 Households

- At Extremely Low Income: 35
- At Very Low Income: 56
- At Low Income: 93
- At Middle Income: 101

2016 Data

What can be done? Extremely low-income renters cannot afford to rent new housing units. In addition, there are not enough older units that are affordable. This
30 means that housing subsidies are required. Housing subsidies come from taxpayer dollars used to support housing needs. Housing subsidies can help to build new affordable housing. They can also provide rental assistance. Subsidies cover what renters cannot afford.

35 However, government officials disagree about housing subsidies. Many officials around the country are cutting subsidies. Those leaders say that taxpayers should not pay for low-income housing. On the other hand, other leaders support housing subsidies. Those leaders insist
40 that subsidies will save taxpayer dollars. They explain how affordable housing creates **stability**. Stability allows people to keep their employment and do better in school. It also improves people's health and well-being. All these factors have economic **benefits**
45 for all taxpayers.

It is up to the voters in the United States. Voters can vote for the political candidates that support housing subsidies. They can also write to their political officials about the **issue**. If you believe all Americans have the
50 right to affordable housing, it's time to take action. Doesn't everyone deserve a home?

Dr. Cecilia Velo, Senior Director, Affordable Housing Advocates (AHA)

B IDENTIFY MAIN IDEAS. Choose the main idea of the article and of Paragraphs 2–4. Find the sentences that best support each main idea. Write the line numbers.

Article Main Idea	Lines
a. Americans need to support housing subsidies to help everyone obtain an affordable home. b. Shelter is one basic right of all human beings, and it should be provided for everyone. c. All Americans deserve to have an affordable home.	
Paragraph Main Ideas	
2 a. Extremely low-income renters make less than 30% the national average. b. Many extremely low-income renters pay less than than 71% of their income on housing. c. Extremely low-income renters have the most difficult time getting affordable housing.	
3 a. Many extremely low-income renters try to pay for housing they cannot afford. b. There are too few housing units available for extremely low-income renters. c. There are only 35 units available for every 100 extremely low-income households.	
4 a. Housing subsidies are needed to help extremely low-income renters. b. Extremely low-income renters cannot afford new housing units. c. Housing subsidies provide rental assistance for extremely low-income renters.	

3 ▸ Close Reading

A **LOCATE DETAILS.** Use the article and the infographics to answer the questions.

1. Which group of renters has the most difficulty finding affordable housing? _____

2. How many extremely low-income households paid 30–50% of their income for housing in 2016? _____

3. How many housing units were available for every 100 very low-income households in 2016? _____

4. How much did extremely low-income households make in 2019? _____

5. What percentage of extremely low-income renters spend more than 50% of their income

   on housing? _____

B **APPLY ACADEMIC READING SKILL.**

Academic Reading Skill: Evaluate the problem and solution presented in an argument
Problem-and-solution texts present a problem and one or more solutions to that problem. Some of these texts are informational. They give the reader information about a problem and some solutions to consider. Others are argumentative text. The purpose of an argument is to convince you to agree with the writer's specific solution. When you read an argument, you need to evaluate it before you decide to agree or disagree.

1. **Is the problem a real problem?** An argument may present a problem that may not be a real problem.

2. **Is the solution a real solution?** An argument may present a solution that may not actually solve the problem.

3. **Are there good reasons to support the solution?** Do the reasons given make sense to you? Are the reasons supported by specific information?

Read the article again. Answer the questions to evaluate this argument.

1. **Problem**

   a. What is the problem? _____

   b. What details show the problem is real? _____

   _____

2. **Solution**

   a. What is the solution? _____

   b. What detail supports the writer's solution? _____

   _____

3. **Reasons to Support the Solution**

   a. What reason is given to support the solution? _____

   b. What detail supports that reason? _____

   _____

4. **Evaluate this argument.**

   a. The problem is a real problem.   Yes/No

   b. The solution is a real solution to the problem.   Yes/No

   c. The reason to support the solution makes sense.   Yes/No

96 Unit 5, Lesson 7

C CALCULATE. Use the statistics from the infographics to answer the questions.

1. How many extremely low-income households spend more than 30% of their income on housing? _____

2. How many more extremely low-income households spend more than 50% of their income on housing than middle income households? _____

3. How many more housing units are available for every 100 middle-income households than every 100 extremely low-income households? _____

4 Prepare for an Academic Presentation

A FOCUS. You will give a formal presentation to describe the affordable housing problem and present a solution to the problem.

B RESEARCH. Find a source that describes a solution to the affordable housing problem. Use the Note-Taking Template on page 253 to take notes from that source. Use the suggestions below to help you include statistics to support your points.

C ORGANIZE. Use the Presentation Template on page 254 to organize your information.

Presentation Checklist	
	The presentation includes...
Organization:	✓ Defined problem and stated solution
	✓ Reasons to support the solution
Support:	✓ Statistics to support your points
Word Choice:	✓ Academic words
	✓ Problem-solution signal words
Delivery:	✓ Speech at appropriate volume and rate
	✓ Speech that is clear and easy to understand
	✓ Eye contact

Statistics to Support Your Points

Statistics use numbers to represent information. Statistics may include total counts, percentages, fractions, changes in amounts, and comparisons of amounts. When presenting a problem and solution, use statistics to convince your audience that the problem is a real problem and that the solution you suggest is a real solution to that problem. Statistics can also provide evidence or reasons to convince others to support your solution. Here are some examples:

- **Statistics to support the problem:** *Every night in the U.S., half a million people go without shelter.*
- **Statistics to support the solution:** *Housing subsidies already help five million people a year obtain affordable housing.*

D REVISE AND PRACTICE. Use the Presentation Checklist to assess your presentation and make revisions. Then practice your presentation until you feel confident.

Apply what you know | **Academic Presentation**

1. **PRESENT EVIDENCE.** Share your presentation with a partner. Remember to give evidence to support your main points. Your teacher may also choose you to present to the class.

2. **EVALUATE.** Have your partner evaluate your performance using the Presentation Checklist.

I can describe the problem of affordable housing and offer a solution. ☐   I need more practice. ☐

For more practice, go to MyEnglishLab.   For audio and video, scan the QR code.

Unit 5, Lesson 7   **97**

Lesson 8 Writing Workshop

Write an effective conclusion

1 What Do You Notice?

A COMPARE. Read the two examples of an essay conclusion. Which example suggests things the reader can do to support the solution and also provides a closing statement?

Example 1:

It is up to the voters in the United States. Voters can vote for the political candidates that support housing subsidies. They can also write to their political officials about the issue. If you believe all Americans have the right to affordable housing, it's time to take action. Doesn't everyone deserve a home?

Example 2:

Affordable housing is a big problem. There are a lot of possible solutions to the problem. Everyone should support the right for people to have housing. People should also support the right for people to access healthcare, just like they should support affordable housing for all.

B ANALYZE. Underline the specific actions suggested in the better example. Circle the closing statement. Cross out the unnecessary idea that was added in the other example.

2 Apply Academic Writing Skill

Academic Writing Skill: Write an effective conclusion
The introduction to an essay usually includes a thesis statement that states the main idea of the entire essay. An effective conclusion connects back to that thesis statement. An effective conclusion helps the reader recognize that the essay is coming to an end. It includes a brief summary of the main points and also tries to provide an interesting wrap up. Imagine the reader asking, "So what?" after reading the essay. An effective conclusion should answer that question.

Do not...
- introduce a new idea in a conclusion.
- simply restate the information from your introduction.
- add in extra facts that would distract from your thesis.

A IDENTIFY. What is the purpose of each sentence? Write *to summarize* or *to take action*.

1. If you support housing subsidies for low-income renters, cast your vote for those who believe the same. _____

2. Affordable housing is one of the biggest challenges in America, and housing subsidies could help eliminate this problem forever. _____

B SELECT. Choose the most effective concluding sentence.

Access to affordable housing continues to be a challenge for extremely low-income renters. Increased housing subsidies are needed. _____

   a. Support the increase of housing subsidies to provide affordable housing for all.
   b. Extremely low-income renters should also pay fewer taxes to make this solution work.

I can write an effective conclusion. ☐ I need more practice. ☐

For more practice, go to MyEnglishLab.

98 Unit 5, Lesson 8

Writing

Lesson **9**

Write a problem-solution essay

1 Model for Writing

STUDY THE MODEL. Use the article on affordable housing in Lesson 7 as a Writing Model. Analyze the structure of that article by filling in the Writing-Model Template on page 255.

2 Prepare Your Writing

A **FOCUS.** You will write an essay to describe the solution to the housing issue you researched in Lesson 7.

B **RESEARCH.** Go online and choose another source that describes a similar solution to the affordable housing issue. Use the same Note-Taking Template you used before (page 253) to take notes from your new source.

3 Write Write a problem-solution essay to describe the housing problem and suggest a solution.

A **ORGANIZE.** Use the structure of the Writing-Model Template from Exercise 1 to organize your writing. Follow the tips below when writing about problems and solutions.

Problem-Solution Essays

Remember that stating a problem and suggesting a solution is an easy way to structure a text, such as a business letter or formal email. First, explain what the problem is and why it is a problem. Then give solutions to the problem. End with a conclusion that briefly summarizes the problem and solution(s). You may also include a call to action that suggests steps for the reader to take.

- Explain why the reader should care about the problem.
- Offer clear, reasonable solutions.
- Use problem-and-solution signal words and phrases, such as *the problem is that, one possible solution is,* and *to solve this problem.*
- Also, remember to give statistics to support your points.

Writing Checklist	
	The text includes...
Structure:	✓ Problem-solution essay
Organization:	✓ Defined problem and stated solution
	✓ Statistics to provide evidence
	✓ Final conclusion
Word Choice:	✓ Academic words
	✓ Problem-and-solution signal words
Writing Skill:	✓ Clearly stated conclusion
Grammar:	✓ Adjective clauses and phrases

B **REVISE.** Use the Writing Checklist to evaluate your writing and make revisions. Remember to include an effective conclusion.

4 Share Your Writing

A **COLLABORATE.** Share your writing with a partner. Use any feedback to improve your writing.

B **PUBLISH.** Create a final document to share with others.

I can write a problem-solution essay. ☐	I need more practice. ☐

For more practice, go to MyEnglishLab.

Unit 5, Lesson 9 **99**

Lesson 10

Workplace Soft Skills

Demonstrate responsibility

1 Expectations

A ▶ **CONSIDER.** Listen to a conversation between a loan applicant and a bank manager. What is the bank manager trying to find out? How does the applicant respond?

B **IDENTIFY EXPECTATIONS.** Describe the bank manager's expectation and the applicant's response. Why does the bank manager ask to see the applicant's paperwork and so many other documents? What was the result?

1. Bank manager's expectation: _____
2. Applicant's response: _____
3. Result: _____

2 Learn from Mistakes

A **DISCUSS.** How could the applicant have prepared for the meeting? Suggest specific things he could have done differently. Have you ever felt that you could have done something to prepare better?

B **ROLE-PLAY.** Give the applicant a "do over." Role-play the conversation, but this time have the applicant meet the bank manager's expectations.

C ▶ **COMPARE.** Listen to the "do over" conversation. How is it similar to your role play? How is it different?

Apply what you know

1. **DEFINE.** In what other contexts would people have to demonstrate that they are responsible? How would you explain this soft skill to a person who is trying to show he or she is responsible?

2. **APPLY.** Record an example from your own life in your Soft Skills Log (page 241) of how you have demonstrated responsibility.

3. **SHARE.** Share your example.
   - *I demonstrated responsibility at _____ when I _____.*

I can demonstrate responsibility. ☐   I need more practice. ☐

For audio and video, scan the QR code.   For more practice, go to MyEnglishLab.

100 Unit 5, Lesson 10

When Nature Is in Charge

6

PREVIEW

Share everything you know about this type of severe weather. Then explain the meaning of the unit title.

UNIT GOALS

Use weather reports to inform decisions

Use a GPS app to choose routes

Identify safety measures for severe weather events

Describe the effects of natural disasters

Explain the science of tornadoes

Write about the process of a severe weather event

Workplace Soft Skill: Exercise leadership

Academic Skills:

- **Listening:** Listen for cause-and-effect relationships
- **Speaking:** Extend the contributions of others
- **Reading:** Mark text to highlight cause-and-effect relationships
- **Writing:** Use complex sentences to create writing that flows

Lesson 1

Listening and Speaking
Use weather reports to inform decisions

1 Before You Listen

A DISCUSS. Where do you see these types of images? What data do they present? How do you use this data to inform your decisions?

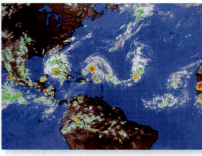

B PREVIEW VOCABULARY.

1. **TOPIC-RELATED WORDS.** These terms are used in the listening. Does anyone know what they mean? For compound words, think about the meaning of each word separately. Also, use roots and affixes to help you.

   | forecast | barometer | radar | flash flooding |

2. **ACADEMIC WORDS.** These sentences are from the listening. Discuss the meaning of each **bolded** word. Use context to help you.

   1. The heavy rains are causing **hazardous** driving **conditions** across the state.
   2. So far this morning, twenty weather-**related** accidents haven been reported.
   3. The Weather Service has issued a severe weather **advisory** for this evening.
   4. The long-range weather forecast looks promising, with **partially** sunny skies expected tomorrow.

C PREDICT. Use the lesson title, vocabulary, and images to make predictions about the listening. What will its purpose be? What information do you expect?

2 Listen

A ▶ LISTEN FOR MAIN IDEAS. Listen to the weather report. List the three important topics in the first column. Then compare your topics with a partner.

Topics	Details

B ▶ LISTEN FOR DETAILS. Listen again. List details that describe each topic.

Listening and Speaking

3 Apply Academic Listening Skill

Academic Listening Skill: Listen for cause-and-effect relationships
Cause-and-effect relationships occur when one event leads to another event. The first event is called the **cause** and the result of that event is called the **effect**. Cause-and-effect signal words and verbs help us identify causes and their effects. Listening for these words will help you identify cause-and-effect relationships.

Cause-and-Effect Signal Words		
Words and Phrases	**Verbs**	
consequently, thus, so…that, since, as a result, the result is, given that, then, due to, because of, thereby	**Cause:** cause, result in, trigger, form, produce	**Effect:** triggered by, result from, caused by, produced by, formed by

A ▶ IDENTIFY. Listen to today's forecast again. Which cause-and-effect signal words or phrases does the speaker use? Underline them in the chart above.

B ▶ TAKE NOTES. Listen to tomorrow's forecast again. Complete the chart with three more cause-and-effect relationships.

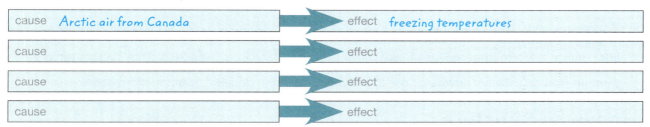

cause: Arctic air from Canada → effect: freezing temperatures
cause: → effect:
cause: → effect:
cause: → effect:

C EXPAND VOCABULARY. Add words to your Word Study Log to show structure and meaning.

4 Real-World Application

A APPLY. How does the weather forecast impact how you get to work or school? Create a chart to list types of weather that impact travel. Support each with an example from your life.

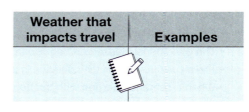

Weather that impacts travel	Examples

B GIVE EXAMPLES. Explain to a partner how the weather forecast impacts your decisions. Provide examples to support each point.

- I decide _____ based on the weather forecast. For example, when it _____, I _____.
- The weather forecast helps me decide _____. For example, if it is going to _____, then I _____.

Academic Speaking Skill: Extend the contributions of others
When other people make statements, ask them questions to draw out more information. This type of questioning will improve your collaboration with others.

- Could you explain that further?
- Why do you think that's the case?
- Could you give me another example of that?

C SUMMARIZE. Describe one way the weather forecast affects a classmate's daily decisions.

- _____ decides _____ based on _____. For example, _____.

I can use weather reports to inform decisions. ☐   I need more practice. ☐

For more practice, go to MyEnglishLab.   For audio and video, scan the QR code.

Unit 6, Lesson 1   103

Lesson 2 — Grammar

Use real conditionals

1 Focus on Usage

A CONSIDER. Read the highlighted sentences in the weather report below. Do the sentences describe something that has actually happened?

> The real conditional refers to a possible situation in the present or future. This possible condition may or may not happen. If the condition does happen, certain results will also happen.

B IDENTIFY. Read the entire weather report. Identify each sentence that states a possible condition and a related result. Underline all the possible conditions. Circle all the related results.

Good afternoon, listeners! If you're going out tonight, you'll need an umbrella. We're expecting scattered showers all evening. We may even see a little snow if temperatures continue to drop. Be careful out there! Streets will be hazardous if the temperature drops below freezing. It's currently 36 degrees. If you have plans for outdoor activities tomorrow, you won't be disappointed. You can expect clear skies and much warmer temperatures by late afternoon. Temperatures will be in the low 60s. Unless a storm front moves in, we'll have beautiful weather all weekend. That's all for today's weather. You can always download our app if you'd like more detailed weather information.

2 Focus on Structure

Real Conditional	
If you're going out tonight,	you'll need an umbrella.
Unless a storm front moves in,	we'll have beautiful weather.
I always drive carefully	if it is snowing.

- The conditional clause can begin with *if, whether,* or *unless. Unless* means "except if."
- The clause that states the condition is a dependent clause. The result clause is an independent clause.
- When a sentence **begins** with the conditional clause, a comma is used to separate the two clauses.

A INVESTIGATE. Analyze all the examples of real conditionals. Choose **all** the correct answers.

1. A conditional clause can begin with _____.
   a. *if*
   b. *because*
   c. *unless*
   d. *before*

2. The verb in the *if* clause may be in the _____.
   a. simple past
   b. simple present
   c. present progressive
   d. future

3. The verb in the result clause may be in _____ tense.
   a. the past
   b. the present
   c. the future
   d. any

104 Unit 6, Lesson 2

Grammar

B **COMPLETE.** Complete the sentences. Use the real conditional.

1. (*rain, carry*) If it _____ for several days, I _____ my umbrella.

2. (*be, go*) If the weather _____ nice next weekend, we _____ to the beach.

3. (*improve, be*) Unless the weather _____ soon, our flight _____ cancelled this evening.

4. (*cancel, not snow*) We _____ our ski plans this weekend if it _____.

5. (*change, get*) If the weather _____ suddenly, I usually _____ a headache.

6. (*not meet, be*) Classes _____ tonight if the tornado watch _____ still in effect.

C **WRITE.** Rewrite each possible situation using the real conditional. Add a result clause.

1. The weather may be very cold tomorrow.

   If the weather is very cold tomorrow, I'll wear my warm coat. _____

2. It might snow this weekend.

   _____

3. Road conditions could be hazardous this evening.

   _____

4. We're expecting sunny skies this afternoon.

   _____

Apply what you know

1. **DESCRIBE.** Discuss the weather with a partner. Use the real conditional.
   1. What will you do if the weather is cold or rainy this weekend?
   2. What will you do if the weather is nice this weekend?

2. **WRITE.** Write a paragraph about your weekend plans. How will your plans change depending on the weather?

   If it's warm and sunny this weekend, I'll play soccer with my friends. If it rains, I'll stay home and watch a movie.

I can use real conditionals for possible situations. ■   I need more practice. ■

For more practice, go to MyEnglishLab.

Unit 6, Lesson 2 **105**

Lesson 3: Workplace, Life, & Community Skills

Use a GPS app to choose routes

1 Solve Transportation Problems

A **REFLECT.** What problems have you had with transportation in the past? What types of weather typically cause transportation problems in your area?

B **PROBLEM-SOLVE.** How do you get to work or school on time in challenging weather and traffic conditions? What suggestions do you have for helping others plan ahead for traffic issues?

2 Consult Resources

GPS Maps

When you are trying to go somewhere, there are often different ways to get there. Using a GPS map can help you see alternate routes and help you choose which one is best. This can be very convenient when weather conditions create traffic problems.

A **SCAN.** A man needed to get from his home in Denver, CO, to a business meeting. He used a GPS map to see his options. Look at the screen.

1. Where is his business meeting? _____
2. How many different route options are shown? _____
3. What are the lengths of time for each route? _____

106 Unit 6, Lesson 3

Workplace, Life, & Community Skills

B **DEFINE KEY WORDS.** Find these words on the screen. Match each word to its definition.

_____ **1.** (n) arrival

_____ **2.** (n) destination

_____ **3.** (adj) estimated

_____ **4.** (n) freeway

_____ **5.** (prep) via

_____ **6.** (n) toll

a. highway with no crossing roads

b. approximate

c. end location or goal

d. by, through

e. fee charged to drive on a road

f. the act of reaching a set place

C **INTERPRET.** Locate information on the GPS map.

1. How many miles long is the shortest route? _____

2. Which of the routes has tolls? _____

3. Which route goes through Wolhurst? _____

4. What three main roads does the second shortest route use? _____

D **CONCLUDE.** Use the GPS map. Discuss the answers to the questions.

1. If you needed to pick something up in Cottonwood, which route would you take?

_____

2. If you wanted to avoid the freeway as much as possible, how much longer would your route take?

_____

3. If there was flooding on the roads in Centennial and Foxfield, which route would you take? _____

4. If you didn't want to take any of the routes shown, could you still get from Denver to Parker?

Draw one alternate route. _____

E **GO ONLINE.** Use the Search Terms to find a GPS mapping app or website. Share your map with a partner. How is it similar to other GPS maps you have used? How has the way you get directions changed in your lifetime?

Search Terms: online maps

Apply what you know

1. **APPLY.** Use one of the GPS mapping apps to show a common route you take. Then find an alternate route to use if your normal route has traffic problems.

2. **SHARE.** Explain your route choice to a partner.

- *When my normal route is _____, I take this route because _____.*
- *If my regular route has a problem, I use this alternate route to _____.*

I can use a GPS app to choose routes. ☐   I need more practice. ☐

For more practice, go to MyEnglishLab.

Unit 6, Lesson 3 **107**

Lesson 4

Reading
Identify safety measures for severe weather events

1 Before You Read

A **IDENTIFY.** What types of severe weather are shown? Which do you have in your area? In your native country?

B **PREVIEW VOCABULARY.**

1. **TOPIC-RELATED WORDS.** These terms are used in the article. Does anyone know what they mean? Use roots and affixes to help you. You can also look for clues in the article.

| severe | nonperishable | evacuation | designated |

2. **ACADEMIC WORDS.** Discuss the meaning of the **bolded** words in the article. Use context to help you. After reading the article, add any words you learned to your Word Study Log.

C **PREDICT.** Preview the article title and images. What is the purpose of the article? What information do you expect?

2 Read for Gist

A **READ.** What aspects of weather safety does the article discuss?

Hope for the Best; Prepare for the Worst: Severe Weather Safety

1   No one wants to think about being caught in the middle of a hurricane or flood. However, knowing what to do during a <u>severe</u> weather event may just save your life. It doesn't take much to prepare, and your preparation could make all the difference.

5   There are many types of severe weather events, such as thunderstorms, snowstorms, and hurricanes. There are also the dangerous conditions they produce like flooding, forest fires, and icy roads. First, know which kinds of severe weather are common in your area. Pay attention to your local weather reports. Also, talk to others in your **community** to find out how they prepare
10 and what they do during severe weather.

Every severe weather event **requires** its own set of precautions. However, there are several things that will come in handy no matter what the event. Having bottled water and <u>nonperishable</u> foods **available** is one such precaution. The most important item is a safety kit. It can help you in your home or if you need to evacuate. Here are some things your kit should include: first-aid supplies, a flashlight, a battery-operated radio, extra batteries, an emergency phone charger,
15 any prescription medications your family needs, toilet paper, a can opener, an extra set of car and house keys, and a list of contact numbers for friends and relatives. If you live in a cold climate, also include a blanket and extra socks, hats, and mittens.

108   Unit 6, Lesson 4

Reading

No matter what the event, you also need a family safety plan. For events that require you to remain indoors, designate an appropriate shelter within your house. In the case of storms, hurricanes, and tornadoes, this should be a windowless
20 room on the lowest level. For events that require <u>evacuation</u>, the shelter should be an area <u>designated</u> by your local government or emergency personnel. This may be a local school, place of worship, business, or community center. If you have friends or relatives outside the affected area, and it is safe to travel there, consider staying with them for the **duration** of the storm. Make sure they are aware of your plan as well.

No one wants to imagine the worst. But being prepared is the best **strategy** if the worst happens to strike. Be aware . . .
25 prepare. That way when nature comes knocking, you'll know you did everything you could to keep your family safe.

B **IDENTIFY MAIN IDEAS.** Choose the main idea of the article. Where is it stated? Lines _____

  a. What types of events are possible
  b. How to prepare for weather-related events
  c. What to include in a safety kit

3 Close Reading

A **RECOGNIZE STRUCTURE.** List the topic of each paragraph in the chart.

Paragraph Topic	Safety Measures
2	
3	
4	

B **LOCATE DETAILS.** Complete the chart with three safety measures from each paragraph.

Apply what you know

1. **APPLY.** Identify a severe weather event you have in your area. Write a list of items to keep in your safety kit for that event. Write a safety plan for that event.

2. **SHARE.** Share your safety kit and safety plan.
   • In case of _____, my safety kit will include _____, _____, _____, and _____.
   • For my safety plan, my family and I will _____.

I can identify safety measures for severe weather events. ☐   I need more practice. ☐

For more practice, go to MyEnglishLab.   For audio and video, scan the QR code.

Unit 6, Lesson 4 **109**

Lesson 5 — Listening and Speaking

Describe the effects of natural disasters

1 Before You Listen

A REFLECT. What event has occurred? What damage will be caused?

B PREVIEW VOCABULARY.

1. **TOPIC-RELATED WORDS.** These terms are used in the listening. Does anyone know what they mean? Use roots and affixes to help you.

   | dams | stranded | FEMA | rescue | power outage |

2. **ACADEMIC WORDS.** These sentences are from the listening. Discuss the meaning of each **bolded** word. Use context to help you.
   1. The amount of rainfall **exceeded** all previous records.
   2. Either **scenario**, staying or leaving, was a disaster.
   3. The human, environmental, and **economic** impact of Hurricane Harvey was staggering.
   4. **Recovery** took over a year.

C PREDICT. Use the lesson title, vocabulary, and images to make predictions about the listening. What will its purpose be? What information do you expect?

2 Listen

A ▶ LISTEN FOR MAIN IDEAS. Listen to the news report. Write 1–4 to order the topics as they are presented in the news report. Then compare your order with a partner.

Order	Topics	Details
	Event description	
	Impact on environment	
	Impact on economy	
	Impact on people	

B ▶ LISTEN FOR DETAILS. Listen again. List details that support each topic.

Listening and Speaking

3 Apply Academic Listening Skill

A ▶ **IDENTIFY CAUSES AND EFFECTS.** Listen to part of the news report again. Add three more cause-and-effect relationships to the chart.

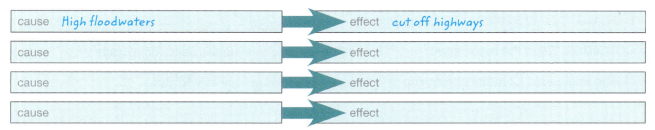

cause	High floodwaters	→	effect	cut off highways
cause		→	effect	
cause		→	effect	
cause		→	effect	

B **EXPAND VOCABULARY.** Add words to your Word Study Log to show structure and meaning.

4 Real-World Application

A **IDENTIFY.** What impact do natural disasters have on people and the environment?

Effects on People	Effects on Environment

B **EXPLAIN.** Describe how natural disasters impact people and the environment. Use your own examples.
- *Natural disasters destroy _____, _____, and _____.*
- *They cause _____, _____, and _____.*
- *They impact _____ by _____-ing _____ and _____-ing. _____.*

C **SUMMARIZE.** Report one classmate's summary of the impact of natural disasters.
- *_____ said the most important impact of disasters was _____.*

I can describe the effects of natural disasters. ☐   I need more practice. ☐

For more practice, go to MyEnglishLab.   For audio and video, scan the QR code.

Lesson **6**

Grammar
Use present and future unreal conditionals

1 ▶ Focus on Usage

A **CONSIDER.** Read the highlighted sentences in the text message below. Do the sentences describe something that has actually happened?

> The unreal conditional is used for improbable or impossible situations. **Improbable** means the situation described is very unlikely to occur.

B **IDENTIFY.** Read the entire text message between two people who just watched a documentary on natural disasters. Identify each sentence that states an improbable situation. Underline all the improbable situations. Circle all the results.

A: If there were a tornado in our city, I would hide in my closet.

B: IDK. I think I'd lie in the bathtub.

A: What if there were a hurricane? I'd make sure I had a lot of canned food and bottled water.

B: We don't have hurricanes in Ohio.

A: But if we had hurricanes, I'd make sure I was prepared.

B: If we had an ocean nearby, we'd have hurricanes. We don't have an ocean.

A: OK. But if we had an ocean, I wouldn't care if we had hurricanes. I'd go surfing every day.

B: And if you went surfing every day, you wouldn't text me about dumb stuff like this.

2 ▶ Focus on Structure

Unreal Conditional	
If there <u>were</u> a tornado in our city,	*I would hide in my closet.*
I would go surfing everyday	*if we had an ocean nearby.*

- In the unreal conditional, a past tense verb is used to express present time.
- *Were* replaces *was* in present unreal conditional clauses.
- If the dependent clause comes first, use a comma to separate the two clauses. Do not use a comma when the dependent clause comes at the end.

112 Unit 6, Lesson 6

Grammar

A **INVESTIGATE.** Analyze all the examples of impossible or improbable conditional clauses. Match to complete each sentence.

_____ **1.** The *if* clause expresses the _____.

_____ **2.** The independent clause expresses the _____.

_____ **3.** In the *if* clause, use _____.

_____ **4.** In the result clause, use _____.

_____ **5.** It is common to make a contraction with _____.

a. a past tense verb

b. *would* + verb

c. the subject + *would*

d. condition

e. response or result

B **COMPLETE.** Complete the sentences. Use the unreal conditional.

1. (*snow, play*) If it _____ in July, I _____ in the snow.

2. (*go, live*) We _____ to the beach every weekend if we _____ near the ocean.

3. (*not carry, not rain*) I _____ an umbrella all the time if it _____ so much.

4. (*not stay, be*) The kids _____ inside the house today if the weather _____ nicer.

C **WRITE.** Read each situation. Write an *if* statement using the unreal conditional.

1. Two friends are talking about what they would do if it snowed in their town where it has never snowed before.

   _____

2. A parent is telling a child what to do in the unlikely event that there is a tornado.

   _____

3. It's a beautiful day. Two co-workers are imagining how they would spend the day if they didn't have to work today.

   _____

4. Two neighbors are discussing what to do in the event of a flood.

   _____

Apply what you know

1. **DISCUSS.** First, decide if the situation described is possible, improbable, or impossible for your location. Then discuss each situation. Remember to use the real conditional for possible situations and the unreal conditional for improbable or impossible situations.

   • A tornado is spotted near your home.
   • An earthquake hits your area.

   • You see someone struck by lightning.
   • You need to get to work in a snowstorm.

2. **WRITE.** Create an emergency plan for some type of severe weather. Use conditionals.

   If a tornado were spotted near my home, I'd go down to the basement. _____

I can use unreal conditionals for improbable or impossible situations. ☐	I need more practice. ☐

For more practice, go to MyEnglishLab.

Unit 6, Lesson 6 **113**

Lesson 7

Reading

Explain the science of tornadoes

1 Before You Read

A DISCUSS. What are tornadoes? Where do they happen? How do they happen? What do you know about the science of tornadoes?

B PREVIEW VOCABULARY.

1. **TOPIC-RELATED WORDS.** These terms are used in the article. Does anyone know what they mean? Use roots and affixes to help you. You can also look for clues in the article.

| funnel | supercell | wind shear | horizontal vortex | mesocyclone | updraft |

2. **ACADEMIC WORDS.** Discuss the meaning of the **bolded** words in the article. Use context to help you. After reading the article, add any words you learned to your Word Study Log.

C PREDICT. Preview the title and diagrams. What is the purpose of the article? What information do you expect?

2 Read for Gist

A READ. Think about the main ideas as you read. Underline any sentences that help you identify main ideas.

The Formation of Tornadoes

From Supercell to Tornado

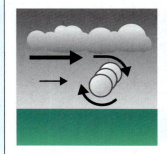
Step 1–Horizontal Vortex

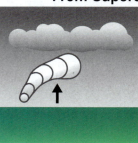
Step 2–Mesocyclone

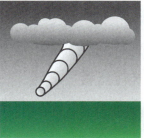
Step 3–Funnel Cloud

Step 4–Tornado

1 Tornadoes are a fearsome sign of nature's power. Each year on average, more than 1,000 tornadoes occur in the U.S. Most of these **occur** within the area known as Tornado Alley. Tornado Alley is roughly **comprised** of the area between the Rocky Mountains and the Appalachian Mountains. Tornadoes cause nearly $400 million in damages and 70 human deaths each year. Once they begin their path along the land, they can destroy large areas up to a mile wide and tens of
5   miles long. The largest tornado ever recorded occurred in El Reno, Oklahoma, in 2013, and it measured 2.6 miles wide and 39 miles long. Given these facts, it is not surprising that many of us want to know more about the science of tornadoes.

   It's helpful to understand what a tornado actually is. Simply put, a tornado is a <u>funnel</u>-shaped cloud of spinning air that moves across the land. The wind within the funnel may spin at speeds up to 300 miles per hour. This funnel of wind
10 crosses the land destroying nearly everything in its path.

114   Unit 6, Lesson 7

Reading

The first step in tornado formation is the making of a supercell. A supercell is a very strong thunderstorm. It is formed when a thunderstorm produces wind shear: winds blowing in different directions or at different speeds. This wind shear causes the lower air of a thunderstorm to spin. This results in a horizontal vortex, or spinning tube of air, the sign of a supercell.

15　　The second step in tornado formation is the creation of a mesocyclone. This happens when the air in the horizontal vortex begins to warm. As the warmer air pushes through the cooler air, an updraft results. An updraft is wind that moves in an upward direction. The updraft pushes the vortex into a vertical position. Consequently, a mesocyclone is formed.

Next, a funnel cloud is formed. In a mesocyclone, the warm air of the thunderstorm increases the speed of the 20 spinning air. Then moisture in the air causes the mesocyclone to form a funnel cloud. However, only when the funnel cloud touches ground does it become a tornado.

How a funnel cloud touches the ground and becomes a tornado is still difficult to understand. Before, scientists believed that the funnel cloud only formed high above the ground and later touched down. Recent **research**, however, shows that spinning air can begin first at ground level and later reach greater heights.

25　　Although much is known about the science of tornadoes, there is still much to learn. Knowing what a tornado is and how it is formed helps us understand a bit more about nature's power. However, no matter how much we learn, we must understand that our knowledge is no match for the power of this fearsome funnel.

B **IDENTIFY MAIN IDEAS.** Choose the main idea of the article and of Paragraphs 2–4. Find the sentences that best support each main idea. Write the line numbers.

Article Main Idea	Lines
a. How tornadoes are an example of nature's power b. How tornadoes destroy nearly everything in their paths c. How tornadoes are formed	
Paragraph Main Ideas	

		Lines
2	a. A description of what a tornado is	
	b. How fast the wind spins within a tornado's funnel	
	c. How a tornado can destroy nearly everything in its path	
3	a. The definition of a supercell	
	b. How a supercell is formed	
	c. How wind shear creates an updraft	
4	a. What causes an updraft	
	b. How the horizontal vortex warms up	
	c. The steps in the formation of a mesocyclone	

Unit 6, Lesson 7　**115**

3 Close Reading

A LOCATE DETAILS. Are the statements true or false? Write the line numbers of your evidence.

	T/F	Lines
1. The largest tornado covered an area one mile wide and ten miles long.	_____	_____
2. The horizontal vortex of a tornado shifts to a vertical position to make a mesocyclone.	_____	_____
3. A funnel cloud is only a tornado when it touches the earth.	_____	_____
4. Scientists know that spinning air at ground level may change a funnel cloud to a tornado.	_____	_____

B APPLY ACADEMIC READING SKILL.

Academic Reading Skill: Mark text to highlight cause-and-effect relationships
Remember that cause-and-effect relationships occur when one event leads to another event. When you read, look for common cause-and-effect signal words, such as *due to* and *consequently*. Also look for cause-and-effect verbs, such as *cause* and *produce*. This skill will improve your reading comprehension, especially for texts that describe cause-and-effect relationships.

1. Reread Paragraph 2. Circle cause-and-effect signal words. Then underline each cause and put a box around its effect. Draw an arrow to connect each cause to its effect.

    It is formed when a thunderstorm (produces) wind shear.

2. Reread Paragraph 3. Record two cause-and-effect relationships that describe supercell formation.

cause	effect
cause	effect

3. Reread Paragraph 4. Record three cause-and-effect relationships that describe mesocyclone formation.

cause	effect
cause	effect
cause	effect

4. Describe the formation of a supercell or a mesocyclone in your own words.

    _____

    _____

C EXPAND UNDERSTANDING. Answer the questions.

1. **DETERMINE.** The title of the article is "The Formation of Tornadoes." What is another title that would be appropriate? _____

2. **SUMMARIZE.** Summarize what scientists believed before about how a funnel cloud becomes a tornado and what recent research has shown.

    _____

    _____

116 Unit 6, Lesson 7

4　Prepare for an Academic Conversation

A GO ONLINE. Read about *Narrowing Online Searches.* Then try it out in YOUR TURN.

| ✓ Search | ✓ Choose Sources | ✓ Evaluate Sources |

Narrowing Online Searches

You can use special commands in online searches to give instructions to the search engines. Here are two common comands.

Quotations: Put quotations around search terms "___" when you want results that contain all the search terms.
Search term example: "tornado science"

Quotation marks should be used around a phrase or concept of two or more words. Doing this ensures that the concept will be searched for as a whole and not picked apart by the search engine. The results will include only websites that contain both the words *tornado* and *science.*

Asterisk: Include an asterisk * for a word you don't remember in a phrase, title, or name.
If you don't remember the last word of the movie title *NYC Tornado Terror,* you can find it online.
Search term example: NYC Tornado *

The results will include the phrases that begin with **NYC Tornado** and end with known options for the missing word.

YOUR TURN…
Try out each command below. Write the number of results you receive and the title of the top result.

1. **Use Quotations**—Enter: "tornado science"

   # of Results: _____   Title: _____

2. **Use an Asterisk**—Enter: NYC Tornado *

   # of Results: _____   Title: _____

B CHOOSE A SOURCE. Choose a severe weather event. Use commands to help you find a source that explains the science of that event.

C TAKE NOTES. Use the Note-Taking Template on page 256 to take notes from the source you chose.

Apply what you know — Academic Conversation

1. **REPORT.** Explain the science of the severe weather event you researched. Remember to explain the cause-and-effect relationships.

2. **EXTEND THE CONTRIBUTIONS OF OTHERS.** Remember to ask questions to encourage your listeners to give additional input.
   - *Can you give me an example of what you mean?*
   - *Could you explain that further?*

I can explain the science of tornadoes. ☐   I need more practice. ☐

For more practice, go to MyEnglishLab.   For audio and video, scan the QR code.

Unit 6, Lesson 7   **117**

Lesson 8

Writing Workshop
Use complex sentences to create writing that flows

1 What Do You Notice?

A COMPARE. Read the two examples. How are they the same? How are they different?

Example 1:

Seventy-five percent of all tornadoes take place in the U.S. Most of those occur within the area known as Tornado Alley. Tornado Alley is roughly comprised of the area between the Rocky Mountains and the Appalachian Mountains. Each year on average, more than 1,000 tornadoes occur in the U.S. They cause upwards of $400 million in damages. They also cause approximately 70 human deaths. Their paths of destruction cover areas up to a mile wide and tens of miles long. The largest tornado ever recorded occurred in El Reno, Oklahoma, in 2013. It measured 2.6 miles wide and 39 miles long.

Example 2:

Seventy-five percent of all tornadoes take place in the U.S. Most of those occur within the area known as Tornado Alley, which is roughly comprised of the area between the Rocky Mountains and Appalachian Mountains. Each year on average, more than 1,000 tornadoes occur in the U.S., which causes over $400 million in damages and 70 human deaths. Their paths of destruction cover areas up to a mile wide and tens of miles long. The largest tornado ever recorded occurred in El Reno, Oklahoma, in 2013, and it measured 2.6 miles wide and 39 miles long.

B ▶ LISTEN AND ANALYZE. Now listen to each example. Count the number of complete stops you hear. How does the number of stops affect the reading?

2 Apply Academic Writing Skill

> **Academic Writing Skill: Use complex sentences to create writing that flows**
> There are three main types of sentences:
> - **Simple** sentences include one independent clause with a complete subject and verb.
> - **Compound** sentences combine two separate independent clauses with a conjunction.
> - **Complex** sentences combine an independent clause and at least one dependent clause.
>
> Writing that flows doesn't have a lot of stop and starts. Texts that include complex and compound sentences have fewer stops and starts than texts that use simple sentences only. Therefore, one way to make your writing flow is to change simple sentences to complex sentences by adding information. Use a relative pronoun or a subordinating conjunction to introduce the information you add.
>
> *For a list of subordinating conjunctions, search online for:* <u>subordinating conjunctions</u>.

A IDENTIFY. Is the sentence complex or compound?

1. The largest tornado ever recorded occurred in El Reno, Oklahoma, in 2013, and it measured 2.6 miles wide and 39 miles long. _____

2. Most tornadoes occur within the area known as Tornado Alley, which is roughly comprised of the area between the Rockies and Appalachian Mountains. _____

B APPLY. Combine the two simple sentences to make a complex sentence.

(which) Consequently, the lighter warm air rises through the cool air, creating an updraft. This updraft triggers the thunderstorm.

_____

I can use complex sentences to create writing that flows. ☐   I need more practice. ☐

For audio and video, scan the QR code.   For more practice, go to MyEnglishLab.

118 Unit 6, Lesson 8

Writing

Write about the process of a severe weather event

Lesson 9

1 ▶ Model for Writing

STUDY THE MODEL. Use the article on tornadoes in Lesson 7 as a Writing Model. Analyze the structure of that article by filling in the Writing-Model Template on page 257.

2 ▶ Prepare Your Writing

A **FOCUS.** You will write an article to explain the science behind the severe weather event you researched in Lesson 7.

B **RESEARCH.** Go online and choose another source that describes that severe weather event. Use the same Note-Taking Template you used before (page 256) to take notes from your new source.

3 ▶ Write Write an article to explain the process and causes of a severe weather event.

A **ORGANIZE.** Use the structure of the Writing-Model Template from Exercise 1 to organize your writing. Follow the tips below to describe any process.

Process Writing

Process writing describes how to do something or how something works. When you write about how something works, first find information to make sure you understand the process yourself. Then you can include important details, facts, and examples to help the reader understand the process.

- State what process you will present and why that process is important to the reader.
- Put all information in your own words.
- Use signal words to show cause-and-effect relationships.
- Use sequence signal words (*first, second, next*) to clarify the order of the steps.

Writing Checklist	
	The text includes…
Structure:	✓ Process essay
Organization:	✓ Introduction with catchy lead-in
	✓ Body of essay and final conclusion
Word Choice:	✓ Academic words
	✓ Cause-effect signal words
	✓ Sequence signal words
Writing Skill:	✓ Complex sentences for writing flow
Grammar:	✓ Real conditionals

B **REVISE.** Use the Writing Checklist to evaluate your writing and make revisions. Remember to include complex sentences to create writing that flows.

4 ▶ Share Your Writing

A **COLLABORATE.** Share your writing with a partner. Use any feedback to improve your writing.

B **PUBLISH.** Create a final document to share with others.

I can write about the process of a severe weather event. ■   I need more practice. ■

For more practice, go to MyEnglishLab.

Unit 6, Lesson 9 **119**

Lesson 10 — Workplace Soft Skills

Exercise leadership

1 Workplace Expectations

A ▶ **CONSIDER.** Listen to a phone conversation between a manager and the shift lead. What does the manager want the shift lead to do? Why doesn't she do it?

B **IDENTIFY EXPECTATIONS.** Describe the manager's expectation and the shift lead's response. What would the shift lead's performance review state?

1. Manager's expectation: _____
2. Shift Lead's response: _____
3. Performance review: _____

2 Learn from Mistakes

A **DISCUSS.** How could the shift lead have improved? Suggest specific things she could have done differently. Share your suggestions with a partner.

B **ROLE-PLAY.** Give the shift lead a "do over." Role-play the conversation, but this time have the shift lead meet the manager's expectations.

C ▶ **COMPARE.** Listen to the "do-over" conversation. How does it compare with your role play?

Apply what you know

1. **DEFINE.** How would you explain this soft skill to a new employee?
2. **APPLY.** Record an example from your own life in your Soft Skills Log (page 241) of how you have exercised leadership.
3. **SHARE.** Share your example. • *I exercised leadership at _____ when I _____.*

I can exercise leadership. ☐   I need more practice. ☐

For audio and video, scan the QR code.   For more practice, go to MyEnglishLab.

Protecting the Planet

7

PREVIEW

What changes in the weather have you seen in your lifetime? Why is a polar bear being shown here? What do you know about global warming?

UNIT GOALS

Describe climate change

Promote responsible waste disposal practices

Describe green jobs

Discuss ways to limit our carbon footprint

Give a presentation to describe an effect of climate change

Write an argument that makes a claim about an effect of climate change

Workplace Soft Skill: Work effectively with a team

Academic Skills:

- **Listening:** Identify components in a causal chain
- **Speaking:** Acknowledge the contributions of others
- **Reading:** Use a graphic organizer to identify components in a causal chain
- **Writing:** Identify components of a valid argument

121

Lesson 1 Listening and Speaking

Describe climate change

1 Before You Listen

A **DISCUSS.** What is climate change? What evidence supports that climate change is happening?

B **PREVIEW VOCABULARY.**

1. **TOPIC-RELATED WORDS.** These terms are used in the listening. Does anyone know what they mean? Use roots and affixes to help you.

| fossil fuels | biodegradable |
| emit greenhouse gases | decomposes |

2. **ACADEMIC WORDS.** These sentences are from the listening. Discuss the meaning of each **bolded** word. Use context to help you.
   1. The World Meteorological Organization has recorded a higher **incidence** of extreme weather events.
   2. The way we **generate** electricity is a significant problem.
   3. Power plants emit, or **release**, huge amounts of greenhouse gases.
   4. And finally, there's deforestation, or cutting down and clearing forests to **convert** the land into farms, ranches, or urban areas.
   5. The crux of the matter is that climate change is **attributed** to all these human activities.

C **PREDICT.** Use the lesson title, vocabulary, and image to make predictions about the listening. What will its purpose be? What information do you expect?

2 Listen

A ▶ **LISTEN FOR MAIN IDEAS.** Listen. In the first column, list the four human activities impacting climate change that the professor discusses. Then compare your list with a partner.

Human Activity	How It Causes Climate Change

B ▶ **LISTEN FOR DETAILS.** Listen again. For each activity, explain how it contributes to climate change.

122 Unit 7, Lesson 1

Listening and Speaking

3 Apply Academic Listening Skill

Academic Listening Skill: Identify components in a causal chain
Speakers use emphasis signal words to highlight key information. Listening for these words will help you recognize when a speaker is making a key point. Tracking key points will help you recognize the overall structure of the information.

One common organization is to link a series of events into a **causal chain**. In a causal chain, each event leads to, or causes, the next event. Thus, the events are linked together like the links in a chain. Listening for emphasis signal words will help you recognize each important event in a causal chain.

Emphasis Signal Words	
Adjectives and Adverbs	**Phrases**
significant, main, primary, key, critical, important, noteworthy, especially, actually, truly, clearly, namely	above all, most of all, the crux of the matter, more than anything else, pay particular attention to

A ▶ IDENTIFY. Listen to part of the lecture again. Which emphasis signal words does the speaker use? Underline those words or phrases in the chart above.

B ▶ IDENTIFY A CAUSAL CHAIN. Listen to the conclusion of the lecture again. Add these phrases to complete the causal chain.

- Climate change
- Warmer temperatures
- Release of carbon dioxide and other gases

C EXPAND VOCABULARY. Add words to your Word Study Log to show structure and meaning.

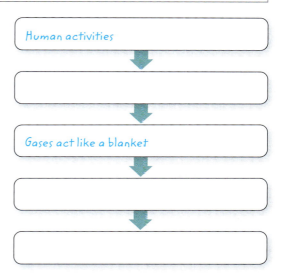

4 Real-World Application

A ANALYZE. Which of the following environmental problems affect your community? How does each of these problems contribute to climate change?

poor waste management	overfishing	energy-inefficient homes
water pollution	acid rain	urban sprawl

B COLLABORATE. Work in a small group to choose one of the environmental problems above. Create a causal chain to visually represent the causes and effects of the problem. Present your causal chain to the group.

Academic Speaking Skill: Acknowledge the contributions of others
When you are working in a group, it is polite to encourage and give credit to others for their ideas. Use statements like these to acknowledge the contributions of others.

- *That's an interesting idea. I hadn't thought about that.*
- *You make a really good point because _____.*

I can describe climate change. ☐   I need more practice. ☐

For more practice, go to MyEnglishLab.   For audio and video, scan the QR code.

Lesson 2

Grammar

Use expressions to state conditions

1 Focus on Usage

A **CONSIDER.** Read the highlighted sentences in the blog below. Which clauses are used to express a condition?

B **IDENTIFY.** Read the entire blog. Underline all clauses that express a condition.

> The expressions *as long as, provided (that), if and only if, on the condition (that),* introduce the event that needs to occur in order for something else to happen. *Even if* and *whether or not* emphasize that something will still be true even if a condition occurs. *Should* can sometimes replace *if,* especially in formal contexts.

Organic waste comes from food and plants. When organic waste decomposes, it produces greenhouse gases. ==As long as we throw organic waste into the trash==, it will end up in a landfill and contribute to more greenhouse gas emissions. ==Should you choose to compost your organic waste, you will help reduce the problem.== Composting is a natural process of recycling leaves and food scraps into a rich soil that provides nutrients to improve plant growth. Many gardeners understand the importance of composting, but whether or not you are a gardener, composting reduces waste and benefits the environment. If you don't need compost for your own garden, you can donate it to a school or community garden. You can compost most of your kitchen scraps provided they come from organic materials such as fruit and vegetables.

2 Focus on Structure

Expressing Condition

	as long as provided (that) if, only if on the condition (that) should	
Your waste will not end up in a landfill		*you compost it.*
You can compost trash	**even if** *you are not a gardener.* **whether or not** *you are a gardener.*	

- The order of the clauses can be reversed. When the conditional clause begins the sentence, the clause is followed by a comma.

    *As long as you compost your organic waste***,** *it will not end up in a landfill.*

A **INVESTIGATE.** Analyze all the examples of conditional sentences. Write *True* or *False.* Correct the false statements.

1. It is possible to omit *that* in the expressions *provided that* and *on the condition that.* _____

2. *Even if* and *only if* have the same meaning. _____

3. *As long as* and *provided that* have the same meaning. _____

4. *If you need help* can be replaced by *You should need help.* _____

5. The conditional clause can go before or after the result clause. _____

124 Unit 7, Lesson 2

Grammar

B **REWRITE.** Rewrite each sentence using the expression shown.

1. Whether we realize it or not, we all emit carbon dioxide through daily activities.

   (*even if*) *Even if we don't realize it, we all emit carbon dioxide through daily activities.*

2. If you need a new recycling bin, call the waste management office.

   (*should*) _____

3. I use detergents on the condition that they are made from natural materials.

   (*provided that*) _____

4. We plug in chargers when it is necessary.

   (*only if*) _____

5. You can open the window only if the AC is turned off.

   (*on the condition that*) _____

6. Even if it is not convenient, she always recycles any useful items.

   (*whether or not*) _____

C **WRITE.** Complete the sentences with your own ideas.

1. Even if I don't have time, _____.

2. I will buy a car provided that _____.

3. Go to this website should _____.

4. You can recycle bottles on the condition that _____.

5. I drive my car only if _____.

Apply what you know

1. **SHARE.** Describe your current environmental practices.

2. **WRITE.** Write a paragraph about an environmental practice you think is important. Use different ways to express conditions and results.

   Cars produce a lot of carbon emissions, so I always ride my bicycle to work even if it is raining. Provided that my destination is less than 10 miles away, I ride my bike every chance I get.

I can use expressions to state conditions. ■   I need more practice. ■

For more practice, go to MyEnglishLab.

Unit 7, Lesson 2   **125**

Lesson 3: Workplace, Life, & Community Skills
Promote responsible waste disposal practices

1 Dispose of Waste Responsibly

A DISCUSS. Do you recycle? What are the recycling rules in your community? Do you agree with those rules? Why or why not?

B PROBLEM SOLVE. What is one way your household could reduce the amount of waste you produce? What suggestions do you have to help your community improve the way waste is disposed of?

2 Consult Resources

Local Recycling Information

Most communities provide residents with options for dealing with waste and unwanted items. Five common options are to recycle, reuse, re-purpose, compost, or throw away. The local community website typically lists drop-off sites, hours, and the kinds of items accepted.

A SCAN. Every fall, the Santos family rakes their yard and cleans out their garage. They want to dispose of the waste they have collected, but they don't know where to take it. They looked online at their community's recycling information.

1. How many sites have Household Hazardous Waste (HHW) collection? _____
2. What do they collect at the Carson Library? _____
3. How many places take medications? _____

Carson Recycling Locations

🔗 http://www.carson.us/residents/recycling-waste/locations

	Location	Hours	Accepted Items
	Carson County Landfill 1182 US Highway 15	Saturday–Sunday, 9 a.m.–4 p.m.	Fill Material – *dirt, rock, sod*
	Carson County Sheriff's Office 711 Distrun Rd.	Monday–Friday, 8 a.m.–5 p.m.	Medication Disposal – *must be in closed containers, personal info will be destroyed*
	Carson Library 998 Minor Dr.	Closed on Holidays	Glass Collection, Paper Shredding – *remove paper clips before drop-off*
	Carson Reuse Center 918 Stalegoat Ln. Suite 320	Hours: Monday–Friday, 8 a.m.–5 p.m.	Items to Re-purpose & Household Hazardous Waste (HHW) – *paints must be solidified with sand or cat litter*

Workplace, Life, & Community Skills

	Coletrip Library 18 6th St. E.	2nd Wednesday of Jan, April, July, and Oct, 1 p.m.–7 p.m.	Electronics, Vehicle Tires – *no rims, limit 5*
	Fire Station #14 316 4th St. E.	4th Wednesdays, Noon–7 p.m.	Medication Disposal – *sharp items must be in closed containers, personal info will be destroyed*
	Fire Station #17 2901 University St.	Wednesday–Friday 8 a.m.–3 p.m.	Household Hazardous Waste (HHW) Collection – *must show proof of residency*
	Woketon Yard Waste Collection Site 1090 French Poppy Dr.	Monday, Wednesday, Friday 9 a.m.–5 p.m., Th closed, Saturday 10 a.m.–2 p.m.	Compost – *no household compost, yard waste only, leaves separated from branches and logs, no tree stumps*

Key to Symbols

natural products	glass	re-purpose	tires
medication	paper	electronics	hazardous waste

B **DEFINE KEY WORDS.** Find the words on the recycling website. Match each word to its definition.

_____ **1.** (v) compost   **a.** unwanted material

_____ **2.** (adj) hazardous   **b.** find a different use for

_____ **3.** (v) re-purpose   **c.** living in a particular location

_____ **4.** (n) residency   **d.** changed from a liquid to a firm object

_____ **5.** (adj) solidified   **e.** use decaying living matter, such as dead leaves, to make fertilizer

_____ **6.** (n) waste   **f.** very dangerous

C **INTERPRET INFOGRAPHICS.** Locate the information on the recycling website.

1. What does the flower symbol represent? Give an example of that type of waste. _____

2. What is collected at Fire Station #17? _____

3. Which location shreds paper? What must be removed? _____

D **GO ONLINE.** Use the Search Terms to find recycling information for your community. Share the site with a partner. When have you used, or could you have used the information provided?

Search Terms: residential recycling website _____ *(name of your community)*

Apply what you know

1. EVALUATE. How easy or hard was it to understand the recycling information on your community's website? What suggestions do you have to make the site better?

2. SHARE. Create a recycling brochure to educate others on the recycling practices in your area.

I can promote responsible waste disposal practices. ■   I need more practice. ■

For more practice, go to MyEnglishLab.

Unit 7, Lesson 3 **127**

Lesson 4 Reading

Describe green jobs

1 Before You Read

A **BRAINSTORM.** Green jobs help protect the environment. What green jobs can you think of?

B **PREVIEW VOCABULARY.**

1. **TOPIC-RELATED WORDS.** These terms are used in the article. Does anyone know what they mean? Use roots and affixes to help you. You can also look for clues in the article.

| renewable | sustainable | resource | recyclables | landfills |

2. **ACADEMIC WORDS.** Discuss the meaning of the **bolded** words in the article. Use context to help you. After reading the article, add any words you learned to your Word Study Log.

C **PREDICT.** Preview the article title, image, and bar graph. What is the purpose of the article? What information do you expect?

2 Read for Gist

A **READ.** What makes each job a green job?

Green Jobs and the People Who Love Them

1   There is a wide range of **diverse** options for living a more eco-friendly life. Some people recycle. Other people buy energy-efficient appliances. And some people do eco-friendly work for a living. This week I interviewed four people with green jobs that support the environment. From generating renewable energy to putting
5   electric cars on the road, these people are making our future more sustainable. Let's take a look at their jobs in more detail.

   Alan López has been a solar panel installer for two years. He installs solar panels on the roofs of houses and buildings. The panels **derive** energy from the sun. They turn that energy into electricity. Before Alan became a solar panel installer, he was a carpenter. He noticed more and
10   more of his customers were asking for solar panels. He realized it was a growing industry. He started working for a contractor specializing in solar energy. Now the company has so many customers it can barely keep up. Alan says he loves his job because the sun is an abundant source of energy. He enjoys helping turn that resource into energy.

   Nada Kabo is a wind turbine technician. She installs, maintains, and repairs wind turbines. Wind turbines convert wind into energy. Nada always wanted to work outdoors. While she was in school, Nada was a ranger at a national park. Since
15   she graduated, Nada has worked for a wind energy company. Nada says her job has unexpected perks. For example, the views from the wind turbines are incredible. Some are as tall as a 20-story building! Nada says she loves her job because she likes helping make clean energy. She thinks the energy industry needs to **integrate** more renewable energy sources into their production plans.

   Abdul Rhal used to be a heating and air-conditioning mechanic. Abdul is now a recycling plant mechanic. He maintains
20   and operates machines in a recycling plant. He says many of the skills required are the same in both jobs. The machines crush recyclables like plastic, paper, and aluminum. His company then ships the materials to manufacturers for reuse. Abdul says he loves his job because he cares about the environment. Americans only recycle 35% of their trash. Abdul enjoys keeping recyclables out of landfills.

128   Unit 7, Lesson 4

Reading

Dan Miller is an electric car technician. He inspects,
25 maintains, and repairs electric cars. Dan was a mechanic for years. Then he got interested in electric and hybrid cars. He got a special certificate to work on electric cars. Now he is a technician at an electric car dealership. Dan loves his job because he feels like he is
30 part of the green movement. Only 2% of the cars in the United States are electric. Experts say electric cars will be more **widespread** soon. As many as 15% of cars could be electric by 2030.

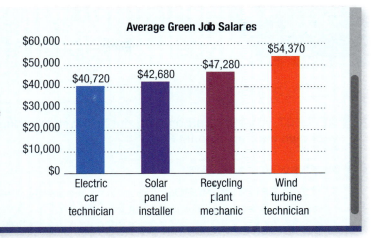

B **IDENTIFY MAIN IDEA.** Choose the main idea of the article. Where is it stated? Lines _____

a. The energy industry needs to use more renewable energy sources.
b. There are many different kinds of green jobs that help protect the environment.
c. Recycling, buying energy-efficient appliances, and working at a green job are all eco-friendly practices.

3 Close Reading

A **RECOGNIZE STRUCTURE.** Create a chart to tell about each person.

Person's Name and Job	Job Person Had Before

B **LOCATE DETAILS.** Are the statements true or false? Write the line numbers of your evidence.

　　　　　　　　　　　　　　　　　　　　　　　T/F　Lines

1. Solar panels derive energy from wind and sun.　____　____
2. Nada is a ranger at a national park.　____　____
3. Americans recycle more than 50% of their trash.　____　____
4. More electric cars will be on the road by 2030.　____　____

C **INTERPRET INFOGRAPHICS.** Use the bar graph to answer the questions.

1. Which person has the job that pays the most? _____
2. How much does a solar panel installer earn? _____
3. Who probably has a higher salary, Alan or Dan? _____

Apply what you know

1. **APPLY.** Research a green job that isn't in the article. What is the job? Why is it a green job?
2. **SHARE.** Would you be interested in a green job? Why or why not?

I can describe green jobs. ■　　　　　　　I need more practice. ■
For more practice, go to MyEnglishLab.　　For audio and video, scan the QR code.

Unit 7, Lesson 4　**129**

Lesson 5

Listening and Speaking
Discuss ways to limit our carbon footprint

1 Before You Listen

A   REFLECT. What is a carbon footprint? How can you limit your own carbon footprint?

B   PREVIEW VOCABULARY.

1. **TOPIC-RELATED WORDS.** These terms are used in the listening. Does anyone know what they mean? For compound words, think about the meaning of each word separately.

| carbon dioxide | hybrid vehicle |
| energy-efficient | ice caps |

2. **ACADEMIC WORDS.** These sentences are from the listening. Discuss the meaning of each **bolded** word. Use context to help you.
   1. The best way to **offset** your carbon footprint is to look for ways to limit the amount of carbon dioxide you produce.
   2. I'd like to highlight four major areas that generate **excess** carbon dioxide.
   3. Look for sustainable ways to **dispose** of waste.
   4. Climate change can cause heat waves that damage crops and livestock, **thereby** limiting food supply.

C   PREDICT. Use the lesson title, vocabulary, and image to make predictions about the podcast. What will its purpose be? What information do you expect?

2 Listen

A   ▶ LISTEN FOR MAIN IDEAS. Listen to the podcast. In the first column, list the four major contributions to your carbon footprint discussed in this podcast. Then compare your answers with a partner.

Contributions	Ways to Reduce Your Carbon Footprint

B   ▶ LISTEN FOR DETAILS. Listen again. Complete the chart with the speaker's suggestions for how to lessen your carbon footprint.

130   Unit 7, Lesson 5

Listening and Speaking

3 Apply Academic Listening Skill

A ▶ **IDENTIFY A CAUSAL CHAIN.** Listen to the speaker's conclusion again. Complete the causal chains.

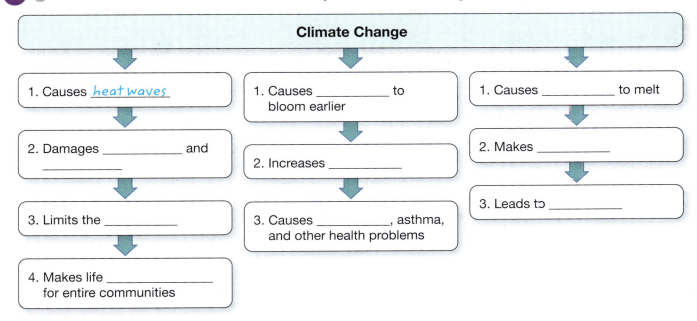

Climate Change

- 1. Causes _heat waves_
- 2. Damages _____ and _____
- 3. Limits the _____
- 4. Makes life _____ for entire communities

- 1. Causes _____ to bloom earlier
- 2. Increases _____
- 3. Causes _____, asthma, and other health problems

- 1. Causes _____ to melt
- 2. Makes _____
- 3. Leads to _____

B **EXPAND VOCABULARY.** Add words to your Word Study Log to show structure and meaning.

4 Real-World Application

A **APPLY.** Create a carbon footprint checklist, using the ideas from the listening. Then add your own ideas. Mark the items you already do and those you plan to do.

B **COLLABORATE.** Present your checklist to a small group. Explain what you already do and what you plan to do and why.

I can discuss ways to limit our carbon footprint. ☐   I need more practice. ☐

For more practice, go to MyEnglishLab.   For audio and video, scan the QR code.

Unit 7, Lesson 5 **131**

Lesson **6**

Grammar

Use past unreal conditionals

1 Focus on Usage

A **CONSIDER.** Read the highlighted sentences from the community newsletter below. Which expressions are used to express regret about an action or event?

Use the past unreal conditional to talk about situations that did *not* happen in the past and to describe what could have happened instead.

B **IDENTIFY.** Read the entire newsletter. Identify each sentence that describes something that did not happen in the past. Underline what did not happen. Circle what could have happened instead.

The recent collapse of our community's fishing industry has been a difficult lesson. Here's the sad part. If we had taken action sooner, the situation could have been avoided. Instead, we allowed commercial fishing companies to use massive nets and hunt for fish in deeper parts of the sea. Some of our fish have declined in population by over 90% in the last decade. If we hadn't allowed overfishing, we would have a healthy fish population today. We could have saved birds and other animals that relied on our fish for food if we had only been more careful. If we had maintained a healthy fish population, we wouldn't have been forced to shut down our fishery. Unfortunately, we had no other choice, and now members of our community are left without jobs. We must learn from our mistakes. Let's support fishing laws and work together to restore our fish population. If our elders had taught us this lesson, we would have protected the most valuable resource in our community, our fish. If we had protected this resource, we could still operate our fishery today.

2 Focus on Structure

Past Unreal Conditional
We _didn't take_ action, so we _can't avoid_ the situation. If we **had taken** action, we **could have avoided** the situation.
No one _taught_ us about overfishing, so we _didn't protect_ our fish. If someone **had taught** us about overfishing, we **would have protected** our fish.
If we **had known** about the problem sooner, **would** we **have made** better decisions?

• Some past unreal conditionals contain mixed tenses. The conditional clause may be in the past, while the result clause is in the present.
    We didn't protect our fish _in the past_, so our fishery isn't open _today_.
    If we **had protected** our resources in the past, our fishery **would be** open today.
• Remember to add a comma after the conditional clause when it comes first.
    If we had known the end result, we would have behaved differently.

132 Unit 7, Lesson 6

Grammar

A **INVESTIGATE.** Analyze all the examples of unreal conditionals. Choose the correct answers.

1. To form the past unreal conditional, use the _____ in the *if* clause.
   a. simple past   **b.** present perfect   **c.** past perfect

2. Use a modal + _____ + past participle in the result clause.
   a. *have*   **b.** *had*   **c.** *has*

3. In a past unreal conditional, you can use _____ to express the idea of *can*.
   a. *is able to*   **b.** *could*   **c.** *might*

B **COMPLETE.** Complete the sentences using the past unreal conditional.

1. (*understand, use*) If we __had understood__ how harmful this fertilizer is for the environment, we __would have used__ something different.

2. (*carpool, be*) I _____ to work at my last job if there _____ other people in my neighborhood who worked at my company.

3. (*tell, choose*) John bought a large SUV. If the salesperson _____ him about the hybrid options, John _____ a hybrid vehicle instead.

4. (*not throw, know*) I _____ my old batteries in the trash if I _____ the metals can get into our groundwater.

C **WRITE.** Write an unreal conditional to describe what would have or could have happened differently.

1. Many animals have lost their habitat because people cut down forests.
   The animals wouldn't have lost their habitat if people hadn't cut down forests.

2. Plastic bags became popular because we didn't know they were bad for the planet.
   _____

3. A chemical oil spill occurred and polluted the water.
   _____

Apply what you know

1. **RESEARCH.** Research one of the following environmental mistakes. Discuss what could have happened if those involved had taken different actions.

   the 2019 Amazon Rainforest wildfires   loss of coral in the Great Barrier Reef
   the Deepwater Horizon oil spill   the Fukushima nuclear power plant disaster

2. **WRITE.** Describe what happened and what could have happened differently. Use past unreal conditionals.
   Deforestation led to more wildfires in Brazil. If government officials had enforced laws against illegal logging activities, they could have prevented some of the fires.

I can use past unreal conditionals. ☐   I need more practice. ☐

For more practice, go to MyEnglishLab.

Unit 7, Lesson 6 **133**

Lesson 7 Reading
Provide examples of the effects of climate change

1 Before You Read

A DISCUSS. What have you learned about climate change? What is causing it?

B PREVIEW VOCABULARY.

1. **TOPIC-RELATED WORDS.** These terms are used in the article. Does anyone know what they mean? Use roots and affixes to help you. You can also look for clues in the article.

| phenomena | emitters | sectors | droughts | coastal |

2. **ACADEMIC WORDS.** Discuss the meaning of the **bolded** words in the article. Use context to help you. After reading the article, add any words you learned to your Word Study Log.

C PREDICT. Preview the article title and image. What is the purpose of the article? What information do you expect?

2 Read for Gist

A READ. Think about the main ideas as you read. Underline any sentences that help you identify main ideas.

How Is Climate Change Affecting the United States?

1   In August 2017, Hurricane Harvey slammed into Texas and Louisiana. More than 100 people were killed. More than 30,000
5 people were **displaced**. They had to leave their homes due to flooding. The storm caused an estimated $125 billion in damages. Just a month later,
10 Hurricane Maria devastated Puerto Rico, Dominica, and the U.S. Virgin Islands. Over 3,000 people died. It cost $91 billion in damages. Both hurricanes were among the deadliest and most expensive storms in U.S. history.

15   Each autumn, several hurricanes hit the United States. But what was different this time was the severity of these storms. The number of severe hurricanes has sharply increased over the past 20 years. This trend of worsening hurricanes is a prime example
20 of how climate change is affecting the United States. Meteorologists say severe storms and other weather phenomena, such as droughts and flooding, will become the **norm** as our planet gets hotter. Human use of fossil fuels contributes to climate change, and the
25 effects, particularly on weather, will be far-reaching.

    Humans make the largest contribution to climate change. Just 150 years ago, humans began burning fossil fuels like
30 oil, coal, and natural gas to generate the power needed to create electricity and run cars. Burning fossil fuels releases carbon dioxide, methane, and
35 nitrous oxide into the atmosphere. Right now, the level of carbon dioxide in our environment is the highest it's been in 400,000 years. These gases are called greenhouse gases. Greenhouse gases trap heat in the
40 atmosphere, causing the planet to heat up. In the United States, the biggest emitters of greenhouse gases are the transportation, energy, and agriculture sectors. Together, those groups are responsible for 60% of carbon dioxide emissions.

45   The effects of climate change, such as severe hurricanes, are just one reality. As record high temperatures become commonplace, we will experience more heat waves. With more heat waves, there will be more droughts. Food and water will be
50 scarce in some areas. Farmers need to plan for how to

134   Unit 7, Lesson 7

Reading

deal with these droughts. Drought-prone cities need to store extra water. Cities need to build shelters to protect people when heat waves occur.

55 Another impact of climate change is flooding. As the Earth heats up, glaciers have begun to melt at the North Pole and South Pole. This melting water is causing sea levels to rise. As a result, many coastal cities in the United States are already experiencing more flooding. For example, 50 years ago, Charleston, 60 South Carolina, flooded four days a year. These days, it floods closer to 40 days a year. By 2045, scientists say Charleston will be flooded 180 days a year, or every other day. Many people will be displaced. They will have to find a new place to live farther from the coast.

65 Cities like Charleston need to prepare for flooding by **constructing** higher roads, building sea walls, and installing pumps. They need to plan for how to take care of people who lose their homes.

This **scenario** might sound scary, but the good news 70 is that we can reduce the impact of climate change. As human contributors to climate change, we can modify our behavior. We can reduce our use of **finite** fossil fuels by adopting renewable energy like wind and solar. We can stop cutting down the forests that clean carbon 75 dioxide from our air. Most importantly, we can talk to our politicians and ask them what their plans are to reduce greenhouse emissions and to prepare for climate change.

B **IDENTIFY MAIN IDEAS.** Choose the main idea of the article and of Paragraphs 2–4. Find the sentences that best support each main idea. Write the line numbers.

Article Main Idea	Lines
a. The United States needs to do more to prepare for climate change. b. Climate change is going to affect the United States in several major ways. c. Climate change is going to cause flooding and severe storms in the United States.	
Paragraph Main Ideas	
2 a. Climate change is going to cause more hurricanes to hit the United States. b. Hurricanes have been getting stronger over the past 20 years. c. Severe storms and other weather phenomena will increase as our planet heats up.	
3 a. Humans are causing climate change by emitting greenhouse gases. b. Carbon dioxide, methane, and nitrous oxide are greenhouse gases. c. Humans began producing greenhouse gases about 150 years ago.	
4 a. Heat waves and droughts are going to become more common in the United States and have significant effects. b. Droughts will cause water to be scarce in some areas. c. Cities need to prepare for droughts and heat waves.	

Unit 7, Lesson 7   **135**

3 Close Reading

A LOCATE DETAILS. Are the statements true or false? Write the line numbers of your evidence.

	T/F	Lines
1. Hurricane Harvey caused $91 billion in damages.	_____	_____
2. The carbon dioxide in the environment is the highest it's been in 600,000 years.	_____	_____
3. Farmers need a plan for how to deal with droughts.	_____	_____
4. Today, Charleston floods four days a year.	_____	_____

B APPLY ACADEMIC READING SKILL.

Academic Reading Skill: Use a graphic organizer to identify components in a causal chain
Remember that in a causal chain, each event leads to, or causes, the next event. A graphic organizer is a helpful way to show the chain of events. The graphic organizer starts with the cause that sets the causal chain in motion and ends with its final result. In this example, *Burning fossil fuels* sets the chain in motion and ends with *climate change* as the final result.

Burning fossil fuels → greenhouse gases → trapped heat in the atmosphere → a warmer planet → climate change

1. Reread Paragraph 4. Complete the causal chain.

Higher temperatures → [ ] → [ ] → [ ]

2. Reread Paragraph 5. Complete the causal chain.

Hotter Earth → [ ] → [ ] → [ ]

3. Reread Paragraph 5 again. What is happening in Charleston? What is the cause that sets the chain in motion? What is the final result?

Cause: _____

Result: _____

C EVALUATE. Which effect of climate change in the United States worries you the most? Explain your answer.

_____

_____

136 Unit 7, Lesson 7

4 Prepare for an Academic Presentation

A FOCUS. You will give a formal presentation to describe an effect of climate change.

B RESEARCH. Find a source that describes one effect of climate change. Use the Note-Taking Template on page 258 to take notes from that source.

C ORGANIZE. Use the Presentation Template on page 259 to organize your information. Use the suggestions below to help you keep your audience's attention when you present.

Presentation Checklist	
	The presentation includes...
Organization:	✓ Stated cause
	✓ Stated results
Support:	✓ Graphic organizer to identify components in a causal chain
Word Choice:	✓ Academic words
	✓ Emphasis signal words
Delivery:	✓ Speech at appropriate volume and rate
	✓ Speech that is clear and easy to understand
	✓ Eye contact
	✓ Poise and effective gestures

Keeping the Audience's Attention Through Poise and Gestures

Good presenters keep the audience's attention with their effective **poise**. This means they look calm and natural. To display poise, keep a good posture with your shoulders back. Look relaxed. Move slowly with purpose and confidence. Let your face mirror your words. For example, keep your face neutral when you are talking about a serious topic. Smile when you say something lighthearted.

Good presenters also use clear, strong **gestures**. For most of your presentation, you should keep your hands by your sides. When you want to make a point, you can use your hands to emphasize what you are saying. Avoid using too many gestures.

Take a video of yourself the next time you practice your presentation. Look at your posture and facial expressions. Do you have poise? Look at your gestures. Are they strong and simple? Do you use too many of them? Take more videos of yourself until you are confident you are using poise and gestures well.

D REVISE AND PRACTICE. Use the Presentation Checklist to assess your presentation and make revisions. Then practice your presentation until you feel confident.

Apply what you know | **Academic Presentation**

1. **PRESENT.** Share your presentation with a partner. Your teacher may also choose you to present to the class.

2. **EVALUATE.** Have your partner evaluate your presentation using the Presentation Checklist.

3. **ACKNOWLEDGE OTHER'S CONTRIBUTIONS.** Remember to let your partner know that you appreciate his or her feedback.
   - *That's a very helpful suggestion.*
   - *You make a good point. Thank you.*

I can provide examples of the effects of climate change. ☐	I need more practice. ☐
For more practice, go to MyEnglishLab.	For audio and video, scan the QR code.

Unit 7, Lesson 7 **137**

Lesson 8

Writing Workshop
Identify components of a valid argument

1 What Do You Notice?

A **COMPARE.** Read the two examples. Which example presents the clearest argument with the most effective evidence?

Example 1:

An increasingly dangerous result of climate change is stronger hurricanes due to warmer sea temperatures. According to the Center for Climate and Energy Solutions, hurricanes in many regions have been increasing in intensity and causing more extensive damage over the past several decades. As the absorption of greenhouse gases from fossil fuels causes sea temperatures to warm, these storms will likely cause even more damage, costing billions of dollars.

Example 2:

Climate change is making weather worse. There are so many more tornadoes, hurricanes, and heat waves than ever before. These weather events are only going to get worse as time goes on. Bad weather costs a lot of money. Everyone needs to stop using fossil fuels because oceans are becoming warmer. Warmer oceans lead to worse weather.

B **ANALYZE.** Underline the writer's main argument in each example. Double underline evidence that effectively supports that argument in the better example.

2 Apply Academic Writing Skill

Academic Writing Skill: Identify components of a valid argument
The purpose of an argument is to persuade someone to take specific action or to accept that a particular point of view is *valid,* or true. A valid argument is made up of three parts:
- **Claim** – the writer's main argument. It is a focused statement that is arguable and includes what the writer wants someone to believe or to do.
- **Key points** – the main reasons why someone should accept that the claim is valid, or true. These reasons, or points, must directly support the claim.
- **Valid evidence** – accurate information that supports each reason or point. Valid evidence may include facts, statistics, examples, statements by experts, studies, and quotations.

In an argument, the claim generally appears in the introduction. The introduction also often includes a description of the issue. Then the argument's main points, each supported by valid evidence, are stated in separate body paragraphs. Finally, the claim is usually restated in the conclusion.

A **IDENTIFY.** Identify each component of the argument as *claim, point,* or *evidence.*

_____ 1. Humans produce 60% of carbon dioxide emissions by burning fossil fuels.

_____ 2. Humans are the main cause of climate change because they create more greenhouse gases.

_____ 3. Burning fossil fuels increases greenhouse gases, such as carbon dioxide.

B **APPLY:** Read the point and evidence. Write a claim that is supported by that point and its evidence.

Claim: _____

Point: Healthy forests absorb greenhouse gases.

Evidence: Each year, forests absorb more than a third of the carbon dioxide that is released from burning fossil fuels.

I can identify components of a valid argument. ☐   I need more practice. ☐

For more practice, go to MyEnglishLab.

138 Unit 7, Lesson 8

Writing

Write an argument that makes a claim about an effect of climate change

Lesson 9

1 ▶ Model for Writing

STUDY THE MODEL. Read the Writing Model on page 260. Analyze that model. Circle the paragraph that describes the causal chain that causes the event. Underline the actions humans can take.

2 ▶ Prepare Your Writing

A ▶ FOCUS. You will write an argument that makes a claim about the effect of climate change that you researched in Lesson 7.

B ▶ RESEARCH. Go online and find another source that describes that effect of climate change. Use the same Note-Taking Template that you used before (page 258) to take notes from your new source.

3 ▶ Write Write an argument that makes a claim about an effect of climate change.

A ▶ ORGANIZE. Use the structure of the Writing-Model Template you completed in Exercise 1 to organize your argument. Follow the tips below to state a clear, concise claim.

State a Clear, Concise Claim

Remember that an effective claim is a focused statement near the beginning of an argument that someone could debate. It is not a personal feeling or opinion. Follow these tips to write an effective claim:

- Choose a claim you can prove and strongly support.
- Include two parts in your claim: your statement of what you believe and why that belief is important.
- Focus on a single argument, though you may make several key points to support it.
- Take a strong stand and avoid claims that begin with "I think," "I believe," or "I feel."
- Research the topic of your claim so that you can include valid evidence to support your claim.

Writing Checklist	
The text includes...	
Structure:	✓ Argument
Organization:	✓ Introduction with claim restated in conclusion
	✓ Body with evidence to support claim
Word Choice:	✓ Academic words
	✓ Emphasis signal words
Writing Skill:	✓ Clearly stated claim
Grammar:	✓ Past unreal conditionals

B ▶ REVISE. Use the Writing Checklist to evaluate your writing and make revisions. Remember to include all three components of a valid argument: claim, point, and evidence.

4 ▶ Share Your Writing

A ▶ COLLABORATE. Share your writing with a partner. Use any feedback to improve your writing.

B ▶ PUBLISH. Create a final document to share with others.

I can write an argument that makes a claim about an effect of climate change. ☐

I need more practice. ☐

For more practice, go to MyEnglishLab.

Unit 7, Lesson 9 **139**

Lesson 10 Workplace Soft Skills
Work effectively with a team

1 Workplace Expectations

A ▶ **CONSIDER.** Listen to the conversation between the manager of a large electrical supply store and the store's owner. What is the manager suggesting?

B **IDENTIFY EXPECTATIONS.** Describe the owner's expectation and the manager's response. What would the manager's performance review state?

1. Owner's expectation: _____
2. Manager's response: _____
3. Performance review: _____

2 Learn from Mistakes

A **DISCUSS.** How could the manager have improved? Suggest specific actions the manager could have said he would take. Share your suggestions with a partner.

B **ROLE-PLAY.** Give the manager a "do over." Role-play the conversation, but this time have the manager meet the owner's expectations.

C ▶ **COMPARE.** Listen to the "do-over" conversation. How is it similar to your role play? How is it different?

Apply what you know

1. **DEFINE.** How would you explain this soft skill to a new employee?
2. **APPLY.** Record an example from your own life in your Soft Skills Log (page 242) of how you have worked effectively with a team.
3. **SHARE.** Share your example.
   - *I worked well with a group at _____ when I _____.*

I can work effectively with a team. ☐

For audio and video, scan the QR code.

I need more practice. ☐

For more practice, go to MyEnglishLab.

The Digital Age

8

PREVIEW
What digital devices do you use? How has your use of digital devices changed over the last ten years? Give examples.

UNIT GOALS

- Identify the pros and cons of the digital age
- Evaluate social media for reliability
- Describe cyberbullying and recommend responses to it
- Describe the dangers of texting and driving
- Discuss the impact of excessive screen time on brain and social development
- Write an argument for or against limiting children's screen time

Workplace Soft Skill: Exercise self-discipline with digital devices

Academic Skills:
- **Listening:** Identify evidence used to support a claim
- **Speaking:** Disagree politely
- **Reading:** Evaluate evidence for relevance and sufficiency
- **Writing:** Use relevant and sufficient evidence to support an argument

Lesson 1 Listening and Speaking
Identify the pros and cons of the digital age

1 Before You Listen

A DISCUSS. What does "digital age" mean? What are some of the pros and cons of living in the digital age?

B PREVIEW VOCABULARY.

1. **TOPIC-RELATED WORDS.** These terms are used in the listening. Does anyone know what they mean? Use roots and affixes to help you.

| distance education | old-school | misinformation |
| interactive | social media | |

2. **ACADEMIC WORDS.** These sentences are from the listening. Discuss the meaning of each **bolded** word. Use context to help you.
   1. With a smartphone, I can **access** information 24/7.
   2. In some **circumstances**, it's simply not appropriate to use your smartphone.
   3. Smartphones have the **potential** to be good or bad.
   4. It depends on how the professor **facilitates** the class.
   5. Interesting **perspective**! I've never really thought about it.

C PREDICT. Use the lesson title, vocabulary, and image to make predictions about the podcast. What will its purpose be? What information do you expect?

2 Listen

A ▶ LISTEN FOR MAIN IDEAS. Listen to the podcast. In the first column, list the topic each speaker discusses and the conclusion **that speaker** reached. Then compare your topics and conclusions with a partner.

Topic and Conclusion	Pros	Cons
Solomon		
Keisha		
Jackson		

B ▶ LISTEN FOR DETAILS. Listen again. For each topic, list at least one pro and one con that was mentioned by any of the speakers.

142 Unit 8, Lesson 1

Listening and Speaking

3 Apply Academic Listening Skill

Academic Listening Skill: Identify evidence used to support a claim
Remember that a claim is a statement that presents an argument. And speakers present evidence to support their claim. For academic conversations, this evidence includes facts, numbers, and information from experts. For less formal conversations, speakers can use their own ideas and experiences as evidence. Speakers often restate their claim in the conclusion. Listening for conclusion words can help you recognize and evaluate the speaker's claim.

Conclusion Signal Words
as a result, therefore, in conclusion, as such, given, for this reason/for these reasons, overall, consequently, all in all, indeed, ultimately

A ▶ IDENTIFY. Listen to part of the podcast again. Which conclusion signal words do the speakers use? Underline those words or phrases in the chart above.

B ▶ IDENTIFY EVIDENCE USED TO SUPPORT A CLAIM. Listen again. List at least one positive personal experience that Keisha or Solomon reported as evidence.

1. Keisha (first speaker) _____
2. Solomon (second speaker) _____

C INTERPRET. What did the student mean when she said they can agree to disagree? What is the purpose of that expression?

D EXPAND VOCABULARY. Add words to your Word Study Log to show structure and meaning.

4 Real-World Application

A SURVEY. Ask your classmates what they consider to be the pros and cons of the digital age. Record their answers in the chart.

Classmate's Name	Pros	Cons

B ANALYZE. Share your survey results with a small group. Compare your class data to the data in the podcast. What overall conclusions do you think can be drawn?

Academic Speaking Skill: Disagree politely
People do not always agree on what conclusion should be drawn from evidence. Therefore, it's important to try to state differences calmly and politely.

- *I understand what you're saying, but _____.*
- *Have you thought about _____?*
- *I think there's another way to look at that.*

I can identify the pros and cons of the digital age. ☐   I need more practice. ☐

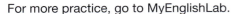

For more practice, go to MyEnglishLab.   For audio and video, scan the QR code.

Unit 8, Lesson 1 **143**

Lesson 2

Grammar
Use the simple future and future continuous to make predictions

1 Focus on Usage

A CONSIDER. Read the highlighted sentences from the blog. Which words make predictions?

> Use the simple future to make predictions about what will occur in the future. Use the future continuous to predict situations or actions that will be in progress at a certain time in the future.

B IDENTIFY. Read the entire blog. Underline all simple future verbs. Circle all future continuous verbs.

Garry Kasparov, who is perhaps the greatest chess player of all time, was defeated in a game of chess in 1997. Who was his opponent? A supercomputer called Deep Blue. At the time, chess was considered the ultimate test for artificial intelligence (AI). But computing power has come a long way since then, and it will continue to improve rapidly in the coming decades. Many computer scientists believe AI will match the intelligence of human beings in the very near future. Some predict that machines are going to be much smarter than humans. These technologists believe we will be using AI to solve the world's most difficult problems. However, not everyone agrees. Some argue that while computers may be better than humans at storing and retrieving information, they won't ever replace human imagination and creativity. What do you think? Will AI ever exceed human intelligence? Is AI going to be taking over the world?

2 Focus on Structure

Simple Future for Predictions
Artificial intelligence **will improve / is going to improve** rapidly in the coming decades.
Machines **will be / are going to be** much smarter in the future.
Computers **won't replace / aren't going to replace** human imagination.
Future Continuous for Predictions
We **will be using / are going to be using** machines to solve the world's problems.
AI **won't be taking over / isn't going to be taking over** the world.
• Time clauses begin with words like *before, after, when, while, once, until,* and *as soon as.* Use the simple present, **not** the simple future, to express the future in a time clause. Use the simple future in the main clause.   *When AI **improves**, it **will transform** the way we live.*

A INVESTIGATE. Analyze all the examples of simple future and future continuous. Choose **all** the correct answers.

1. Use _____ + the base form of a verb to make predictions in the simple future.
   a. *will*　　　　**b.** *is going to*　　　　**c.** *are going to*　　　　**d.** *will be*

2. Use *will* or *am/is/are going to* + _____ to make predictions in the future continuous.
   a. *be* + verb + *-ing*　　**b.** base form of the verb　　**c.** *won't*　　　**d.** the simple present

144 Unit 8, Lesson 2

Grammar

3. Use _____ to make negative statements in the simple future or future continuous.
    a. the simple present   **b.** *won't*   **c.** *isn't*   **d.** *aren't*

4. Use _____ to express the future in time clauses.
    a. the simple future   **b.** the future continuous   **c.** the simple present   **d.** the past

B **COMPLETE.** Look at each prediction. Then complete the next sentence to restate the prediction in a different way. Change the negative verbs to affirmative and the affirmative verbs to negative.

1. In 100 years, we **won't be doing** our own housework. Robots _____*will be doing*_____ all our chores.

2. Cars in the future **will be** much safer. There _____ any more car accidents.

3. Most people **are going to work** from home. They _____ work in office buildings.

4. Drones **will be delivering** our mail. Mail carriers _____ the mail any longer.

5. Some people **aren't going to be living** on Earth. They _____ on Mars.

C **WRITE.** Write future predictions about the given topics.

1. drones

    Drones will deliver all our mail.

2. virtual reality

3. space tourism

4. cars

Apply what you know

1. DISCUSS. Share your predictions about technology use in the future.

2. WRITE. Write a paragraph about one of your predictions.
    I think more and more companies are going to be using virtual reality to train new employees.

I can use the simple future and future continuous to make predictions. ◻   I need more practice. ◻

For more practice, go to MyEnglishLab.

Unit 8, Lesson 2 **145**

Lesson 3 — Workplace, Life, & Community Skills

Evaluate social media for reliability

1 Use Social Media Sites

A DISCUSS. What social media sites have you used? What types of problems can occur on social media? What are some reasons to stay away from social media?

B PROBLEM-SOLVE. How can you be sure that the news you get on social media is reliable? What suggestions do you have to help recognize fake news?

2 Consult Resources

Fact-Checking

The fastest-growing form of communication throughout the world is social media. Social media is not only being used to connect with others, it is also being used as a source of information. The majority of Americans today receive their news online, and nearly half of those people rely on social media. However, researchers have found that fake headlines frequently fool people. Because of this, the need to check how believable an article is has grown. An article is reliable only when the facts are accurate. The information stated in an article isn't necessarily reliable just because it s in print.

Fortunately, there are many different fact-checking sites. Some sites check on the accuracy of an article or a fact. Other sites can tell if an image or a video has been modified. You can usually email the item in question to these sites. You can also search the information already published on the site using keywords.

A SCAN. A man is not sure if an article he read on social media is accurate. He went online to check if **all** Disney films would really be available on TV in 2020. Read his search results.

1. What search terms did he use? _____

2. How many results did he get? _____

3. Which of the results answered his question? What was the answer? _____

FULL FACTS *All the news you need to know*

Disney movies 🔍	**You searched for:** *Disney movies* 22 results

Category: All ▼   From: Date ▼ ✓ All Time / Last Week / Last Month / Last Year

Did Walt Disney's will require his movies to be remade every 10 years?
12/5/2018 – That method is a marketing strategy and was never part of the founder's will.

New Disney park puts parkgoers in a *Star Wars* movie.
3/7/2019 - The article in *Media* states: "You will not think you're in a theme park. You will play the character from the movie."

Deal makes Disney films available for TV viewing.
6/3/2016 – The deal that provides for exclusive rights to Disney films does not include the entire Disney film archive.

Is Winnie the Pooh actually a girl?
6/18/2018 – Winnie the Pooh was inspired by a female bear named Winnifred. The character was written as a boy bear.

Rubber duck navy
Fauxtography: A photograph showing thousands of rubber ducks lost at sea has been manipulated and was not from a Disney film.

Is there an image of a sand dune hidden in *The Lion King*?
2/15/2020 – Hidden images in Disney films do not appear as often as people think.

Workplace, Life, & Community Skills

B **DEFINE KEY WORDS.** Find the words in the information on fact-checking or on the fact-checking site. Match each word to its definition.

_____ **1.** (n) article   **a.** images that show inaccurate events or scenes

_____ **2.** (n) archive   **b.** worthy of being trusted

_____ **3.** (adj) believable   **c.** the ability to be depended on for accuracy and honesty

_____ **4.** (n) reliability   **d.** published text or document

_____ **5.** (n) "fauxtography"   **e.** place where records or documents are kept

C **INTERPRET.** Locate information on the fact-checking site.

1. What fact did the man learn? _____

2. What time frame did he use to narrow the search results? _____

3. Which of the results says that a posted image had been altered? _____

4. What additional search term could he have added to get results that more closely matched his question?

_____

D **CONSIDER.** Why do you think people post false information? What can they gain by spreading inaccurate stories?

E **GO ONLINE.** Use the Search Terms to find a fact-checking site. Share your site with a partner. How is the site you found similar to or different from your partner's site?

Search **Terms:** fact-check

Apply what you know

1. **APPLY.** Find a news article on social media and use a fact-checking site to evaluate its reliability.

2. **SHARE.** Discuss the results of your evaluation with a partner.

- _The article says _____. I think this information is/isn't reliable because _____._
- _According to the article, _____. I fact checked those results, and they are/aren't reliable._

I can evaluate social media sources for reliability. ☐   I need more practice. ☐

For more practice, go to MyEnglishLab.

Unit 8, Lesson 3 **147**

Lesson 4 Reading
Describe cyberbullying and recommend responses to it

1 Before You Read

A **DISCUSS.** What does the term *cyberbullying* mean? Have you or anyone you know ever been cyberbullied? Describe what happened.

B **PREVIEW VOCABULARY.**

1. **TOPIC-RELATED WORDS.** These terms are used in the article. Does anyone know what they mean? Use roots and affixes to help you. You can also look for clues in the article.

| cruel | threatening | rumors | harass | privacy |

2. **ACADEMIC WORDS.** Discuss the meaning of the **bolded** words in the article. Use context to help you. After reading the article, add any words you learned to your Word Study Log.

C **PREDICT.** Preview the article title and image. What is the purpose of the article? What information do you expect?

2 Read for Gist

A **READ.** How does the author define cyberbullying?

Parenting Today
What every parent needs to know

Home ⌄   Featured Articles ⌄   News ⌄   Tips ⌄

What Is Cyberbullying? How Should We Respond to It?

1   In 2006, a young teenage girl named Megan Meier opened an account on the social media website MySpace. She began to receive messages from a mysterious boy named Josh. He said that he had just moved to her town and was homeschooled. Megan was lonely and unpopular. She didn't have many
5   friends at school. She was eager to befriend Josh. They began writing messages to one another. What Megan didn't know was that Josh wasn't real. Megan's next-door neighbors had created Josh's fake account to make fun of her and bully her.

A few months after he first wrote to Megan, Josh's messages became <u>cruel</u>. He told her that she was a bad person. He
10   said the world would be a better place without her. Megan was **devastated**. On October 17, just three weeks before her 14th birthday, Megan committed suicide.

Megan's parents were shocked when they discovered that their neighbors were the people who had been bullying their daughter. They founded the Megan Meier Foundation to honor their daughter's memory. The foundation provides cyberbullying trainings and resources for people across the country.

15   Cyberbullying is defined as any of the following:
   • sending cruel or <u>threatening</u> messages to another person
   • spreading **inaccurate** or false <u>rumors</u> about a person online
   • posting sensitive or private information about a person to hurt or embarrass him or her
   • pretending to be someone else in order to <u>harass</u> a person

20   The statistics on cyberbullying are shocking. One in four teenagers say they have been cyberbullied. Approximately 90% of teenagers say cyberbullying is a major problem in schools. Teenagers who have been cyberbullied are twice as likely to commit suicide. Surprisingly, the problem is not limited to children and teenagers. Nearly half of adults say they have been harassed on social media.

148   Unit 8, Lesson 4

Reading

So, what can we do about cyberbullying? Experts recommend that the first step for children, teenagers, and adults alike
25 is to protect their <u>privacy</u> online. One easy way to do this is to turn on your privacy settings on social media sites. Also, keep your email address and phone number private. Use passwords that are hard to guess.

Parents should keep an eye out for signs their child is being cyberbullied. For example,
- has a sudden fear of using the phone or computer;
- is secretive about his or her computer use;
- acts nervous when receiving text messages;
- becomes withdrawn or depressed.

30 If parents find out their child is being cyberbullied, they should **react** calmly. Parents should explain to the child that it is not his or her fault. Bullied children should know they didn't do anything wrong.

Regardless of whether the person who is cyberbullied is a child, teenager, or adult, the person should follow these steps:
1. Stop engaging with the bully immediately. The bully is often looking for a reaction.
2. Block or ban the bully on social media.
35 3. Take a screenshot and print out or download the **evidence** of cyberbullying before the bully can delete it.
4. Report the cyberbullying to the moderators of the website where it happened.

Many schools and workplaces **enforce** anti-bullying policies. If you have evidence of cyberbullying, take it to your child's school or to your workplace for guidance on how to deal with it. While we can't end cyberbullying entirely, we can honor the memory of people like Megan Meier. We can increase our awareness of how common cyberbullying is
40 and take steps to protect ourselves and our family members from it.

B **IDENTIFY MAIN IDEA.** What is the main idea of the article?

Cyberbullying _____.

3 Close Reading

A **RECOGNIZE STRUCTURE.** Read each suggested response. Where is it stated? Write the line numbers.

Lines	Suggested Response to Cyberbullying	Details
	Safeguard online privacy.	
	Watch for signs a child is being cyberbullied.	
	People who are cyberbullied should take specific actions.	

B **LOCATE DETAILS.** Provide at least one detail about each suggested response.

C **ANALYZE.** Describe at least three things that have contributed to the increase in cyberbullying.

Apply what you know

1. **APPLY.** Describe an occurrence of cyberbullying. How did you or would you handle the situation?

2. **SHARE.** Share the experience and suggested response.
   - *I knew someone who was being cyberbullied at _____. I recommended that the person _____.*
   - *I don't know anyone who has been cyberbullied, but if I did, I would tell him or her to _____.*

I can describe cyberbullying and recommend responses to it. ☐   I need more practice. ☐

For more practice, go to MyEnglishLab.   For audio and video, scan the QR code.

Unit 8, Lesson 4 **149**

Lesson 5 Listening and Speaking
Describe the dangers of texting and driving

1 Before You Listen

A REFLECT. How common is texting and driving? What are some possible consequences of texting while driving?

B PREVIEW VOCABULARY.

1. **TOPIC-RELATED WORDS.** These terms are used in the listening. Does anyone know what they mean? Use roots and affixes to help you.

distraction	navigation system	diverts attention	tragedy

2. **ACADEMIC WORDS.** These sentences are from the listening. Discuss the meaning of each **bolded** word. Use context to help you.
   1. I know it was wrong. There's no **justification**.
   2. I was reading a short text, just one **brief** text.
   3. Any distraction can **pose** serious dangers for drivers.
   4. Anything that diverts your attention away from the **task** of driving, even for a second, is a dangerous distraction.
   5. Please **refrain** from texting and driving.

C PREDICT. Use the lesson title, vocabulary, and images to make predictions about the listening. What will its purpose be?

150 Unit 8, Lesson 5

Listening and Speaking

2 Listen

A ▶ **LISTEN FOR MAIN IDEAS.** Listen to the public service announcement. What did the first two speakers say they had done? What is the purpose of the announcement?

_____

B ▶ **LISTEN FOR DETAILS.** Listen again. List other causes of distracted driving besides texting.

_____

3 Apply Academic Listening Skill

A ▶ **IDENTIFY EVIDENCE USED TO SUPPORT A CLAIM.** Listen to part of the public service announcement again. List one statistic reported as evidence for each claim.

1. Distracted driving is dangerous but common. _____
2. Distracted driving is especially dangerous for teens. _____
3. Texting is possibly the most dangerous distraction. _____

B **EXPAND VOCABULARY.** Add words to your Word Study Log to show structure and meaning.

4 Real-World Application

A **CONSIDER.** What would you say to someone who texts and drives?

B **COLLABORATE.** Work with a small group to create an ad to convince others not to text and drive. Use supporting evidence such as facts and statistics to support your claim.

I can describe the dangers of texting and driving. ☐   I need more practice. ☐

For more practice, go to MyEnglishLab.   For audio and video, scan the QR code.

Unit 8, Lesson 5 **151**

Lesson 6 Grammar

Use the simple past, past continuous, and past perfect

1 Focus on Usage

A **CONSIDER.** Read the highlighted sentences from the company memo. Why does the writer shift from the simple past to the past continuous and past perfect?

> The simple past indicates an action that began and ended at a definite time in the past. The past continuous indicates an action was in progress when another action occurred in the past. The past perfect indicates an action occurred before another action in the past.

B **IDENTIFY.** Read the entire memo. Underline all simple past verbs. Double underline all past continuous verbs. Circle all past perfect verbs.

Dear team,

Last month we adopted virtual reality (VR) tools to train new employees. We had spent months researching this new technology. VR allows us to create safe environments for trainees to learn from their mistakes without taking risks. We are excited to offer these opportunities to our workers. However, it comes with some risks. Last week, while an employee was training with VR, she tripped and injured her ankle. Two other employees reported that they got headaches and felt dizzy when they were using the new technology. We had not considered these side effects when we adopted the new technology, but we want to assure our employees that we are investigating these incidents. We had not planned on these unfortunate results when we approved the new methods.

Best, John

2 Focus on Structure

Simple Past
Last month, we **adopted** virtual reality tools to train new employees.
I **didn't feel** dizzy when I **tried** the new technology.
Past Continuous
We **were taking** notes while the trainer **was explaining** the new VR tools.
While she **was training**, she fell.
Past Perfect
I **had heard** about VR before I worked here.
We **had not considered** the side effects when we adopted the technology.

- Use the simple past with the past continuous to show that an action interrupted another action. The action being interrupted is in the past continuous. The interruption is in the simple past.
- Use the simple past with the past perfect to show an action occurred before another action in the past. The first action is in the past perfect. The second action is in the simple past.
- When you use *before* or *after* to clarify the order of two events in the past, you can also just use the simple past for both verbs.

  I **had heard** about VR before I worked here. **or** I heard about VR before I worked here.

152 Unit 8, Lesson 6

Grammar

A **INVESTIGATE.** Analyze all the uses of verbs. Complete the sentences with *simple past, past continuous,* or *past perfect.*

1. Use *had* + past participle to form the _____.

2. For _____ verbs, add *-ed* to the verb or use the irregular form. Use *didn't* + the base form for negative statements.

3. Use *was* or *were* + verb + *-ing* to form the _____.

4. Use the _____ to show an action occurred before another action.

B **DECIDE.** Read the sentences. Check the action that occurred first.

1. Some of the new technology failed as soon as we had purchased it.
   ☐ Some of the technology failed.
   ☑ We purchased it.

2. Alex was entering an address in his GPS when he ran a red light.
   ☐ He entered an address.
   ☐ He ran a red light.

3. Khalid began having vision problems after he had upgraded to a larger computer monitor.
   ☐ He began having vision problems.
   ☐ He upgraded his monitor.

4. Cindy's phone crashed when she installed a new app.
   ☐ Her phone crashed.
   ☐ She installed a new app.

C **WRITE.** Combine the sentences by using time clauses starting with *while, before,* or *after.* Use simple past, past continuous, or past perfect to show which action occurred first or was in progress.

1. John used a payment app on his smartphone. During that time, his identity was stolen.
   While John was using a payment app on his smartphone, his identity was stolen.

2. First, I didn't think about privacy concerns. Second, I bought a smart speaker.
   _____

3. First, Chris bought a new game console. Then he became addicted to video games.
   _____

4. The hospital upgraded its server. During that time, it lost some records.
   _____

Apply what you know

1. **REFLECT.** Describe a past experience using technology that produced an unexpected result.

2. **WRITE.** Write about an experience using technology that resulted in an unexpected result. Use the simple past, past continuous, or past perfect.
   I bought a smartwatch because I didn't like carrying my phone all the time. I had never been interested in fitness trackers, but now that I have a smartwatch, I use the fitness tracker all the time. I began to exercise more, and I lost a lot of weight.

I can use the simple past, past continuous, and past perfect. ☐   I need more practice. ☐

For more practice, go to MyEnglishLab.

Unit 8, Lesson 6   **153**

Lesson 7 Reading
Discuss the impact of excessive screen time on brain and social development

1 Before You Read

A DISCUSS. How many hours a day do you watch TV or use digital devices like a laptop, smartphone, or tablet? How does that amount of time compare to people you know, both older and younger?

B PREVIEW VOCABULARY.

1. **TOPIC-RELATED WORDS.** These terms are used in the article. Does anyone know what they mean? Use roots and affixes to help you. You can also look for clues in the article.

| milestones | motor skills | neural | cortex | predictors | downtime |

2. **ACADEMIC WORDS.** Discuss the meaning of the **bolded** words in the article. Use context to help you. After reading the article, add any words you learned to your Word Study Log.

C PREDICT. Preview the article title, image, and infographic. What is the purpose of the article? What information do you expect?

2 Read for Gist

A READ. Think about the main ideas as you read. Underline any sentences that help you identify main ideas.

Parenting 101 Your guide to raising a happy family

Home ⌄   Family Topics ⌄   Tips ⌄   Tools ⌄

How Screen Time Affects Children's Brains and Behavior
March 25, 2020

1 Think about what you did in your childhood. Now think about how much time kids spend in front of screens today. Did you know the average teenager checks his or her phone 150 times a day? And spends nine hours a day online? Even young children ages two to five typically spend three hours a day
5 in front of screens. Too much screen time has a profound impact on children's brains and behavior. As a society, we need to help children have a more balanced relationship with **technology**.

Sheri Madigan, a researcher at the University of Calgary, is a leading expert on how screen time impacts children. Madigan has studied thousands of families to determine the relationship between
10 screen time and development. In 2016, she began following 2,441 families with children ages two to five. She followed them for three years. She tracked how much time
15 the children spent on digital devices each day. She also asked the parents questions about their children's development.

Madigan **published** her findings in
20 2019. They were disturbing. She found that children who spent more than two hours in front of a screen a

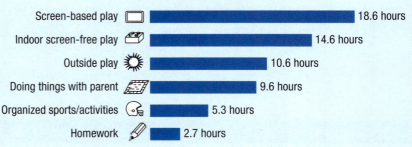

U.S. Children's Screen Time
Average hours per week

- Screen-based play — 18.6 hours
- Indoor screen-free play — 14.6 hours
- Outside play — 10.6 hours
- Doing things with parent — 9.6 hours
- Organized sports/activities — 5.3 hours
- Homework — 2.7 hours

154 Unit 8, Lesson 7

Reading

day weren't meeting major <u>milestones</u>. Their communication, problem-solving, and language skills were lagging. Many of them also had delayed <u>motor skills</u>. They weren't outside learning to ride a bike or throw a ball. They were inside
25 playing on their devices instead.

Young children need constant stimulation to develop their brains. The more children **interact** with others, the more their brains build new <u>neural</u> connections. In 2016, the National Institutes of Health started studying how screen use affects children's brains. So far, researchers have scanned the brains of thousands of nine- and ten-year-olds. They have found that children who spend more than seven hours on screens a day have a thinner <u>cortex</u>. One **theory** is that their
30 cortex is thin because they don't have as many diverse experiences as other children do.

Another growing concern is how screen use impacts children's social lives. A 2016 National Survey of Children's Health studied children who spend seven hours or more a day in front of screens. The survey found those children are twice as likely to be depressed or anxious. They struggle to make friends. They don't develop emotional intelligence because they spend a lot of time alone. Unfortunately, this can create a self-**reinforcing** cycle. Children who feel isolated or
35 anxious may want to spend even more time alone on their devices.

Fortunately, research has shown that reducing screen time can have an immediate effect on feelings of isolation. In 2018, researchers asked a group of students at the University of Pennsylvania to cut back their screen time. The students' screen time was limited to 30 minutes or less a day. Within just a few weeks, the students reported feeling less lonely and depressed.

40 Parents who wonder how much screen time to give their children should take note of a surprising fact. One of the best <u>predictors</u> of a how much time a child spends in front of screens is how much time their parents do. Experts suggest families eat regular screen-free meals together. Parents can plan screen-free group activities during <u>downtime</u> after school and on weekends.

If you are a parent, try following some of those suggestions this week and see what works. Plan activities that get you
45 and your kids offline and out into the real world.

About the author: Linda Gold is a neuroscientist at Mountainside Hospital. She is the author of the book *How Technology Has Changed Our Lives*.

B **IDENTIFY MAIN IDEAS.** Choose the main idea of the article and of Paragraphs 2–4. Find the sentences that best support each main idea. Write the line numbers.

Article Main Idea	Lines
a. How parents' screen time impacts their children	
b. How screen time affects children's brains and behavior	
c. How parents can monitor their children's screen time	
Paragraph Main Ideas	

		Lines
2	a. Madigan studied how screen time impacts children's brains and bodies.	
	b. Madigan tracked 2,441 families with young children.	
	c. Parents answered questions about their children's development.	
3	a. Too much screen time impacted children's gross motor skills.	
	b. Too much screen time slowed children's communication skills.	
	c. Too much screen time delayed children's developmental targets.	
4	a. Children with seven hours or more of screen time had a thinner cortex.	
	b. Children need plenty of diverse experiences to develop their brains.	
	c. The National Institutes of Health researchers also studied children's development.	

3 ▶ Close Reading

A **LOCATE DETAILS.** Are the statements true or false? Write the line numbers of your evidence.

                                                                                T/F   Lines

1. Sheri Madigan's study showed too much screen time can delay a
   child's development.   _____   _____

2. Children who spend more than two hours a day in front of screens have a thinner
   cortex than children who don't.   _____   _____

3. Teenagers who spend a lot of time on their devices are more likely to be anxious
   and depressed.   _____   _____

4. University of Pennsylvania students reported being lonelier after increasing their
   screen time.   _____   _____

B **APPLY ACADEMIC READING SKILL.**

> **Academic Reading Skill: Evaluate evidence for relevance and sufficiency**
> Remember that valid evidence includes facts, numbers, and information from experts. Strong
> evidence is both **relevant** and **sufficient**. Evidence is relevant when it connects to the topic and
> supports the author's points. It is sufficient when there is enough strong evidence to support the
> author's points. Use these criteria to evaluate the strength of the evidence presented in a text:
>
> - The evidence is relevant to the topic.
> - The evidence clarifies, describes, or gives examples to support the author's points.
> - There is enough evidence, at least two or three details, to support each point.

1. Read the article again. Circle all the facts that state evidence using specific numbers. (Remember to
   also look for numbers spelled out as words.)

   Did you know the average teenager checks his or her phone 150 times a day?

2. Reread Paragraph 3. What evidence to support the author's point is presented? How is that evidence
   relevant to the topic?

   _____

   _____

3. Reread Paragraph 4. What evidence to support the author's point is presented? In what way is that
   evidence strong and sufficient?

   _____

   _____

4. Describe in your own words how screen time can impact a child's social skills.

   _____

   _____

C **INTERPRET INFOGRAPHICS.** Look at the bar graph.

1. On which activity do children spend the most time? The least time? _____

2. Why was this infographic included in the article? _____

   _____

156 Unit 8, Lesson 7

4 Prepare for an Academic Conversation

A **GO ONLINE.** Read about *Evaluating the Reliability of a Source.* Then try it out in **YOUR TURN**.

✓ Search	✓ Choose Sources	✓ Evaluate Sources

Evaluating the Reliability of a Source
To evaluate the reliability of a source, ask these questions:

1. *What is the source?* Common sources are books, newspapers, websites, magazines, radio shows, and podcasts. Sources can be in print or online.
2. *When was the source published?* More recent publications may be more relevant.
3. *What evidence does the author use to make his or her point?* Make sure it is relevant and objective.
4. *Who is the author?* A reliable author is an expert on the subject or well-known for reporting on the topic.

YOUR TURN...
Now try evaluating the reliability of a source. Search for "screen time for children." Open the top result and evaluate its reliability.

1. Where and when was the source published? _____
2. Would you consider the author an expert? Why or why not? _____

_____

B **CHOOSE A SOURCE.** Find a reliable source that gives advice on screen time for children.

C **TAKE NOTES.** Use the Note-Taking Template on page 261 to take notes from the source you chose.

Apply what you know — Academic Conversation

1. **REPORT.** Describe the advice on screen time to a small group. Remember to explain the evidence that supports the author's point. Talk about how you know the source is reliable.

2. **DISAGREE POLITELY.** Ask your listeners to state their own opinions on screen time. Remember to encourage people to discuss their differing views politely.
   - *I think there may be another way to look at that.*
   - *I understand what you're saying but _____.*

I can discuss the impact of excessive screen time on brain and social development. ☐

I need more practice. ☐

For more practice, go to MyEnglishLab.

For audio and video, scan the QR code.

Unit 8, Lesson 7   157

Lesson 8

Writing Workshop
Support an argument with relevant and sufficient evidence

1 What Do You Notice?

A COMPARE. Read the two examples. Which example provides evidence that supports the author's claim?

Example 1:

Fortunately, research has shown that reducing screen time can have an immediate effect. In 2018, researchers asked a group of students at the University of Pennsylvania to cut back their screen time. They limited it to 30 minutes or less a day. Within just a few weeks, the students reported feeling less lonely and depressed.

Example 2:

Fortunately, research has shown that reducing screen time can have an immediate effect. Many students who reduce screen time are probably less lonely and depressed. They should try to limit their screen time to 30 minutes a day and cut down on the games they play online. In all likelihood, they should stay completely off social media apps.

B ANALYZE. Underline the specific evidence provided in the better example. Circle the words in the other example that show the evidence is based on opinions, not on facts.

2 Apply Academic Writing Skill

Academic Writing Skill: Use relevant and sufficient evidence to support an argument
Remember, an effective argument must be supported by relevant and sufficient evidence. In order to do this, the author presents a claim, or statement of the argument, and then provides valid evidence. That evidence must be both relevant and sufficient in order to persuade others to support the claim.

- **Relevant evidence:** The evidence supports the author's claim and does not go off topic. All evidence relates to the claim.
- **Sufficient evidence:** There is enough evidence to support the claim well. More evidence is usually better, as long as it is relevant to the author's claim.

A IDENTIFY. Check the sentence that is relevant to the claim given.

Children younger than 18 months should have little to no screen time.

☐ **a.** Young children develop language and social skills through interacting face-to-face with others.
☐ **b.** Educational videos can help young children learn a variety of skills.

B SELECT. Check the sentence that could be added to the paragraph to provide more sufficient evidence.

Fortunately, research has shown that reducing screen time can have an immediate effect. In 2018, researchers asked a group of students at the University of Pennsylvania to cut back their screen time. They limited it to 30 minutes or less a day. Within just a few weeks, the students reported feeling less lonely and depressed.

☐ **a.** These effects lasted only a few days.
☐ **b.** The students also reported improved relationships with friends and family.

I can support an argument with relevant and sufficient evidence. ☐

I need more practice. ☐

For more practice, go to MyEnglishLab.

158 Unit 8, Lesson 8

Writing

Lesson 9

Write an argument for or against limiting children's screen time

1 ▶ Model for Writing

STUDY THE MODEL. Use the article on children's screen time in Lesson 7 as a model. Analyze the structure of that article by filling in the Writing-Model Template on page 262.

2 ▶ Prepare Your Writing

A **FOCUS.** You will write an argument for or against limiting children's screen time.

B **RESEARCH.** Go online and find another source that gives advice on screen time for children. Use the same Note-Taking Template (page 261) that you used before to take notes from your new source.

3 ▶ Write Write an argument for or against limiting children's screen time.

A **ORGANIZE.** Use the structure of the Writing-Model Template you completed in Exercise 1 to organize your argument. Follow the tips below to incorporate evidence to support your claim.

Incorporating Evidence

Remember, an effective argument incorporates relevant and sufficient evidence to convince the reader that the claim is valid. Use the following sentence starters to introduce evidence to support your claim:

- *One piece of evidence...*
- *One reason that...*
- *This evidence supports the claim because...*
- *This evidence is strong because...*
- *The writer of the article states...*

Writing Checklist	
	The text includes...
Structure:	✓ Argument
Organization:	✓ Introduction with claim
	✓ Body with evidence
	✓ Conclusion
Word Choice:	✓ Academic words
	✓ Conclusion signal words
Writing Skill:	✓ Relevant and sufficient evidence
Grammar:	✓ Future predictions
	✓ Simple past, past continuous, past perfect

B **REVISE.** Use the Writing Checklist to evaluate your writing and make revisions. Remember to include relevant and sufficient evidence to support your argument.

4 ▶ Share Your Writing

A **COLLABORATE.** Share your writing with a partner. Use any feedback to improve your writing.

B **PUBLISH.** Create a final document to share with others.

I can write an argument for or against limiting children's screen time. ☐
I need more practice. ☐

For more practice, go to MyEnglishLab.

Unit 8, Lesson 9 **159**

Lesson

Workplace Soft Skills
Exercise self-discipline with digital devices

1 Workplace Expectations

A ▶ **CONSIDER.** Listen to the conversation between a sales clerk and a customer. What is happening? Why is the customer upset?

B **IDENTIFY EXPECTATIONS.** Describe the customer's expectation and the sales clerk's response. What would the customer write on a complaint card?

1. Customer's expectation: _____
2. Sale's clerk's response: _____
3. Customer's complaint: _____

2 Learn from Mistakes

A **DISCUSS.** How could the sales clerk have improved? Suggest specific things she could have done differently. Share your suggestions with a partner.

B **ROLE-PLAY.** Give the employee a "do over." Role-play the conversation, but this time have the sales clerk meet the customer's expectations.

C ▶ **COMPARE.** Listen to the "do-over" conversation. How is it similar to your role play? How is it different?

Apply what you know

1. **DEFINE.** How would you explain this soft skill to a new employee?

2. **APPLY.** Record an example from your own life in your Soft Skills Log (page 242) of how you have exercised self-discipline with a digital device.

3. **SHARE.** Share your example.
   • I exercised self-discipline with a digital device at _____ when I _____.

| I can exercise self-discipline with digital devices. ☐ | I need more practice. ☐ |

For audio and video, scan the QR code.　　For more practice, go to MyEnglishLab.

160　Unit 8, Lesson 10

Health in the Balance

9

PREVIEW
What form of exercise are these people doing? What forms of exercise have you tried? What other factors besides exercise build good health?

UNIT GOALS

Identify tips for promoting well-being

Identify benefits of preventive healthcare

Describe community practices that support public health

Identify ways to manage mental health

Give a presentation to describe one possible solution to the obesity problem

Write a problem-solution essay about obesity

Workplace Soft Skill: Display a positive attitude

Academic Skills:

- **Listening:** Differentiate between fact and opinion
- **Speaking:** Paraphrase the contributions of the group
- **Reading:** Differentiate between fact and opinion
- **Writing:** Use passive voice to create an academic tone

Lesson 1 Listening and Speaking

Identify tips for promoting well-being

1 Before You Listen

A DISCUSS. How do you define "well-being"? Why is well-being important?

B PREVIEW VOCABULARY.

1. **TOPIC-RELATED WORDS.** These terms are used in the listening. Does anyone know what they mean? Use roots and affixes to help you.

| nutritionist | unprocessed foods |
| cardio and strength training | nutrients |

2. **ACADEMIC WORDS.** These sentences are from the listening. Discuss the meaning of each **bolded** word. Use context to help you.
   1. Most of you are probably **aware** of the importance of well-being.
   2. **Maintaining** a healthy lifestyle will help you be the best, most productive student or employee you can be.
   3. A good gym offers a variety of fitness **equipment**, such as weights and exercise machines.
   4. If everyone ate ten servings of fruits and vegetables every day, approximately 7.8 million **premature** deaths could be prevented.
   5. I can think of lots of simple ways to **modify** your diet.

C PREDICT. Use the lesson title, vocabulary, and image to make predictions about the podcast. What will its purpose be? What information do you expect?

2 Listen

A ▶ LISTEN FOR MAIN IDEAS. Listen to the podcast. List the four main tips for well-being in the first column. Then compare your tips with a partner.

Tips	Suggestion for Practicing That Tip

B ▶ LISTEN FOR DETAILS. Listen again. In the second column, list at least one suggestion to put each tip into practice.

162 Unit 9, Lesson 1

Listening and Speaking

3 Apply Academic Listening Skill

Academic Listening Skill: Differentiate between fact and opinion
A fact can be verified and proven true or false with objective evidence. An opinion expresses a feeling, attitude, belief, or judgment. An opinion may feel true for some people and false for others. Speakers use fact and opinion signal words to indicate whether they are stating facts or opinions. Listening for these words will help you recognize whether an argument is based on a fact or on an opinion

Fact and Opinion Signal Words	
Facts	**Opinions**
the fact is…, in fact, as a matter of fact, experts/ researchers… say/estimate, evidence/research/ statistics/data… proves/shows/indicates	in my opinion, personally, in my experience, my recommendation is…, I… recommend/suggest/agree/ disagree/think/feel/believe

A ▶ **IDENTIFY.** Listen to part of the podcast again. Which fact and opinion signal words does the speaker use? Underline those words or phrases in the chart above.

B ▶ **DIFFERENTIATE BETWEEN FACT AND OPINION.** Listen again. List one fact and one opinion that the nutritionist stated.

1. **Nutritionist fact:** _____

2. **Nutritionist opinion:** _____

C **EXPAND VOCABULARY.** Add words to your Word Study Log to show structure and meaning.

4 Real-World Application

A **EVALUATE.** How is your health and well-being? Rate your well-being based on the tips given in the podcast (5 = excellent; 1 = poor). Discuss your ratings with a group. Then share your own ideas about improving well-being.

1.	Some physical activity per day	5	4	3	2	1
2.	8–10 glasses of water per day	5	4	3	2	1
3.	Grains, protein, and 5 or more fruits/vegetables per day	5	4	3	2	1
4.	8 hours of sleep per night	5	4	3	2	1

B **COLLABORATE.** Summarize your group's ratings into factual statistics about the well-being of the group. Then discuss opinions on how to improve well-being.

Academic Speaking Skill: Paraphrase the contributions of the group
When you are working in a group, many differing facts and opinions will be stated by the members of the group. If the group is trying to reach agreement, occasionally restate the ideas expressed by the group. These paraphrases of the group's contributions will help the members agree.

- *It sounds like we agree that _____.*
- *If I understand correctly, _____.*

I can identify tips for promoting well-being. ☐   I need more practice. ☐

For more practice, go to MyEnglishLab.   For audio and video, scan the QR code.

Unit 9, Lesson 1 **163**

Lesson 2 Grammar

Use the passive voice

1 Focus on Usage

A **CONSIDER.** Read the highlighted sentences in the company newsletter. Who completed the action described in the verbs?

B **IDENTIFY.** Read the entire newsletter. Underline all passive verbs.

> The active voice tells what a person or thing does. The passive voice tells what is done to someone or something. Use passive voice when it is not important or not known who or what is performing the action.

A successful company supports its workers. Because we recognize the importance of our employees' health, we are making some changes to support a healthy lifestyle. <u>Last month, each staff member was given a reusable water bottle, and water coolers were installed in every hallway. The salty and sugary snacks in our vending machines have been replaced with more nutritious options.</u> Next month, we will finally open our company cafeteria. Healthy breakfast and lunch options will be served every day. Finally, we are proud to announce that our gym is now open. Employees are encouraged to take advantage of our free classes and fitness equipment. Tai chi and yoga classes are being taught every morning. A cycling class is offered three nights a week. While we are aware that more improvements are needed, we believe this is a healthy start. We would like to hear from all staff members. What other measures should be introduced?

2 Focus on Structure

Passive Voice	
Simple present	Healthy lunch options **are offered** at the cafeteria.
Present continuous	Several free classes **are being offered** at the gym.
Simple past	Employees **were offered** free nutrition counseling.
Past continuous	Yoga classes **were being offered** last month.
Present perfect	I **have been offered** a job at the gym.
Simple future	More classes **will be offered** next month.
Modals	An aerobics class **should be offered**. A new class **might be offered** soon.

- In a passive sentence, the object of an active sentence becomes the subject.
    Active – The fitness center **is offering** <u>free classes</u>.
    Passive – <u>Free classes</u> **are being offered** at the fitness center.

A **INVESTIGATE.** Analyze all the examples of passive sentences. Choose the correct answers.

1. A passive sentence can take _____ verb tenses.
   a. only simple   b. only present   c. all
2. Look at the form of the _____ to determine the tense of a passive sentence.
   a. verb *be*   b. past participle   c. subject
3. In a passive sentence, the main verb is _____.
   a. verb + *ing*   b. the past participle   c. the base form

Grammar

B **COMPLETE. Read the first sentence. Complete the second sentence with the passive form of the verb. Use the same verb tense or modal as in the first sentence.**

1. Daily activities **affect** our health. Our health _____*is affected*_____ by almost everything we do.

2. Sitting for long hours **reduces** blood flow. Blood flow _____ when we sit at a desk all day.

3. Blue light from computer screens and devices **has impaired** my vision. My vision _____ from using my computer so often.

4. A heavy purse or backpack **will damage** certain muscles. Your shoulder muscles _____ by carrying heavy bags.

5. Drinking coffee late last night **disrupted** my sleep schedule. My sleep _____ by caffeine.

6. Getting enough sleep **may prevent** some physical and mental health issues. A number of health problems _____ by getting a good night's rest.

C **WRITE. Write a passive sentence about how our health is affected by each item.**

1. tobacco products, such as cigarettes and vaping

   Serious health problems are caused by smoking cigarettes.

2. junk food and fast food

   _____

3. walking and other light physical activity

   _____

4. pets, such as cats and dogs

   _____

Apply what you know

1. **SHARE.** Choose one of the items from Exercise 2C. Discuss how you personally have been affected—positively or negatively.

2. **WRITE.** Write a paragraph about how you have been affected. First, discuss the effects on people in general. Then write about your own personal experience. Use passive voice when possible.

   It has been said that people who have pets get sick less often and are less depressed. I personally have experienced the benefits of pet ownership. Whenever I feel tired or stressed out, I am always cheered up when I take my dog for a walk.

I can use the passive voice. ■   I need more practice. ■

For more practice, go to MyEnglishLab.

Unit 9, Lesson 2   **165**

Lesson 3: Workplace, Life, & Community Skills

Identify benefits of preventive healthcare

1 Access Low-Cost Preventive Care

A **REFLECT.** Have you or anyone you know been diagnosed with a disease? Could anything have been done to prevent the disease from developing? Explain your answer.

B **PROBLEM-SOLVE.** People often seek medical care once they have a disease or get injured. What suggestions do you have to help people avoid disease or injury?

2 Consult Resources

Online Preventive Care Resources

Modern medicine is constantly improving. Doctors are getting better at diagnosing and curing diseases. However, many people are taking steps to prevent disease before it occurs. Eating right and getting exercise are both known to help prevent disease. Such steps are part of preventive healthcare. It's also important to get other preventive healthcare, such as screenings and vaccinations.

A **SCAN.** A woman wants to make good choices to prevent health problems, so she looked at an online site for preventive healthcare. Read her search results.

1. What is one preventive care choice she can make for her children? _____
2. What are two types of cancer screenings? _____
3. What five vaccinations are available? _____

166 Unit 9, Lesson 3

Workplace, Life, & Community Skills

B **DEFINE KEY WORDS.** Find the words on the preventive healthcare website. Match each word to its definition.

_____ **1.** (n) immunization

_____ **2.** (adj) eligible

_____ **3.** (n) intervention

_____ **4.** (n) counseling

_____ **5.** (n) vaccination

a. meeting the requirements for joining

b. similar to vaccination; anything to prevent a specific disease

c. typically a shot to protect against a specific disease

d. licensed help in coping with personal problems

e. an action that is meant to help someone

C **INTERPRET.** Locate information on the preventive healthcare website.

1. What type of medical care can help ensure a healthy pregnancy? _____

2. What ages are included in well-baby or well-child visits? _____

3. Would intervention happen before you begin smoking or after you have started? _____

_____

4. What does a colonoscopy screen for? _____

D **GIVE EXAMPLES.** Describe any preventive healthcare steps you have taken.

E **GO ONLINE.** Use the Search Terms to find a preventive healthcare resource. Share your site with a partner. How is your site similar to or different from your partner's?

Search Terms: preventive healthcare services

Apply what you know

1. **APPLY.** Think about preventive healthcare for your family. Which types of screenings should you or your family members be getting and why?

2. **SHARE.** Discuss the benefits of preventive healthcare practices as it relates to your work and your personal life.

- *I feel that preventive practices are especially important in my career because _____.*
- *I want to _____, so preventive care can help me reach that life goal.*

I can identify benefits of preventive healthcare. ■   **I need more practice.** ■

For more practice, go to MyEnglishLab.

Unit 9, Lesson 3 **167**

Lesson 4 Reading
Describe community practices that support public health

1 Before You Read

A IDENTIFY. Look at the community health practices shown. Which do you have in your community? In your native country?

health fair

free flu shots

community garden

B PREVIEW VOCABULARY.

1. TOPIC-RELATED WORDS. These terms are used in the article. Does anyone know what they mean? Use roots and affixes to help you. You can also look for clues in the article.

| obese | diabetes | initiatives | vaccinations | outbreaks |

2. ACADEMIC WORDS. Discuss the meaning of the **bolded** words in the article. Use context to help you. After reading the article, add any words you learned to your Word Study Log.

C PREDICT. Preview the article title and image. What is the purpose of the article? What information do you expect?

2 Read for Gist

A READ. What did Brownsville, Texas, do to make the community healthier?

Brownsville, Texas: A Model for Improving Public Health

1 Ten years ago, the city of Brownsville, Texas, faced a public health crisis. More than half of the population was <u>obese</u>. The rate of <u>diabetes</u> was three times the national average. Many families lived in poverty. Most people did not have health insurance. To solve this problem, the city created a Community
5 Advisory Board. The board's job was to make the city healthier. More than 200 local businesses, politicians, and doctors joined the board. They determined that the two most urgent issues in the community were obesity and diabetes.

To combat obesity, the board promoted **physical** fitness. The board wanted it to be easy for people to lose weight by
10 getting more exercise. Gym and health centers started offering free exercise classes. The exercise classes became very popular. Brownsville even hosted the world's largest free outdoor Zumba® class. More than 1,200 people attended!

Brownsville's focus on physical fitness had a profound **impact** on the community. Companies encouraged their employees to join sports teams. The teams competed against one another in tournaments. Elementary schools created clubs for many different team sports. This emphasis on team sports helped people get healthier and also helped build
15 community spirit.

168 Unit 9, Lesson 4

Reading

Another result of the focus on physical fitness to combat obesity was that running and biking became more popular. Volunteers cleaned up the city's jogging trails so citizens can run through natural surroundings. The city also added bike and pedestrian lanes to the streets. In addition, each month, the city closes some of its streets. Thousands of people now bike, run, and walk throughout the city.

20 The board's next task was to reduce the rate of diabetes. It started by advocating access to healthy food. Brownsville opened a weekly farmers' market. The farmers' market has been an **enormous** success. The city is building a permanent home for the market. People who receive food vouchers can use them at the market.

In addition, the city built four community gardens. The city gave low-income families plots of land in the gardens. Farmers then trained the families to grow vegetables. The families kept some of the vegetables, and they sold the rest at 25 the farmers' market. These two <u>initiatives</u>, the farmers' market and the community gardens, have encouraged people in Brownsville to eat more fruits and vegetables. Eating these healthy foods is a key step in preventing diabetes.

The next step in lowering the rate of diabetes was to improve diabetes education and provide support for people who had diabetes. Health centers offered free or low-cost diabetes tests. Health workers held free classes on how to manage life with diabetes. These community health workers also gave free nutritional counseling.

30 Brownsville has started other initiatives to keep the community healthy. The city hosts regular health fairs. People can get free flu shots and other <u>vaccinations</u> there. Brownsville **communicates** news of any disease <u>outbreaks</u> on TV and the radio. Weight loss programs have also been introduced and supported by the University of Texas. In 2019, 7,500 people participated in the programs.

Brownsville, Texas, has received acclaim for its efforts to build a healthier community. In 2014, the city won the Robert 35 Wood Johnson Foundation Culture of Health prize. Brownsville is proud that other cities have copied its public health initiatives. The board has advice for these cities. It suggests focusing on the people with the least access to health services. One way to do this is by creating programs for low-income families. It also advises cities to utilize their existing resources—for example, adding bike lanes to roads or asking health centers to offer free nutrition counseling.

Which of Brownsville's public health initiatives would you like to see in your community?

B **IDENTIFY MAIN IDEA.** What is the main idea of the article?

Brownsville, Texas, deserves credit _____.

3 ▸ Close Reading

A **RECOGNIZE STRUCTURE AND LOCATE DETAILS.**
Create a chart to list Brownsville's two main goals and the specific steps taken to support each goal.

Combat	Reduce
_____	_____

B **CITE EVIDENCE.** People have become more focused on health. What have you done to improve your health?

Apply what you know

1. **PRIORITZE.** Look online for upcoming public health events in your community. Make a list of 3–4 events. Which ones would you most like to attend?

2. **SHARE.** Share your findings.
   - *I'm interested in _____, so I'd really like to attend the _____.*

I can describe community practices that support public health. ☐   I need more practice. ☐

For more practice, go to MyEnglishLab.   For audio and video, scan the QR code.

Unit 9, Lesson 4 **169**

Lesson 5 Listening and Speaking

Identify ways to manage mental health

1 Before You Listen

A **REFLECT.** Think about mental health.
- How does mental health impact a person's life?
- What factors influence a person's mental health?
- How can people manage their own mental health?

B **PREVIEW VOCABULARY.**

1. **TOPIC-RELATED WORDS.** These terms are used in the listening. Does anyone know what they mean? Use roots and affixes to help you.

| psychologist | therapist | anxiety | mood |

2. **ACADEMIC WORDS.** These sentences are from the listening. Discuss the meaning of each **bolded** word. Use context to help you.
   1. My doctor couldn't identify any **underlying** health issues.
   2. A **distinction** is often made between mental and physical health.
   3. Not all sadness **constitutes depression**. It's perfectly healthy to feel a little sad and upset sometimes.
   4. True depression **persists** for weeks or months.

C **PREDICT.** Use the lesson title, vocabulary, and image to make predictions about the listening. Who will participate in the conversation? What will the purpose of the conversation be?

2 Listen

A ▶ **LISTEN FOR MAIN IDEAS.** Listen to the conversation. Why is Omar visiting a therapist?

_____

B ▶ **LISTEN FOR DETAILS.** Listen again. Complete the therapist's tips for managing stress.

1. Talk to a therapist in order to _____.
2. _____ increases endorphins and helps people manage stress.
3. Spending time with friends _____.
4. _____ also helps you deal with stress and avoid becoming irritable.
5. Taking breaks _____.

170 Unit 9, Lesson 5

Listening and Speaking

3 Apply Academic Listening Skill

A ▶ **DIFFERENTIATE BETWEEN FACT AND OPINION.** Listen to part of the conversation again. Does the therapist present the information as fact or opinion? Check the correct column.

	Fact	Opinion
1. Moderate stress can be a good thing.		
2. Exercise increases the production of endorphins.		
3. Running is the best way to deal with stress.		
4. Quality sleep helps you deal with stress.		

B **EXPAND VOCABULARY.** Add words to your Word Study Log to show structure and meaning.

4 Real-World Application

A **APPLY.** How can mental health impact your work? Make a list of the five most stressful aspects of your life. Consider how those stressors affect your job or your studies.

B **COLLABORATE.** Work with a small group. Share opinions about how mental health issues can impact job performance. Discuss strategies for managing those issues.

I can identify ways to manage mental health. ☐   I need more practice. ☐

For more practice, go to MyEnglishLab.   For audio and video, scan the QR code.

Unit 9, Lesson 5   **171**

Lesson **6**

Grammar
Use active and passive voice strategically

1 Focus on Usage

A **CONSIDER.** Read the highlighted sentences from a nutritionist's blog. Why does the writer use active voice in some sentences and passive voice in others?

Use active sentences most of the time. Active sentences are clearer and more concise than passive sentences. The person or thing that completes the action of the verb is called the agent. Use passive sentences only when the agent is not known or not important or when it is obvious.

B **IDENTIFY.** Read the entire blog. Underline all active verbs. Circle all passive verbs.

The link between our diet and our physical health has been established, but what about our mental health? Is our mental well-being also affected by our dietary choices? How exactly does diet affect our brains? A recent study was conducted through an anonymous online survey. The survey was sent to hundreds of professional and social group networks. Participants who reported eating fast food more than three times a week had higher scores of anxiety and depression. Those who consume a healthy, balanced diet reported higher levels of energy and general contentment. In particular, a Mediterranean diet, which includes lots of fruits, vegetables, whole grains, and fish or poultry, seems to protect against depression. Overall, the results indicate that a healthy diet is important for our brain as well as our body.

2 Focus on Structure

Active	Passive
Experts **recommend** *a balanced diet.*	*A balanced diet* **is recommended**.
Someone **conducted** *a study.*	*A study* **was conducted**.
Does our diet **affect** *our mental health?*	**Is** *our mental health* **affected** *by our diet?*
I **went** *to the health food store.*	

- When the agent is unknown or unimportant, it is not included in a passive sentence.
  A study was conducted. (Who conducted the study? It is unknown.)
- Sometimes passive voice is used to focus on the result of the action instead of the agent. In these sentences, the agent is often included as a *by*-statement after the verb.
  A study was conducted **by university researchers**. (The focus of the sentence is the study, not the researchers.)
- An intransitive verb does not take a direct object. Some common examples of intransitive verbs include *arrive, go, happen*, and *sit*. Intransitive verbs can never be passive.

A **INVESTIGATE.** Analyze all the examples of passive sentences. Write *True* or *False.* Correct the false statements.

1. All active sentences can be changed to passive. _____

2. In an active sentence, the agent is the subject of the sentence. _____

3. The agent is important in passive sentences. _____

4. Passive sentences focus on the result of the action. _____

172 Unit 9, Lesson 6

Grammar

B **COMPLETE.** Complete the sentences with the active or passive form of the verb. Use the simple present tense.

1. *associate*   A poor diet _____ with emotional and mental health issues.

2. *reduce*   Exercise _____ your risk of heart disease.

3. *produce*   Organic food _____ without the use of chemical pesticides and fertilizers.

4. *contain*   Fruits and vegetables _____ many vitamins and nutrients.

5. *have*   Dark chocolate _____ some health benefits.

6. *recommend*   Natural whole foods _____ by nutritionists.

C **REWRITE.** Change the active sentences to passive and the passive sentences to active. Do not change the verb tense. Do not include the agent in the passive sentences. If it is not possible to change the sentences, write *Not possible*.

1. You **should wash** fruits and vegetables before you **eat** them.
   Fruits and vegetables should be washed before they are eaten.

2. Fitness trackers **are used** by many people to track calories.
   _____

3. Doctors **have linked** a vegetarian diet to lower health risks.
   _____

4. I **arrived** a few minutes late for my exercise class.
   _____

5. You **can find** tofu products at the health food store.
   _____

6. Doctors **do not recommend** fasting for more than 24 hours.
   _____

Apply what you know

1. DISCUSS. What do you and your classmates believe about the following topics?

dark chocolate	caffeinated beverages	yoga	intermittent fasting
fitness trackers	organic food	probiotics	meditation

2. RESEARCH. Choose one of the topics above. Go online to find more information and to check what you and your classmates believed.

3. WRITE. Write a paragraph about the topic. Include a few specific facts. Use both active and passive sentences.
   Dark chocolate has been proven to have many health benefits. For example, it may improve brain function and lower the risk of diabetes. Chocolate is packed with antioxidants, which fight various diseases.

I can use active and passive voice strategically. ☐	I need more practice. ☐

For more practice, go to MyEnglishLab.

Unit 9, Lesson 6   **173**

Lesson 7 Reading

Describe the causes of obesity and its impact

1 Before You Read

A **DISCUSS.** Many people in the United States are overweight. Why do you think this is? What can we do about it?

B **PREVIEW VOCABULARY.**

1. **TOPIC-RELATED WORDS.** These terms are used in the article. Does anyone know what they mean? Use roots and affixes to help you. You can also look for clues in the article.

| physical education | vending machines | nutritional | addictive | pedometers |

2. **ACADEMIC WORDS.** Discuss the meaning of the **bolded** words in the article. Use context to help you. After reading the article, add any words you learned to your Word Study Log.

C **PREDICT.** Preview the article title and image. What is the purpose of the article? What information do you expect?

2 Read for Gist

A **READ.** Think about the main ideas as you read. Underline any sentences that help you identify main ideas.

How Should We Handle the Obesity Epidemic?

1   In 2010, Michelle Obama founded the *Let's Move!* campaign to reduce childhood obesity. She believed schools were the best place to tackle obesity. Nearly 50 million children eat at least one meal at school every day. *Let's Move!* encouraged schools to serve more whole grains, fruits, and vegetables.
5   It worked and proved that schools could change children's eating habits. Salad bars were added in thousands of schools. Soda machines and dessert trays were taken away. *Let's Move!* also urged schools to get students moving. At least an hour of physical education was added to the daily schedule at many schools.

As first lady, Michelle Obama focused on obesity because she believed it was a big problem. The numbers show that she
10   is right. In the United States, one in five children is obese. More than one in three adults is obese.

Obesity is defined as a weight that is excessive for a person's gender and height. Obesity contributes to health problems such as diabetes, high blood pressure, and heart disease. These diseases cause millions of premature deaths each year. Obesity is also a very expensive problem. It leads to more than $147 billion in additional healthcare costs each year.

Dr. Dariush Mozaffarian is the dean of the School of Nutrition Science and Policy at Tufts University. He believes the
15   responsibility for healthy eating shouldn't be left up to consumers. He wants doctors to help their patients eat better. Mozaffarian thinks people eat junk food because it is less expensive than healthy food. He also points out that sodas, candy, and fast food are not only cheap, they're everywhere. Nearly every school and office has vending machines. Drugstores and gas stations sell candy at the checkout counter. There are more than 247,000 fast food restaurants in the country.

In contrast, many communities across the country lack grocery stores that sell fruits and vegetables. This **phenomenon**,
20   in which a place lacks healthy food sources, is especially **predominant** in low-income neighborhoods. Dr. Mozaffarian believes "farmacies" may offer a solution to a lack of healthy food sources. The word is a play on *pharmacy*, a place where you buy medicine to make you better or keep you healthy. So a farmacy would be a place where you can buy foods to keep you healthy. It would be a place where people could buy fresh fruits, vegetables, and lean meats.

174   Unit 9, Lesson 7

Reading

25 One example of a farmacy that is becoming more common is farmers' markets. In Dr. Mozaffarian's vision, doctors should encourage their obese patients to buy groceries from "farmacies".

Dr. Mozaffarian also argues that obese patients should attend <u>nutritional</u> counseling. He wants them to learn that sodas, candy, and fast food are <u>addictive</u>. When a person eats fat and sugar, it stimulates the reward centers in the person's brain. This makes the person want to **consume** more fat and more sugar. He also thinks patients should learn how to eat
30 better and make healthy **substitutions**. For, example, three cups of popcorn are **equivalent** to just six potato chips. That kind of knowledge would help obese patients lose weight.

If you want to address obesity in your community, there are many things you can do. Ask your workplace to change the food in the vending machine. Suggest that juices be sold instead of soda and that healthy snacks be offered instead of candy. Find out if your manager is interested in setting up a *Steps to Wellness* contest. You and your co-workers can wear
35 <u>pedometers</u> and see who walks the most steps. Ask your child's school to serve healthy meals and offer physical education programs. Together, we can all work to tackle the obesity epidemic in our country.

B **IDENTIFY MAIN IDEAS.** Choose the main idea of the article and of Paragraphs 2–4. Find the sentences that best support each main idea. Write the line numbers.

Article Main Idea	Lines
a. Dr. Mozaffarian has innovative solutions to the problem of obesity. b. Obesity contributes to several serious diseases. c. Obesity is a major health problem in the United States.	
Paragraph Main Ideas	
2 a. Michelle Obama was the first person to focus on obesity. b. One in five children in the United States is obese. c. Michelle Obama focused on obesity because it is a big problem.	
3 a. Obesity contributes to premature deaths in the United States. b. Obesity causes many diseases and leads to high healthcare costs. c. It is estimated that obesity costs the country $147 billion a year.	
4 a. Dr. Mozaffarian thinks people eat junk food because it is cheap and available everywhere. b. Many schools and offices sell junk food in vending machines. c. Healthy food should be less expensive than unhealthy food.	

Unit 9, Lesson 7 **175**

3 Close Reading

A LOCATE DETAILS. Are the statements true or false? Write the line numbers of your evidence.

	T/F	Lines
1. One in five adults is obese.	_____	_____
2. Obesity leads to $147 billion in healthcare costs each year.	_____	_____
3. There are 427,000 fast food restaurants in the country.	_____	_____
4. Fat and sugar stimulate the reward centers in the brain.	_____	_____

B APPLY ACADEMIC READING SKILL.

Academic Reading Skill: Differentiate between fact and opinion

Remember that a fact refers to something that is true or accurate. Facts are based on evidence that can be checked. To find facts, look for numbers, dates, and observable information. This type of data is often included in facts. You can also look for phrases like *This **proves**..., This **shows**..., He **demonstrated**....*

Remember that an opinion is what a person believes or thinks about something. To find opinions, look for statements that express a single person's view. These statements often include personal examples and judgments. Look for phrases like *She **thinks**..., He **argues**..., They **believe**..., We **should**..., He **wants**....*

1. Read the article again. Look for words that indicate facts. Put a box around them. Look for words that indicate opinions. Circle them.

   Nearly 50 million children eat at least one meal at school every day.

   She believed schools were the best place to tackle obesity.

2. Reread Paragraph 4. Write one fact and one opinion stated in this paragraph.

   Fact: _____

   Opinion: _____

3. Reread Paragraph 5. Write one fact and one opinion stated in this paragraph.

   Fact: _____

   Opinion: _____

4. What do you think we should do to tackle obesity? Use words that indicate an opinion.

   _____

   _____

C SUMMARIZE. What does Dr. Mozaffarian think we should do to fight obesity? List his two key opinions in the first column. What facts does he base those opinions on? List the facts in the second column.

Opinions	Facts
He believes that healthy food should be cheaper and more available.	

176 Unit 9, Lesson 7

4 Prepare for an Academic Presentation

A **FOCUS.** You will give a formal presentation to describe a possible solution to the obesity problem. You will use visuals for support.

B **RESEARCH.** Find a source that describes the obesity problem and suggests solutions. Also look for sources that include helpful visuals. Use the Note-Taking Template on page 263 to take notes from those sources.

C **ORGANIZE.** Use the Presentation Template on page 264 to organize your information. Use the suggestions below to help you use infographics to support your points.

	Presentation Checklist
	The presentation includes...
Organization:	✓ Defined problem
	✓ Stated solution
	✓ Reasons for the solution
Support:	✓ Infographics to support your points
Word Choice:	✓ Academic words
	✓ Fact and opinion signal words
Delivery:	✓ Speech at appropriate volume and rate
	✓ Speech that is clear and easy to understand
	✓ Eye contact
	✓ Poise and effective gestures

Infographics to Support Your Points

Remember, an infographic is a visual representation of information or data. Infographics may include data, percentages, changes in amounts, and comparison of amounts. Infographics present information clearly. They take advantage of our ability to process information with our eyes. When presenting a problem and solution, use infographics to support your points. Suppose you wanted to give a visual to support these facts. You could use either of the two examples below.

- **Infographics to show a problem:**

Junk Food and Obesity

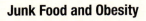

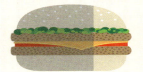
80% OF PEOPLE
eat junk food on a daily basis

ONLY 19% OF PEOPLE
get the recommended amount of physical activity

- **Infographics to show a solution:**

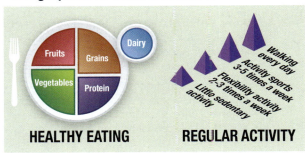
HEALTHY EATING   REGULAR ACTIVITY

D **REVISE AND PRACTICE.** Use the Presentation Checklist to assess your presentation and make revisions. Then practice your presentation until you feel confident.

Apply what you know — Academic Presentation

1. **PRESENT.** Share your presentation with a partner. Your teacher may also choose you to present to the class.
2. **EVALUATE.** Have your partner evaluate your presentation using the Presentation Checklist.
3. **PARAPHRASE OTHER'S CONTRIBUTIONS.** When you get feedback from another person, it often helps to restate the feedback in your own words. These paraphrases will make sure you understand the person's suggestion.

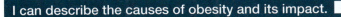

I can describe the causes of obesity and its impact. ☐   I need more practice. ☐

For more practice, go to MyEnglishLab.   For audio and video, scan the QR code.

| Lesson **8** | # Writing Workshop
Evaluate the impact of passive voice on writing tone |

1 ▶ What Do You Notice?

A **COMPARE.** Read the two examples. Which example do you think uses more formal language? Explain your choice.

Example 1:

Obesity affects almost all U.S. adults. We all probably know someone who is obese. The problem of obesity can result in a lot of problems, including death. We all have to learn how to eat healthier and exercise to stop the obesity problem in our country.

Example 2:

According to the Centers for Disease Control and Prevention, 93.3 million U.S. adults are affected by obesity. Examples of obesity can be seen everywhere. The results of obesity are higher medical costs and severe health issues, including death. If the goal is to reduce obesity then increased education about healthy eating and exercise must be provided by communities.

B **ANALYZE.** Look at the more formal example. Underline two specific facts that support the claim that obesity is a major problem. Circle the three examples of passive voice.

2 ▶ Apply Academic Writing Skill

Academic Writing Skill: Use passive voice to create an academic tone
Passive voice creates a more academic tone. An academic tone focuses on facts and not opinions. Passive voice is especially useful for academic writing that provides objective information or supporting evidence, such as the results of a study or the description of a process.

Use passive voice in order to
- focus on the result of an action instead of who or what is performing the action;
- emphasize the most important information by placing it at the beginning of a sentence;
- avoid using personal pronouns like *I, you,* or *we* in academic writing.

A **IDENTIFY.** Check the sentence that uses the passive voice to focus on the results of an action instead of who or what is performing it.

☐ **a.** When a person eats fat and sugar, the fat and sugar stimulate the brain's reward centers.

☐ **b.** When a person eats fat and sugar, the brain's reward centers are stimulated.

B **APPLY.** Rewrite the following sentences in the passive voice to emphasize a different item in the sentence. Make that item the subject of the sentence.

1. Nearly every school and office provides vending machines.

_____

2. Drugstores and gas stations sell candy at the checkout counter.

_____

| I can evaluate the impact of passive voice on writing tone. ☐ | I need more practice. ☐ |

For more practice, go to MyEnglishLab.

178 Unit 9, Lesson 8

Writing

Write a problem-solution essay about obesity in the United States

Lesson **9**

1 Model for Writing

STUDY THE MODEL. Use the article on obesity in Lesson 7 as a model. Analyze the structure of that article by filling in the Writing-Model Template on page 265.

2 Prepare Your Writing

A **FOCUS.** You will write an essay proposing a solution to the obesity problem in the United States.

B **RESEARCH.** Go online and find another source that describes a solution to the obesity problem. Use the same Note-Taking Template (page 263) that you used before to take notes from your new source.

3 Write Write an essay proposing a solution to the obesity problem in the United States.

A **ORGANIZE.** Use the structure of the Writing-Model Template you completed in Exercise 1 to organize your essay. Follow the tips below to use passive voice effectively in your essay.

Using Passive Voice Effectively

Remember to use passive voice when who or what performed an action is not known or not needed: *Obesity has been carefully studied for over 30 years.* The reader will understand that researchers have performed the action, so it's not necessary to focus on them. Also remember to use passive voice when you want to highlight certain information at the beginning of a sentence: *Obesity was determined to be a huge problem by university researchers.* Obesity is the focus, not the university researchers.

Writing Checklist	
	The text includes...
Structure:	✓ Problem-Solution essay
Organization:	✓ Defined problem
	✓ Stated solution
	✓ Facts for support
Word Choice:	✓ Academic words
	✓ Fact and opinion signal words
Writing Skill:	✓ Effective use of passive voice
Grammar:	✓ Strategic use of passive vs. active voice

Passive voice helps in certain situations, but active voice generally uses fewer words. Active voice is usually clearer and more direct. A balance of active and passive voice creates sentence variety and is more interesting to read.

B **REVISE.** Use the Writing Checklist to evaluate your writing and make revisions. Remember to use passive voice to create an academic tone.

4 Share Your Writing

A **COLLABORATE.** Share your writing with a partner. Use any feedback to improve your writing.

B **PUBLISH.** Create a final document to share with others.

I can write a problem-solution essay about obesity in the United States. ■
I need more practice. ■

For more practice, go to MyEnglishLab.

Unit 9, Lesson 9 **179**

Lesson 10 — Workplace Soft Skills
Display a positive attitude

1 Workplace Expectations

A ▶ **CONSIDER.** Listen to the conversations between a bank teller and her customers. What is happening? Why does the bank manager intervene and come over to talk to the teller?

B **IDENTIFY EXPECTATIONS.** Describe the manager's expectation. What would the bank teller's performance review state?

1. Manager's expectation: _____
2. Performance evaluation: _____

2 Learn from Mistakes

A **DISCUSS.** How could the bank teller have improved? Suggest specific things she could have done or said differently. Share your suggestions with a partner.

B **ROLE-PLAY.** Give the bank teller a "do over." Role-play the conversation, but this time have the bank teller meet the manager's expectations.

C ▶ **COMPARE.** Listen to the "do-over" conversation. How is it similar to your role play? How is it different?

Apply what you know

1. **DEFINE.** How would you explain this soft skill to a new employee?

2. **APPLY.** Record an example from your own life in your Soft Skills Log (page 242) of how you have displayed a positive attitude.

3. **SHARE.** Share your example.
   • I displayed a positive attitude at _____ when I _____

I can display a positive attitude. ☐   I need more practice. ☐
For audio and video, scan the QR code.   For more practice, go to MyEnglishLab.

180 Unit 9, Lesson 10

Navigating Healthcare

10

PREVIEW

What is the meaning of *healthcare*? Why does the title use the word *navigating*? Describe any experiences you have had receiving or paying for healthcare services in the United States.

UNIT GOALS

Contact the right specialist for specific health needs
Follow medication instructions
Interpret healthcare plans
Describe the factors that increase the cost of healthcare
Evaluate a strategy for making healthcare accessible
Write an argument to support accessible healthcare

Workplace Soft Skill: Demonstrate professionalism
Academic Skills:
- **Listening:** Evaluate soundness of reasoning
- **Speaking:** Provide direction for the group
- **Reading:** Evaluate the soundness of reasoning in a text
- **Writing:** Revise fragments and run-on sentences

181

Lesson 1

Listening and Speaking
Contact the right specialist for specific health needs

1 Before You Listen

A **DISCUSS.** A doctor who focuses on a particular part of the body or type of illness is called a specialist. How do you find the right doctor or specialist for your health needs?

B **PREVIEW VOCABULARY.**

1. **TOPIC-RELATED WORDS.** These terms are used in the listening. Does anyone know what they mean? Use roots and affixes to help you.

| blurred vision | cancerous |
| tumor | high blood pressure |

2. **ACADEMIC WORDS.** These sentences are from the listening. Discuss the meaning of each **bolded** word. Use context to help you.
   1. My vision is blurry. Actually, my vision has been a little **distorted** for a few days now.
   2. You should go to the optometrist to have your eyes **evaluated**.
   3. I'm **reluctant** to have surgery on my eyes.
   4. Did you fall or hit your head recently, or do anything else that could cause a brain **injury**?
   5. A specialist will most likely want to **confer** with your regular doctor.

C **PREDICT.** Use the lesson title, vocabulary, and image to make predictions about the listening. Who will participate in the conversation? What will the purpose of the conversation be?

2 Listen

A ▶ **LISTEN FOR MAIN IDEAS.** Listen to the conversation. What symptoms has Hana been having? What does her sister ultimately recommend she do about it?

1. Hana's symptoms: _____
2. Her sister's recommendation: _____

B ▶ **LISTEN FOR DETAILS.** Listen again. The speakers mention several types of specialists. Listen carefully and match the specialists with the conditions they treat.

_____ 1. cardiologist   a. conditions that affect the eyes
_____ 2. dermatologist   b. medical conditions that require operations
_____ 3. neurologist   c. problems with skin, hair, or nails
_____ 4. oncologist   d. heart diseases
_____ 5. ophthalmologist or optometrist   e. disorders that affect the brain or nerves
_____ 6. surgeon   f. cancer or pre-cancerous conditions

Listening and Speaking

3 Apply Academic Listening Skill

Academic Listening Skill: Evaluate soundness of reasoning
A **sound argument**, also called a **logical** argument, consists of a list of reasons that leads to a conclusion. The reasons are called **premises**. For the reasoning to be sound, or logical, the premises must be true, be supported by evidence, and lead directly to the **conclusion**.

Speakers use reasoning signal words to introduce their premises and conclusions. Listening for these words will help you follow the speaker's reasoning and evaluate the soundness of the argument.

Reasoning Signal Words	
Premise	**Conclusion**
because, since, for this reason, given that, granted	it follows that, therefore, so, hence, consequently

A ▶ **IDENTIFY.** Listen to part of the conversation again. Which reasoning signal words do the speakers use? Underline those words or phrases in the chart above.

B ▶ **EVALUATE REASONING.** Read the information below about *Logical Fallacies.* Then listen to parts of the conversation again. Which logical fallacy does the speaker make?

1. _____   2. _____   3. _____

Logical Fallacies

Logical fallacies are examples of unsound, or illogical, reasoning. It is easy to make a logical fallacy when you have strong feelings about a topic or if a conclusion seems obvious. Here are three logical fallacies to avoid.

- **Bandwagon** - This argument presents what most people, or a large group of people, think in order to persuade someone to think the same way. *I'm going to try that new diet because everyone says it's great.*

- **Either/or** - This reduces an argument to only two sides or choices. The speaker ignores a wide range of choices in between. *You can either stop eating fatty foods or suffer from heart disease.*

- **Slippery Slope** - This argument assumes if one thing happens, then a series of other things will necessarily happen and lead to a terrible conclusion. *If you feed your kids fast food, they'll never eat vegetables again.*

C **EXPAND VOCABULARY.** Add words to your Word Study Log to show structure and meaning.

4 Real-World Application

A **APPLY.** Choose either of these symptoms: *loss of appetite* **or** *sharp chest pains.* Convince a partner of the cause of that symptom and the specialist you should see.

B **COLLABORATE.** Work in a small group. Role-play your conversation. Have other members of the group evaluate the soundness of your reasoning and check that you avoid any logical fallacies.

Academic Speaking Skill: Provide direction for the group
When working with a group, it's important to help the group move toward a common goal. When others are not sure what to do next, offer suggestions to move the group forward.

- *I believe we should _____ because _____.*   • *How about we _____ so that _____.*

| I can contact the right specialist for specific health needs. ☐ | I need more practice. ☐ |

For more practice, go to MyEnglishLab.   For audio and video, scan the QR code.

Unit 10, Lesson 1 **183**

| Lesson **2** | **Grammar** |

Use embedded *Wh*-questions

1 Focus on Usage

A **CONSIDER.** Read the highlighted sentences in the conversation below. How do the speakers ask for more information without asking the questions directly?

> A direct question asks a question directly. An embedded question asks for information more subtly or politely. Speakers often use embedded questions to indicate uncertainty about a topic.

B **IDENTIFY.** Read the entire conversation. Underline all embedded questions.

Dr. Kim: Hi, Sofie. You look very healthy. I wonder what brings you in today.

Sofie: Right. I'm not sick, but my arm is bothering me, and I don't know which doctor I should see. I was hoping you could refer me to a specialist. Should I see an orthopedist?

Dr. Kim: That depends. Could you tell me what's wrong with your arm?

Sofie: Sure. I have this shooting pain up the side of my arm and around my elbow. It hurts to hold or lift anything. I'm not sure what happened. I didn't fall or anything.

Dr. Kim: Sounds like you have tennis elbow.

Sofie: I don't understand how I could have tennis elbow. I've never played tennis in my life!

Dr. Kim: Plenty of people with tennis elbow have never played tennis. It's a common injury that can result from any repetitive motion in your arm. You're a professional piano player, right?

Sofie: Yes. That's why this condition is so annoying! I'm afraid to ask what the treatment plan will be. Will I need to have surgery?

Dr. Kim: Probably not. First, I'll give you some pain management techniques. We'll see how it goes.

2 Focus on Structure

Wh-questions	
Direct Questions	**Embedded Questions**
What is tennis elbow?	*Could you explain **what tennis elbow is**?*
Who should I call?	*I'm not sure **who/whom I should call**.*
When did the pain first start?	*Do you remember **when the pain first started**?*
How long has this been going on?	*Please tell me **how long this has been going on**.*
Why didn't you call your doctor sooner?	*I wonder **why you didn't call your doctor sooner**.*

- An embedded question can be introduced by a statement and end with a period.
- An embedded question can be part of a longer question and end with a question mark.
- Use statement word order in embedded questions.
   I'm not sure when I first noticed it.
- Notice the word order does **not** change when the *Wh*-word is the subject of the question.
   What happened?   *Can you tell me **what happened**?*

184 Unit 10, Lesson 2

Grammar

A **INVESTIGATE.** Analyze all the examples of *Wh*-questions. Choose the correct answers.

1. Embedded questions use _____ word order.
   - **a.** statement
   - **b.** question
   - **c.** statement or question

2. When an embedded question is inside a longer question, use a(n) _____ at the end of the sentence.
   - **a.** period
   - **b.** question mark
   - **c.** exclamation point

3. When an embedded question is inside a statement, use a _____ at the end of the sentence.
   - **a.** period
   - **b.** question mark
   - **c.** comma

B **REWRITE.** Change the direct questions to embedded questions. Begin each embedded question with *Can you tell me...*

1. When did you start having headaches?
   Can you tell me when you started having headaches?

2. What medications do you take every day?
   _____

3. What can I do to lower my blood pressure?
   _____

4. Where does your arm hurt?
   _____

5. Which specialist did you see?
   _____

6. Why do I need an X-ray?
   _____

C **WRITE.** Complete the sentences to form embedded questions about your own health. End your questions with the correct punctuation (question mark or period).

1. Do you know why _____
2. I wonder what _____
3. Can you tell me when _____
4. I'm not sure how _____
5. I have no idea where _____

Apply what you know

1. **DISCUSS.** Why is it a good idea to prepare a list of questions before you have a medical exam? What kinds of questions should you ask a doctor when you have a regular checkup?

2. **LIST.** Make a list of general questions that patients might ask their doctors during a routine annual exam. Share your list with the class.
   - *Could you tell me what screening tests I need?*
   - *I'd like to know what I should do before my next visit.*

I can use embedded *Wh*-questions. ☐   I need more practice. ☐

For more practice, go to MyEnglishLab.

Unit 10, Lesson 2 **185**

Lesson 3: Workplace, Life, & Community Skills

Follow medication instructions

1 Use Medication

A **RELATE.** What types of medications do you or a family member take? Did a doctor prescribe them or were they over the counter (OTC)? What side effects are likely with those medications?

B **PROBLEM-SOLVE.** What steps do you take to help you use medication correctly?

2 Consult Resources

Interpreting Medication Information

When taking a medication, you need to know the answers to several important questions:

- What is the purpose of the medication?
- Who can take the medication? (adults, children, infants, pregnant women)
- How much and how often should you take the medication? This is called the **dosage**.
- What are the possible side effects of the medication?
- Can you take the medication with other medications, or are there harmful drug interactions?

A **SCAN.** A woman received a new prescription for Percocet. She read the label on her medication bottle carefully. She is already taking Benadryl for her allergies, so she found additional information online to see if using the two drugs together is safe. Read all the information.

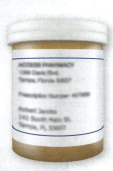

ACCESS PHARMACY
1099 Davis Blvd.
Tampa, Florida 33607

Phone: 888-294-7336
Fax: 888-294-1765

Prescription Number: 457889

Date Filled: 4/16/20
Date Written: 4/14/20

Robert Jacobs
141 South Main St.
Tampa, FL 33607

DOSAGE: 10mg oxycodone/325MG acetaminophen TAB

DOSAGE INSTRUCTIONS: Take 1 to 2 tablets every 8 hours as needed for pain.

PERCOCET

GENERIC FOR: oxycodone/acetaminophen

USES: PERCOCET is indicated for the relief of moderate to moderately severe pain.

WARNINGS: You should avoid or limit the use of alcohol while being treated with these medications. Also avoid activities requiring mental alertness, such as driving or operating hazardous machinery, until you know how the medications affect you. It is important to tell your doctor about all other medications you use, including vitamins and herbs. Administration of PERCOCET (Oxycodone and Acetaminophen Tablets, USP) tablets should be closely monitored for potentially serious adverse reactions and complications.

SIDE EFFECTS: Serious adverse reactions that may be associated with PERCOCET tablet use include respiratory depression, apnea, respiratory arrest, circulatory depression, hypotension, and shock.

Dr. Campos, Eric

QUANTITY: 100
DRUG EXPIRES: 09/23

Refills: None

Drug Interaction Report
This report displays the drug interactions for the following two drugs:
~Percocet (acetaminophen/oxycodone)
~Benadryl Allergy (diphenhydramine)

Level of Concern: Moderate

Interaction Effects: Using diphenhydramine together with oxycodone may increase side effects such as dizziness, drowsiness, confusion, and difficulty concentrating. Some people, especially the elderly, may also experience impairment in thinking, judgment, and motor coordination. You should avoid or limit the use of alcohol while being treated with these two medications.

Workplace, Life, & Community Skills

1. How many tablets can she take every eight hours? _____

2. How many tablets are in a bottle? _____

3. List three things to avoid while taking Percocet. _____

4. What is the level of concern for taking Percocet and Benadryl together? _____

B **DEFINE KEY WORDS. Find the words on the medication label or the drug interaction report. Match each word to its definition.**

_____ 1. (n) interaction effects

_____ 2. (n) prescription

_____ 3. (adj) generic

_____ 4. (n) side effects

_____ 5. (n) refill

a. additional medication given after prescription is used up

b. what can happen if two medicines are taken together

c. common undesirable results

d. not of a specific brand

e. instruction written by a doctor for medicine or treatment

C **INTERPRET. Locate information on the medication label or the drug interaction report.**

1. If this woman begins to take a daily multivitamin, what does she need to do? _____

2. List three side effects of taking Percocet. _____

3. The woman followed the dosage instructions, but she is still in pain and has no more tablets. What will she need to do? Why? _____

D **CONCLUDE.**

1. Why do drug companies state the possible side effects in such detail? Give two reasons.

2. Labels often mention specific concerns for children, pregnant women, and the elderly. What other groups of people might be mentioned in a warning?

E **GO ONLINE. Use the Search Terms to find information about a particular medication. What types of important information are given online? Share at least two examples with a partner.**

Search Terms: medication information _____ *(name of medication)*

Apply what you know

1. **APPLY.** Continue to research the medication you searched for in Exercise 2E. What is it used for?

2. **SHARE.** Describe the common uses of that medication.
   - *The most common use of _____ is _____. It is also used for _____.*
   - *According to the medication information, _____. I also found that _____.*

I can follow medication instructions. ☐   I need more practice. ☐

For more practice, go to MyEnglishLab.

Unit 10, Lesson 3 **187**

Lesson 4 Reading

Interpret healthcare plans

1 Before You Read

A **IDENTIFY.** When have you used your health insurance to help cover medical costs? What kind of insurance was it? What type of plan did you have?

B **PREVIEW VOCABULARY.**

1. **TOPIC-RELATED WORDS.** These terms are used in the article. Does anyone know what they mean? Use roots and affixes to help you. You can also look for clues in the article.

| dependent | emergency room | network | specialist | primary-care doctor |

2. **ACADEMIC WORDS.** Discuss the meaning of the **bolded** words in the article. Use context to help you. After reading the article, add any words you learned to your Word Study Log.

C **PREDICT.** Preview the article title and image. What is the purpose of the article? What information do you expect?

2 Read for Gist

A **READ.** A health insurance plan pays for medical expenses, but certain costs are paid for by the individual. What types of costs does the person have to pay?

How to Interpret Health Insurance Plans

1 Navigating health insurance plans can be tricky. It's important to know as much as you can about insurance plans. This includes information about costs, types of plans, and where you can get insurance. The more you know, the better you'll be able to choose the right plan for you.

5 Let's start by looking at the most common health insurance costs.
- The *monthly premium* is how much you pay for insurance each month. You can get plans for an individual or for a family. The cost of your premium will **vary** due to many **factors**. If you are covering a spouse or a dependent, your premium will be more expensive. Your premium can also
10 go up if you are older or if you smoke. Where you live has an effect on premiums, too. Some states and cities have a more competitive health insurance marketplace. Health insurance may be cheaper in those places.
- A *deductible* is how much you have to pay before your insurance starts to pay. For example, if your deductible is $750, you pay for the first $750 of your medical costs. After that, your insurance kicks in to help pay costs over
15   that amount.
- *Co-insurance* is the percent of costs you pay after you have paid your deductible. This percentage often applies to doctors' visits and medicines. For example, if your co-insurance on a doctors' visit is 20% and a visit costs $100, you pay $20.
- An *Emergency Room (ER) co-payment* is how much money you pay if you go to the emergency room at the hospital.
20 - An *out-of-pocket expense limit* is the maximum amount of money you have to pay for health services in a given year. To see if you reach this limit on expenses, the plan would total up the amounts you had spent on your deductible, co-insurance payments, and emergency room visits. If your out-of-pocket expenses limit is $5,000, once you reach that limit, you do not have to spend any more money that year.

188 Unit 10, Lesson 4

Reading

Now let's look at the two most common types of health insurance plans. We'll start with HMOs. With an HMO (Health
25 Maintenance Organization), you have a given <u>network</u> of doctors. You must choose your doctor from within that
network. If you need to see a <u>specialist</u>, your <u>primary-care doctor</u> will help you find one.

The second type of plan is a PPO (Preferred Provider Organization). With a PPO, you also have a network of doctors.
However, you can see doctors outside of that network, too. It's easier to choose and see specialists. Your primary care
doctor doesn't have to help you find those doctors.

30 One big difference between HMOs and PPOs is that HMOs are typically less expensive than PPOs. They have lower
premiums and deductibles. An HMO may be right for you if cost is more important to you than flexibility. If you see a lot
of specialists and go to the doctor often, a PPO might be better for you.

There are three common places where you can **obtain** health insurance. The first is through your job. The second is
through a private health insurance company. The third is through the government. The government insurance is
35 especially helpful for people who are unemployed, 65 or older, or living at the poverty line.

Choosing a health insurance plan can be hard, but knowing more information is a good place to start. Then you can
get several **quotes** and compare them. Hopefully the information in this overview will help you find the best plan for you.

B **IDENTIFY MAIN IDEA. What is the main idea of the article?**

Finding a health insurance plan is easier when you know _____.

3 Close Reading

A **RECOGNIZE STRUCTURE. Write the numbers 1–7. Restate the main idea of each paragraph in your own words.**

B **LOCATE DETAILS. Match each item to its definition.**

_____ **1.** (n) monthly premium

_____ **2.** (n) deductible

_____ **3.** (n) co-insurance

_____ **4.** (n) out-of-pocket expense limit

a. percent of costs you pay after you have paid your deductible

b. how much you pay for insurance each month

c. maximum amount of money you have to pay in a year

d. how much you pay before your insurance starts to pay

C **EVALUATE. What are the advantages and disadvantages of an HMO plan? Of a PPO plan?**

Apply what you know

1. **ASSESS. Which of the following expenses in a healthcare plan would be the most important to you? Why? Which type of plan, HMO or PPO, do you think is better for you? Explain your answer.**

   - monthly premium
   - deductible
   - ER co-payment
   - out-of-pocket expenses limit
   - co-insurance

2. **SHARE. Share your preferences in healthcare plans with a partner.**

   - *My deductible is _____. I like that because _____.*
   - *I don't like my ER co-payment because _____.*

| I can interpret healthcare plans. ☐ | I need more practice. ☐ |

For more practice, go to MyEnglishLab.

For audio and video, scan the QR code.

Unit 10, Lesson 4 **189**

Lesson 5

Listening and Speaking
Describe the factors that increase the cost of healthcare

1 Before You Listen

A BRAINSTORM. Why is healthcare so expensive in the United States?

B PREVIEW VOCABULARY.

1. **TOPIC-RELATED WORDS.** These terms are used in the listening. Does anyone know what they mean? Use roots and affixes to help you.

| administrative costs | prescription drugs | pharmaceutical | residency |

2. **ACADEMIC WORDS.** These sentences are from the listening. Discuss the meaning of each **bolded** word. Use context to help you.
   1. Healthcare **administration** services include lots of different activities: processing patient bills and payments, working with insurance companies, finding and hiring doctors and other employees, and maintaining up-to-date technology.
   2. Hospitals must also protect patient privacy and set up security **procedures**.
   3. Administrative costs are only one **component** of our expensive healthcare system.
   4. If the government **regulates** prescription prices, it's true that it would help reduce costs.
   5. There are **rigid** requirements for getting into medical school.

C PREDICT. Use the lesson title, vocabulary, and image to make predictions about the podcast. What will its purpose be? What information do you expect?

190 Unit 10, Lesson 5

Listening and Speaking

2 Listen

A ▶ LISTEN FOR MAIN IDEAS. Listen to the podcast. In the first column, list the three factors behind the high cost of healthcare discussed in the podcast. Then compare your list with a partner.

Factor	Reason or Cause

B ▶ LISTEN FOR DETAILS. Listen again. List at least one reason or cause for each factor.

3 Apply Academic Listening Skill

A ▶ EVALUATE REASONING. Recall the three types of logical fallacies described in Lesson 1: *bandwagon, either/or,* and *slippery slope.* Listen to parts of the podcast again and name the logical fallacy that each speaker makes.

1. Professor's argument about administrative costs: _____
2. Professor's argument about doctors' salaries: _____
3. Nurse's argument about doctors' salaries: _____

B EXPAND VOCABULARY. Add words to your Word Study Log to show structure and meaning.

4 Real-World Application

A EVALUATE. What do you consider to be the most significant factors in the high cost of healthcare? What would you suggest we do to reduce these costs? Make a list of factors and suggestions.

B COLLABORATE. Share your list with a small group. Support your suggestions with sound reasoning.

| I can describe the factors that increase the cost of healthcare. ☐ | I need more practice. ☐ |

For more practice, go to MyEnglishLab.   For audio and video, scan the QR code.

Lesson 6 Grammar

Use embedded *yes/no* questions

1 Focus on Usage

A **CONSIDER.** Read the highlighted sentences in the text messages below. How do the writers ask *yes/no* questions without asking the question directly?

> Use embedded *yes/no* questions to politely ask for information or to express information you don't know or aren't sure about.

B **IDENTIFY.** Read the entire message. Underline all embedded *yes/no* questions.

A: I'll be a little late. I need to call my insurance company. **I'm not sure whether my hospital bill is correct.** I hope it's not right! It's almost five times the price I expected.

B: Medical bills keep getting higher and higher, don't they? **I don't know if there is any end in sight.**

A: Exactly. And it's not just doctor's visits and hospital stays. My prescription medications have doubled in price.

B: I've had the same problem.

B: The movie starts in an hour. Do you know whether you will be here by then? I wonder if we should change our plans.

A: No, I can definitely make it by then. I just need to check on this one bill. It will take only a few minutes.

B: OK. Good luck. Let me know whether or not you resolve it.

2 Focus on Structure

Yes/No Questions	
Direct Questions	**Embedded Questions**
Is this bill correct?	I'm not sure **if this bill is correct or not**.
Did you call the insurance company?	Let me know **if you called the insurance company**.
Does this bill include everything?	I need to know **whether or not this bill includes everything**.
Will there be a discount?	Do you know **whether there will be a discount or not**?

- Embedded *yes/no* questions begin with *if* or *whether*.
- It is possible to include *or not* immediately after *whether* or at the end of the embedded question. Do not use *or not* immediately after *if*.

192 Unit 10, Lesson 6

Grammar

A **INVESTIGATE.** Analyze all the examples of embedded *yes/no* questions. Choose **all** the correct answers.

1. Embedded *yes/no* questions are introduced by _____.
   a. *what*   **b.** *if*   **c.** *whether*   **d.** *who*

2. Use _____ in embedded questions.
   a. question word order   **b.** statement word order

3. The following patterns are possible in embedded *yes/no* questions.
   a. *if or not*   **b.** *if … or not*   **c.** *whether or not*   **d.** *whether … or not*

B **REWRITE.** Change the direct questions to embedded questions. Begin each embedded question with *I wonder….*

1. Do medications cost too much?

   I wonder if medications cost too much.

2. Does the United States have the most expensive healthcare in the world?

   _____

3. Do healthcare providers order unnecessary medical tests?

   _____

4. Are there any other treatment options?

   _____

5. Do insurance companies charge fair prices?

   _____

6. Is there any way to cut administrative costs?

   _____

C **WRITE.** Complete the sentences to include embedded questions about the cost of healthcare.

1. Do you know if _____?
2. I'm not sure whether _____.
3. Can you tell me if _____ or not.
4. I can't tell whether or not _____.
5. I really don't know whether _____ or not.

Apply what you know

1. **DISCUSS.** Discuss your questions from Exercise 2C in a small group.

2. **WRITE.** Write about the rising costs of healthcare. Use embedded *yes/no* questions.

   I wonder if the cost of healthcare will continue to rise. I don't know whether or not there is a solution to this problem.

I can use embedded *yes/no* questions. ☐	I need more practice. ☐

For more practice, go to MyEnglishLab.

Unit 10, Lesson 6   **193**

Lesson 7 Reading
Evaluate a strategy for making healthcare accessible

1 Before You Read

A DISCUSS. When did you last go to the doctor? How long did you have to wait to get an appointment? How long did you wait to see the nurse or doctor?

B PREVIEW VOCABULARY

1. **TOPIC-RELATED WORDS.** These terms are used in the article. Does anyone know what they mean? Use roots and affixes to help you. You can also look for clues in the article.

| telemedicine | glucose | physician's assistant |
| vitals | generalist | flat fee |

2. **ACADEMIC WORDS.** Discuss the meaning of the **bolded** words in the article. Use context to help you. After reading the article, add any words you learned to your Word Study Log.

C PREDICT. Preview the article title, image, and infographic. What is the purpose of the article? What information do you expect?

2 Read for Gist

A READ. Think about the main ideas as you read. Underline any sentences that help you identify main ideas.

How Telemedicine Could Change Healthcare

1   What if you could have your next doctor's appointment in your living room? The **concept** might sound strange. However, "telemedicine" is a promising new trend. All you need is a computer or phone at home. Then you
5   could talk to your doctor by video or phone. Almost 90% of households in the U.S. have computers. And 96% of Americans have cell phones. Telemedicine could be an easy new way for patients to get medical care. Telemedicine could also solve problems with our
10 healthcare system.

   One issue telemedicine could address is that general **practitioners** spend too much time on minor illnesses. Patients with colds, flus, and allergies wouldn't need to see a doctor in person. They could see a doctor online.
15 Patients could even use telemedicine for their **annual** physicals. It would be simple for patients to track their vitals at home. They could take their temperature and weigh themselves. They could wear inexpensive smartwatches. These watches would monitor their oxygen,
20 pulse, and blood pressure. Patients with diabetes could test their glucose. Patients with asthma could use peak flow meters to track their breathing. Doctors would then use that information to suggest the appropriate treatment.

   Another big problem in healthcare is that the average
25 wait time to see a doctor, who is not a specialist, is almost three weeks. Telemedicine would shorten the time it takes to see a generalist. One reason for the long wait time is a shortage of doctors. Experts predict the shortfall will get worse as the baby boomer **generation** retires.
30 The line graph shows the projected shortage of doctors. By 2032, the country could be short 121,900 doctors. Telemedicine would help ease this shortage because patients using telemedicine might see a nurse or a physician's assistant instead of a doctor. This would help
35 free up more doctors and thus reduce wait times.

194 Unit 10, Lesson 7

Reading

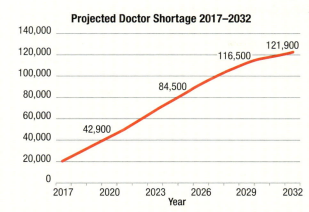

Yet another issue telemedicine would solve is a lack of doctors in rural areas. One in five Americans lives in rural areas. However, only one in ten doctors practices in rural areas. Rural patients often drive a long distance to see a
40 doctor. Telemedicine could save them time and gas money.

Perhaps the biggest benefit of telemedicine is that it would be less expensive. Telemedicine doctors could work from home without renting an office or hiring support staff. Because they could control their costs
45 better, doctors might be able to charge a flat fee, for example, $50 per appointment. This is a quarter of the average cost for an appointment with a general practitioner. This would benefit the 43 million Americans without **adequate** health insurance. Even people with
50 insurance struggle to pay for doctor's visits because of high deductibles or co-pays. Flat fee appointments could help people with or without insurance afford medical care.

Think about telemedicine the next time you have a doctor's appointment. Do you really need to go there in
55 person? Or could you talk to your doctor from your home or office instead? If the answer is yes, talk to your insurance company. Maybe you can get them to consider adopting this exciting new form of healthcare.

B **IDENTIFY MAIN IDEAS.** Choose the main idea of the article and of Paragraphs 2–4. Find the sentences that best support each main idea. Write the line numbers.

Article Main Idea	Lines
a. Telemedicine could solve many problems in the healthcare system. b. Using telemedicine could save patients time and money. c. Soon you will be able to talk to your doctor by video or phone.	
Paragraph Main Ideas	
2 a. Patients with minor illnesses use up a lot of doctor time. b. Telemedicine is ideal for minor illnesses and annual physicals. c. Many patients have minor illnesses like colds, flus, or allergies.	
3 a. The average wait time to see a general practitioner is three weeks. b. There is going to be a big shortage of doctors by 2030. c. Telemedicine could shorten appointment wait times.	
4 a. Telemedicine would address the lack of doctors in rural areas. b. There are more people than doctors in rural areas. c. People who live in rural areas drive far to get to the doctor.	

3 Close Reading

A **LOCATE DETAILS.** Are the statements true or false? Write the line numbers of your evidence.

	T/F	Lines
1. Nearly 90% of Americans have cell phones.	_____	_____
2. The country is currently short 121,900 doctors.	_____	_____
3. Over 43 million Americans have high deductibles.	_____	_____
4. Telemedicine would help both those with insurance and those without.	_____	_____

B **APPLY ACADEMIC READING SKILL.**

Academic Reading Skill: Evaluate the soundness of reasoning in a text
Remember, a sound, or logical, argument consists of a list of premises that are true, are supported by evidence, and lead directly to a conclusion.

To evaluate the reasoning of an argument, first break down the argument into its premises. Then pay attention to the conclusion. Evaluate how directly the premises lead to the conclusion. Keep in mind that the conclusion is often stated first and the premises that support that conclusion follow later.

Here is an example of a sound argument from the article about telemedicine.

> Premise 1: One in five Americans lives in a rural area.
> Premise 2: Only one in ten doctors practices in a rural area.
> Conclusion: There is a shortage of doctors in rural areas.

1. Read the article again. Circle the arguments that state problems telemedicine could help fix.

   General practitioners spend too much time on minor illnesses.

2. Reread Paragraph 2. What is one of the author's arguments? Use the standard form of a sound argument.

   Premise 1: _____

   Premise 2: _____

   Conclusion: _____

3. Reread Paragraph 5. What is one of the author's arguments? Use the standard form of a sound argument.

   Premise 1: _____

   Premise 2: _____

   Conclusion: _____

C **INTERPET INFOGRAPHICS.** Look at the graph in the article.

1. In what year will the shortage of doctors be the greatest? What will the shortage be that year? _____

2. If the highest range of the projections proves true, how much will the shortage increase between 2020 and 2029? _____

3. Why was the line graph included in the article? _____

196 Unit 10, Lesson 7

4 Prepare for an Academic Conversation

A **GO ONLINE.** Read about *Evaluating a Source for Sound Reasoning.* Then try it out in **YOUR TURN**.

| ✓ Search | ✓ Choose Sources | ✓ Evaluate Sources |

Evaluating a Source for Sound Reasoning

When you read any online source or printed article, you must evaluate the author's reasoning. Find each argument. Note the premises and the conclusion. Make sure to verify the evidence given to support the premises. Then ask yourself:

1. Are the premises true?
2. Do the premises lead to the conclusion?
3. Are the premises different from the conclusion?
4. Is the conclusion true?

If the answer to all the questions is *yes,* then the reasoning is sound. If the answer to any of the questions is *no,* then the reasoning is not sound.

YOUR TURN...
Now try out evaluating a source. Search for a source on telemedicine. Open the top result and evaluate the reasoning.

Premise 1: _____

Premise 2: _____

Conclusion: _____

Is the argument sound? ☐ Yes   ☐ No

B **CHOOSE A SOURCE.** Use the search term *accessible healthcare* to find an argument about how to make healthcare more affordable.

C **TAKE NOTES AND EVALUATE.** Use the Note-Taking Template on page 266 to take notes from the source you chose. Remember to evaluate the source's reasoning.

| Apply what you know | Academic Conversation |

1. **REPORT.** Explain one possible solution to make healthcare more accessible. Describe your source and the soundness of its reasoning.

2. **PROVIDE DIRECTION FOR THE GROUP.** Work in a group to choose one possible solution to make healthcare more accessible. Remember to make specific suggestions to help move the group forward.
   - *I was thinking we should _____.*
   - *My idea is _____.*

I can evaluate a strategy for making healthcare accessible. ☐   I need more practice. ☐

For more practice, go to MyEnglishLab.

For audio and video, scan the QR code.

Unit 10, Lesson 7   **197**

Lesson 8 Writing Workshop

Revise fragments and run-on sentences

1 What Do You Notice?

A COMPARE. Read the two examples. Which example uses full sentences and correct punctuation?

Example 1:
One benefit of telemedicine is that it would be less expensive. In-person doctor visits can cost a lot of money. Many Americans don't have insurance or have insurance that requires they pay high deductibles or co-pays. Telemedicine is an option that could have financial benefits for patients.

Example 2:
Because of a shortage of doctors and increased wait time for appointments. Telemedicine could be a helpful option to ease these issues. Doctors could fit more patients into a day, telemedicine would make appointments shorter. People wouldn't have to wait up to three weeks to see a doctor.

B ANALYZE. Underline the sentences in the other example that are written incorrectly.

2 Apply Academic Writing Skill

> **Academic Writing Skill: Revise fragments and run-on sentences**
> A **sentence fragment** is a group of words that does not express a complete thought. Some fragments are missing the subject of the sentence. Some fragments leave out the verb. Other fragments use the wrong verb form so that the action expressed is incomplete.
>
> *To fix a sentence fragment:*
> • Add the missing subject or verb, or correct the verb form.
> • Connect the fragment to the sentence before or after it. Then add the correct punctuation.
>
> A **run-on sentence** has two or more independent clauses that are not connected correctly. The most common run-on sentences use the wrong punctuation or are missing a connecting word and a comma.
>
> *To fix a run-on sentence:*
> • Separate the two independent clauses with a period.
> • Add a comma and a coordinating conjunction, such as *and, but, or,* or *so* between the two clauses.

A IDENTIFY. Tell whether each sentence is a fragment, run-on, or complete sentence.

_____ 1. Telemedicine uses a computer and phone, then you can talk to a doctor.

_____ 2. If patients need something specific. Such as a prescription or a specialist for a certain problem.

_____ 3. To help doctors, patients could keep track of vitals at home.

B APPLY. Rewrite the fragments or run-on sentence to create a complete sentence.

1. Many people lack the money to see a doctor, they may delay getting help for a medical problem.

_____

2. Healthcare could be more convenient. If telemedicine were available for everyone with a computer and a phone.

_____

I can revise fragments and run-on sentences. ☐   I need more practice. ☐

For more practice, go to MyEnglishLab.

Writing

Write an argument to support accessible healthcare

Lesson 9

1 ▶ Model for Writing

STUDY THE MODEL. Use the article on telemedicine in Lesson 7 as a model. Analyze the structure of that article by filling in the Writing-Model Template on page 267.

2 ▶ Prepare Your Writing

A **FOCUS.** You will write an essay to support one strategy for making healthcare accessible to all.

B **RESEARCH.** Go online and find another source that describes a possible solution for making healthcare accessible. Use the same Note-Taking Template (page 266) that you used before to take notes from your new source.

3 ▶ Write Write an argument supporting one strategy for making healthcare accessible to all.

A **ORGANIZE.** Use the structure of the Writing-Model Template you completed in Exercise 1 to organize your argument. Remember to state your points in complete sentences. Follow the tips below to make sure you use logical reasoning.

Logical Reasoning

Remember that a sound argument is built on logical reasoning.

For each premise:
1. State the premise clearly.
2. Support the premise with evidence.
3. Establish a direct connection between the premise and the conclusion.

Use reasoning signal words such as *because, since, given that,* and *the reason that* to indicate a premise. Use words such as *so, therefore, we may conclude,* and *as a result* to indicate a conclusion. Finally, support your logical reasoning by making the connection between the premise and the conclusion clear and direct.

Writing Checklist	
The text includes...	
Structure:	✓ Argument
Organization:	✓ Introduction with thesis
	✓ Body with evidence
	✓ Conclusion
Word Choice:	✓ Academic words
	✓ Reasoning signal words
Writing Skill:	✓ Complete sentences without fragments or run-on sentences
Grammar:	✓ N/A – Not Applicable

B **REVISE.** Use the Writing Checklist to evaluate your writing and make revisions. Remember to revise any fragments and run-on sentences.

4 ▶ Share Your Writing

A **COLLABORATE.** Share your writing with a partner. Use any feedback to improve your writing.

B **PUBLISH.** Create a final document to share with others.

I can write an argument to support accessible healthcare. ☐   I need more practice. ☐

For more practice, go to MyEnglishLab.

Unit 10, Lesson 9 **199**

Lesson 10 — Workplace Soft Skills

Demonstrate professionalism

1 Workplace Expectations

A ▶ **CONSIDER.** Listen to the phone conversation between a supervisor and a human resources (HR) representative. Why does the HR rep call? Why is the supervisor upset?

B **READ.** Read the email from the HR representative to the supervisor's manager.

> Karla,
> I just wanted to make you aware of a conversation I had with your night supervisor. I called to bring him up to speed on some of the changes in the new benefits package, and he was quite upset. He was rude and impatient with me, and he displayed a complete lack of professionalism. Maybe someone should talk to him.
> Thanks!
> Ting

C **IDENTIFY EXPECTATIONS.** Describe the HR representative's expectation and the supervisor's response. State the result.

1. HR representative's expectation: _____
2. Supervisor's response: _____
3. Result: _____

2 Learn from Mistakes

A **DISCUSS.** How could the supervisor have improved? Suggest specific things he could have done differently. Share your suggestions with a partner.

B **ROLE-PLAY.** Give the supervisor a "do over." Role-play the conversation, but this time have the supervisor meet the HR representative's expectations.

C ▶ **COMPARE.** Listen to the "do-over" conversation. How does it compare to your role play?

Apply what you know

1. **DEFINE.** How would you explain this soft skill to a new employee?
2. **APPLY.** Write an example from your own life in your Soft Skills Log (page 242) of how you have demonstrated professionalism.
3. **SHARE.** Share your example.
   - *I demonstrated professionalism at _____ when I _____.*

I can demonstrate professionalism. ☐   I need more practice. ☐

For audio and video, scan the QR code.   For more practice, go to MyEnglishLab.

Citizenship 11

PREVIEW
What type of ceremony do you think these people are taking part in? What do you know about the process of becoming a citizen in the United States?

UNIT GOALS
Describe the process and benefits of becoming a citizen
Interpret time zone maps
Identify workers' rights and the laws that protect them
Describe how a bill becomes law
Give a presentation to describe one branch of the United States government
Write a formal email to an elected official to request a specific action

Workplace Soft Skill: Respect individual differences
Academic Skills:
- **Listening:** Identify steps in a process
- **Speaking:** Keep collaboration guidelines in mind
- **Reading:** Identify steps in a process
- **Writing:** Use clear and concise language

Lesson 1: Listening and Speaking
Describe the process and benefits of becoming a citizen

1 Before You Listen

A CONSIDER. What are your feelings about becoming or having become a U.S. citizen? What advantages do U.S. citizens have that non-citizen residents do not have?

B PREVIEW VOCABULARY.

1. **TOPIC-RELATED WORDS.** These terms are used in the listening. Does anyone know what they mean? Use roots and affixes to help you.

| Constitution | USCIS | naturalization | allegiance | patriotism |

2. **ACADEMIC WORDS.** These sentences are from the listening. Discuss the meaning of each **bolded** word. Use context to help you.
   1. I'll discuss the **series** of steps that must be taken in order to become a citizen.
   2. Applicants have to wait patiently for USCIS to either **grant** or deny citizenship.
   3. Applying for citizenship is a lengthy process that requires **commitment** and determination.
   4. I've **resided** in this country for over a decade.
   5. I plan to **register** to vote right away.

C PREDICT. Use the lesson title, vocabulary, and image to make predictions about the podcast. What will its purpose be? What information do you expect?

2 Listen

A ▶ LISTEN FOR MAIN IDEAS. Listen to the podcast. Complete the information in the first column.

Steps to Citizenship	Specific Details
First, meet the _____ requirements.	1. be at least _____ years old 2. be a permanent resident for at least _____ 3. speak, read, and write _____ 4. understand and agree with the ideas in the U.S. _____
Download and complete the _____ and provide personal information.	1. current and past _____ 2. _____ history 3. _____ status 4. number of _____
Attend a _____ and answer questions about several factors.	1. application 2. background 3. _____ 4. willingness to _____
Benefits	**Specific Details**
Fully participate as a _____.	1. register to _____ 2. become an _____
Get assistance when dealing with _____.	1. hold a U.S. _____ 2. bring _____ from overseas

B ▶ LISTEN FOR DETAILS. Listen again. Complete the second column with specific details.

202 Unit 11, Lesson 1

Listening and Speaking

3 Apply Academic Listening Skill

Academic Listening Skill: Identify steps in a process
A **process** is a series of steps or events that leads to a final result or goal. Speakers often describe a process by listing the steps or events in order, or **in sequence**. Speakers often use process and sequence signal words to clarify the order of the steps or events. Listening for these words will help you recognize when one step in a process ends and another step begins.

Process/Sequence Signal Words
process, sequence, step, first, second, third…
then, before, after, next, since, prior to, during, finally, once, when

A ▶ **IDENTIFY.** Listen to part of the podcast again. Which process/sequence signal words does the speaker use? Underline those words in the chart above.

B **PUT IN ORDER.** Write 1–6 to put the steps in order.

_____ Download and complete the citizenship application.

_____ Send the application and fees to the USCIS office.

_____ Check to see that all eligibility requirements are met.

_____ Have fingerprints taken and get a criminal background check.

_____ Take the Oath of Allegiance to the United States.

_____ Attend a naturalization interview.

C **EXPAND VOCABULARY.** Add words to your Word Study Log to show structure and meaning.

4 Real-World Application

A **APPLY.** Prepare interview questions about U.S. citizenship. Get information about citizenship status, reasons for becoming or wanting to become a citizen, or reasons for not becoming a citizen.

B **COLLABORATE.** Work in a small group. Use your questions to interview one person. Then have that person ask his or her questions of another person. Continue until everyone has participated.

A: Why do you want to become a citizen?
B: I consider the United States my home and want to participate as a citizen by voting and serving on juries.

Academic Speaking Skill: Keep collaboration guidelines in mind
When working in a group, be sure to include all group members. Everyone should have a chance to speak and be heard. If one or two people tend to take over the conversation, try using these friendly reminders.

- *Let's make sure everyone has time to participate.*
- *Remember to include everyone in the group.*

I can describe the process and benefits of becoming a citizen. ☐   I need more practice. ☐

For more practice, go to MyEnglishLab.   For audio and video, scan the QR code.

Unit 11, Lesson 1 **203**

Lesson 2

Grammar
Use nouns and possessive nouns as adjectives

1 ▸ Focus on Usage

A **CONSIDER.** Read the highlighted sentences in the paragraph below. Which nouns are used as adjectives? Which nouns show possession?

B **IDENTIFY.** Read the entire paragraph. Underline all nouns that are used as adjectives. Circle all possessive nouns.

> When a word does not have an adjective form, a noun is often used as an adjective to describe another noun.
>
> A possessive noun expresses possession, or the idea of belonging to someone or something. The possessive noun names who or what the noun that follows it belongs to.

In the 1800s, millions of immigrants arrived in the United States from Europe to begin a new life. The United States government needed a system to handle the immigrants' arrival. Congress built a large center at Ellis Island in 1892 to process the thousands of immigrants who were arriving in the United States each day. Upon the newcomers' arrival, they would pass through the center and receive health examinations before entering the country. The first immigrant to arrive was a 17-year-old girl named Annie Moore in 1892. Ellis Island's peak years were from 1900 to 1914, when the island had its own power station, hospital, laundry facilities, and cafeteria. The immigration station closed in 1954. Today, it is part of the Statue of Liberty National Monument. Park visitors can tour the history museum and find their ancestors through the immigration records made public in 2001. It has been estimated that nearly 40% of all current U.S. citizens can trace at least one ancestor to Ellis Island. Visiting the island gives millions of Americans an opportunity to learn more about their country's history and, in many cases, about their own family's story.

2 ▸ Focus on Structure

Nouns as Adjectives
Immigration officials conducted **health** exams.
The journey from Europe took 12 days. The **12-day** journey was difficult.
She was 17 years old. The **17-year-old** girl immigrated to the United States.
Possessive Nouns as Adjectives
Annie's brothers immigrated with her to the United States.
The two **brothers'** names appeared after **their sister's** name in the first registry book.
The **children's** parents had already immigrated to the United States.

- A noun used as an adjective indicates a specific type or kind, not possession.
- When a noun used as an adjective includes a number, use hyphens to separate the words in the adjective. Do not use a hyphen between the adjective and the main noun.

  three-story house   **three-year-old** house

- For possessive nouns, if a singular noun ends in -s, there are two possible forms. Add an apostrophe + s, **or** add only an apostrophe.

  Samuel Ellis's heirs **or *Samuel Ellis'*** heirs inherited his island and sold it to New York State.

204   Unit 11, Lesson 2

Grammar

A **INVESTIGATE.** Analyze all the examples of nouns and possessive nouns used as adjectives. Complete the sentences with *singular* or *plural.*

1. Use a _____ noun + 's to express possession.

2. Use a _____ noun + ' to express possession.

3. For irregular _____ nouns, use 's.

4. Always use a _____ noun when it functions as an adjective.

B **COMPLETE.** Complete the second sentence using the words from the first sentence. Some phrases will include possessive nouns, and some will include nouns as adjectives.

1. My grandfather owned a **store** that sold **shoes**. He owned a _____*shoe store*_____.

2. My **aunt** has a **house** near Ellis Island. My _____*aunt's house*_____ is very old.

3. John is a **worker** at a **factory**. He is a _____.

4. We need to book a **room** at the **hotel**. We need to book our _____ soon.

5. My **doctor** has an **office** downtown. I need to go to the _____ today.

6. The **movie** lasted **three hours**. We watched the whole _____.

7. **Mary** has two **sisters**. _____ live in New York.

C **LIST.** Make a list of common expressions with the given noun + another noun.

1. (*immigration*) *immigration center, immigration papers, immigration lawyer, immigration facts, immigration interview, immigration office*

2. (*history*) _____

3. (*government*) _____

4. (*airplane*) _____

5. (*computer*) _____

Apply what you know

1. **RESEARCH.** Research a historical place or event that you want to know more about. Describe it to a classmate. Use nouns and possessive nouns as adjectives.

2. **WRITE.** Write about the historical place or event. Use nouns and possessive nouns as adjectives.
   The Statue of Liberty is a copper statue on Liberty Island in New York. The statue was a gift from the people of France. The figure is modeled after a Roman liberty goddess. She holds a torch above her head with one hand. In the figure's other hand, she holds a tablet that represents the law. She wears a crown. The crown's seven rays represent the seven continents and seven seas of the world.

I can use nouns and possessive nouns as adjectives. ■   I need more practice. ■

For more practice, go to MyEnglishLab.

Unit 11, Lesson 2 **205**

Lesson 3 — Workplace, Life, & Community Skills

Interpret time zone maps

1 Use Time Zone Maps

A MAKE CONNECTIONS. There are many standards that impact all citizens of a country. One example is time zones. When have you tried to call someone in a different part of the country or world and the time was different? Describe the situation.

B PROBLEM-SOLVE. What suggestions would you give for connecting with people in other time zones?

2 Consult Resources

Time Zone Maps

A **time zone** is a region of the world that follows a standard time for all legal and social interactions. Time zones tend to follow the boundaries of countries instead of set vertical, longitude lines because it is easier for the citizens of a country to keep the same time. The world is divided into 24 times zones. The International Date Line, where one day ends and another begins, is in the middle of the Pacific Ocean.

A SCAN. A man wants to call his daughter, but he doesn't know what time it is where she lives. He looked at a time zone map to know when he should call her. Use the map to answer the questions.

1. What color are the states in the Eastern time zone? _____
2. Which time zone is orange? _____
3. Which two states don't observe daylight savings time? (HINT: Look at the inset.) _____

206 Unit 11, Lesson 3

Workplace, Life, & Community Skills

B **INTERPRET GRAPHICS.** Use the time zone map and key. Match each symbol to its meaning.

_____ **1.** ⎯

_____ **2.** ⎯ (red)

_____ **3.** ▬ (yellow)

_____ **4.** ▬ (orange)

_____ **5.** ▬ (green)

_____ **6.** ▬ (blue)

_____ **7.** ▬ (pink)

_____ **8.** ▬ (light blue)

_____ **9.** ////

a. Pacific time zone

b. state boundary

c. central time zone

d. time zone boundary

e. Hawaii time zone

f. areas that do not observe daylight savings time

g. mountain time zone

h. eastern time zone

i. Alaska time zone

C **INTERPRET.** Locate information on the time zone map.

1. How many time zones are included in the United States? _____

2. Which states include more than one time zone? _____

3. The Eastern and Central time zones split which two Great Lakes? (Use an online map showing the Great Lakes, if necessary.) _____

D **CALCULATE.** Use the time zone map.

1. Your friend Dan moved to Oregon and wants to watch the Super Bowl. The game begins at 7:00 p.m. in central Texas. What time does Dan need to turn on his TV?

2. You are on the east side of North Dakota. You drive 400 miles west. Which time zone are you in?

3. You live in California. Your sister lives in Vermont. You need to call her at 8:00 p.m. her time. What time do you need to make the call?

E **GO ONLINE.** Use the Search Terms to find a time zone map. Share your map with a partner. How are the symbols used in your map similar to or different from the symbols used in the map above or in your partner's map?

🔍 **Search Terms:** time zone map

Apply what you know

1. APPLY. Find another U.S. map that shows state capitals, national parks, highest mountains, or anything else you are interested in.

2. SHARE. Explain any symbols used on your map to a partner.
- *This map uses the _____ symbol for _____.*
- *The symbols show _____ to represent _____.*

I can interpret time zone maps. ▪ | I need more practice. ▪

For more practice, go to MyEnglishLab.

Unit 11, Lesson 3   **207**

Lesson 4 Reading

Identify workers' rights and the laws that protect them

1 Before You Read

A BRAINSTORM. There are many laws that protect American workers. Which laws do you know?

B PREVIEW VOCABULARY.

1. **TOPIC-RELATED WORDS.** These terms are used in the article. Does anyone know what they mean? Use roots and affixes to help you. You can also look for cues in the article.

| humane | act | minors | hazards | elderly | seniors |

2. **ACADEMIC WORDS.** Discuss the meaning of the **bolded** words in the article. Use context to help you. After reading the article, add any words you learned to your Word Study Log.

C PREDICT. Preview the article title and image. What is the purpose of the article? What information do you expect?

2 Read for Gist

A READ. What four laws are discussed?

A Brief History of Workers' Rights

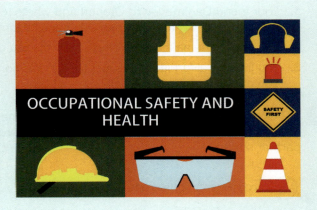

1   Every day, more than 125 million Americans go to work. Yet few of us think about the laws that protect us while we're there. Over the past century, many politicians have fought to create safer and more humane working
5   conditions. We can thank these leaders for our 40-hour workweek, overtime pay, and unemployment benefits. It's important for all workers to know the laws that protect workers' rights. These laws make sure that all workers are safe and treated fairly when they are at work.

10 Let's start by taking a look at one of the early workplace laws. In 1938, the government passed the Fair Labor Standards Act (FLSA). This law said employers had to pay employees a minimum wage. It also required employers to pay hourly employees time-and-a-half if
15 they worked more than 40 hours a week.

Before the FLSA was passed, millions of children worked in factories. They were often injured by machinery. The FLSA limited the number of hours minors could work each week. It also **constrained**
20 employers from hiring children under 14. The FLSA has been revised many times in the past century. In 2009, the FLSA updated the minimum wage to $7.25 per hour.

Right now, the FLSA doesn't protect vacation or sick time. Several politicians have proposed amendments to
25 the FLSA to guarantee time off. They want to protect workers' rights to time away from work.

Next, let's look at one of the most important workplace safety laws. In the late 1960s, many workers faced dangerous workplace conditions. Each year, around
30 14,000 employees were killed by hazards at work like toxic chemicals or machinery. Another 2 million were injured. The Occupational Safety and Health Act (OSHA) was passed in 1970. This law guaranteed employees an environment free from hazards. If
35 employees were exposed to dangerous chemicals, machines, or conditions, they could submit a complaint. Today, workplaces have gotten a lot safer. Far fewer

208 Unit 11, Lesson 4

Reading

people are injured or killed at work. Most workplaces must display an OSHA poster. This poster explains some
40 of the OSHA laws that protect workers.

Another law that keeps workplaces safe is the Whistleblower Protection Act (WPA) of 1989. When you blow a whistle, you are trying to call attention to something. A *whistleblower* is an employee who calls
45 attention to something his or her employer is doing wrong and files a complaint. The WPA protects the millions of people who work for the government. If they see something illegal or dangerous, they can report it. The law **inhibits** the government from penalizing the
50 employee for speaking up on behalf of other workers. The WPA makes it illegal for the government to try to silence the whistleblower. Most private companies have **similar** whistleblower policies in place.

What about employees who lose their jobs? In 1935, the
55 government passed the Social Security Act. This act grew out of social unrest following the Great Depression. During the Depression, unemployment rose as high as 25%. Many people who lost their jobs also lost their homes. Some starved to death. The Social Security Act
60 guaranteed an income to people who lost their job. Today, you can get unemployment benefits for up to 26 weeks if you are laid off or fired.

Before the Social Security Act, millions of <u>elderly</u> Americans didn't have enough money to retire. They
65 spent their last years in poverty. The act required the government to **distribute** monthly payments to <u>seniors</u>. Today, the government sends 60 million Americans over the age of 65 checks each month.

Today, more than 180 laws protect American workers.
70 These laws define our minimum income. They keep our workplaces safe. They safeguard our retirement. Because of these important laws, workers in our country are safer than ever and can hope to be treated fairly.

B IDENTIFY MAIN IDEA. What is the main idea of the article?

_____

3 ▶ Close Reading

A RECOGNIZE STRUCTURE. Record the year that each law was passed in the first column.

Year	Law	Details
	Fair Labor Standards Act	
	OSHA Act	
	Whistleblower Protection Act	
	Social Security Act	

B LOCATE DETAILS. Complete the chart. Describe the type of protection provided by each law.

Apply what you know

1. **PUT IN ORDER.** Create a time line showing the order and year in which each law was passed.

2. **SHARE.** Describe your time line to a partner. Summarize the type of protection provided by each law.
   - *The Fair Labor Standards Act was passed in _____. This law protects _____.*
   - *The _____ was passed in _____. This law guards against _____.*

| I can identify workers' rights and the laws that protect them. ☐ | I need more practice. ☐ |

For more practice, go to MyEnglishLab.

For audio and video, scan the QR code.

Unit 11, Lesson 4 **209**

Lesson 5 — Listening and Speaking

Describe how a bill becomes law

1 Before You Listen

A **DESCRIBE.** Lawmakers in Congress propose bills regarding important issues such as immigration, environmental regulations, and healthcare reform. How does an idea become a bill? How does a bill become a law?

B **PREVIEW VOCABULARY.**

1. **TOPIC-RELATED WORDS.** These terms are used in the listening. Does anyone know what they mean? Use roots and affixes to help you.

| petition | sponsors | chamber | veto | override |

2. **ACADEMIC WORDS.** These sentences are from the listening. Discuss the meaning of each **bolded** word. Use context to help you.
   1. How is a **federal** law made?
   2. If you get an **adequate** number of signatures, you can send a petition to a congressperson.
   3. A bill may eventually go back to the original committee for **revision**.
   4. When the president signs the proposed **legislation**, it does indeed become a law.
   5. A two-thirds **majority** in both chambers of Congress is needed to override the president's veto.

C **PREDICT.** Use the lesson title, vocabulary, and image to make predictions about the podcast. What will its purpose be? What information do you expect?

2 Listen

A ▶ **LISTEN FOR MAIN IDEAS.** Listen to the podcast. In the first column, list each person or group involved in the process of getting a bill passed. Then compare your answers with a partner.

People or Group	Steps
sponsor in Congress	
	votes to approve the bill
Senate and House	

B ▶ **LISTEN FOR DETAILS.** Listen again. In the second column, list the first step that each person or group will take to pass the bill.

Listening and Speaking

3 Apply Academic Listening Skill

A **PUT IN ORDER.** Complete the diagram to show the steps in the passage of a bill. Write each letter in the appropriate box.

A. The sponsor's chamber accepts the bill and sends it to the other chamber of Congress.
B. The signed petition is sent to a congressperson.
C. The president passes the bill.
D. The idea is proposed as a bill and sent to the appropriate committee.
E. The other chamber rejects the bill.

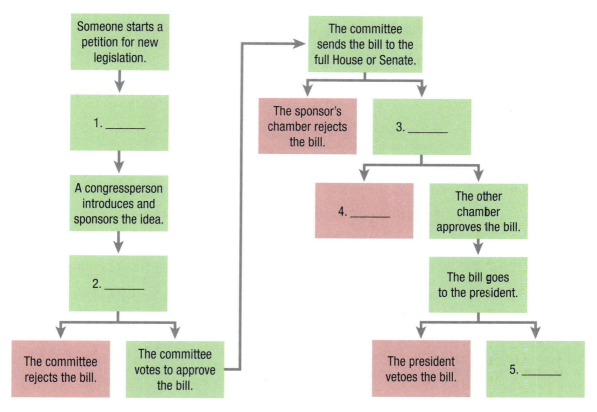

B **EXPAND VOCABULARY.** Add words to your Word Study Log to show structure and meaning.

4 Real-World Application

A **APPLY.** Research a bill that has been proposed in Congress. Where is it currently in the process of becoming a law?

B **REPORT.** Present the bill you researched. Describe where it is in the process and what will happen next.

I can describe how a bill becomes a law. ☐   I need more practice. ☐

For more practice, go to MyEnglishLab.   For audio and video, scan the QR code.

Lesson 6 Grammar

Use participial adjectives

1 Focus on Usage

A **CONSIDER.** Read the highlighted sentences in the text messages below. Which participial adjectives are used to describe nouns?

B **IDENTIFY.** Read the entire message. Underline all present participial adjectives. Circle all past participial adjectives.

> The present participle is the *-ing* form of a verb. The past participle usually uses the *-ed* form of the verb. Both participles can be used as adjectives. Generally, the present participial adjective describes an event or experience, and the past participial adjective describes a person or group.

A: Are you taking any interesting classes next semester?

B: Yes! I signed up for 5 classes. I'm especially interested in my political science class.

A: Political science!? That's a boring class.

B: Not to me. I'm fascinated by government and history.

A: I took political science with Dr. Andrews last year. I was not excited about the subject, but the professor was amazing.

B: Dr. Andrews will be teaching my class, too.

A: I think you'll like her. She tells a lot of entertaining stories and gives students thought-provoking assignments. For my favorite assignment, we chose an issue that we were concerned about and wrote letters to our elected officials.

B: That's exciting. I can't wait for the next semester to begin!

2 Focus on Structure

Present Participle	Past Participle
The students had a **frustrating** experience.	The **frustrated** students asked for help.
I watched an **interesting** movie about a politician.	I'm **interested** in politics.

- Irregular verbs have irregular past participles.
    broken record   **unknown** history   **misunderstood** quote
- Some verbs do not have both a present and a past participial form. For example, there is no present participle form for *scare* or *stress*. Instead, use *scary* and *stressful*.
    It was a **scary** movie. We were **scared**.
    It was a **stressful** situation. I was very **stressed**.
- Some present participial adjectives are preceded by a noun that tells more about it. These forms are usually hyphenated. There is generally no past participle equivalent.
    It was a **time-consuming** project.

212 Unit 11, Lesson 6

Grammar

A **INVESTIGATE.** Analyze all the examples of participial adjectives. Complete the sentences with *present* or *past*.

1. The _____ participial form of a verb ends with *-ing.*

2. The _____ participial form of a verb ends with *-ed* or has an irregular form.

3. Use the _____ participle to describe how someone feels.

4. Use the _____ participle to talk about something that causes a feeling.

B **COMPLETE.** Complete the sentences with the present or past participle.

1. (*elect*) We expect our _____*elected*_____ officials to have integrity.

2. (*inspire*) The senator delivered an _____ speech.

3. (*divide*) Our nation is more _____ than ever on this issue.

4. (*divide*) Political boundaries are the _____ lines between cities, counties, states, and countries.

5. (*surprise*) The representative made a _____ decision.

C **WRITE.** Write your own sentences using the present and past participles shown.

1. shocking / shocked

   _____

2. confusing / confused

   _____

3. amazing / amazed

   _____

4. frightening / frightened

   _____

5. thrilling / thrilled

   _____

Apply what you know

1. **BRAINSTORM.** Discuss concerns that affect your local community.

2. **WRITE.** Write an email to a community official or board member to express a concern. Use present and past participles.

   Obesity is a growing problem among children in our community. I am deeply concerned about this issue. Part of the problem is vending machines in schools that are filled with junk food. I would like you to prohibit vending machines in schools.

| I can use participial adjectives. ■ | I need more practice. ■ |

For more practice, go to MyEnglishLab.

Unit 11, Lesson 6 **213**

Lesson

Reading
Describe the organization of the U.S. government

1 Before You Read

A DISCUSS. You have learned a lot about the purpose and structure of the American government. Describe what you know about how the U.S. government works.

B PREVIEW VOCABULARY.

1. **TOPIC-RELATED WORDS.** These terms are used in the article. Does anyone know what they mean? Use roots and affixes to help you. You can also look for clues in the article.

blueprint	checks and balances	branches	stool	cabinet

2. **ACADEMIC WORDS.** Discuss the meaning of the **bolded** words in the article. Use context to help you. After reading the article, add any words you learned to your Word Study Log.

C PREDICT. Preview the article title and infographic. What's the purpose of the article? What information do you expect?

2 Read for Gist

A READ. Think about the main ideas as you read. Underline any sentences that help you identify main ideas.

How Is the United States Government Organized?

1   The United States Constitution is a remarkably stable document. Our world couldn't be more different than it was two centuries ago. However, the Constitution continues to be the <u>blueprint</u> for how we run the country.

    When the Constitution was written in 1787, the United States was recovering from the Revolutionary War with Britain. The founding fathers wrote the Constitution with Britain's domination and tyranny in mind. James Madison
5 defined tyranny as "all powers, legislative, executive, and judiciary, in the same hands." John Adams agreed, adding that "power must never be trusted without a check." Because they recognized the importance of shared power, our founders created the three branches of government and the <u>checks and balances</u> that regulate, or control, them.

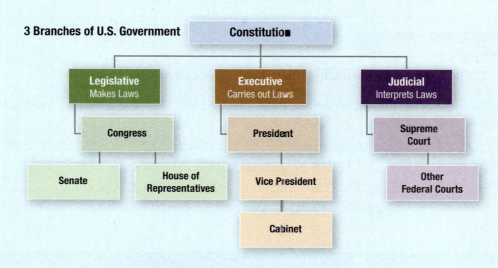

214   Unit 11, Lesson 7

Reading

The three <u>branches</u> of government include the legislative branch, the executive branch, and the judicial branch. These branches of government are like a three-legged <u>stool</u>. Each has an equal amount of power. Each has **discrete**
10 responsibilities. The Constitution sets up a system of checks and balances. Each branch can *check* - that is, challenge or veto - the power of the other branches. This system **minimizes** the chance of one branch becoming more powerful than the others and causing the stool to fall over.

- The **legislative branch**, or Congress, has the primary responsibility of passing laws. It also manages the money needed to operate the government and oversees the military. Congress is made up of the Senate and the House of
15 Representatives. The Senate has 100 senators. Each state elects two senators. Senators serve six-year terms. The House has 435 representatives. The number of representatives elected in each state depends on the population of that state. States with more people get more representatives. Representatives serve two-year terms.

- The **executive branch** completes and puts into action the laws passed by the legislative branch. It also appoints federal judges to be approved by Congress. The executive branch is run by the president, the vice president, and the
20 president's <u>cabinet</u>. A president can serve no more than two four-year terms.

- The **judicial branch**, as Alexander Hamilton said, has "neither force nor will, but merely judgment." The judicial branch interprets the laws passed by the legislative branch. It also interprets the Constitution for the other two branches. The judicial branch includes the Supreme Court and other federal courts. The Supreme Court is the top court in the United States. There are nine justices on the Supreme Court.

25 To understand how the system of checks and balances works, think about how the three branches of government work together to pass a law. First, Congress discusses a bill. Then it votes on it. For the bill to pass, the majority of each house of Congress, which means both the Senate and the House of Representatives, must support it. Then the president can pass or veto the bill. If the president vetoes the bill, two-thirds of Congress must support the bill in order to override the president's veto. Only then can it become a law. Once a bill becomes a law, the judicial branch decides whether the
30 law is fair or unfair.

Sometimes, these checks and balances create **overlap** between the branches. This can cause **tension**. This is especially true when different political parties run different branches. Tension is a natural part of living in a democracy. Fortunately, our constitution **unifies** us as Americans. We can all agree that the Constitution continues to provide a guiding light for how our government should run.

B **IDENTIFY MAIN IDEAS.** Choose the main idea of the article and of Paragraphs 2–4. Find the sentences that best support each main idea. Write the line numbers.

Article Main Idea	Lines
a. The United States has used the same constitution since 1787.	
b. The United States' government is organized into three branches.	
c. The United States Constitution was written to prevent tyranny.	
Paragraph Main Ideas	

		Lines
2	a. The checks and balances system regulates the government.	
	b. The United States was recovering from war with Britain in 1787.	
	c. The founding fathers shared an important vision for the checks and balances system.	
3	a. Each branch of the government has its own specific members.	
	b. The legislative, executive, and judicial branches can veto one another.	
	c. The legislative, executive, and judicial branches are equally strong.	
4	a. Congress is made up of the Senate and House of Representatives.	
	b. Each state gets two senators, but the number of representatives varies.	
	c. The legislative branch oversees the creation of the country's laws.	

Unit 11, Lesson 7 **215**

3 Close Reading

A **LOCATE DETAILS.** Are the statements true or false? Write the line numbers of your evidence.

	T/F	Lines
1. Senators serve two-year terms.	_____	_____
2. The president can serve four two-year terms.	_____	_____
3. There is an even number of justices on the Supreme Court.	_____	_____
4. Congress can pass a bill even if the president vetoes it.	_____	_____

B **APPLY ACADEMIC READING SKILL.**

> **Academic Reading Skill: Identify steps in a process**
> Remember that a process is a series of steps or events that leads to a final result or goal. When you are reading, look for words that introduce steps in a process like *first, next, then,* and *last.* That will help you recognize and understand the sequence of the steps in the process.

1. Reread Paragraph 7. Circle the words that indicate the steps in the process of passing a law.

> To understand how the system of checks and balances works, think about how the three branches of government work together to pass a law. First, Congress discusses a bill.

2. Reread Paragraph 7 again. Summarize how each branch is involved in passing laws.

Legislative: _____

Executive: _____

Judicial: _____

3. Reread Paragraph 7 again. How is this process an example of checks and balances?

_____

_____

C **SUMMARIZE.** Write, in your own words, the important details of Paragraph 4.

_____

_____

_____

216 Unit 11, Lesson 7

4 Prepare for an Academic Presentation

A FOCUS. You will give a formal presentation on one branch of the U.S. government.

B RESEARCH. Choose one branch of the U.S. government and find a source that describes that branch. Use the Note-Taking Template on page 268 to take notes from that source.

C ORGANIZE. Use the Presentation Template on page 269 to organize your information. Use the suggestions below to help you use quotations from primary sources to support your points.

Presentation Checklist	
	The presentation includes...
Organization:	✓ Introduction
	✓ Three main points or sections
Support:	✓ Quotations from a primary source
Word Choice:	✓ Academic words
	✓ Process/Sequence signal words
Delivery:	✓ Speech at appropriate volume and rate
	✓ Speech that is clear and easy to understand
	✓ Eye contact
	✓ Poise and effective gestures

Quotations for Support

A **primary source** is an immediate, first-hand account of a topic. Primary sources are usually written by people who participated in or observed a historical event. You can use a quote from a primary source to strengthen your presentation.

For example, James Madison was one of the people who wrote the Constitution. His description of tyranny is striking: "all powers, legislative, executive, and judiciary, in the same hands." Madison's words provide a glimpse into what he was thinking when he worked on the Constitution. The quote is especially useful because it is equally true today.

When you use a primary quote to support a point, ask yourself these questions:
1. Does the quote contain important points or dramatic language?
2. Does the quote make your presentation more interesting?
3. Did you include the name or source of the quotation?

D REVISE AND PRACTICE. Use the Presentation Checklist to assess your presentation and make revisions. Then practice your presentation until you feel confident.

Apply what you know — **Academic Presentation**

1. **PRESENT.** Share your presentation with a partner. Your teacher may also choose you to present to the class.

2. **EVALUATE.** Have your partner evaluate your presentation using the Presentation Checklist.

3. **KEEP COLLABORATION GUIDLELINES IN MIND.** Remember to show appreciation for your partner's feedback. Use positive statements to show that you value his or her comments.
   - *Thank you. I think that suggestion will really help.*
   - *Your comments definitely improve my presentation.*

I can describe the organization of the U.S. government. ☐   I need more practice. ☐

For more practice, go to MyEnglishLab.   For audio and video, scan the QR code.

Unit 11, Lesson 7 **217**

Lesson	**8**	# Writing Workshop

Revise writing to be clear and concise

1 What Do You Notice?

A COMPARE. Read the two examples. Which example uses clearer language?

Example 1:

Please vote to increase federal funding for adult education. Over 40 million adults in the United States lack the skills to get the fastest growing and highest paying jobs. Adult education can improve people's English fluency and also strengthen their academic and workplace skills. These skilled adults will ultimately help our country's economy.

Example 2:

It is my opinion that Congress should increase the amount of funding needed to educate our nation's under-skilled adults. Indeed, very many people who live in the United States of America cannot get jobs that are growing quickly or paying high wages. Skills gained from the adult education system will increase the economic success of this country, which is of great importance.

B ANALYZE. Underline words and phrases in the other example that make the sentences too wordy or unclear.

2 Apply Academic Writing Skill

Academic Writing Skill: Use clear and concise language
Clear language uses words and phrases that state your message accurately and precisely.
Concise language uses only words and phrases that are essential. Clear and concise writing requires careful attention to word choice and sentence structure. Clear, concise writing avoids using too many words or including awkward sentences that may confuse or distract the reader.

Follow these tips for using clear and concise language:
- Express meaning with the most straightforward words.
- Do not use long phrases when fewer words will work.
- Write in the active voice.
- Avoid adverbs such as *very, really,* and *just.* Those words don't add much to your message.
- Limit your use of the pronouns *it* and *they.* Readers often get confused about who or what those words refer to.

The most important thing to remember is *when in doubt, leave it out!*

A IDENTIFY. Check the sentence that uses clear, concise language.

☐ **a.** It is often the case that adults who lack the needed skills often find themselves in situations where they can't find work or get sick all the time.

☐ **b.** Under-skilled adults are more likely to be unemployed, underemployed, or unhealthy.

B APPLY. Rewrite each sentence to reduce wordiness and awkward wordings.

1. It seems to me that increasing how much money goes into adult education is a solution which would be practical.

_____

2. There are over seven million employee positions that need skilled employees to fill them.

_____

I can revise writing to be clear and concise. ■	I need more practice. ■

For more practice, go to MyEnglishLab.

218 Unit 11, Lesson 8

Writing

Write a formal email to an elected official to request a specific action

Lesson **9**

1 ▶ Model for Writing

STUDY THE MODEL. Read the Writing Model for an email on page 270. Analyze the structure of that email by labeling the sections: *Greeting, Request for action, Background on issues, Reasons for action, Conclusion, Polite ending, Closing,* and *Contact information.* Then use those labels to create your own email template.

2 ▶ Prepare Your Writing

A FOCUS. You will write a formal email to an elected official to request a specific action.

B RESEARCH. Go online and find a source on an issue you care about. Choose a source that suggests specific action steps. Take notes from that source.

3 ▶ Write
Write a formal email to an elected official to request a specific action on an issue you care about.

A ORGANIZE. Use the email template you completed in Exercise 1 to organize your email. Follow the tips below to maintain formal email structure and tone.

Formal Email Structure and Tone

In the U.S., sending a formal email to an elected official is an important way to participate in the democratic process. Provide a short, clear subject line. State your request for action clearly at the beginning of the email. Use first-person pronouns such as *I* and *we,* but keep a formal tone overall. End your email in a polite way.

Other tips for creating a formal email to request an action:
- Use a respectful greeting and closing.
- Include a brief background on the issue.
- Clearly explain the problem.
- Suggest a specific solution and describe the necessary action steps.

Writing Checklist	
	The text includes...
Structure:	✓ Persuasive email
Organization:	✓ Structure of a formal email
Word Choice:	✓ Academic words
Writing Skill:	✓ Clear, concise language
Grammar:	✓ Nouns used as adjectives
	✓ Participial adjectives

B REVISE. Use the Writing Checklist to evaluate your writing and make revisions. Remember to use clear, concise language. And always remember: *When in doubt, leave it out.*

4 ▶ Share Your Writing

A COLLABORATE. Share your writing with a partner. Use any feedback to improve your writing.

B PUBLISH. Create a final document to share with others.

I can write a formal email to an elected official to request a specific action. ■

I need more practice. ■

For more practice, go to MyEnglishLab.

Unit 11, Lesson 9 **219**

Lesson 10 Workplace Soft Skills
Respect individual differences

1 Workplace Expectations

A READ. Read an email from a shift supervisor to a personnel manager about an employee. What is the problem? What is the shift supervisor worried about?

> John,
> I just wanted to let you know about a conversation I overheard between a couple of the employees. As you know, we've been really busy and had to hire five new line workers a few months ago. We haven't had any issues with them despite the last-minute hire.
>
> The problem is that one of the other line workers, Nadia, has become increasingly frustrated with the new employees, all recent immigrants. She complains (loudly) about the smell of their food in the lunchroom and makes inappropriate cultural jokes. I even overheard her yesterday saying that they should learn English or get a different job. I don't really understand her attitude. It's causing a lot of stress on the line, so I thought you should know.
> Yuki

B ▶ CONSIDER. Listen to a conversation between the employee, Nadia, and the personnel manager, John. Why is the personnel manager upset? How does the personnel manager plan to solve the problem?

C IDENTIFY EXPECTATIONS. Describe the personnel manager's expectation. What would Nadia's performance review state?

1. Personnel manager's expectation: _____
2. Performance review: _____

2 Learn from Mistakes

A DISCUSS. What should Nadia have done differently? Suggest specific things Nadia could have done differently. Share your suggestions with a partner.

B ROLE-PLAY. Give Nadia a "do-over." First, role-play a conversation between Nadia and her co-worker, but this time have Nadia meet the personnel manager's expectations. Then role-play a conversation between the personnel manager and Nadia now that she has changed her behavior toward her co-worker.

C ▶ COMPARE. Listen to the two conversations. How do they compare to your role plays?

Apply what you know

1. **DEFINE.** How would you explain this soft skill to a new employee?

2. **APPLY.** Record an example from your own life in your Soft Skills Log (page 242) of how you have displayed respect for individual differences.

3. **SHARE.** Share your example. • *I displayed respect for individual differences when I _____.*

I can respect individual differences. ☐   I need more practice. ☐

For audio and video, scan the QR code.   For more practice, go to MyEnglishLab.

220 Unit 11, Lesson 10

Rights and Responsibilities

12

PREVIEW
What are the people in this photo doing? Describe what you know about the election process in the United States.

UNIT GOALS

Identify civic responsibilities
Interpret citations and law enforcement resources
Identify the rights described in the Bill of Rights
Identify the rights of people accused of crimes
Evaluate campaign propaganda
Write an evaluation of a news article

Workplace Soft Skill: Take initiative
Academic Skills:
- **Listening:** Make inferences and support with evidence
- **Speaking:** End collaborative tasks on a positive note
- **Reading:** Make inferences
- **Writing:** Use qualifiers to avoid hasty generalizations

221

Lesson 1

Listening and Speaking

Identify civic responsibilities

1 Before You Listen

A **REFLECT.** A civic responsibility is a duty expected from all members of society. What civic responsibilities do you have? How do you fulfill those responsibilities?

B **PREVIEW VOCABULARY.**

1. **TOPIC-RELATED WORDS.** These terms are used in the listening. Does anyone know what they mean? Use roots and affixes to help you.

| punishable | jury duty |
| predecessors | Selective Service |

2. **ACADEMIC WORDS.** These sentences are from the listening. Discuss the meaning of each **bolded** word. Use context to help you.

1. Citizens may **assemble**, or gather, for any purpose, as long as it's a peaceful gathering.
2. Free and fair elections are the **foundation** of our democracy.
3. If you're a citizen, please make it a **priority** to vote for your elected officials.
4. A jury listens to a court trial and decides the **outcome** of a trial.
5. Everyone pays taxes. The government uses that **revenue** to pay the nation's debts.

C **PREDICT.** Use the lesson title, vocabulary, and image to make predictions about the podcast. What will its purpose be? What information do you expect?

2 Listen

A ▶ **LISTEN FOR MAIN IDEAS.** Listen to the podcast. List the five civic responsibilities in the first column. Then compare your answers with a partner.

Responsibility	Who Must Do It	What It Means

B ▶ **LISTEN FOR DETAILS.** Listen again. For each responsibility, list who is required to fulfill that duty and what it means.

222 Unit 12, Lesson 1

Listening and Speaking

3 Apply Academic Listening Skill

> **Academic Listening Skill: Make inferences and support with evidence**
> Making inferences involves using personal knowledge and experience to make assumptions about what is **not** said or written. Speakers and writers use inference signal words to show they are making an educated guess or drawing their own conclusions. Listening for these words will help you recognize when someone is making an inference about something that was not actually stated or known.

Inference Signal Words	
Words	**Verbs**
clues, probably, educated guess, assumption, judging from, based on	infer, imagine, guess, assume, believe, think, feel, figure, suppose

A ▶ **IDENTIFY.** Listen to part of the podcast again. Which inference signal words do the speakers use? Underline those words or phrases in the chart above.

B ▶ **INFER.** Listen again. Make inferences to decide whether the statements are *True* or *False*. Then explain to a partner why you made that inference.

  • *Based on what the attorney said, _____.*   • *The lawyer said, "_____," so he must feel _____.*

1. The attorney considers voting to be a responsibility.   T   F
2. Not responding to a jury summons is punishable by law.   T   F
3. Women are required to register with the Selective Services. T   F
4. The attorney believes people do not like to pay taxes.   T   F
5. It's not possible to pay taxes after the April 15 deadline. T   F

C **INTERPRET.** What does the speaker mean when he says, "I'll get off my soapbox"? What can you infer?

D **EXPAND VOCABULARY.** Add words to your Word Study Log to show structure and meaning.

4 Real-World Application

A **ANALYZE.** Individuals can feel differently about rights and responsibilities. What one person sees as a privilege that can be enjoyed if desired, another might see as a duty that should be fulfilled. Decide whether you think each of these items is a Right (R) or a Duty (D).

Attend a peaceful demonstration _____   Know your senator's views _____

Practice any religion _____   Register to vote _____

Start a petition on a key issue _____   Serve on a jury _____

B **COLLABORATE.** Share your responses with a group. Work together to compile the group's responses into a table or graph to summarize the group's results.

> **Academic Speaking Skill: End collaborative tasks on a positive note**
> When working with others, try ending on a positive note by expressing your appreciation.
>   • *I enjoyed working with you. I hope we have the opportunity to work together again.*
>   • *I learned a lot from you on this project. Thanks for contributing so much.*

I can identify civic responsibilities. ☐   I need more practice. ☐

For more practice, go to MyEnglishLab.   For audio and video, scan the QR code.

Lesson 2 Grammar

Use modals of deduction

1 Focus on Usage

A CONSIDER. Read the highlighted sentences in the text messages below. Which modals express a guess or a theory?

> Modals of deduction express a guess or a theory about a situation. The modals *may*, *might*, *could*, *can*, and *must* express different degrees of certainty about a theory.

B IDENTIFY. Read the entire message. Underline all modals that express a guess or a theory.

A: How's the apartment search going? <mark>You must have found something by now.</mark> You've been looking for two weeks.

B: We found the perfect place, but it didn't work out. When I called, the landlord said he had seven units available. But when we arrived an hour later, he said everything was rented.

A: That doesn't sound right. <mark>He couldn't have rented out all seven apartments in only an hour.</mark>

B: Exactly. He seemed uncomfortable when we told him we're refugees. He must not like refugees.

A: That's illegal! You need to talk to an attorney.

B: It's OK. He might have leased all the apartments.

A: You must be joking! You need to stand up for your rights!

2 Focus on Structure

Modals of Deduction	
Weak Theory	
Present	I'm <u>not sure</u> about this website. It **may/might/could contain** wrong information.
Continuous	I <u>don't know</u> where Lee is. He **may/might/could be meeting** with his attorney.
Past	<u>Maybe</u> she went to court. She **may/might/could have gone** to court.
Strong Theory	
Present	I'm <u>sure</u> that's incorrect. It **must be** a mistake.
Continuous	I'm <u>almost positive</u> he has jury duty today. He **must be sitting** in court right now.
Past	There's <u>no way</u> he rented every apartment. He **must have lied** to you.

- Contractions are often used in past modals, such as *could've*. It is possible to use *must've* and *might've* in spoken English, but it's unusual in writing. Do not use a contraction with *may have*.
- *Could have* has a very different meaning than *couldn't have*.
  She **could have** been at the meeting, but I didn't see her.   She **couldn't have** been there.

224 Unit 12, Lesson 2

Grammar

A **INVESTIGATE.** Analyze all the examples of deductive modals. Choose the correct answers.

1. Use a deductive modal + _____ to express present time.
   a. base form of a verb   **b.** *have* + present participle   **c.** past participle

2. For continuous modals, use modal + _____.
   a. base form of a verb   **b.** *be* + verb *-ing.*   **c.** past participle

3. To make a deductive modal express past time, use modal + _____ + past participle.
   a. *has*   **b.** *had*   **c.** *have*

B **REWRITE.** Use the modal shown to rewrite each sentence.

1. I think that was illegal.

   (*might*) *That might have been illegal.*

2. It's possible that he is filing a complaint.

   (*could*) _____

3. I'm sure she is looking for an attorney.

   (*must*) _____

4. Maybe your rights were ignored.

   (*may*) _____

C **WRITE.** Read each sentence. Write a second sentence using the modal shown.

1. Jin didn't show up for work today.

   (*might be*) *She might be sick.*

2. Andy wasn't allowed to vote in the last election.

   (*could have*) _____

3. My car was towed.

   (*may have*) _____

Apply what you know

1. **CONCLUDE.** Read the following situations. For each situation, discuss what must have happened. What might each person do next?
   - Maya got a divorce two years ago and received custody of her children. The court ordered her husband to pay child support payments. Her husband never paid anything.
   - Fatima's manager asked her not to wear a headscarf, but Fatima explained it is for religious reasons. A few days later, Fatima was fired from her job.

2. **WRITE.** Choose one situation. What might have happened and might happen next?
   Maya's ex-husband might not have understood the court orders. Maya could take him to court again. He might have to pay more money. He could go to jail.

I can use modals of deduction. ☐   I need more practice. ☐

For more practice, go to MyEnglishLab.

Unit 12, Lesson 2   **225**

Lesson	3	**Workplace, Life, & Community Skills**

Workplace, Life, & Community Skills
Interpret citations and law enforcement resources

1 Pay or Dispute Citations

A **MAKE CONNECTIONS.** *Citation* is the more official word for a ticket. What have you or someone you know ever received a citation for? Where can someone go to pay for a citation?

B **PROBLEM-SOLVE.** If you don't know where to pay for a citation or how to disagree with a citation, how could you find this information?

2 Consult Resources

Citations

There are many reasons for which a person might receive a citation, such as littering, loitering (standing around with no purpose), speeding, parking or other traffic offenses, or jaywalking (crossing street unlawfully). If you know you are guilty and want to pay the ticket right away, it's easy to pay online. The appropriate website is usually shown on the citation. However, if you think the citation is unfair, you can also follow certain steps to disagree with the ticket. Those steps will also be on the law enforcement website.

A **SCAN.** A woman was issued a speeding citation. She went online to pay her ticket. Use the website below to answer the questions.

1. Where does she click to make a payment? _____

2. How many days does she have to make a payment? _____

3. When can she use the website to make a payment? _____

City of Riverville   Court Services

Home | **Pay or Dispute** | Public Notices | Feedback | Translate | 🔍 Search

In Person
Online ▸
By Mail
Over the Phone

Online Payments

Payment for a citation in the city of Riverville must be made within 20 days of the infraction. El Paso Municipal Court offers four ways to make a payment for your violation. By paying your fine on this website, you agree to the following:

• A plea of No Contest will be entered and a plea of Guilty will be entered on your case.
• Citations paid after hours, on weekends, or on holidays, will not post until the following work day.
• Failure to make payment by the due date will result in additional fees.

You may pay online for your citation 24/7. You may pay by credit or debit card. Visa, Mastercard, and Discover are accepted. Print your receipt for proof of payment.

Click Here to Make Payment

If you don't respond to the traffic citation within 20 days, the DMV will send you a letter stating you are in default, and if you do not pay your fine and fees within 30 days of that letter, your driver's license will be suspended. You can pay the fine in full, or you can **appeal and request a hearing**.

Contact DMV (Department of Motor Vehicles)

Call the DMV
Email the DMV
Visit the DMV

226 Unit 12, Lesson 3

Workplace, Life, & Community Skills

B **DEFINE KEY WORDS.** Find the words on the city website. Match each word to its meaning.

_____ **1.** (v) appeal   **a.** not valid for a period of time

_____ **2.** (n) default   **b.** act of breaking a law

_____ **3.** (n) violation   **c.** another word for violation

_____ **4.** (phr) no contest   **d.** saying you accept the punishment but not saying you are guilty

_____ **5.** (adj) suspended   **e.** apply for review to a higher court

_____ **6.** (n) infraction   **f.** failure to do what is needed in time

C **INTERPRET.** Locate information on the city website.

1. What are the four different ways to pay for a ticket? _____

2. What should she also do if she pays the ticket online? _____

3. If her ticket is paid on a weekend, when will the payment actually be made? _____

4. What will happen if the ticket is not paid by the due date? _____

5. What will be the result if the woman does not respond to the citation within 20 days? _____

_____

D **RELATE.** Why is it important to fight a ticket that you think is unfair? How comfortable or uncomfortable would you be disputing a ticket? Explain.

E **GO ONLINE.** Use the Search Terms below to access online information on how to pay a ticket for a large city in another state. Share the information with a partner. Explain which of the payment options you would choose and why.

Search **Terms:** citation payment _____ *(name of city in another state)*

Apply what you know

1. APPLY. Find out how to pay for a traffic citation in your own community.

2. SHARE. Explain your results to a partner. Discuss whether or not you would feel comfortable paying for a citation online.

- *Paying a citation online would/wouldn't be easy since I _____.*
- *I feel that I know/don't know how to pay for a citation online because _____.*

I can interpret citations and law enforcement resources. ☐   I need more practice. ☐

For more practice, go to MyEnglishLab.

Unit 12, Lesson 3 **227**

Lesson 4 Reading
Identify the rights described in the Bill of Rights

1 Before You Read

A **BRAINSTORM.** What freedoms does the United States government protect?

B **PREVIEW VOCABULARY.**

1. **TOPIC-RELATED WORDS.** These terms are used in the article. Does anyone know what they mean? Use roots and affixes to help you. You can also look for clues in the article.

| protest | search warrant | trial | convicted |

2. **ACADEMIC WORDS.** Discuss the meaning of the **bolded** words in the article. Use context to help you. After reading the article, add any words you learned to your Word Study Log.

C **PREDICT.** Preview the title and image. What is the purpose of the article? What information do you expect?

2 Read for Gist

A **READ.** What is the purpose of the Bill of Rights?

What Is the Bill of Rights?

1 In the United States, we take many of our freedoms for granted. Yet those freedoms were not always a given. When Congress adopted the constitution in 1789, the Constitution didn't state what freedoms and rights
5 Americans had. Thomas Jefferson encouraged a group of politicians to put together a list of Americans' rights. The politicians debated which freedoms to include. Finally, in 1791, they agreed on a list of ten freedoms. That list was called the Bill of Rights. The Bill of Rights
10 **complemented** the Constitution and made it more thorough and complete. The freedoms stated in the Bill of Rights are called **amendments** to the Constitution because those freedoms changed the original Constitution. The best way to protect these important
15 rights is for you to know the freedoms provided to all Americans by the Bill of Rights.

The First Amendment protects many of Americans' most **fundamental** freedoms. This amendment is perhaps most famous for protecting free speech. That means the
20 government can't tell people or the media what to think or say. It also guarantees Americans the right to <u>protest</u> peacefully to show that they object to something. The amendment also allows Americans to practice whatever religion they choose. It says the government can't make
25 laws favoring one religion over another.

The Second Amendment says the government can't stop people from having weapons. This means Americans can buy guns. People can keep guns in their homes. This freedom is called *the right to bear arms*.

30 The Fourth Amendment protects people from **arbitrary** searches. This means police officers can't randomly search a person or his or her house, car, or papers. Police officers must have proof from a judge that they have a good reason to search someone. This proof is called a
35 <u>search warrant</u>.

The Fifth Amendment **clarifies** how a <u>trial</u> works if a person goes to court. This amendment protects the person accused of or charged with a crime. If a jury decides a

228 Unit 12, Lesson 4

Reading

person is innocent, the government can't try the person
40 again for the same crime with a different jury. The person charged can't be forced to admit that he or she is guilty of a crime. The person doesn't have to say anything at the trial if he or she doesn't want to. Lastly, a person can't be put in jail, fined, or sentenced to death unless he or she
45 was <u>convicted</u> of a crime by a jury.

The Sixth Amendment lays out the **protocol** or set of steps that should be followed if a person is arrested. According to the amendment, a person has the right to know what he or she is accused of having done wrong.
50 The person also has the right to a public trial so that everyone knows what's happening. The trial must include a jury of ordinary people. The jury decides if the accused person is innocent or guilty. The accused person also has the right to a lawyer. If the person can't pay for a lawyer,
55 the government will pay.

Since the original Bill of Rights was passed, the government has added 17 additional amendments. Several of these amendments were very important. The Twelfth Amendment changed how the president and vice
60 president are elected. The Thirteenth Amendment made slavery illegal. The Fifteenth Amendment gave African Americans the right to vote. The Nineteenth Amendment gave women the right to vote.

The Bill of Rights is a living document that has changed
65 throughout history. It is updated to reflect change and progress in the country. Many Americans cherish the Bill of Rights. They are proud that their freedoms were an integral part of the country's birth. Knowing about these rights is the best way to protect them.

B IDENTIFY MAIN IDEA. What is the main idea of the article?

---

3 ▶ Close Reading

A RECOGNIZE STRUCTURE. Read the article again. Write a summary of each amendment discussed.

B LOCATE DETAILS. Match each amendment to one of the freedoms it protects.

_____ **1.** First Amendment

_____ **2.** Second Amendment

_____ **3.** Fourth Amendment

_____ **4.** Fifth Amendment

_____ **5.** Sixth Amendment

a. The government can't prevent people from having weapons.

b. If a person is arrested, he or she has the right to a lawyer.

c. The government can't tell news reporters what to say.

d. A person doesn't have to say anything against him- or herself.

e. Law officers need a search warrant before they can search.

C EVALUATE. Which of the amendments do you think is the most important? Why?

Apply what you know

1. APPLY. Find a current event related to each of the amendments below. Describe the event.

First Amendment   Fourth Amendment   Fifth Amendment

2. SHARE. Share your examples with a partner.

- *I heard on the news that _____. Freedom to _____ is protected by the _____.*
- *I heard an example of the _____ Amendment. That amendment protects _____. In this news story, _____.*

I can identify the rights described in the Bill of Rights. ☐   I need more practice. ☐

For more practice, go to MyEnglishLab.   For audio and video, scan the QR code.

Unit 12, Lesson 4 **229**

Lesson 5

Listening and Speaking
Identify the rights of people accused of crimes

1 Before You Listen

A **DISCUSS.** What rights do people who are accused of crimes have? Why might a suspect want to speak to a lawyer before answering a police officer's questions?

> **Miranda Warning**
> 1. You have the right to remain silent.
> 2. Anything you say can and will be used against you in a court of law.
> 3. You have the right to an attorney.
> 4. If you cannot afford an attorney, one will be provided for you.
> 5. Do you understand the rights I have just read to you? With these rights in mind, do you wish to speak to me?

B **PREVIEW VOCABULARY.**
   1. **TOPIC-RELATED WORDS.** These terms are used in the listening. Does anyone know what they mean? Use roots and affixes to help you.

| suspected | protections | defense attorney | confession | interrogating |

   2. **ACADEMIC WORDS.** These sentences are from the listening. Discuss the meaning of each **bolded** word. Use context to help you.
      1. If you watch a television crime show, you'll likely hear a police officer spell out a person's rights by **citing** the well known Miranda warning.
      2. Miranda admitted that he was guilty and had **committed** the crime.
      3. He had not been told that he could use or **invoke** his Fifth Amendment right, which is the right to remain silent.
      4. The Supreme Court **reversed** the decision of the lower court.
      5. Television has helped make the Miranda rights well known, but crime dramas have also contributed to some **misconceptions**.

C **PREDICT.** Use the lesson title, vocabulary, and numbered list above to make predictions about the podcast. What will its purpose be? What information do you expect?

2 Listen

A ▶ **LISTEN FOR MAIN IDEAS.** Listen to the podcast. What police procedures did the case against Ernesto Miranda establish and are now part of the Miranda warning?

_____

_____

B ▶ **LISTEN FOR DETAILS.** Listen again. Answer the questions.
   1. What can happen if a suspect answers a police officer's questions?

   _____

   2. What two Constitutional rights does the *Miranda* decision support?

   _____

   3. In the *Miranda v. Arizona* case, what had the lower court decided?

   _____

230 Unit 12, Lesson 5

Listening and Speaking

4. What happened to Ernesto Miranda after the Supreme Court ruling at the second trial?

_____

5. What information **can** the police ask about without stating the Miranda warning?

_____

3 ▶ Apply Academic Listening Skill

A ▶ **INFER.** Read each inference. Then listen to part of the podcast again. State the information on which each inference is based.

1. When a Supreme Court decides a case, the ruling from the lower court is no longer correct.

The Supreme Court reversed the decision of the lower court.

2. The narrator believes that Miranda deserved to go to prison.

_____

_____

3. The narrator thinks the *Miranda* case improved the judicial system.

_____

_____

4. The narrator does not consider television crime dramas to be realistic.

_____

_____

B **EXPAND VOCABULARY.** Add words to your Word Study Log to show structure and meaning.

4 ▶ Real-World Application

A **APPLY.** Imagine a friend calls you from the police station. Your friend was accused of vandalizing school property by spray-painting a wall, but your friend says he didn't do it. He was never in the location the police accused him of vandalizing, and he has never bought or used spray paint. The police did not cite his Miranda rights. They asked him to come with them to the station, and he is now in a waiting room.

What advice would you give your friend?

B **ROLE-PLAY.** Role-play the conversation with a partner. Then switch roles.

I can identify the rights of people accused of crimes. ☐	I need more practice. ☐

For more practice, go to MyEnglishLab.

For audio and video, scan the QR code.

Unit 12, Lesson 5 **231**

Lesson 6 Grammar

Punctuate adjective clauses

1 Focus on Usage

A CONSIDER. Read the highlighted sentences in the paragraph below. Which adjective clause is necessary to identify the noun it describes? Which adjective clause provides additional information that is not needed to identify the noun?

B IDENTIFY. Read the entire paragraph. Underline all restrictive adjective clauses. Circle all non-restrictive adjective clauses.

> Do not use commas with restrictive adjective clauses. A restrictive clause identifies the noun it describes. The sentence is not clear or does not make sense without the clause.
>
> Use commas to separate non-restrictive adjective clauses. A non-restrictive clause merely provides additional information about the noun. The sentence still makes sense if the clause is omitted.

There are three levels of courts that make up the judicial system in the United States. These three levels are the district courts, circuit courts, and the Supreme Court. The Supreme Court, which is the highest court in the United States, receives about 10,000 petitions a year. Of those petitions, the court will hear about 80 cases. The Supreme Court consists of nine justices, who review the petitions. These justices look for cases that are important for the whole nation and involve the Constitution. At least five of the nine justices must agree on a Supreme Court decision. The justice who serves as the head of court publishes the court's final decision for the public. That decision, which represents the majority's decision, then becomes law.

2 Focus on Structure

Punctuating Adjective Clauses	
Restrictive Clauses	**Non-Restrictive Clauses**
The Supreme Court hears **cases** that/which are of national importance.	**The nine justices**, who hear several appeals each year, have a very important job.
The chief justice is **the person** that/who is the head of the court.	**Judge Sánchez**, whom/who everyone respects, has served as a district judge for 20 years.
A person that/whom/who/Ø the president nominates as a Supreme Court justice must be approved, or confirmed, by the U.S. Senate.	**The Supreme Court**, which hears appeals, may overturn decisions from lower courts.

- A restrictive adjective clause is usually introduced by a relative pronoun such as *who, whom, that,* or *which*. The relative pronoun may be deleted when the pronoun is the object of the clause.
- In a non-restrictive adjective clause, do not use the relative pronoun *that* or omit the pronoun.
- Compare the following sentences. The use of commas means that **all** the jury members agreed. The lack of commas means that only some of the jury members agreed:

    The jury members, who agreed on the verdict, went home early.
    The jury members who agreed on the verdict tried to convince **the ones** who did not agree.

232 Unit 12, Lesson 6

Grammar

A **INVESTIGATE.** Analyze all the examples of adjective clauses. Check the correct column(s) to indicate whether the statements are true for restrictive adjective clauses, non-restrictive adjective clauses, or both.

	Restrictive	Non-Restrictive
Commas separate the clause from the rest of the sentence.		
Commas are not used to separate the clause.		
The clause may be introduced by *who, whom,* or *which.*		
The clause may be introduced by *that.*		

B **DECIDE.** Underline the adjective clause. Decide if the clause is necessary, or if it merely provides additional information. If it merely provides additional information, add commas.

1. Legal clerks who work for the Supreme Court justices help decide if a case should be heard.

2. A Supreme Court justice, who is appointed for life, may retire any time.

3. The Supreme Court reviews several cases which have been appealed in lower courts.

4. At least four of the justices who review a written appeal must agree to hear the case.

5. *Miranda v. Arizona* which was decided by the Supreme Court set critical rules for police officers.

6. The first Hispanic justice on the Supreme Court was Sonia Sotomayor who was appointed in 2009.

C **REWRITE.** Make the second sentence an adjective clause. Use commas when necessary.

1. The defendant was happy about the ruling. The ruling was in his favor.
   The defendant was happy about the ruling, which was in his favor.

2. Sandra Day O'Connor retired in 2006. She was the first female justice.

3. The justices receive briefs. The briefs provide details about both sides of a case.

4. The case got a lot of attention. The case went all the way to the Supreme Court.

Apply what you know

1. **LOCATE INFORMATION.** Research one of the following landmark Supreme Court cases.
   - *Dred Scott v. Sanford*
   - *Brown v. Board of Education*
   - *Roe v. Wade*
   - *Regents of the University of California v. Bakke*

2. **WRITE.** Describe the Supreme Court case. Use adjective clauses.
   Dred Scott versus Sandford, which was a landmark Supreme Court case in 1857, was about a black couple who wanted to live in freedom in Missouri, which was still a slave state.

I can punctuate adjective clauses. ☐   I need more practice. ☐

For more practice, go to MyEnglishLab.

Unit 12, Lesson 6 **233**

Lesson 7 Reading

Evaluate campaign propaganda

1 Before You Read

A DISCUSS. Describe a political ad. What was the purpose of the ad? What was your reaction to the ad?

B PREVIEW VOCABULARY

1. **TOPIC-RELATED WORDS.** These terms are used in the article. Does anyone know what they mean? Use roots and affixes to help you. You can also look for clues in the article.

campaign	endorse	positions	testimonial

2. **ACADEMIC WORDS.** Discuss the meaning of the **bolded** words in the article. Use context to help you. After reading the article, add any words you learned to your Word Study Log.

C PREDICT. Preview the article title and image. What is the purpose of the article? What information do you expect?

2 Read for Gist

A READ. Think about the main ideas as you read. Underline any sentences that help you identify main ideas.

Propaganda or Plain Facts?

1 During the 2008 presidential election, Barack Obama released his famous "Yes We Can" ad. The video featured 30 celebrities singing the words of his speeches. It quickly went viral. Twenty-six million people watched it within a few days. The positive message and famous faces in the ad brought attention
5 to Obama's campaign. As a result, his fundraising dramatically increased. He went on to beat John McCain later that year with 68% of the vote.

Politicians create their campaign speeches and ads for one reason, and only one reason: to get people to vote for them. This means that campaign messages are specifically designed to **manipulate** the audience and get them to believe certain things. Any information
10 deliberately spread to help or harm a person or group is called *propaganda*. That is not to say that all propaganda is bad. Barack Obama's "Yes We Can" ad had a very positive message. However, its primary goal was to convince the audience to support his political campaign. As responsible citizens, we need to take control of our own political decisions. It's important to evaluate any campaign propaganda for yourself.

The first step is to think about how the ad presents the candidate. Which of the candidate's values does the ad highlight?
15 Honesty? Intelligence? Business experience? Leadership skills? What important issues does the candidate plan to address? How has the candidate voted on those issues in the past?

The second step is to look for who paid for the ad. You usually hear this at the end of an ad on TV or radio. You can look for that information on any printed material. This will give you an idea of which groups endorse the candidate. Ask yourself: What is their **motive**? Why do these groups want to win votes? Remember that candidates are often loyal to
20 the groups who funded their campaign.

The third step is to look for emotional appeals. Many political ads appeal to the audience's emotions. The ad may try to make you angry, sad, anxious, or hopeful. The ad may also use images, music, or data to produce strong emotions. Ask yourself: What emotions am I feeling? And then ask yourself: Why am I feeling that?

234 Unit 12, Lesson 7

Reading

The fourth step is to identify any **logical** fallacies. A logical fallacy is any
25 argument that uses unsound reasoning. The fallacy is used to get you to
believe something that is not supported by the facts. Here are three
common logical fallacies often used in political campaigns and questions
to help you identify them:
- **ad hominem:** In this fallacy, a politician attacks the opponent as
30 a person instead of attacking the opponent's positions. To identify
   this fallacy, ask yourself: What is the politician attacking? Is he or
   she saying mean things about the opponent?
- **celebrity testimonial:** You shouldn't support a candidate just
   because some celebrities do. Does the campaign propaganda try to
35 convince you to vote for the candidate because celebrities do?
- **bandwagon:** A *bandwagon* was once a wagon that carried a big group of people. This fallacy says you should
   support a candidate because other people do. Is the campaign filled with data saying how many people already
   support the candidate? Do you plan to vote for a candidate just because other people do?

The United States government was founded on the belief that informed citizens choose the best candidates. When you
40 take time to evaluate campaign propaganda, you become a more **rational** voter. You become a part of the Founding
Fathers' dream for America.

B **IDENTIFY MAIN IDEAS.** Choose the main idea of the article and of Paragraphs 2–4. Find the sentences that best support each main idea. Write the line numbers.

Article Main Idea	Lines
a. All politicians use political propaganda to support their campaigns. b. It's important to carefully evaluate campaign propaganda. c. Ads and speeches are all types of campaign propaganda.	
Paragraph Main Ideas	

2   a. Campaign propaganda is designed to spread information.
      b. Barack Obama's "Yes We Can" ad is an example of propaganda.
      c. Propaganda is designed to manipulate the audience.	

3   a. Think about how the ad describes the candidate's skills.
      b. Think about the candidate's business experience and leadership skills.
      c. Check whether the ad mentions how the candidate has voted.	

4   a. It's important to find out who pays for campaign propaganda.
      b. Candidates are loyal to people who give money to their campaign.
      c. Powerful groups and individuals often endorse political candidates.	

3 Close Reading

A LOCATE DETAILS. Are the statements true or false? Write the line numbers of your evidence.

		T/F	Lines
1.	Barack Obama's "Yes We Can" ad featured 26 celebrities.	____	____
2.	A commercial with moving music is an example of an emotional appeal.	____	____
3.	You can usually find who paid for campaign ads.	____	____
4.	An *ad hominem* fallacy says you should vote for a candidate because other people do.	____	____

B APPLY ACADEMIC READING SKILL.

Academic Reading Skill: Make inferences
Remember, making inferences involves using personal knowledge and experience to make assumptions about what is **not** said or written. When you make an inference, you fill in information that is not directly presented. You use the information given **plus** what you already know to make the inference.

- Look at Example 1. Think about what's in the ad and what you already know. What inference could you make?
- Now look at Example 2. Think about what the candidate said and what you already know. What inference could you make?

Given in the ad	What I already know	Inference
Example 1 American flag in the background.	Flags are a symbol of patriotism and loyalty.	I should vote for the candidate because he or she is patriotic, and so am I.
Example 2 "I firmly believe in all the interests of my supporters."	Candidates are often loyal to the people who funded them.	I should give money to the candidate so he or she will support my beliefs.

1. Reread Paragraph 1. What kind of inference could you make from Obama's "Yes We Can" ad?

Given in the ad	What I already know	Inference
30 celebrities sang Obama's speeches.	I admire and respect those celebrities.	

2. Reread the concluding paragraph. What inference can you make about the author's belief about voter responsibility in the United States?

Given information	What I already know	Inference
When you evaluate campaign propaganda, you become a more logical voter.	Campaign propaganda manipulates voters to support candidates.	

C SUMMARIZE. Read the article again. Create an evaluation checklist by listing the four steps you should follow to evaluate a source.

1. _____
2. _____
3. _____
4. _____

4 Prepare for an Academic Conversation

A **GO ONLINE.** Read about *Wide and Deep Research*. Then try it out in **YOUR TURN**.

| ✓ Search | ✓ Choose Sources | ✓ Evaluate Sources |

Wide and Deep Research

Not all campaign propaganda is bad. To find reliable information on political candidates, your research should be both wide and deep. **Wide research** involves looking at many different sources to make an overall informed decision. **Deep research** involves looking carefully at each source and evaluating it for its reliability and use of sound reasoning.

YOUR TURN...
Try doing some wide and deep research. Find different sources of campaign propaganda. Use the search term to help you.
- **Website**—Search for the websites of candidates running for election in your city or state.
    Search Terms: (elected position) candidates (state or city)
- **Speech**—Find a transcript or a video of a speech online.
    Search Terms: (candidate name) speech
- **Debate**—Find a video of a political debate online.
    Search Terms: (elected position) debate (location) (year)
- **Commercial**—Find a political ad in support of a candidate.
    Search Terms: (candidate name) political ad

B **CHOOSE A SOURCE.** Find a source of campaign propaganda for one political candidate.

C **EVALUATE.** Use the evaluation checklist you created in Exercise 3C to complete deep research on the campaign propaganda you chose.

Apply what you know | **Academic Conversation**

1. **REPORT.** Present an example of campaign propaganda to a small group.

2. **EVALUATE.** Describe the steps you took to evaluate it. Remember to tell your listeners about any inferences you made while you were reading or watching it.

3. **END COLLABORATIVE TASKS POSITIVELY.** Remember to end your conversation on a positive note.
    - *I enjoyed sharing my ideas with you.*
    - *I look forward to sharing ideas with you again.*

I can evaluate campaign propaganda. ☐   I need more practice. ☐

For more practice, go to MyEnglishLab.   For audio and video, scan the QR code.

Unit 12, Lesson 7   **237**

Lesson **8**

Writing Workshop

Recognize hasty generalizations in an argument

1 What Do You Notice?

A **COMPARE.** Read the two examples. Which example presents valid evidence to support its argument?

Example 1:

In the United States, people don't care about voting anymore. Most eligible voters did not cast a vote in the last election. Clearly, people are either lazy or are satisfied with the way things are. Who knows who will win in the next election since so few people will actually show up to vote. The structure of government must change completely.

Example 2:

In the last election, about 55% of eligible voters voted, according to the Pew Research Center. There may be many reasons for low turnout. For example, some eligible voters do not have the proper identification necessary to vote. Others may have trouble getting to the polls. Certainly, some voters feel that they don't have the power to change anything. All these reasons are cause for concern.

B **ANALYZE.** Underline words and phrases in the other example that present invalid evidence.

2 Apply Academic Writing Skill

Academic Writing Skill: Use qualifiers to avoid hasty generalizations
The **hasty generalization** fallacy occurs when someone bases a general conclusion on insufficient evidence. A hasty generalization is presented as being true for everyone and everything rather for a limited number. Hasty generalizations are usually incorrect and can lead to negative results, such as stereotyping.

Congress didn't approve the bill I support. Politicians never want what I want!

Should all politicians be labeled as people who don't care about others because a vote didn't go the way you wanted it to? Adding a qualifier like *some, few, often, likely,* or *probably* can change a hasty generalization to something more specific and believable, such as:

Congress didn't approve the bill I support. **Some** *politicians think differently than I do.*

A **IDENTIFY.** Check the sentence that demonstrates the hasty generalization fallacy.

☐ People never vote anymore because they are angry at the government.

☐ Some people choose not to vote because they are unhappy with the actions of the government.

B **APPLY.** Change hasty generalizations to credible claims by using the qualifiers shown.

1. (*some, likely*) Everyone thinks the government should get rid of the Electoral College system, but nothing will ever change.

   _____

2. (*few, probably*) No one supports this city's mayor, so she won't be reelected.

   _____

| I can recognize hasty generalizations in an argument. ■ | I need more practice. ■ |

For more practice, go to MyEnglishLab.

238 Unit 12, Lesson 8

Writing

Lesson 9

Write an evaluation of a news article

1 ▶ Model for Writing

STUDY THE MODEL. Read the Writing Model for an evaluation on page 271. Analyze the structure of that evaluation by filling in the Writing-Model Template on page 272.

2 ▶ Prepare Your Writing

A **FOCUS.** You will evaluate the reliability of a news article.

B **RESEARCH.** Go online and choose a news article to evaluate.

3 ▶ Write Write an evaluation of a news article, arguing that it is either reliable or unreliable.

A **ORGANIZE.** Use the structure of the Writing-Model Template you completed in Exercise 1 to organize your own writing. Follow the steps below to evaluate the news article.

Evaluating a News Article

The role of the news media is to communicate what is happening in our world and to provide information that allows readers to make informed decisions. However, like campaign propaganda, the news in the media is not always reliable. In fact, some news is false and is called *fake news.* Fake news gives us false information. It is designed to manipulate how we feel and act. Here are some ways to evaluate how reliable a news article is:

- Read the entire article, not just the headline.
- Check for valid evidence. Verify any sources or quotes used in the story.
- Determine if the author's claims are supported by sound reasoning.
- Identify any logical fallacies.
- Check to see whether other news articles are reporting the same story.
- Ask yourself if the story seems believable.

Writing Checklist	
	The text includes...
Structure:	✓ Evaluative essay
Organization:	✓ News story summary
	✓ Claim and evaluation
	✓ Conclusion
Word Choice:	✓ Academic words
	✓ Inference signal words
Writing Skill:	✓ Qualifiers to avoid hasty generalizations
Grammar:	✓ Modals of deduction
	✓ Adjective clauses

B **REVISE.** Use the Writing Checklist to evaluate your writing and make revisions. Remember to avoid making any hasty generalizations.

4 ▶ Share Your Writing

A **COLLABORATE.** Share your writing with a partner. Use any feedback to improve your writing.

B **PUBLISH.** Create a final document to share with others.

I can write an evaluation of a news article. ☐   I need more practice. ☐

For more practice, go to MyEnglishLab.

Unit 12, Lesson 9 **239**

Lesson 10 Workplace Soft Skills
Take initiative

1 Workplace Expectations

A **READ.** Read the memo. What hospital policy is changing? How do the employees feel about the new policy?

B ▶ **CONSIDER.** Listen to the conversation between an employee, Susan, and her co-worker, Mark. What problem does the policy create for Susan? Why doesn't Susan want to do anything about it?

> ♥ **White City Hospital**
> Care you can trust.
>
> **Attention: White City Hospital Employees**
>
> **From:** Hospital Employee Manager
> **Subject:** Employee Break Times
>
> Effective immediately, employee breaks will be taken divided into a 30-minute break for lunch and two additional 15-minute breaks, to be taken throughout the day.
>
> Please direct any concerns to your shift supervisor.

C **IDENTIFY EXPECTATIONS.** Describe Mark's expectations and Susan's response. Why is Susan's response not helpful for herself or for the hospital?

1. Mark's expectations: _____
2. Susan's response: _____
3. Why is Susan's response not helpful? _____

2 Learn from Mistakes

A **DISCUSS.** Suggest specific things Susan could have done differently. Share your suggestions with a partner.

B **ROLE-PLAY.** Give Susan a "do-over." Role-play a later conversation between Susan and Mark. In this conversation, Susan says she changed her mind and followed Mark's advice. She spoke to her supervisor.

C ▶ **DISCUSS.** Listen to the "do-over" conversation. How is it similar to your role play? How is it different?

Apply what you know

1. **DEFINE.** How would you explain this soft skill to a new employee?

2. **APPLY.** Write an example from your own life in your Soft Skills Log (page 242) of how you have shown initiative.

3. **SHARE.** Share your example.
   - *I showed initiative at _____ when I _____.*

I can take initiative. ☐   I need more practice. ☐

For audio and video, scan the QR code.   For more practice, go to MyEnglishLab.

240 Unit 12, Lesson 10

My Soft Skills Log

Developing soft skills will help you participate more effectively in your workplace and in your community. Identifying your soft skills and providing real-life examples of those skills can help you succeed in an interview and in workplace performance reviews.

Unit 1: Demonstrate a willingness to learn

For example, _____

_____

_____

_____

Unit 2: Project self-confidence

For example, _____

_____

_____

_____

Unit 3: Respond effectively to customer needs

For example, _____

_____

_____

_____

Unit 4: Negotiate to resolve conflict

For example, _____

_____

_____

_____

Unit 5: Demonstrate responsibility

For example, _____

_____

_____

_____

Unit 6: Exercise leadership

For example, _____

_____

_____

_____

My Soft Skills Log

Unit 7: Work effectively with a team

For example, _____

_____

_____

_____

Unit 8: Exercise self-discipline with digital devices

For example, _____

_____

_____

_____

Unit 9: Display a positive attitude

For example, _____

_____

_____

_____

Unit 10: Demonstrate professionalism

For example, _____

_____

_____

_____

Unit 11: Respect individual differences

For example, _____

_____

_____

_____

Unit 12: Take initiative

For example, _____

_____

_____

_____

Unit 1

Note-Taking Template
Lesson 7 (page 16)

Note-Taking Template	Student Name _____
Famous Person I Admire	

Search Terms: _____   Search Date: _____

Source URL: _____   Date Published: _____

Basic information	
Reason for fame	
Key life events	
Key achievements	
Reasons to admire	

Unit 1 Note-Taking Template **243**

Presentation Template

Lesson 7 (page 16)

Unit 1

Presentation Template	
Famous Person I Admire	
Title Mother Teresa	**Presenter**

Introduction	
Presentation Main Idea	She shared many life lessons throughout her time to the Wor
Section 1	
Section 2	
Section 3	

Section 1 – Description of Person	
Main Idea	
Basic information	
Reason for fame	

Section 2 – Life Events and Achievements	
Main Idea	
Key life events	
Key achievements	

Section 3 – Reasons I Admire Him or Her	
Main Idea	
Reason to admire 1	
Reason to admire 2	
Reason to admire 3	

Unit 1

Writing Model

Interests, Skills, and Goals – Lesson 9 (page 19)

A High-Tech Nature Lover

I have a wide variety of interests, but my main interests are science and nature. Even as a child, I always loved spending time outdoors. For example, I enjoy gardening, and I'm interested in organic gardening methods. I grow vegetables, herbs, and flowers in the community garden in my neighborhood and often teach others who are new to gardening.

I have many skills. I'm good at math, and working with computers has always been easy for me. In addition, I keep up with new computer programs, and I do a lot of things online, including buying and selling items and building simple websites. I think my interpersonal skills are good, too. I'm outgoing and patient. I often help my friends with their computer problems.

I want to work at something that combines my interests and skills. My career goal is to work as a landscape architect for the City Parks and Recreation Department. Right now I'm taking ESL classes at the community college. After I finish my ESL classes, I want to enroll as a credit student and study landscape architecture. While I'm taking classes, I hope to work in a job related to landscaping, such as a tree pruner in the city parks. Once I have my landscaping degree, I believe those practical skills combined with my computer knowledge will make me a great candidate for a job at Parks and Recreation.

Andrea Fernández

Writing Model

Cover Letter Responding to Job Posting – Lesson 9 (page 39)

Unit 2

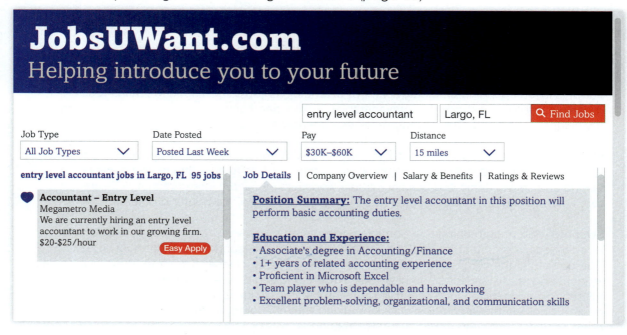

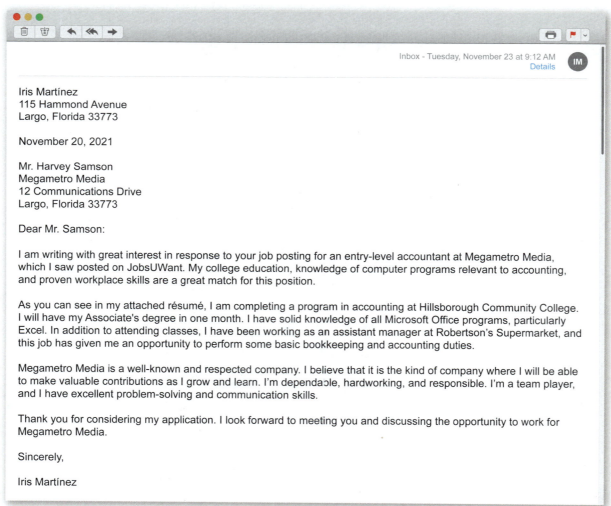

Unit 2

Note-Taking Template
Lesson 9 (page 39)

Note-Taking Template	**Student Name** _____
Job That Matches Your Experience, Skills, and Interests	

Job Title and Company: _____   Search Date: _____

Job-Search Website: _____

Job Requirements	**My Qualifications (Experience and Skills)**

Unit 2 Note-Taking Template **247**

Note-Taking Template

Unit 3

Lesson 7 (page 57)

Note-Taking Template	Student Name _____
	Compare and Contrast Two Jobs

Search Terms: _____ Search Date: _____

Source URL: _____

Job	Job 1	Job 2
Education required		
Experience needed		
Expected income		
Venn diagram		

248 Unit 3 Note-Taking Template

Unit 3

Presentation Template
Lesson 7 (page 57)

Presentation Template	
Compare and Contrast Two Jobs	
Title _____ **Presenter** _____	
Introduction	
Presentation Main Idea	
Section 1	
Section 2	
Section 3	
Section 1 – Description of Job 1	
Main Idea	
Education required	
Experience needed	
Expected income	
Section 2 – Description of Job 2	
Main Idea	
Education required	
Experience needed	
Expected income	
Section 3 – Compare and Contrast the Two Jobs	
Main Idea	
Similarities	
Differences	

Unit 3 Presentation Template **249**

Writing Model

Compare-and-Contrast Essay – Lesson 9 (page 59)

Unit 3

Dental Hygienists Versus Dental Assistants

To many people, the jobs of dental hygienist and dental assistant may seem to be the same. However, when the two jobs are compared, there are some definite similarities and some marked differences.

Dental hygienists and dental assistants have many job similarities. Both work with patients and dentists. Also, these two jobs are alike in that both hygienists and assistants must have some knowledge of medicine and dentistry. Dental hygienists should be dependable, cooperative, and attentive to detail, which is also true for dental assistants. The job of dental hygienist requires postsecondary training, which is any training after high school. Similarly, the job of dental assistant requires some level of postsecondary training. Both career pathways have projected growth into the next decade.

Although these dental jobs have much in common, they also have some major differences. Dental assistants help dentists who work with patients' teeth and gums. In contrast, dental hygienists work directly with patients' teeth and gums to protect each patient's oral health. Though both jobs require postsecondary training, a dental hygienist typically has a two-year degree, but a dental assistant may work with only a certificate or college diploma. Probably the biggest difference between the two jobs is the pay. Dental hygienists have a median annual wage of about $75,000. However, the median annual wage of a dental assistant is about $39,000.

The jobs of dental hygienist and dental assistant can differ in required education, duties, and income, but both jobs would be good choices for people who like to work with others in a professional environment.

Unit 4

Writing Model
Incident Report – Lesson 9 (page 79)

INCIDENT REPORT	Employee Report
	Description of accident

Employee Name:	Department:
Jeff Nolan	Maintenarce

Location:	Supervisor:
2nd floor supply room	Lela Martin

Date:	Time:
10/13/21	11:15 a.m.

Injury Involved?	Type of Injury (Be specific: muscle pull, bruise, cut, etc.)
___X___ Yes _____ No	Lower back muscle pull

Incident Details (Be as specific as possible: how the incident happened, what led to the incident, who was involved, etc.)

I received an urgent request for copy paper from Uma Green the morning of 10/13. I was attempting to pick up and carry a full box of copy paper from the second floor supply room to the copy machine in the second floor accounting office. When I lifted the box, I felt pain in my lower back. I set the box down and immediately reported my injury to my supervisor, Lela Martin.

Supervisor Recommendation
Actions taken, next steps to prevent recurrence of issue

Jeff reported the copy paper incident to me on 10/13. Although Jeff injured his back, he stated he could fill out an incident report form immediately. He then requested to go home to rest and did not want medical treatment. Jeff took the workers' compensation paperwork offered and was advised he must file a formal workers' compensation claim and could seek medical treatment if the back pain worsens. To prevent a future lifting injury, all maintenance employees will be required to attend a training even if they have not sustained a lifting injury during employment. This training will review factors that contribute to lifting injuries and provide practice with safe lifting procedures.

Unit 4 Writing Model **251**

Writing-Model Template

Incident Report – Lesson 9 (page 79)

Unit 4

Writing-Model Template	Student Name _____

INCIDENT REPORT

Employee Report
Description of accident

Employee Name:	Department:

Location:	Supervisor:

Date:	Time:

Injury Involved? _____ Yes _____ No	**Type of Injury** (Be specific: muscle pull, bruise, cut, etc.)

Incident Details (Be as specific as possible: how the incident happened, what led to the incident, who was involved, etc.)

Supervisor Recommendation
Actions taken, next steps to prevent recurrence of issue

Unit 5

Note-Taking Template
Lesson 7 (page 97) and Lesson 9 (page 99)

Note-Taking Template	Student Name _____
Solution to the Affordable Housing Problem	

Search Terms: _____ Search Date: _____

Source URL: _____ Date Published: _____

Source URL: _____ Date Published: _____

	Lesson 7	**Lesson 9**
Problem with examples		
Problem statistics		
Solution with examples		
Solution statistics		
Reason to support the solution		

Presentation Template

Lesson 7 (page 97)

Unit 5

Presentation Template	
Solution to the Affordable Housing Problem	
Title _____	**Presenter** _____

Introduction	
Presentation Main Idea – Thesis	
Section 1	
Section 2	
Section 3	

Section 1 – The Problem	
Main Idea	
Description of the problem	
Other information and examples	
Statistics of support	

Section 2 – One Solution	
Main Idea	
Description of the solution	
Other information and examples	
Statistics of support	

Section 3 – Reason to Support This Solution	
Main Idea	
Description of reason	
Other information and examples	
Statistics of support	

Unit 5

Writing-Model Template
Problem-Solution – Lesson 9 (page 99)

Writing-Model Template
Solution to the Affordable Housing Problem

Title _____   Student Name _____

Introduction	
Thesis Statement	
Background Information	

Description of the Problem
Main idea, statistics of support, and examples

Description of the Solution
Main idea, statistics of support, and examples

Reasons to Support the Solution
Main idea, statistics of support, and examples

Conclusion	
Summary	
Call to Action	

Source URL: _____

Source URL: _____

Unit 5 Writing-Model Template **255**

Note-Taking Template

Unit 6

Lesson 7 (page 117) and Lesson 9 (page 119)

Note-Taking Template	Student Name _____
Severe Weather Event	

Search Terms: _____   Search Date: _____

Source URL: _____   Date Published: _____

Source URL: _____   Date Published: _____

	Lesson 7	**Lesson 9**
Basic information: facts and statistics		
Definition or explanation of what the event is		
What causes the beginning of the event?		
What are the middle steps in the formation of the event?		
How does the event end?		

256 Unit 6 Note-Taking Template

Unit 6

Writing-Model Template
Process – Lesson 9 (page 119)

Writing-Model Template
Causes of a Severe Weather Event

Title: _____   Student Name: _____

Introduction	
Thesis statement	
Background information	

Paragraph 2
Main idea and explanation of process

Paragraph 3
Main idea and explanation of process

Paragraph 4
Main idea and explanation of process

Conclusion	
Restatement of thesis	
Closing statement	

Source URL: _____

Source URL: _____

Note-Taking Template

Lesson 7 (page 137) and Lesson 9 (page 139)

Unit 7

Note-Taking Template		Student Name _____
Effect of Climate Change		

Search Terms: _____   Search Date: _____

Source URL: _____

Source Title: _____   Date Published: _____

	Lesson 7	Lesson 9
What is one unavoidable effect of climate change?		
How has climate change caused that effect?		
How will this effect impact humans in the future?		
How can humans slow down or lessen this effect?		

Unit 7

Presentation Template
Lesson 7 (page 137)

Presentation Template
Effect of Climate Change

Title _____   Presenter _____

Introduction

Presentation Main Idea – Thesis	
Section 1	
Section 2	
Section 3	

Section 1 – Description of One Effect of Climate Change

Main Idea	
Description of effect	
Example 1	
Example 2	

Section 2 – How Will This Effect Impact Humans in the Future?

Main Idea	
Effect 1	
Effect 2	
Effect 3	

Section 3 – How Humans Can Slow Down or Lessen This Effect

Main Idea	
Behaviors to change	
Possible results of changes	
Call to action	

Writing Model

Argument – Lesson 9 (page 139)

Unit 7

Flooding: One Effect of Global Warming

Flooding causes incredible damages to people, property, and the natural environment. For example, flooding from Hurricane Sandy in 2012 caused $70 billion in damages, while flooding from Hurricane Harvey in 2017 caused $125 billion in damages. As global warming increases, the effects of flooding will be more severe. How does global warming cause flooding? How can we protect ourselves and our communities from this increased flooding? These are questions we must answer in order to respond to global warming and its harmful effects.

Due to global warming, Glaciers have begun to melt because Earth is warming. The melting water from glaciers causes sea levels to rise. In the past century, sea levels have risen eight inches. As sea levels rise, flooding results. In fact, more flooding is happening on more days in a year than ever before. For example, 50 years ago, Charleston, South Carolina, flooded four days a year. These days, it floods closer to 40 days a year. By 2045, scientists say Charleston will be flooded 180 days a year, or every other day.

The impact on human lives, property, and their surrounding environments will be devastating. As sea levels rise, homes and entire communities will flood. People will need to live farther from the coast. Cities will need to build higher roads and sea walls, and use pumps to control the water levels. Cities will also need to take care of people who lose their homes to flooding. Implementing these responses will cost billions of dollars.

It's true that climate change is happening. We see it as glaciers continue to melt more and more each year. We see it as flooding increases on a yearly basis. How can we do our part to decrease the harmful effects of global warming? First, we can adopt renewable energy sources. We can stop cutting down forests. Finally, we can talk to our politicians about their plans to lower greenhouse gases and support politicians who have good plans in mind. It is time to do our part to protect the planet and its inhabitants.

Unit 8

Note-Taking Template

Lesson 7 (page 157) and Lesson 9 (page 159)

| Note-Taking Template | Student Name _____ |
| **Advice on Screen Time for Children** | |

Search Terms: _____   Search Date: _____

Source URL: _____   Date Published: _____

Source URL: _____   Date Published: _____

	Lesson 7	Lesson 9
What advice does the author give on screen time for children?		
What evidence does the author use to make that point?		
What source does the evidence come from? Is it recent? Is it relevant? Is it objective?		
Who is the author? Does he or she have training in the subject?		

Unit 8 Note-Taking Template **261**

Writing-Model Template

Unit 8

Argument – Lesson 9 (page 159)

Writing-Model Template
Advice on Screen Time for Children

Title: _____   Student Name: _____

Introduction

Description of the issue	
Claim	

Supporting Point 1
Main idea, relevant and sufficient evidence

Supporting Point 2
Main idea, relevant and sufficient evidence

Supporting Point 3
Main idea, relevant and sufficient evidence

Supporting Point 4
Main idea, relevant and sufficient evidence

Conclusion

Summary	
Call to action	

Source URL: _____

Source URL: _____

Unit 9

Note-Taking Template

Lesson 7 (page 177) and Lesson 9 (page 179)

Note-Taking Template	Student Name _____
Solution to the Obesity Problem	

Search Terms: _____   Search Date: _____

Source URL: _____   Date Published: _____

Source URL: _____   Date Published: _____

	Lesson 7	Lesson 9
Problem		
Infographic URL and description to support problem		
Solution		
Infographic URL and description to support problem		
Reasons to support this solution		

Presentation Template

Lesson 7 (page 177)

Unit 9

Presentation Template	
Solution to the Obesity Problem	
Title _____	Presenter _____

Introduction	
Presentation Main Idea – Thesis	
Section 1	
Section 2	
Section 3	

Section 1 – The Problem	
Main Idea	
Description of the problem	
Other information and examples	
Description of supporting infographic	

Section 2 – One Solution	
Main Idea	
Description of the solution	
Other information and examples	
Description of supporting infographic	

Section 3 – Reasons to Support This Solution	
Main Idea	
Description of reason	
Other information and examples	

264 Unit 9 Presentation Template

Unit 9

Writing-Model Template
Problem-Solution – Lesson 9 (page 179)

Writing-Model Template
Solution to the Obesity Problem

Title: _____   Student Name: _____

Introduction	
Thesis statement	
Background information	

Description of the Problem
Main idea, statistics of support, and examples

Description of the Solution
Main idea, statistics of support, and examples

Reasons to Support the Solution
Main idea and examples

Conclusion	
Summary	
Call to action	

Source URL: _____

Source URL: _____

Unit 9 Writing-Model Template **265**

Note-Taking Template

Unit 10

Lesson 7 (page 197) and Lesson 9 (page 199)

Note-Taking Template	Student Name _____
Making Healthcare Accessible	

Search Terms: _____   Search Date: _____

Source URL: _____   Date Published: _____

Source Title: _____   Date Published: _____

	Lesson 7	**Lesson 9**
What argument(s) does the author make for how to make healthcare accessible?		
Restate the argument(s). Use the standard form of a sound argument.		
Are the premises and conclusion true? How do you know?		
Is the argument sound? How do you know?		

266 Unit 10 Note-Taking Template

Unit 10

Writing-Model Template
Argument – Lesson 9 (page 199)

Writing-Model Template
Making Healthcare Accessible

Title: _____   Student Name: _____

Introduction	
Description of the issue	
Argument for solution	

First Body Paragraph (Paragraph 2)	
Premise 1, premise 2, conclusion	
	☐ Each premise is true. ☐ Premises lead to conclusion.

Second Body Paragraph (Paragraph 3)	
Premise 1, premise 2, conclusion	
	☐ Each premise is true. ☐ Premises lead to conclusion.

Third Body Paragraph (Paragraph 4)	
Premise 1, premise 2, conclusion	
	☐ Each premise is true. ☐ Premises lead to conclusion.

Fourth Body Paragraph (Optional)	
Premise 1, premise 2, conclusion	
	☐ Each premise is true. ☐ Premises lead to conclusion.

Final Conclusion	
Summary	

Source URL: _____

Source URL: _____

Note-Taking Template

Lesson 7 (page 217)

Unit 11

| **Note-Taking Template** | **Student Name** _____ |
| **Branch of the U.S. Government** | |

Search Terms: _____   Search Date: _____

Source URL: _____   Date Published: _____

Which branch of the U.S. government did you choose? Why?	
What are its primary responsibilities?	
What is a quotation from a primary source about that branch of government?	
How can you use the quotation to make your presentation more interesting?	

Unit 11

Presentation Template
Lesson 7 (page 217)

Presentation Template	
Branch of the U.S. Government	
Title _____	Presenter _____

Introduction	
Presentation Main Idea – Thesis	
Section 1	
Section 2	
Section 3	

Section 1 – Description of This Branch of Government	
Main Idea	
Primary responsibility of this branch	
Other responsibilities	
Optional quotation	

Section 2 – Who Makes Up This Branch of Government?	
Main Idea	
Primary members of this branch	
How members are chosen	
Optional quotation	

Section 3 – How This Branch Checks the Other Branches	
Main Idea	
How this branch checks _____ branch	
How this branch checks _____ branch	
Optional quotation	

Unit 11 Presentation Template **269**

Writing Model

Email to Elected Official – Lesson 9 (page 219)

Unit 11

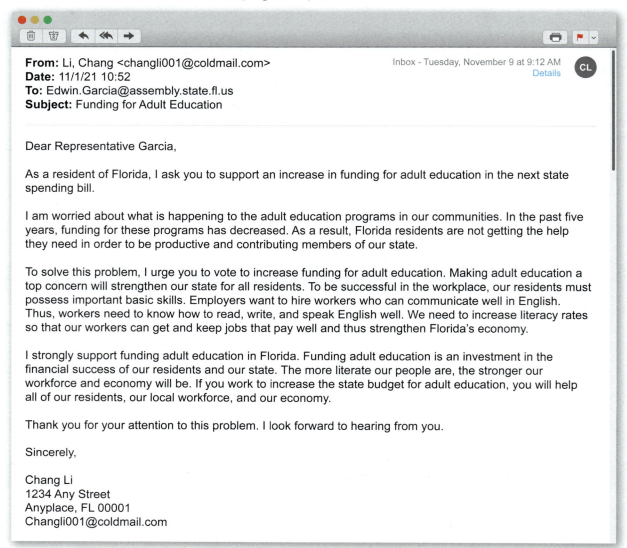

From: Li, Chang <changli001@coldmail.com>
Date: 11/1/21 10:52
To: Edwin.Garcia@assembly.state.fl.us
Subject: Funding for Adult Education

Inbox - Tuesday, November 9 at 9:12 AM
Details

Dear Representative Garcia,

As a resident of Florida, I ask you to support an increase in funding for adult education in the next state spending bill.

I am worried about what is happening to the adult education programs in our communities. In the past five years, funding for these programs has decreased. As a result, Florida residents are not getting the help they need in order to be productive and contributing members of our state.

To solve this problem, I urge you to vote to increase funding for adult education. Making adult education a top concern will strengthen our state for all residents. To be successful in the workplace, our residents must possess important basic skills. Employers want to hire workers who can communicate well in English. Thus, workers need to know how to read, write, and speak English well. We need to increase literacy rates so that our workers can get and keep jobs that pay well and thus strengthen Florida's economy.

I strongly support funding adult education in Florida. Funding adult education is an investment in the financial success of our residents and our state. The more literate our people are, the stronger our workforce and economy will be. If you work to increase the state budget for adult education, you will help all of our residents, our local workforce, and our economy.

Thank you for your attention to this problem. I look forward to hearing from you.

Sincerely,

Chang Li
1234 Any Street
Anyplace, FL 00001
Changli001@coldmail.com

Unit 12

Writing Model
Evaluation – Lesson 9 (page 239)

Don't Accept This Friend Request! – An Evaluation of the Article

Jen Fisher
December 1/2/21

The article "Don't Accept This Friend Request" reports on a virus that is spreading through email accounts. It explains how the virus will affect users' computers and claims that in order to protect against the virus readers should delete their email accounts. This article is not trustworthy because the source doesn't seem believable, the evidence isn't reliable, and the argument isn't sound.

The article appears on the website Technology123. The website is recent and many of the posted articles are current. However, the majority of the articles are intended to scare people about cyberattacks. The purpose of these articles seems to be to make readers fearful of both the attacks and the people who may be responsible for them. In addition, no information is given about the writer of the article. Therefore, it is impossible to judge the writer's qualifications.

Another significant problem with the article is that the evidence isn't strong. Much of it sounds like the opinion of the writer. The writer says that the expert included in the article works for a "well-known software company," but for which company? Is that expert qualified to give advice? Furthermore, some of the evidence doesn't make logical sense. For example, if the virus is spreading worldwide and these kinds of viruses have caused large power outages in major cities, why is there no information about these events on other news sources? Even more confusing is the writer's claim that if a computer gets the virus, "everything on the user's computer will be deleted." How can creators of the virus steal any valuable and sensitive information if everything has been deleted? The claims make the article hard to believe.

Finally, the article contains three logical fallacies. First, the writer uses emotional appeals to scare the readers and persuade them to delete their email accounts. Words like "destroy America" and warnings that future cyberattacks like this one will become more common are merely included to create fear. Second, the writer uses the bandwagon fallacy to make the reader believe that millions of people have already deleted their email accounts because of this virus, so the reader should, too. Third, the article includes a hasty generalization when it claims that "most countries want to use these cyberattacks to destroy America." Maybe some countries want to attack America in this way, but certainly not most. There are too many problems with logic to believe this article is actually true.

The article "Don't Accept This Friend Request!" is not trustworthy because the source and writer aren't believable, and the evidence presented isn't reliable. In addition, the article contains logical fallacies in its claims about the virus and why it was created that are both questionable and unsound.

Writing-Model Template

Evaluation – Lesson 9 (page 239)

Unit 12

Writing-Model Template **Evaluating a News Article**	**Student Name** _____

Source Title: _____   Author: _____

Source URL: _____   Date Published: _____

Article Summary

Article Claim

	☐ Reliable ☐ Unreliable

Article Description
Details about the source and qualifications of the author

Evaluation
Is evidence relevant and sufficient and supported by reliable sources?

Logical Fallacies

	☐ Ad hominem ☐ Emotional appeals ☐ Bandwagon ☐ Slippery slope ☐ Celebrity testimony ☐ Hasty generalization

Conclusion

Grammar Review

Unit 1

A **PUT IN ORDER.** Unscramble the words and phrases to make sentences. Use the simple present with gerunds and infinitives.

1. prefer / Zora / in a large office / work

   Zora prefer to work in a large office.

2. enjoy / Mr. Jung / blueprints / read

   Mr. Jung enjoys reading blueprints.

3. take / Dennis and Mark / plan / a coding course

   Dennis and Mark plan to take a coding course.

4. not mind / Angie / check / the budget

   Angie does not mind to checking budget

5. would like / improve / his communication skills / Rodrigo

   Rodrigo would like to improve improving his communication skills

6. John / be / a manager / not want

   John does not want to be a manager.

7. hope / Larry and Rita / the problem / solve

   Larry and Rita hope to solve the problem.

8. need / get / Dina / a business degree

   Dina needs to get a business degree.

B **COMPLETE.** Match to create logical sentences.

c	1. Choi is good	a.	about getting a degree in data science.
f	2. He is interested	b.	taking more English classes.
a	3. He is thinking	c.	at solving math problems.
e	4. He met a career counselor	d.	for helping him.
g	5. The counselor advised	e.	to discuss his goals.
b	6. He'll begin by	f.	in finding a job as a programmer.
h	7. He also hopes	g.	him to start with small achievable goals.
d	8. He thanked the counselor	h.	to find an internship.

Grammar Review **273**

Grammar Review

Unit 2

A **CHOOSE.** Use the words in the box to complete the message from a career counselor to her client.

could help	may be	maybe	might consider	should ask	shouldn't send

Dear Kelly,

I'm following up after our meeting last week. Have you finished writing your résumé yet? You

_____ it to any companies until you have reviewed it carefully. You _____

scheduling another appointment with me next week. I _____ you with your résumé, or

_____ you _____ your English teacher to check it for spelling and grammar

mistakes. I also wanted to remind you to check the job finder app every day. There _____

new postings that interest you. With a solid résumé and some interview practice, I believe you'll find a job

soon. Please let me know if I can be of further assistance.

Best,

Jan Smith

Heights College Career Counselor

B **COMPLETE.** Complete the sentences with the present perfect or present perfect continuous.

1. (*work*) Jackson _____ never _____ in a restaurant.

2. (*look*) My roommate _____ for a job for over a month. I hope he finds one soon.

3. (*submit*) I _____ already _____ an application to that company.

4. (*not, graduate*) Chris _____ from college yet.

5. (*wait*) Sophie _____ all day for her career counselor to return her call. She is beginning to feel impatient.

6. (*have*) _____ you ever _____ a job overseas?

7. (*work*) Alex seems really tired. He _____ the night shift lately. Is he getting enough sleep?

8. (*promote*) Clara is excited because her company _____ her to a management position.

Unit 3

DECIDE. Complete the conversations with the adjective given. Decide whether to use the comparative or superlative.

1. (*nice*)

   A: I like this furniture store. It has _____ furniture than the other stores we have visited.

   B: Sure, they have the _____ furniture we have seen today, but it is also the most expensive.

274 Grammar Review

2. (*important*)

A: When we shop for a car, we should consider safety first. It is _____ to have a safe car than a beautiful one.

B: I agree, but the _____ thing to consider is the price. It doesn't matter how safe or beautiful a car is if we can't afford it.

3. (*hard*)

A: Buying a new car is the _____ decision we have ever made together. I think we need to take our time and do some more research.

B: I think it will be even _____ if we wait. We need a car now, and we've saved up enough money.

4. (*bad*)

A: This car dealership has the _____ customer service. Let's go somewhere else.

B: But they offer very reasonable prices. The customer service isn't great, but I've been to

_____ places.

5. (*good*)

A: I don't think this is the _____ loan option for us. The interest rate seems very high.

B: You're right. We should look for a _____ loan.

Unit 4

A COMPLETE. Match to create logical sentences.

_____ **1.** Maddie didn't get a promotion

_____ **2.** Amy got the position

_____ **3.** Leah is qualified because of

_____ **4.** Emma missed the training due to

_____ **5.** Jane went back to school in order to

_____ **6.** Nora takes leadership classes so that

a. get a business degree.

b. her business degree.

c. because she works hard

d. even though she works hard.

e. she can become a manager.

f. illness.

B COMPLETE. Complete the requests with *if I* + the past tense **or** the *-ing* form of the verb

1. (*repeat*) I didn't hear you. Would you mind _____ that?

2. (*leave*) I have an appointment this afternoon. Would you mind _____ a little early today?

3. (*ask*) Would you mind _____ a personal question?

4. (*help*) I don't know how to use this new printer. Would you mind _____ me?

5. (*not, attend*) I need to finish this project today. Would you mind _____ the meeting today? Could you take notes for me while I stay here to work on my project?

6. (*not, take*) I can't concentrate on my work. Would you mind _____ personal calls in the office?

Grammar Review **275**

Grammar Review

Unit 5

REWRITE. Complete the adjective clauses with *that, which, who, whom,* or *whose.* When more than one answer is possible, list both choices. Then rewrite each sentence with an adjective phrase if possible. If not possible, write *Not Possible.*

1. This apartment complex is for people _____*who / that*_____ live on a limited income.
   This apartment complex is for people living on a limited income.

2. We have a handout _____ explains the eligibility requirements.
   _____

3. Everyone _____ attends the meeting will receive a free book.
   _____

4. I have a friend _____ mother is the director of a homeless shelter.
   _____

5. Students _____ are enrolled in classes may apply for financial aid.
   _____

6. The university offers several resources _____ students can access free of charge.
   _____

7. I'd like to speak with the person _____ is in charge of this office.
   _____

8. The person _____ I spoke with last week was very helpful.
   _____

Unit 6

COMPLETE. Complete the sentences.

1. (*play*) If the weather is nice tomorrow, we _____ soccer.

2. (*eat*) If the weather were nice today, I _____ my lunch outside.

3. (*be*) I would evacuate the city if there _____ a hurricane.

4. (*be*) I always stay indoors and away from the windows if there _____ a tornado.

5. (*not, go*) If it rains this weekend, we _____ to the beach.

6. (*not, wear*) If it weren't so cold today, I _____ this huge coat.

7. (*not, have*) I'm lucky I have snow tires on my car. If I _____ snow tires, I wouldn't be able to drive to work today.

8. (*not, snow*) I haven't checked next week's weather forecast. If it _____, we won't go skiing.

276 Grammar Review

Unit 7

A CHOOSE. For each item, choose the two possible answers to complete the sentence.

1. I believe in recycling as much as possible. I try to recycle _____ it's inconvenient.
   a. even if   **b.** only if   **c.** whether or not   **d.** provided that

2. Do not put medical waste or other non-recyclable items in the recycle bin. You may put trash in the recycle bin _____ it is made from recyclable materials.
   a. even if   **b.** only if   **c.** whether or not   **d.** as long as

3. You don't need any special training to volunteer to clean up the park. You can volunteer _____ you have no experience.
   a. only if   **b.** as long as   **c.** even if   **d.** if

4. Here is the phone number for the recycling office, just in case you need it. Call this number _____ you need more information. They are very friendly and always willing to answer questions.
   a. only if   **b.** should   **c.** if   **d.** even if

5. We do not want a car that runs on gasoline and has a negative impact on the environment. We'll buy a car _____ it's environmentally friendly.
   a. even if   **b.** provided that   **c.** should   **d.** only if

6. We must take action to save our planet. Climate change will remain a problem _____ we continue our bad habits.
   a. as long as   **b.** should   **c.** whether or not   **d.** even if

B COMPLETE. Use past unreal conditionals to complete the sentences.

1. (*prevent, know*) We ___could have prevented___ the disaster if we _____had known_____ about the problem.

2. (*start, realize*) I _____ carpooling to work years ago if I _____ how easy it is.

3. (*told, take*) If someone _____ us about the technology recycling center, we _____ our old computers there.

4. (*have, not ban*) The city of Bangladesh banned plastic bags due to flooding. They _____ much worse problems with flooding if they _____ plastic bags.

5. (*not recycle, go*) I'm glad we threw our plastic bottles in the recycle bin. If we _____ the bottles, they _____ to a landfill.

6. (*not complain, not change*) The company used to dump its wastewater into the ocean, but many people wrote letters and complained. If so many people _____, the company _____ its policies.

Grammar Review **277**

Grammar Review

Unit 8

COMPLETE. Circle the correct verb.

Electric and hybrid vehicles are growing in popularity, but they are still not as widespread as business analysts **expect / had expected**. When the first mass-produced hybrid vehicle **was released / had been released** in 1997, some experts believed most cars would be hybrid or fully electric within the next 20 years. That **didn't happen / wasn't happening**, but as governments look for ways to tackle carbon emissions, automakers **release / will be releasing** more and more electric vehicles in the next few years.

The move from fuel to electric engines is not the only prediction experts missed. Where are all the self-driving cars? Twenty years ago, automakers **were saying / will say** that we would soon be able to read a book or take a nap as our cars drove us to work. In fact, many people **predict / had predicted** that all cars would be fully autonomous, or self-driving, by 2020. Again, that prediction **didn't come / wasn't coming** true. Still, some analysts remain optimistic that in the very near future, people **won't be driving / aren't driving** their own cars and that the majority of all vehicles **are being / will be** autonomous. However, others disagree and argue that self-driving cars **aren't going to / won't be** take over the automobile market any time soon. What do you think? How soon **will / do** we all have self-driving cars?

Unit 9

REWRITE. Change the active sentences to passive. Do not change the verb tense. Do not include the agent. If it is not possible to change the sentence, write *Not Possible.*

1. The doctor conducted a health assessment.

   _____

2. Our diet may affect our mental health.

   _____

3. I will arrive at the doctor's office an hour early.

   _____

4. People have always considered nuts healthy.

   _____

5. Whole grains have many health benefits.

   _____

6. You can use this app to create a diet plan.

   _____

Unit 10

REWRITE. Rewrite the direct questions as embedded questions. Use the prompts given.

1. What's wrong with Pat?

   (*Do you know?*) _____

2. Does he have a doctor's appointment?

   (*Could you tell me?*) _____

3. Who is his healthcare provider?

   (*I wonder*) _____

4. When is his appointment?

   (*I don't know*) _____

5. Will he take medicine for his cold?

   (*I have no idea*) _____

6. What are his symptoms?

   (*I'm not sure*) _____

Unit 11

COMPLETE. Complete the second sentence using the words from the first sentence. Some phrases will include nouns or possessive nouns as adjectives. Some phrases will include participial adjectives.

1. Hawa is preparing to take an **exam** on **civics** in order to become a U.S. citizen. Her

   _____ is next week.

2. She has learned a lot about the **rights** of **citizens**. The test may include questions about

   _____ and responsibilities.

3. The **test** consists of **two parts**. The _____ has an English component and a civics

   component.

4. There are several **tests** available online for **practice**. Hawa has taken some of the

   _____.

5. Some of the **questions confused** Hawa. She asked her friends for help with the

   _____.

6. **Naturalization** is a long **process**. The exam is only one part of the _____.

7. Hawa hopes to pass the exam. Failing the exam can **complicate** the **process**. It can be a

   _____.

8. When she completes all the steps, **Hawa** will invite her **friends** to attend her naturalization ceremony.

   _____ will go to her ceremony.

Grammar Review **279**

Grammar Review

Unit 12

A REWRITE. Change each statement to express a guess or a theory by using the modal given.

1. Trespassing on school property is illegal.

    (*might*) _____

2. You don't need an attorney.

    (*may*) _____

3. The defendant is talking to the judge.

    (*must*) _____

4. The trial was last week.

    (*might*) _____

5. My car wasn't towed.

    (*could*) _____

6. She wasn't speeding.

    (*may*) _____

B IDENTIFY. Underline the adjective clauses. Add commas when necessary.

Ruth Bader Ginsburg who is a well-known American judge became the second woman to earn the title of

Supreme Court Justice. She studied at Cornell which is a prestigious university in New York. She finished

her bachelor's degree, got married, and had children. In 1956, she made a decision that was unusual

for women at the time. She enrolled in law school at Harvard University and became one of only eight

other women in a class which consisted of about 500 men. Ginsburg who has always cared deeply about

women's rights has earned a national reputation as an advocate for gender equality. In a 2015 speech at

Harvard University, Ginsburg advised students, "Fight for the things that you care about, but do it in a way

that will lead others to join you."

Audio Script

UNIT 1 — THE POWER OF GOALS

Pages 2 and 3, Exercises 2A, 2B, 3A, 3B, and 3C

Main announcer: Welcome to "Getting Started," the podcast for people who want to take steps to plan their careers. In order to maintain a satisfying work-life balance, it's important to pursue a career that's right for you. In today's episode, we ask people to tell us why they chose their career. Our reporter, Sherri Davis, went downtown to speak with people headed home after a busy day at work. Let's listen to what they had to say.

Sherri: Hello, listeners! I'm speaking with Henry, a barber at Great Cuts. Henry, how did you choose your career?

Henry: It's a funny story. My uncle owns a barbershop. When I was a teenager, I wanted to earn some money to save for college, so I worked at my uncle's shop. I answered calls, swept the floor, that sort of thing. Eventually, I started helping clients choose haircuts and styles. I really enjoyed it. A couple years later, I decided to get a barber's license. I like getting to know my clients, and I love seeing them gain extra confidence after a good haircut.

Sherri: What advice would you give to someone trying to choose a career?

Henry: Find your passion. We all have certain strengths. The key is to figure out what you're inherently good at and what you enjoy doing. Maybe you like cutting hair. Or perhaps you love cooking. Do you like teaching people? Do you enjoy being outside? Identify your passion and find a way to pursue it in a career.

Sherri: It's great advice to follow your passions! That ensures that your ambitions and aspirations will match what you like to do. Thanks, Henry.

Sherri: Now I'm talking to Jessica, an instructional designer at a tech company. Jessica, what do instructional designers do?

Jessica: They develop course content to train students or employees. Instructional designers can work for any organization. Take for instance, medical clinics and hospitals. They need instructional designers to create training for their medical staff. There are lots of places an instructional designer might work. For example, schools, government agencies, and corporations all need instructional designers. To illustrate, I create online training materials for the sales team at a large corporation. I basically teach the sales associates about our new products so they can sell them.

Sherri: Interesting! How did you choose your career?

Jessica: I consulted with a career counselor at my college. The counselor gave me several assessments to identify my skills and strengths. These tests helped me clarify what type of work I would be good at.

Sherri: What kind of assessments?

Jessica: The counselor collected information using several tests. For instance, I took a personality test, which gave me all kinds of information about myself, such as my communication style, interests, abilities, and values. Another example of an assessment was a career test. A career test is very similar to a personality test, but it provides a little more information, including a list of the best careers for your particular interests. A career test also helps make sure you will like the job you get.

Sherri: Very useful information. Thanks, Jessica.

Sherri: Finally, I'm speaking with Emma, a purchasing manager for a construction company. Emma, can you tell us a little about your job?

Emma: Sure. I make bids, work with vendors, and prepare documents and agreements in order to process large purchases and deliveries for my company.

Sherri: How did you decide to become a purchasing manager?

Emma: I discovered it by accident. I was looking at job postings and saw an internship with good advancement opportunities. The internship helped me see that purchasing was a good fit for me because I'm very detail oriented, I like talking to people, and I'm a good at negotiating. Now, ten years later, I've worked my way up the career ladder from intern to manager.

Sherri: That's an inspiring story and good advice for our listeners. An internship is an excellent opportunity to see how a particular job feels and whether the work environment is right for you. It also allows you to build expertise as you begin your career.

Main announcer: So there you have it, listeners. There are many ways to find the right career. You can start by identifying your passion, talking to a career counselor, or by getting an internship.

Pages 10 and 11, Exercises 2A, 2B, 3A, and 3B

Counselor: Hi, Ruben. Come in and have a seat.

Ruben: Thank you.

Counselor: So, you're here to talk about career options, right?

Ruben: That's right.

Counselor: Do you have any ideas of what you might like to do?

Ruben: Yes. I really enjoy cooking, and I've always wanted to own a small business, so I've been thinking about starting my own catering business someday.

Counselor: Do you have any experience in catering or business management?

Ruben: No, not yet.

Counselor: Well, I don't want to discourage you, but starting and running a business can be very difficult. You'll have to spend a lot of time preparing.

Ruben: Yes, I know. It may take several years.

Counselor: It's important for you to have a clear plan. You can do that by setting up some SMART goals. SMART stands for specific, measurable, achievable, relevant, and time-bound. A goal that is specific is very clear. To demonstrate, it's not enough to say you're going to take some classes. An example of a specific goal might be to take a business management class at the community college.

Ruben: Got it. What do the other words mean?

Counselor: Measurable means you have a way to see the goal has been reached. For instance, you'll have a college transcript listing all the classes you took. Achievable means the goal is possible. You want to set goals that you can actually accomplish, such as finding a job and taking specific classes. Relevant means the goal will help you achieve your long-term goal. For example, talking to people who own catering companies might be helpful. And time-bound simply means there's a specific date for finishing the goal, such as a month, a semester, a year, or even five years. OK, so what's the first goal?

Ruben: That's easy. I need to pass my final ESL class.

Counselor: What's step two?

Ruben: I'm not sure. I'll probably look for a job with a catering company.

Counselor: OK, good. What about school? Are you going to continue taking classes at the college?

Ruben: Yes, definitely. I need to acquire some cooking techniques, so I'll take some culinary arts classes. Running a business also requires management and accounting skills. I'll need to take some business classes as well.

Counselor: Let's work on making that goal a little more specific and time-bound. Have you chosen specific classes? When do you plan on taking them?

Ruben: I think I'll start by taking two classes this semester and see how I do working and going to school at the same time.

Counselor: It sounds like Step 2 has two parts that need to be coordinated: You're going to work for a catering company and take college classes in culinary arts and business.

Ruben: Yes.

Counselor: I suggest searching and applying for jobs right away. You need to figure out how achievable that goal is. You don't know how many jobs are available in catering. You also need to decide if you want to work full time or part time.

Ruben: Initially, I want to start out working part time so that I have time to study.

Counselor: Sounds good. OK, you'll apply for jobs and see what the possibilities are there. For your college classes, I'd like you to meet with an academic advisor to determine specific classes that will help you become a catering manager. Think about whether or not you want to complete a degree plan. Pursuing a degree could be your third step.

Ruben: And my fourth step could be to work in upper management at the catering company where I'll work. And at the same time, I could collect more information about starting a small business. After getting enough training and saving enough money or getting a small-business loan, my fifth step would be to open my catering business near the campus.

Counselor: That sounds great. Stay focused on the achievable goals. For now, shift your energy to finding a catering job and choosing your college classes. Why don't we meet again in two weeks? I'd like to hear how the job search goes and to find out what plans you've made with your academic advisor.

Ruben: That sounds great. Thanks!

Page 20, Exercise 1A

Interviewer: So, my next question has to do with your future goals. Where do you see yourself in five years?

Candidate: Um… I don't know. I haven't really thought about that.

Interviewer: Do you think you would still be working at Fresh n' Fast?

Candidate: Sure. I guess. This is a good company to work for.

Interviewer: If you get the job, do you think you would still be in the same position in five years, or would you like to move higher in the company?

Candidate: It doesn't really matter to me. I'm fine with anything.

Interviewer: OK. But, are there any skills you think would help you improve as an employee?

Candidate: Hmm. I'm not really sure.

Page 20, Exercise 2C

Interviewer: So, my next question has to do with your future goals. Where do you see yourself in five years?

Candidate: That's a great question. I'm really interested in learning more about how Fresh n' Fast trains new employees. I've always enjoyed learning more about how people develop new skills for their jobs. Things are always changing in this business, and employees have to work with new technology.

Interviewer: Do you think you would still be working at Fresh n' Fast?

Candidate: Oh, yes. I'm very excited about this opportunity.

Interviewer: If you get the job, do you think you would still be in the same position in five years?

Candidate: In five years, I really want to be a part of the training team. That way I can support new employees and share the skills I've gained.

Interviewer: OK. And are there any skills you think would help you improve as an employee?

Candidate: Hmm. I think I would like to develop communication skills and leadership skills.

UNIT 2 – GETTING A JOB

Pages 22 and 23, Exercises 2A, 2B, and 3A

Main announcer: Welcome back to "Getting Started." Our guest today is Michael Chen, a career advisor. Michael, could you give our listeners a few tips to help them prepare for a job search?

Michael: Of course! My first tip is to do volunteer work. The more experience you can accumulate, the better, and one great way to get experience is through volunteer work. For example, if you're a computer programmer, you might help develop a website for a local business or charity. If you're a great chef, you could volunteer at a community center for the homeless. In short, volunteering can help fill in a gap in your experience, and it will show employers that you are passionate about your work.

My next tip is to compile a list of names of all the people who might help you. If you belong to any community organizations, such as a school or religious organization, you should make a list of people who could help you find a job. Perhaps someone might be able to introduce you to

Audio Script **281**

Audio Script

an employee at a business you're interested in. You also need to identify the people who you can use as references on your résumé. Almost all employers will ask for two or three references. Good references might include your college professors, previous employers, and the people you have met through your volunteer work. In other words, be sure to think about all the people you know when you are deciding who might help you and when choosing your references.

The third tip is to make a file of important documents. This file should include diplomas, certificates, and reference letters from teachers and employers. You don't need to have a copy of every single document, but these documents will help you write a great résumé. Ultimately, it is these documents that will help make sure that all the details on your résumé are accurate.

Now that you have your résumé, references, and documents ready, my next tip is to research companies you're interested in. Learn as much as you can about what the company values and what it's like to work there. You can often find out about a company's vision and goals online. Reach out to anyone who works there and ask that person questions about his or her work and about the company's goals. If you can, find out who is responsible for hiring. If possible, approach that person directly and tell him or her that you're interested in a job. Sometimes it's not enough to submit an application online and wait for someone to contact you. The more you know about what a company wants, the more you can make sure it's you that they want.

Finally, my last tip is to read about interview skills and prepare answers to common interview questions. I can't stress enough how important this is. A job interview is often your one chance to make a great impression. It's a good idea to practice your interview skills. Do a mock interview with a friend or career counselor. The career counselor can comment on your interview responses and suggest improvements. Practicing your interview will also help you feel more confident when the time for the real interview comes.

To conclude and sum up, as you prepare for your job search, you should increase your experience by volunteering, get help from all the people you know, collect your important documents, find out all you can about the company, and, lastly, practice your interview.

Main announcer: Thank you for sharing these wonderful tips with our listeners.

Page 30, Exercises 2A and 2B
Employment Counselor: Hello. I'm Dr. Williams from Career Courage—an employment agency. I'm here to talk about the important dos and don'ts for job interviews.

Your answers to interview questions are very important, but there are several other aspects, or key elements, that can affect your performance in a job interview.

The first important aspect is your clothing. First impressions are very important, so be sure to dress appropriately for the job you want. For example, you can wear more casual clothes for a construction job interview, but wear business clothes for an office job. In either case, wear clean clothes that are not wrinkled. Do not wear anything that is too tight or revealing. If you're not sure what to wear, be conservative. Always be clean and well-groomed. Don't wear heavy perfume or cologne.

Second, pay attention to your body language; it is extremely important. Your body language should indicate that you are interested but relaxed. Sit and stand up straight. Use a firm handshake when you meet your interviewer. Look at your interviewer, make eye contact when he or she speaks, and smile and nod to show that you are listening. Don't make nervous movements, such as tapping your fingers or your feet. In other words, remember that your body says as much as your words.

The next important aspect is your voice. Speak clearly so that the interviewer can understand you—don't mumble! Your voice should indicate interest. Relax so that you don't sound nervous, and don't speak too quickly or too slowly. Don't use too many sounds like "uh" or "um." On the whole, always try to sound confident and enthusiastic.

Finally, show respect during your interview. For example, the way you address an interviewer is very important. Always use "Mr." and "Ms.," unless the interviewer specifies some other preference. Do not use a lot of slang or informal language. Say "please" and "thank you" if the interviewer offers to do something for you. Ultimately, being polite and respectful in the interview shows that you will be polite and respectful if you get hired.

To conclude, appearance, body language, voice, and respect are all important. Let me add just a few other dos and don'ts: Make sure you arrive on time. Don't bring anything except the materials you need for your interview. Always turn off your phone before you walk into the building where you'll be interviewed. Although pay is obviously important, don't ask about compensation right away. Ideally, the interviewer will bring up the salary and benefits first so you don't have to. Any questions?

Page 31, Exercise 3A
Narrator: Conversation 1: Beatriz
Interviewer: Have a seat, Beatriz.
Beatriz: Thank you.
Interviewer: I see in your résumé that you're getting a certificate in computer programming.
Beatriz: Um…yes. I'll get my certificate in…uh…six weeks.
Interviewer: I'm sorry. I didn't hear that.
Beatriz: I'm sorry. I'm getting my programming certificate in six weeks.
Interviewer: I see. And I see that you've been working at a web development company.
Beatriz: Yes. I've been…um…I've had an internship there for the past year.
Interviewer: You know it's a little hard to hear you with that air conditioner on. Did you say you were a receptionist there?

Narrator: Conversation 2: Sam
Interviewer: Hello. You must be Sam. I'm Karen Mathews.
Sam: Hey, Karen! How's it going?
Interviewer: Fine, thank you. Please have a seat.
Sam: Thanks, man.
Narrator: Conversation 3: Bruno
Interviewer: Hello, Bruno. It's very nice to meet you. Let's start with this: Why did you choose to apply for a job here?
Bruno: Well, the place where I work now doesn't pay nearly enough. I have a family to support and need to make more money. Could you tell me what the salary and benefits package are like here?
Narrator: Conversation 4: Jin
Interviewer: Hello, Jin. I'm happy you could finally make it. Please come in and have a seat.
Jin: Thank you so much! Sorry I was running a little late today… Oh no…I really need to take this call. Could you excuse me for just a minute?
Interviewer: Actually, I have another candidate waiting. Perhaps we should just reschedule your interview for another day.

Page 33, Exercise 2B
Narrator: B. COMPLETE. Listen and complete the sentences. Then check whether the action is completed or continuing.
1. I've been working on my résumé.
2. I've been attending night classes.
3. My friend has proofread my résumé.
4. I've been applying for full-time jobs.
5. Miriam has taken classes in landscape design.
6. Shelly has finished all of her classes for her degree.
7. We've been studying all day for our math exam.
8. She's finally completed her applications for college.

Page 40, Exercise 1A
Interviewer: So, now I'd like to know what your greatest strengths and weaknesses are. Let's start with strengths.
Candidate: Oh, well, I haven't thought about that too much. Um. I guess I… I have been able to get things done when they needed to get done.
Interviewer: Can you give an example?
Candidate: Uh. I'm not sure I can think of a specific example. Uh, I am usually just happy to help out when it's necessary. I don't know if I always do the best job, but I try.
Interviewer: OK. Anything else?
Candidate: I don't think so.
Interviewer: How about your weaknesses?
Candidate: This one is easy! I am very shy, which makes it hard for me to talk to people or ask questions.

Page 40, Exercise 2C
Interviewer: So, now I'd like to know what your greatest strengths and weaknesses are. Let's start with strengths.
Candidate: Sure. Well, I am determined and persistent. I am able to get things done when they need to get done. For example, at my last job I was working on a presentation when my co-worker got sick. I taught myself his parts of the presentation, even though I had to stay late to make sure I was prepared. The presentation ended up going really well and we won the bid!
Interviewer: OK, great. How about your greatest weakness?
Candidate: I am naturally very shy, which makes it hard for me to talk to people or ask questions. This affected my work and I couldn't have imagined giving a presentation like I mentioned before. I took more English classes as well as some public speaking classes and that helped me to become confident and share my ideas with my team. I'm also not afraid to ask questions anymore and can usually get the quietest person in the room to speak up!

UNIT 3 – THE THOUGHTFUL CONSUMER

Pages 42 and 43, Exercises 2A, 2B, and 3A
Announcer: Good afternoon, listeners! Welcome to "Money Matters." Our guest today is Beth Howard, a financial consultant at Smart Investments. Beth is going to talk to us about strategies for successful money management. Thanks for joining us, Beth.
Beth: Thanks for having me.
Announcer: We all know that some people are better at managing money than others. Can you tell us what makes someone more successful at money management?
Beth: Of course. First of all, in order to manage your finances successfully, you need to start with a budget. Make a list of all your monthly expenses. Are there any expenses you can reduce or eliminate? Make cuts where you can, but be careful. Many people are unsuccessful because they try to cut back too much.

If your budget is very tight and restrictive, it may be impossible for you to stick to it. Then, when you find yourself going over your spending limit each month, you give up on your budget because it didn't work.

On the other hand, if you cut back in just a few areas at a time, instead of completely eliminating all extra expenses, you will be more likely to stick to your budget. Likewise, you should plan to spend a little more than your monthly average. For instance, if your electricity bill is usually $86 a month, write $90 on your budget sheet. You want to be ambitious, but you must also remain realistic. Make a budget that you can actually put into practice.

Second, make a list of goals. Just as athletes set goals to help keep them on track, you can set goals to help you keep your finances on track. However, if your goals are very broad, you'll be less successful because

282 Audio Script

it's hard to stay on track. Although saving money just to get rich might be a good goal, it's too broad.

In contrast, if you have a more specific goal, such as buying a new car, you'll stay more motivated. Similarly, you can increase motivation by setting some mini goals along the way to reward yourself. After you save a certain amount of money, you might reward yourself with a new pair of shoes or dinner at a nice restaurant.

Third, make adjustments each month. I see a lot of people who are unsuccessful because they never adjust their budget. Successful budget makers understand it is a trial and error process. Most expenses will differ from month to month. Remember that your utility bills will vary depending on the season. The cost of gasoline and groceries can also fluctuate. Change those items on your expense sheet whenever the prices go up or down.

Next, set aside an emergency fund. Not anticipating emergencies is a big reason why so many people are unsuccessful in managing their money. A budget works great until your car breaks down, your son needs braces, or you lose your phone and have to replace it. Emergency expenses can completely destroy even the most carefully detailed budget. Those who anticipate emergency situations recognize the need to set money aside for emergencies. If possible, have six months of living expenses saved. You never know when you'll need it.

Finally, it's important to give your budget enough time. Many people aren't successful because they become impatient and give up. You shouldn't expect immediate results from a budget. On the contrary, budgets take time and practice, and some trial and error before they produce results.

Everyone who sets a budget has the same goal: to save money. You might not meet your goal if you are impatient or inflexible. However, if you make smarter financial choices, have a reasonable budget, make budget adjustments when necessary, and really stick to it, you'll see good results.

Page 43, Exercise 3B
Narrator: 1.
Beth: Second, make a list of goals. Just as athletes set goals to help keep them on track, you can set goals to help you keep your finances on track.

Narrator: 2.
Beth: Although saving money just to get rich might be a good goal, it's too broad. In contrast, if you have a more specific goal, such as buying a new car, you'll stay more motivated.

Narrator: 3.
Beth: Many people aren't successful because they become impatient and give up. You shouldn't expect immediate results from a budget. On the contrary, budgets take time and practice, and some trial and error before they produce results.

Pages 50 and 51, Exercise 2A, 2B, and 3A
Narrator: Conversation 1
Jeff: Our car needs a lot of repairs. I think the best solution is to trade it in for a new car.
Lily: I think we need a different plan. We won't get much money for a trade-in. The car has too many problems. And we haven't saved enough money for a new car.
Jeff: Our car is very old, so it will inevitably break down soon, and that will be very expensive, probably more expensive than buying a new car.
Lily: A new car does sound great. On the other hand, I really don't like to borrow money.
Jeff: I think we will have to take out an auto loan. That's the easiest way.
Lily: Why don't we get a lease instead of a loan? A lease is similar to a loan, but a lease usually has less expensive payments.
Jeff: True, but unlike a loan, you don't own the car at the end of a lease. When a lease ends, you have to return the car. Another difference is that with a lease you have mileage limits that say how far you can drive in a year. And with a lease you can be charged if the car is damaged, like if the seats get torn. So I think the smartest strategy is to get a loan and then drive the car for several years after we pay off the loan. It's a good investment.
Lily: I see your point. Perhaps the smartest option is to invest in a new car, even if we have to take out a loan.
Jeff: We can choose a loan with the longest term, probably five years. That way, we can make the smallest payments possible.
Lily: That's a very long time. I would prefer a short-term loan over a long-term loan. Like you said, we could pay off the loan quickly and then drive the car for a few years after it has been paid off.
Jeff: That's true. Still, a short-term loan will mean larger payments. What if we have an emergency and can't make our payments? We need smaller payments so we can still set aside some money for emergencies.
Lily: Hmm. Let's go to a bank tomorrow and see what our options are. We need to think about which type of loan will make sense for us.

Narrator: Conversation 2
Chris: Our car needs some repairs. We should have it inspected to see which repairs are the most important. We'll fix what we have to now, and we'll start saving for a new vehicle. If we save carefully, we can buy a new car in a year or two.
Amy: Should we purchase a new car or a used one?
Chris: I'm not sure which option is the best. What do you think?
Amy: Let's take it one step at a time. First, we'll see how much money we can save in a year. Then we'll go to a car dealership and compare the least expensive new car to the nicest used car. I think a used car will be the best deal.

Chris: But I just remembered something. A lot of dealerships offer special incentives for purchasing new cars, such as free oil changes for a year. I think we should shop for the most reasonably priced new car.
Amy: Good point, but a used car will cost a lot less than a new car.
Chris: That's true, but when you buy a used car, you may be buying someone else's car problems.
Amy: Here's a plan. Let's save first, and then figure out the best value for our money. We can research to see if a new car or a used car will be best for us.

Page 60, Exercise 1A
Customer: Excuse me.
Customer Service Representative (CSR): Yes, how can I help you?
Customer: This iron hasn't worked right since I bought it. I need a refund.
CSR: OK, let me see your receipt…. Oh, it's too late to get a refund.
Customer: But it doesn't work! Surely you can do something about this.
CSR: No, I can't. That's our policy. Can I help the next customer?
Customer: I'm not done here! I expect better customer service than this. Where is your manager?
Manager: Can I help you, ma'am? Is there a problem?
Customer: Yes! This iron is clearly broken and I need a refund. Your employee isn't even listening to me.
CSR: I know the policy. You can't return it because it's been too long since you bought it.
Manager: True, that is the policy, but we can replace the product even after the refund date…. We always aim to please our customers. Would it be all right with you to get an exchange instead of a refund?
Customer: Thank you! That's all I really wanted.
Manager: We're always happy to help.

Page 60, Exercise 2C
Customer: Excuse me.
CSR: Yes, how can I help you?
Customer: This iron hasn't worked right since I bought it. I need a refund.
CSR: I'm sorry to hear that. OK, let me see your receipt…. Oh, I'm sorry. It's too late to get a refund. But we may be able to do something else. Let me check with my manager.
Customer: OK, sure.
CSR: All right, I just spoke with my manager, and she said I can offer you a replacement instead of a refund. Would that be OK?
Customer: Yeah, that's great.
CSR: Perfect. Let's get you checked out.

UNIT 4 – AT PEAK PERFORMANCE

Pages 62 and 63, Exercises 2A, 2B, 3A, and 3B
Main announcer: Hello! And welcome back to "Getting Started." Are you seeking a promotion or trying to work your way up the career ladder at your company but you don't know what steps to take to improve your chances of getting a promotion? Then today's episode is for you. Our guest today is Roger Chambers, a human resources director for a large corporation. He's here to talk about factors that influence job promotion. Roger, what are some actions employees can take in order to earn a promotion?
Roger: First of all, the length of time an employee works at a company is an important factor when it comes to promotions. Try to stay with the same company so that you can build relationships and prove your value to the managers. A recent report claimed that it usually takes months, or even years, to be promoted. The study explained that there are good reasons for this. First, an employee has to work long enough in order to master the skills required for his or her current job. Second, the employers claim that they need a chance to see how the employee might respond in a variety of situations—especially situations that might come up in the employee's next position.
Main announcer: So if you stay with a company long enough, you'll eventually be promoted?
Roger: Well no, not necessarily. According to that same study, many employees spend years at a company without ever receiving a promotion. Length of time is only one of many factors.
Main announcer: Right. There are several other dimensions, such as arriving to work on time, doing a good job, and staying out of trouble.
Roger: Sure, but that's still not enough. Those are basic factors that employers expect of all workers. In order to get a promotion, you need to go above and beyond the basic job expectations.
Main announcer: But how exactly can an employee go above and beyond the usual job requirements?
Roger: I believe that teamwork is the most important factor in proving your value to a company. Studies show that collaboration is highly valued in today's workplace. Based on that information, anyone who wants to be a leader or supervisor should put the success of the team or the company ahead of his or her own personal success. It's important to acknowledge co-workers for their work, share credit for ideas, and encourage and mentor others. Managers want to know that the people they promote are team players.

Another important factor is flexibility. A recent study indicated that flexibility and a willingness to learn new things are important factors. Employers want to promote people who are flexible and will adapt to new responsibilities easily. They select people who are eager to learn more about the organization. Employers also tend to promote employees who have developed the skills necessary for their current job and who have started to learn the skills that they may need in the future.

Communication skills is yet another factor. According to a recent article in "Business Report," companies want leaders with excellent speaking and writing skills. A leader or supervisor needs to be able to

Audio Script **283**

Audio Script

choose the right words to explain, to offer criticism, to inspire or motivate, and to persuade. Good listening skills are important, too. A supervisor needs to communicate with people from different backgrounds and in various positions. Whether dealing with customers, co-workers, or managers, having communication skills is important.

One final important factor is taking the initiative in solving problems. In almost any workplace, you can find people who avoid dealing with problems. They may think, "That's not my job." Or they may be afraid of becoming involved or making a mistake—so they wait for someone else to solve the problem. Employees who take the initiative to solve problems stand out. These people are more likely to be considered for promotion than colleagues who don't take action when problems arise.

Main announcer: This is very helpful, Roger. Thank you for sharing this information today. Is there anything else you would like to add before we end our interview?

Roger: Yes! One last thing, and this is related to taking the initiative. If you want a promotion, you need to ask for one. Don't sit around and wait for your employer to offer you a promotion. Gather plenty of evidence to indicate why you deserve a promotion. Then request a meeting with your manager.

Pages 70 and 71, Exercises 2A, 2B, and 3A
Narrator: Conversation 1
Speaker A: Hey, Dan?
Speaker B: Yes?
Speaker A: I got a message that explained that you and the other new hires need to watch some training videos today, but the noise is a little distracting. Would you mind using headphones?
Speaker B: Of course not. Now that you mention it, I had to attend an orientation for new employees yesterday, and the director indicated that we should always use headphones when viewing videos in the office. I completely forgot. Sorry about that.
Speaker A: No problem. I really appreciate your cooperation!
Speaker B: Thanks again for bringing up the problem in such a friendly way.

Narrator: Conversation 2
Speaker A: I wasn't able to take a lunch break today because I had to cover the front desk while you were on your break.
Speaker B: Oh, I'm sorry! I didn't realize I was out so long.
Speaker A: It's OK this time, but according to our company policy, we each get only 30 minutes for lunch.
Speaker B: I feel terrible. How about I cover the desk tomorrow so that you can have a long lunch break?
Speaker A: No, that's OK. I want everyone to have a lunch break. Why don't we come up with a consistent break schedule, and then we can all stick to it?
Speaker B: Sounds like a good plan.

Narrator: Conversation 3
Speaker A: Could you turn off that music? I'm trying to work over here.
Speaker B: Well, I'm trying to work, too, and I'm more productive when I listen to music.
Speaker A: Then get some headphones. We all have to share this office space. I can't concentrate with that noise.
Speaker B: I turned the volume very low. You make a lot more noise on your personal calls. We all have to listen to you make a dentist appointment or talk to your wife.
Speaker A: I just make a few calls during my break. You listen to music all day. And it's very inconsiderate.
Speaker B: I'm not trying to be inconsiderate. I'll use headphones since it bothers you so much, but I wish you had just asked a little more politely.
Speaker A: Sorry about that; it's been a long day. I'll try to ask more politely next time. And I'll make my personal calls outside from now on.

Narrator: Conversation 4
Speaker A: I'm sorry to bring this up, Jenn, but when you eat at your desk, our whole office smells like a fast food restaurant.
Speaker B: So I'm not allowed to eat lunch?
Speaker A: That's not what I said. Don't get so defensive!
Speaker B: You don't like the smell of my food. Is that what you're saying?
Speaker A: No, that's not it. I'm just asking if you could please eat your lunch in the break room, not at your desk.
Speaker B: Well, why didn't you say that to begin with? Of course, I can eat in the break room.
Speaker A: Great. Thanks. I'm glad we talked and worked this out.

Page 80, Exercise 2C
Julie: Hi Manny. I'm having a problem. The new equipment at this jobsite is so loud that it's hurting my ears. I feel like we should be wearing some kind of hearing protection.
Manny: You know that we have noise at all our jobsites.
Julie: Yes, but the noise here is really, really loud.
Manny: Well, perhaps that new machine is especially noisy. Do you feel that the noise is hurting your hearing?
Julie: Yes. Even after I go home, I hear ringing in my ears.
Manny: Then I should definitely order everyone some hearing protection. I'll put the order in at the office this afternoon. Thanks for letting me know about the problem.

UNIT 5 – AFFORDABLE HOUSING

Pages 82 and 83, Exercises 2A, 2B, 3A, and 3B
Announcer: On today's podcast, we're examining a serious concern in our society: homelessness. Our guest today is Bill Sizemore, director of a nonprofit organization whose goal is to fight homelessness. Welcome to our program, Bill. Could you start by telling us what homelessness looks like?

Guest: That's a great question. What does homelessness look like in our community? It's actually not as apparent as you might expect. Many people don't realize just how large the homeless population is because the homeless are often not visible. The homeless people that you see living and sleeping on the sidewalks or city park benches make up only a small percentage of the total homeless population. The majority of the homeless population are people who move around from place to place, sleeping in cars, shelters, motels, or staying with friends or family. They do not have a permanent place that they can call home. They have no idea where they will go from one day to the next. The homeless population consists of both men and women, young and old, individuals and families.

According to the National Coalition for the Homeless, in the United States, more than 550,000 people experience homelessness on a single night. That's 17 out of every 10,000 people in the U.S. About 67% of the homeless population consists of individuals, while 33% are people with children. Of the total homeless population, people under the age of 25 living on their own make up 7%. Veterans make up another 7% of the homeless population. About 18% of the homeless population are chronically homeless, which means they have experienced homelessness repeatedly or for an extended period of time.

Announcer: What causes homelessness, and what can we do about it?

Guest: That's a very complicated question. There are several problems that may lead to homelessness, but two concerns that are largely responsible for the rise in homelessness over the past few decades are insufficient income and lack of affordable housing. Clearly, the solution to lack of income is to help all individuals earn a wage that allows them to move above the poverty line. A raise in the minimum pay per hour would move more people in that direction.

The lack of affordable housing is an equally significant problem. In our city, for example, 38% of the homeless citizens were evicted from their residence because they couldn't pay their rent or house payments. Another 21% were evicted by their friends or families due to overcrowded living conditions. Nine percent were living in substandard buildings that the city closed or tore down. Seven percent lost their homes in a disaster, such as a fire. So, three-quarters of our homeless population simply needs housing. Providing more affordable housing, therefore, is one obvious way to solve the problem.

Announcer: But that seems like a very big challenge. Who provides the affordable housing?

Guest: One answer is the government. Government subsidy houses are built by the government and given to low-income families. There are also private companies and nonprofit organizations that raise money to provide more affordable housing solutions.

But for some homeless people, housing is only part of the problem. Other challenges that lead to homelessness include domestic violence, substance abuse, and mental illness. This group makes up at least 25% of the homeless population here in our city. And there is no clear resolution. The challenges for people in this group are very difficult problems on their own, but the challenges become even more difficult to address when a person is homeless. Most organizations are concerned only with putting a roof over someone's head before they even consider the other issues.

The bottom line is that there are no simple solutions to homelessness. Homeless people are often trapped in a vicious cycle. They can't pay rent unless they get a job. They can't apply for a job unless they have an address.

Fighting this problem will take much more than an individual or even a government effort. We all need to work together to solve this problem in our community.

Page 90, Exercises 2A and 2B
Loan Officer: Hi, Eric. Hello, Monica. Please come in and have a seat. I understand you're interested in a home loan, right?
Eric: Yes, that's correct.
Loan Officer: Have you already found a home that you want to buy?
Monica: No, not yet. We still have three months left on our apartment lease. We're just looking around at houses now.
Eric: We want to make sure we can secure a loan before we make an offer on a house. We're worried our loan application will be rejected. We've never applied for a home loan before. And we're not sure how much money we can borrow. So we want to see what kind of loan we can get and what the payments will look like.
Loan Officer: That's very smart. The first thing we'll do is determine whether or not you're eligible for a mortgage, or a home loan. First, we need to calculate your net worth. Your net worth is the amount remaining after you have subtracted your total liabilities from your assets. Then—
Eric: Sorry to interrupt you, but could you explain what you mean by liabilities and assets?
Loan Officer: Sure. Assets refer to money or anything that you own. For example, your checking and savings account are assets. So are any vehicles or property you own. Liabilities include things that you're still paying for, or money that you owe someone. Any type of debt, such as a credit card or school loan, is a liability. Does that make sense?
Eric: Yes. Thanks!
Loan Officer: So, you need to calculate assets and liabilities. Then, you need to determine how much you have for a down payment. The down payment is the amount of money that you pay as a lump sum. The higher your down payment, the lower your mortgage will be. Finally, you will be ready to work out the monthly mortgage payment you can afford. Your mortgage payment should not be more than 32% of your gross monthly

income, at the very most. The amount of mortgage you can qualify for at a bank will be determined by your net worth and the amount of your down payment, as well as your credit score. If you successfully meet all the requirements, the bank will pre-qualify you for a loan.

Monica: What is the credit score range needed to pre-qualify for a loan?

Loan Officer: Your credit score is a number ranging from 300 to 850. It shows how likely you are to repay debt. You'll need at least a 650 to get a loan with our bank. Do you happen to know what your credit score is?

Monica: No, we don't. What if our score is below 650?

Loan Officer: Then you would need to try another bank or a credit union. Some places offer loans for people with lower credit scores. Before you submit a complete loan application, I can see if you prequalify for a loan. This means you'll know if you meet our eligibility requirements, and I can provide you with an estimate of how much financing you could receive. That way, you can decide if you want to continue with your application.

Eric: Sounds good. What will we need for the complete application?

Loan Officer: You'll need to submit tax returns for the past two years, current pay stubs or other proof of income, bank statements for the past six months, a letter from your landlord stating that you have paid your rent on time, and of course we'll order a complete credit report. After you've filled out a loan application and our bank has analyzed your credit more thoroughly, we can provide you with a "pre-approval." That's a written letter stating how much money you can borrow. That letter will confirm your ability to borrow that amount of money. Getting pre-approved lets you and others see in writing that you qualify for a specific home loan amount. With your pre-approval in hand, you're ready to start shopping for your new home. We'll finalize the loan later on in the process, after you've found the home you want to buy.

Page 91, Exercise 3A

Eric: I'm looking at these different options our loan officer gave us, but I'm not sure I understand. Do you?

Monica: Yes, I think so. The term is how long it will take us to pay off the loan. The interest rate shows the additional amount we'll pay on top of what we owe. We want a fixed interest rate so the percentage doesn't change over time.

The minimum down payment is the amount we have to pay up front, when we get our loan. The minimum credit score is the lowest score we need to qualify for the loan. And mortgage insurance is an extra fee the bank charges to guarantee our loan in case we stop making payments. It's usually about 1% of the amount of the loan. So option 1 with no mortgage insurance and a low interest rate is clearly the best option.

Eric: But our credit score isn't quite high enough for option 1.

Monica: That's right. Together, our score is right at 700. And the other problem is we don't have that much money for a down payment. Most of the houses we're interested in cost around $200,000. That means we would need to put down $40,000. We only have about half that amount.

Eric: So maybe we should renew our apartment lease for another year. In the meantime, we can save up for a bigger down payment and work to increase our credit score. Our loan officer said there are some steps we can take to improve our credit scores, such as closing credit card accounts we don't use and checking our credit report for mistakes.

Monica: Yes, waiting is definitely one solution. We could also start with a less expensive house. We can always sell it in a couple of years and buy our dream home later.

Eric: True, but it's expensive to buy and sell a house. We still have to pay bank fees and closing costs. And we would need to hire a realtor when we sell. It seems more complicated than renting.

Monica: Maybe. I'm not sure. We need to investigate more.

Eric: We can also consider the other loan options. We have the down payment and the credit score we need for options 2 and 4.

Monica: Yes, but we would also have a higher interest rate, and we would need to pay mortgage insurance.

Eric: This is going to be a much harder decision than I thought.

Page 100, Exercise 1A

Bank Manager: Hi there! How can I help you today?

Applicant: I want to buy a house, so I'd like to apply for a loan.

Bank Manager: I can help you with that. Have you completed the loan application paper work?

Applicant: Oh, I got started, but I haven't finished it yet.

Bank Manager: OK, well, that will be the first step. Unless you've finished the application, we can't really go much further. As you're working on it, keep in mind that you'll need to show that you have a good credit score so the bank can see that you've paid past debts back regularly and on time.

Applicant: OK.

Bank Manager: Also, when you come back with the completed paperwork, you will need to attach copies of your tax returns and your pay stubs or some other proof of income.

Applicant: Wow. That's a lot of paperwork.

Bank Manager: Yes, but it all helps to show that you are responsible and likely to pay back the loan. So, when you complete the application and gather your documents, come back and we'll talk again.

Page 100, Exercise 2C

Bank Manager: Hi there! How can I help you today?

Applicant: I want to buy a house, so I'd like to apply for a loan.

Bank Manager: I can help you with that. Have you completed the loan application paper work?

Applicant: Yes. Here it is.

Bank Manager: Great! Let's have a look. OK, it looks like the application itself is complete. That's good. Now, what have you brought in for supporting documentation?

Applicant: First, here are my tax returns from last year.

Bank Manager: OK.

Applicant: Also, here are 12 months of my pay stubs. I changed jobs three months ago, so I'm making more money now.

Bank Manager: Congratulations! That will affect how much money the bank will lend you, so that's good.

Applicant: Also, I printed off some of my credit card statements to show you that I have made all my payments on time.

Bank Manager: That's really important.

Applicant: Finally, although I know you will confirm it yourself, I checked my credit score online and it's 760.

Bank Manager: That's a strong score. OK, I'll have a look at all this paperwork and, in a couple of days, I will let you know if the application is approved and for how much. Between the two of us, though, this is a strong application. I think it'll be a slam dunk.

Applicant: Thanks so much. I'll check back with you in two days.

UNIT 6 – WHEN NATURE IS IN CHARGE

Pages 102 and 103, Exercises 2A, 2B, 3A, and 3B

And now for today's weather forecast ….

Be sure to give yourself plenty of time to travel to work this morning. It's cold and rainy out there. As a result, you can expect major traffic delays. The heavy rains are causing hazardous driving conditions across the state. So far this morning, 20 weather-related accidents have been reported. The barometer indicates very low pressure, and our radar map shows even more rain heading this way. The heaviest rainfall is expected this evening. Due to these conditions, the Weather Service has issued a severe weather advisory for this evening, with an increased chance of severe thunderstorms that may trigger flash flooding. Thus, if you don't need to travel this evening, we encourage you to stay in place.

And now let's take a look at tomorrow's forecast. Rainfall is expected to end by midnight, but temperatures will continue to fall. Arctic air from Canada could produce freezing temperatures by morning. This cold front may result in temperatures falling more than 20 degrees below normal. Consequently, standing water on roads and highways may freeze into ice. Icy roads are, of course, extremely dangerous and may cause serious accidents. Please allow plenty of time for travel and continue to exercise caution tomorrow.

And finally, for some good news, the long-range weather forecast looks promising, with partially sunny skies expected by Friday. We're expecting clear skies and warmer temperatures for the weekend, so hang in there! But for now, stay safe and dry, everyone.

Pages 110 and 111, Exercises 2A, 2B, and 3A

Newscaster: Recent hurricanes have caused great destruction and much suffering. It is important to look at these storms as learning opportunities. In many cases, storms cause more damage because residents and city officials do not take the threat of the storm seriously. If residents understood the risks, they would make better preparations for natural disasters. And if city officials set aside more emergency funds, recovery efforts could go faster and smoother. Cities might be better equipped to handle natural disasters if the residents and government officials learned from past mistakes. Hurricane Harvey is an example of a storm that taught some very difficult lessons.

Harvey was a Category 4 hurricane that hit Texas on August 25, 2017. The floods from the storm devastated the city of Houston, Texas. The amount of rainfall exceeded all previous records, with 51 inches of rain in some parts of Houston. The U.S. military released water from two major dams in order to control water flow along the main river in Houston, but the water level was so high that it flowed over the top of the dams and flooded homes in the area. Some parts of the city were completely under water.

The enormous impact Harvey had on people was due to both its power and its location, with over 6 and a half million people living in Houston. Thousands of people tried to leave the city but found travel was impossible because highways around the city were cut off due to high floodwaters. Many residents who tried to stay in their homes became stranded as the water rose and they couldn't get out of their homes. Either scenario was a disaster. Because so many people were forced to go up to their roofs, The Federal Emergency Management Agency, or FEMA, arranged rescue plans, sending boats to residential areas and flying helicopters over the city to rescue residents from rooftops. Over 30,000 people were left homeless immediately after the storm, and at least 68 people died. Thousands of residents had no electricity in their homes or access to food and clean water. Since the businesses also had no electricity or water, schools and businesses were shut down for several days.

The impact on the environment was also severe. Because the floodwaters carried bacteria and various chemicals, residents were advised to avoid contact with the water. The quality of the drinking water became an urgent health concern since water treatment plants were also affected by the storm. While floodwater caused most of the environmental damage, the air quality was also affected. Many oil refineries and chemical plants were forced to shut down quickly due to flooding, power outages, and lightning strikes. These sudden outages caused the release of millions of pounds of air pollution.

Finally, the economic impact of Harvey was staggering. Harvey caused about $125 billion in damage, making it one of the most expensive natural disasters in U.S. history. Over 200,000 homes, 1 million vehicles, and tens of thousands of businesses were damaged by the storm. Recovery took over a year. As a result, many businesses remained closed for months.

The human, environmental, and economic impact of Hurricane Harvey was devastating. Many Houston residents were not prepared for or even aware of the risk of flooding. Because of their experience with

Audio Script

Harvey, Houston residents may be more prepared to deal with storms in the future. It has also triggered public officials to examine how the city can prepare for and protect against this kind of flooding in the future.

Page 120, Exercise 1A
Manager: Did you get the severe-weather alert?
Shift Lead: Yes, I did. Thank you.
Manager: Is everyone where they need to be?
Shift Lead: Excuse me?
Manager: Did you get everyone to the designated severe-weather area?
Shift Lead: What do you mean?
Manager: What do I mean? Didn't you get my email last week marked "Urgent"? I told you to carefully review the information because severe weather was predicted for this week.
Shift Lead: Sorry. I'm behind in checking my email.
Manager: A week behind? That's not acceptable. You know the expectation is that you check your email every morning when the shift starts. You are the shift lead. I count on you to exercise leadership. And now we're in a severe weather alert and nobody is where they need to be!
Shift Lead: Sorry. I'll check my email now.
Manager: There's no time for that! We need to get everyone to a safe location now. The cafeteria is the designated severe-weather area. Take everyone there now have them sit under the tables. You'll get an "all-clear" on your phone when the severe weather has passed. Do it now!

Page 120, Exercise 2C
Manager: Did you get the severe-weather alert?
Shift Lead: Yes I did. Thank you.
Manager: Is everyone where they need to be?
Shift Lead: Absolutely. We are all in the designated severe-weather area now.
Manager: Is everyone sitting under the cafeteria tables?
Shift Lead: Yes. Just like you instructed in your email.
Manager: Excellent. I was really worried. I'm glad you are all safe.
Shift Lead: We'll stay here until I get the "all clear" message on my phone.
Manager: That's exactly right. I appreciate you being on top of this. I know I can count on you to exercise leadership.
Shift Lead: Yes, you can. We'll all be fine. Thanks for checking in.

UNIT 7 – PROTECTING THE PLANET

Pages 122 and 123, Exercises 2A, 2B, 3A, and 3B
Many people think of climate change as a distant future threat, but actually, scientific data shows the Earth's climate is already changing. In the last five years, the World Meteorological Organization has recorded a higher incidence of extreme weather events such as droughts, heatwaves, rainfall, hurricanes, wildfires, melting of sea ice, and many other signs that clearly indicate the Earth's climate has changed. Most scientists agree that the cause of global warming is human activity. The primary human activities that contribute to climate change include: generating electricity, using transportation, discarding waste, and cutting down forests.

The way we generate electricity is a significant problem because most electricity comes from power plants that run on fossil fuels like coal or gas. These power plants emit, or release, huge amounts of greenhouse gases, especially carbon dioxide and methane. These gases are like the glass in a greenhouse. They allow the sunlight to pass in, but they block the heat from escaping into space.

We must also pay particular attention to our means of transportation. Like power plants, most cars, buses, trains, and planes also run on fossil fuels and emit pollutants. Every time we drive a car, carbon dioxide comes out of the exhaust pipe and floats up into the air and gets trapped in the atmosphere.

Disposing of waste is another key activity because most trash ends up in landfills. About two-thirds of landfill waste is biodegradable. As the waste rots and decomposes, it releases methane gas into the atmosphere.

And finally, there's deforestation, or cutting down and clearing forests to convert the land into farms, ranches, or urban areas. We also cut down trees to use the wood for building materials. This is a noteworthy activity because when we cut down forests, the trees can no longer absorb carbon dioxide from the atmosphere, and they add new carbon dioxide (CO_2) to the air as they decompose.

So the crux of the matter is that climate change is attributed to all these human activities. Human activities are causing more carbon dioxide and other gases to be released into the air. These gases cover the planet like a big blanket. This blanket then traps in more greenhouse gases because they can't escape into space. These trapped gases make the planet warmer. And a warmer planet causes climate change.

Pages 130 and 131, Exercises 2A, 2B, and 3A
Host: Hello! And welcome back to the show. Today we're going to talk about our carbon footprint, or the amount of carbon dioxide each of us produces with every action. We all have a carbon footprint. If your carbon footprint is small, you have an environmentally friendly lifestyle. But what should you do if you have a big carbon footprint? That's our question for our guest, Claire Henderson, a climatologist. Welcome, Dr. Henderson!
Dr. Henderson: It's my pleasure.
Host: So what can we do if we have a big carbon footprint?
Dr. Henderson: The best way to offset your carbon footprint is to look for ways to limit the amount of carbon dioxide you produce. I'd like to highlight four major areas that generate excess carbon dioxide: electricity, transportation, personal habits, and waste. There are some easy ways you can reduce your carbon footprint in each of the four areas.

Let's start with electricity. Always turn off the lights, TV, or anything you're not using. You can go a step further and replace old lightbulbs with energy-efficient bulbs that consume less electricity, and when it's time to replace big appliances such as your refrigerator or washer and dryer, look for the most energy-efficient appliances. You'll reduce your carbon footprint *and* your electric bill. Another important way to cut down on electricity and save money is to get a programmable thermostat to turn your heating or air-conditioning up and down automatically depending on the time of day.
Host: That's a great idea. If I had installed a programmable thermostat last summer, I would have saved hundreds of dollars. My electricity bill was crazy.

Dr. Henderson. Right. It was a very hot summer. And if your electricity bill was higher, you were also contributing to more carbon emissions.
Host: Good point. Can you tell us about the next area, transportation?
Dr. Henderson: Of course. All gasoline-powered cars emit carbon dioxide. The bigger the car, the more carbon dioxide it emits. When you purchase your next car, consider an electric or hybrid vehicle, and think about getting a smaller car to conserve energy. And when possible, walk or take a bicycle instead of the car.

The next area is waste. Look for sustainable ways to dispose of waste. Remember the three R's: reduce, reuse, recycle. Only buy what you need and will actually use. If you no longer need something, see if you can donate it to someone. And if you can't reuse it, find out if it's recyclable, and then dispose of it in a recycle bin.

And last, let's talk about personal habits. Think about your food and where it comes from. Growing, processing, packaging, and delivering food requires energy from farms, factories, delivery trucks, and stores. If you buy locally grown food from the farmer's market, you'll support local farmers and reduce your carbon footprint. Another personal habit to consider is your water use. When water goes down the drain, it is processed through water treatment plants, even if it's clean. Use only the amount of water you really need.
Host: Thank you, Dr. Henderson. These are wonderful suggestions. If I had known about some of them sooner, I could have made better choices myself. To conclude, could you explain why it's so important to reduce our carbon footprint?
Dr. Henderson: A big carbon footprint contributes to climate change. And climate change causes all sorts of problems. It can cause heat waves that damage crops and livestock, thereby limiting food supply and making life more difficult for entire communities. The warmer air of climate change can cause flowers to bloom earlier and this increase the pollen in the air, which in turn causes allergies, asthma and other health problems. It can also cause ice caps to melt, which then makes sea levels rise. Higher sea levels can lead to flooding.

It is urgent that we all do our part to reduce our own carbon footprint.

Page 140, Exercise 1A
Manager: Hey! Do you have a minute?
Owner: Sure!
Manager: I just wanted to talk to you all about a problem I've noticed at your store.
Owner: Oh no! What's the problem?
Manager: Well, we get boxes and boxes of our products every day, right? And, what do we do with all the packaging material when we unpack the boxes, all the bubble wrap and the packing peanuts? We throw it all in the garbage dumpster behind the building. The packaging alone generates a lot of the trash we throw away every day.
Owner: Yes, that's true.
Manager: That's not very environmentally friendly. I think we can find better ways to dispose of or repurpose our trash.
Owner: You're probably right. How do you feel about putting together a team to come up with some ideas for solving this problem? I'd like a solution that doesn't cost too much money.
Manager: Actually, I don't think that's necessary. I already know what we should do.
Owner: Hmmm. I'm sure you have some good ideas, but if you involve some people from other departments, like customer service and repairs, you'll get a variety of ideas. In my experience, a team is a better problem-solver than any one person.
Manager: Well, maybe. But I'm going to work on this on my own for a while.

Page 140, Exercise 2C
Manager: Hey! Do you have a minute?
Owner: Sure!
Manager: I just wanted to talk to you all about a problem I've noticed at your store.
Owner: Oh no! What's the problem?
Manager: We throw a lot of boxes and packing materials away every day. It's not very environmentally friendly. I think we can find better ways to dispose of or repurpose our trash.
Owner: You're probably right. How do you feel about putting together a team to come up with some ideas for solving this problem? I'd like a solution that doesn't cost too much money.
Manager: That's a great idea! I'll come up with a list of names of people from different departments that might be interested in working on this problem. I should probably reach out someone from Accounting, so we can keep an eye on the budget while we try to solve this problem.
Owner: You know I like that idea!
Manager: I might also want to put together a survey so all of the employees can respond with their own suggestions.
Owner: A survey is a good way to involve everyone.
Manager: If we get a lot of responses on the survey, we'll have a nice variety of suggestions. Once we get the responses, I'll schedule some time for the team to brainstorm some solutions. We'll try to have a proposal with several cost-effective options on your desk by next week.

Owner: That sounds great. Thanks for noticing this problem and taking the lead on finding a solution. I'm also really impressed with your interest in working with a team of people.

UNIT 8 – THE DIGITAL AGE

Pages 142 and 143, Exercises 2A, 2B, 3A, and 3B

Announcer: Modern technology has changed our lives, but has it made our lives better or worse? Our reporter, Ellen Larsen, visited a community college to ask students to discuss the pros and cons of the digital age. Here's what they had to say.

Ellen: Hello! I'm here at Central Community College talking to Solomon, Keisha, and Jackson, a group of new college students. These students have grown up using digital technology all their lives. I wanted to know how they felt about living in the digital age. Let's start with you, Solomon. What's the best thing about the digital age?

Solomon: Oh, that's easy. The best thing is smartphones. I can't imagine living without my phone. It has everything I need at the touch of a button. I can check my email, watch videos, take and edit pictures, use a navigation app to get directions, do my homework, and access information 24/7. All that plus I can easily stay in touch with my family. My parents and siblings live in Ethiopia, where I'm from. I love being able to video call them every week. My smartphone makes me feel like we're all in the same place... For all these reasons, I think smartphones are absolutely the best thing about living in the digital age, and smart phone technology will only get better and better in the future.

Ellen: Do you think there are any disadvantages to smartphones?

Solomon: Sure. They can be a huge distraction, and in some circumstances, it's simply not appropriate to use your smartphone. A lot of students in my classes play on their phones, even while the professor is talking. It's very rude. And I don't like it when I see a family eating out at a nice restaurant, but instead of talking and enjoying their time together, everyone is staring at their phones. Indeed, smartphones have the potential to be good or bad. Smartphones can bring people closer together or create more distance. It all depends on how you use them.

Ellen: Great point. How about you, Keisha? What do you consider to be the pros and cons of living in the digital age?

Keisha: I think distance education is the biggest pro. I like having the ability to take classes online. I recently got a new job, and I'll be working full-time next semester. It's going to be impossible for me to be on campus every single day. For this reason, online classes will be essential because they will give me the flexibility I need.

Ellen: Do you think online classes are as good as your face-to-face classes?

Keisha: Yes. Sometimes I think they're even better. It depends on how the professor facilitates the class. Some online classes are very interactive and require group projects. Therefore, the students get to know each other just as well as they do in face-to-face classes. All in all, when it comes to distance education, I don't see any cons.

Solomon: Hmmm. I don't know about that. Can I add something here?

Ellen: Sure, Solomon. What are your thoughts about distance education?

Solomon: I understand what Keisha's saying, but I still think nothing beats face-to-face classes. When it comes to education, I'm a little old-school. I like to see my professors and classmates in person. I've taken a couple online classes, and I found it really hard to stay motivated. The professors weren't very engaging, and there was almost no social interaction among the students. As a result, I consider distance education to be boring. Ultimately, there's nothing like the traditional college experience, being on a real campus and making lifelong friends.

Keisha: Well, I've had great experiences and made lifelong friends in all of my online classes. As I said, I've made some really close friends as we worked together on online projects. I guess we're going to have to agree to disagree.

Ellen: Interesting perspective! I've never really thought about it. Thank you both for sharing your ideas. So what are your thoughts, Jackson? What do you see as the pros and cons of the digital age?

Jackson: I think social media is definitely a big plus. I can spend just a few minutes checking my social media accounts each day and find out what's happening in the world. I use social media to check my friends' posts and status updates, so I can celebrate their accomplishments, like a graduation or a new job. I would certainly have lost contact with many of my childhood friends without social media. I really like seeing all their pictures of weddings and new babies. Plus, I like getting reminders of friends' birthdays and other important dates. Given these reasons, I think social media is great. However, the con is that social media makes it very easy to spread misinformation. I'm concerned about all the rumors, fake news, and other misleading information that spreads through social media. Therefore, I believe that the digital age and access to social media can have both pros and cons.

Ellen: You all bring up excellent points. Thank you for talking with me today!

Page 151, Exercises 2A, 2B, and 3A

Speaker 1: I didn't mean to do it. I wasn't even driving very fast. I know it was wrong. There's no justification. But it all happened so quickly. I was reading a short text, just one brief text. And when I looked up, it was too late. I had already hit the other car. I never meant to hurt anyone. I'm so sorry...

Speaker 2: I was driving home after school, and my best friend was in the car. Someone texted her a funny picture, and she wanted me to look at it. I glanced at it for just a second. I didn't see the red light. It was an accident....

Speaker 3: Any distraction can pose serious dangers for drivers. According to The National Highway Traffic Safety Administration, in 2015, distracted driving caused over 3,000 deaths and almost 400,000 injuries, making up 10% of all fatal crashes and 15% of injury crashes. Furthermore, because teenagers are not very experienced drivers, they are especially at risk. The fatal crash rate for teenagers is three times higher than it is for drivers over the age of 20. Talking, texting, eating, drinking, changing a song on your stereo, looking at your navigation system, anything that diverts your attention away from the task of driving, even for a second, is a dangerous distraction.

But texting is perhaps the most alarming distraction. Drivers who are sending or reading text messages are 20 times more likely to be involved in a car crash than other drivers. Why does texting cause so many accidents? Sending or reading a text takes your eyes off the road for 5 seconds or more. Close your eyes and slowly count to five. Imagine what tragedy could have occurred in those five seconds. You wouldn't close your eyes for five seconds while you're driving, right? But texting has the same effect. That's why thousands of people are killed or seriously injured in texting-related accidents every year. It takes only a few seconds, and then it's too late.

Please refrain from texting and driving, not just for you, but for everyone on the road.

Page 160, Exercise 1A

Sales Clerk: Oh, wow! Then what happened?

Customer: Excuse me. Do you have this t-shirt in a smaller size?

Sales Clerk: I'm sorry. What did you say?

Customer: Can you get me a smaller size in this?

Sales Clerk: Oh, yeah. Just a second. No way! I can't believe it! What are you going to do? Do you think you should text him back? — Ma'am? Here you are.

Customer: Hmmm. I'm not sure about it. My daughter is about your size. Which one do you think would fit you?

Sales Clerk: Huh? Me? I don't know.

Customer: I think I'll get the smaller one. Can you ring it up for me?

Sales Clerk: Umm, sure…Well I think you should text him back. I mean, it's not your fault… Let me text you what I think you should do.

Customer: Could you please put your phone down for a minute while you ring up my purchase? It's really rude and you should be working, not talking or texting on the phone.

Sales Clerk: Oh, yeah. Sorry. My friend is having a problem and we're not really that busy right now.

Customer: You might not be very busy, but you really should learn to exercise some self-discipline when it comes to staying attached to your friends digitally!

Page 160, Exercise 2C

Sales Clerk: Oh, wow! Then what happened?

Customer: Excuse me. Do you have this t-shirt in a smaller size?

Sales Clerk: I'm sorry. What did you say?

Customer: Can you get me a smaller size in this?

Sales Clerk: Oh, yeah. Just a second. I'll have to call you back on my break. Ma'am? Here you are.

Customer: Hmmm. I'm not sure about it. My daughter is about your size. Which one do you think would fit you?

Sales Clerk: I think I would wear the smaller one. Would you like to look at any sweaters or jeans while you are here?

Customer: Hmm. No, I don't think so.

Sales Clerk: Okay. I'll ring this up for you. Oh, I m so sorry. I'll put this under the counter.

Customer: My daughter can't even ignore her phone for a couple of minutes. Congratulations on exercising such impressive self-discipline!

Sales Clerk: Thanks! Do you think you could tell my mother that?

UNIT 9 – HEALTH IN THE BALANCE

Pages 162 and 163, Exercises 2A, 2B, 3A, and 3B

Announcer: Hello, listeners! And welcome back to "Getting Started." Most of you are probably aware of the importance of well-being and the impact it has on our daily routines. Maintaining a healthy lifestyle will help you be the best, most productive student or employee you can be.

Joining us today are two health experts who will share a few tips for well-being. Anna Martin teaches fitness classes at a local gym, and Kenzo Jin is a family nutritionist and author of several cookbooks for healthy eating. Thanks for joining us today!

Anna, let's start with you. Can you share a few health tips with our listeners?

Anna: Sure! I believe the most important key to well-being is to engage in regular physical activity. Studies show that major health problems such as obesity, diabetes, and heart disease are often caused by lack of physical activity. Exercising every day can help you live a long, healthy life. That's why, in my opinion, a gym membership is the best gift you can give yourself. A good gym offers a variety of fitness equipment, such as weights and exercise machines, as well as a variety of group exercise classes, like yoga, Pilates, aerobics, cycling, and dance. I recommend following a balanced exercise plan, with a combination of cardio and strength training. If you don't have the time or money to join a gym, then try walking as much as possible. Research indicates that you should walk at least 10,000 steps per day, or about five miles total. Some experts even claim walking is a miracle cure for diabetes and heart disease.

Another extremely important health tip is to drink plenty of water. Most people don't drink enough water every day. Studies show we need about 8-10 glasses of water a day. Your body uses water to regulate its temperature and maintain bodily functions. We lose water in almost every activity, including breathing and digesting food but even more is lost when we're working and sweating, so it's especially important to drink lots of water and stay hydrated while exercising I suggest always

Audio Script **287**

Audio Script

carrying a water bottle, especially when you go to the gym. Another tip is to set up a reminder on your phone to drink some water every hour.

Announcer: Thanks, Anna. Those are great tips. Now, let's turn to Kenzo. What are your best tips for promoting well-being?

Kenzo: Well, I agree with Anna that exercise is important, but I disagree that it's the most important aspect of well-being. I think the most significant tip is to stick to a healthy diet. You should start by eating whole, unprocessed foods as often as possible. It's a fact that fresh fruits and vegetables contain more nutrients than canned or processed foods. Experts say we need at least five servings of fruits and vegetables per day, but I personally feel we should aim for nine or ten. Researchers estimate that if everyone ate ten servings of fruits and vegetables every day, approximately 7.8 million premature deaths could be prevented. I know ten servings of fruit and vegetables sounds like a big goal, but it is easily achieved by adding some delicious chopped fruit to your breakfast cereal, putting lettuce and tomatoes on your sandwich for lunch, having a nice salad before dinner, or serving a refreshing fruit smoothie for dessert.

I can think of lots of simple ways to modify your diet. For example, in my experience, it is helpful to have fruits and vegetables washed, cut, and ready to eat. That way, when you're tempted to snack on potato chips, you can reach for some tasty strawberries or carrot sticks instead. You also need to include grains and protein in your diet. When choosing grains, remember to look for whole food. Research shows that whole wheat bread is better than white bread, and brown rice is better than white rice. As far as protein goes, I recommend lean meat that is baked or broiled instead of fried. Fish and chicken are great options. Boiled eggs are another easy source of protein. If you're a vegetarian, nuts and beans can be used to satisfy your daily protein needs.

One more tip, in addition to diet and exercise: get a good night's sleep. Sleep is vital to our overall health and well-being. Experts say we need about 8 hours of sleep each night. It's good for your memory and good for your heart. And some studies show that sleep may help prevent weight gain. I believe a key recommendation for healthy diet *and* sleep is to avoid eating close to bedtime. And it's also important to avoid digital monitors and screens when you're trying to go to sleep. Don't watch TV or use your phone or tablet in bed. Instead, try reading a book.

Announcer: So it seems the key to well-being starts with exercise, water, a healthy diet, and sleep. Thank you again to our guests today for sharing their expert health advice.

Pages 170 and 171, Exercise 2A, 2B, and 3A

Therapist: Hello, Omar! Please come in and have a seat. What brings you in today?

Omar: I'm not sure. I've never been to a psychologist or therapist. My doctor suggested I seek counseling because I haven't been sleeping well, and I've been having headaches and chest pains. My doctor couldn't identify any underlying health issues. She thinks my problems are caused by stress and anxiety. But I don't agree. I'm having physical health symptoms, not mental problems. In my opinion, counseling won't solve my problems.

Therapist: Hmmm. That's a common misconception. A distinction is often made between mental and physical health, but the mind and body are more connected than you might think. Scientific evidence indicates that stress and anxiety may lead to the physical health problems you've described. Why don't we try to figure out what's going on?

Omar: Sure.

Therapist: Could you describe your typical mood? Do you feel generally happy or sad, or do your moods go up and down like a roller coaster?

Omar: Up and down, I guess. Sometimes I'm happy, but most of the time, I'm tired and stressed out. I don't even want to get out of bed some mornings. I guess I'm suffering from depression, but I'm not sure. How can you tell when someone is depressed?

Therapist: Great question. Not all sadness constitutes depression. It's perfectly healthy to feel a little sad and upset sometimes. Common life events, such as the end of a relationship or financial troubles, can cause periods of depression. But true depression persists for weeks or months and might occur with no obvious trigger or event. A depressed person often has no idea where the sadness comes from. Does this sound like you?

Omar: No, not at all. I always know exactly why I'm sad.

Therapist: Good. Let's start there. What makes you feel sad?

Omar: Well, I've been working towards a promotion at work for years, but now that I've finally been promoted to manager, I don't like my new role. The work is very demanding. I'm trying to finish my master's degree, but I can't keep up with both school and work. I worry that I'm letting my employer down.

Therapist: It sounds like you're dealing with a lot of stress. In my opinion, a moderate amount of stress can be a very good thing. It provides healthy motivation. But the key word is *moderate*. When your stress levels rise too high, you may experience sleep loss and physical health problems, just as you've described.

Omar: So what do I do?

Therapist: Learn how to manage your stress. You're taking the first step by talking to a therapist. A therapist will help you think through your problems and ask questions such as: Is your stress helping you by pushing you to work hard, or is it overwhelming you? A therapist can also help you put a positive spin on a problem. And if you can't find a positive spin, he or she can help you think of ways to change the situation.

Another helpful tip is to exercise. For stress management, doctors recommend exercise because it increases the production of endorphins, which are your brain's feel-good neurotransmitters. Personally, I find running to be the best way to deal with my own stress. Do you play sports or do any kind of physical activity?

Omar: I used to play in a soccer league, but I quit because I didn't have enough time.

Therapist: Can you try to make time? A soccer league provides physical activity, plus it gives you an opportunity to socialize with friends. That's another tip. Spend time with your friends. It gives you a chance to talk and helps you avoid feeling alone.

Omar: You're right. I did feel a lot better when I was playing soccer, and I was sleeping a lot more.

Therapist: Sleep is another important factor. Research shows that quality sleep helps you deal with stress. When you're tired, you become more irritable. Try to put your worries on pause when you go to sleep.

One last thing – it's important to give yourself breaks. Make some time for yourself each week to do something for fun. It could be watching a movie, going to the beach, hiking, anything that you enjoy and look forward to.

Omar: That sounds awesome, but I would feel guilty. I have way too much work.

Therapist: I understand why you feel that way, but remember your mental health affects your physical health. If you are happier and healthier, you'll be a better student and employee.

Page 180, Exercise 1A

Bank Teller: Next.

Customer 1: Good morning. I'd like to deposit my paycheck into my checking account, please.

Bank Teller:] Did you fill out a deposit slip?

Customer 1: Oh, no. I'm sorry.

Bank Teller: I'll do it, but you should remember to do it before you stand in line next time.

Customer 1: Okay. Well, thanks.

Bank Teller: Yep. Right. Who's next?

Customer 2: I need some change. Can I get 5 rolls of quarters, 5 of dimes and …

Bank Teller: Whoa! Slow down.

Customer 2: 5 rolls of quarters, 5 rolls of dimes, and 5 rolls of nickels. Also, I need 100 ones.

Bank Teller: That's going to take some time… Huh. Here you are.

Bank Manager: Excuse me, Ellen. Can I speak with you for a moment?

Bank Teller: Of course.

Bank Manager: Are you okay today?

Bank Teller: Uh, no. Not really.

Bank Manager: Are you still having problems at home?

Bank Teller: Yes. Things are really hard right now.

Bank Manager: Okay, well, while I understand things aren't going well at home, I still expect you to display a positive attitude at work. You need to be more pleasant to our customers - no matter how you are feeling. Representing the bank with a cheerful manner is part of your job.

Page 180, Exercise 2C

Bank Teller: Can I help the next customer?

Customer 1: Good morning.

Bank Teller: Good morning! How can I help you today?

Customer 1: I'd like to deposit my paycheck into my checking account, please.

Bank Teller: I can help you with that. Did you fill out a deposit slip yet?

Customer 1: Oh, no. I'm sorry.

Bank Teller: No problem at all. I'll take care of it for you.

Customer 1: Thanks so much!

Bank Teller: My pleasure! See you next time.

Customer 2: I need some change. Can I get 5 rolls of quarters, 5 of dimes and…

Bank Teller: Oh, I'm sorry. I'm moving a little slowly today. Can you repeat that?

Customer 2: 5 rolls of quarters, 5 rolls of dimes, and 5 rolls of nickels. Also, I need 100 ones.

Bank Teller: Let me work on that for you…. Here you are.

Customer 2: Thanks!

Bank Teller: No problem at all! Have a great day.

Bank Manager: Excuse me, Ellen. Can I speak with you for a moment?

Bank Teller: Of course.

Bank Manager: I just wanted to check in with you. How are things today?

Bank Teller: Ahhh… Things are really hard at home right now.

Bank Manager: I'm sorry to hear that. But you're doing a very good job of showing a positive attitude at work.

Bank Teller: Thanks. It actually helps me to be here. It's keeping my mind off the situation at home. What do they say, umm, "fake it until you make it"?

Bank Manager: Well, I certainly appreciate it, and the customers do, too.

UNIT 10 – NAVIGATING HEALTHCARE

Pages 182 and 183, Exercises 2A, 2B, and 3A

Amira: What's wrong, Hana? You're squinting and making funny faces.

Hana: My vision is blurry. Actually, my vision has been a little distorted for a few days now. I'm not sure what's going on.

Amira: Well, since you're having vision problems, you should go to the optometrist to have your eyes evaluated.

Hana: Given that I went to the eye doctor just a few weeks ago, I'm sure nothing is wrong with my eyes. I had a complete exam, and the doctor updated the prescription for my contact lenses. Therefore, my eyes are fine. Either my eyes are totally healthy, or they're not.

Amira: Granted you just saw the optometrist, but the prescription might not be right for you. Sometimes doctors make mistakes, so maybe that's the problem. I wonder why you even wear contacts. If I were you, I would go to an ophthalmologist and ask about Lasik surgery because it's so easy and affordable these days.

Hana: What's the difference between an optometrist and an ophthalmologist?

Amira: An optometrist can examine your eyes and prescribe glasses or contacts. An ophthalmologist can actually perform operations on the eyes.

Hana: So an ophthalmologist is both an eye doctor and a surgeon?

Amira: Basically, yes. As I was saying, you should get Lasik surgery. Nobody wears contacts or glasses anymore. These days, everyone gets laser surgery to correct their vision.

Hana: I don't think so, Amira. I'm reluctant to have surgery on my eyes. I'm happy with my contacts, and I know plenty of people who still wear glasses or contacts.

Amira: Well, if I needed glasses, I would get Lasik surgery like everyone else I know. But in any case, you should see a different eye doctor to figure out why your eyes are bothering you.

Hana: But it might not be my eyes. I'm also having headaches, and I feel a little dizzy. I think something is possibly wrong with my brain.

Amira: That's scary! Did you fall or hit your head recently, or do anything else that could cause a brain injury?

Hana: Well, no. But I've been reading a lot of health blogs, and I learned that blurred vision and headaches can mean you have a brain tumor.

Amira: That seems a bit extreme. Brain tumors are extremely rare.

Hana: I definitely think that's what this is. I'm worried it will spread to other parts of my brain and maybe to other organs. Tumors spread quickly. I need to get this taken care of immediately. Since it's a problem with my brain, I should probably see a neurologist. Or should I call an oncologist first, since it's probably cancerous?

Amira: You're jumping to a lot of conclusions. Blurred vision and headaches are common symptoms for a lot of conditions, aren't they? It could be high blood pressure, or diabetes, or any number of health issues. We could call Uncle Yusef and ask for advice. He's a doctor.

Hana: But he's a dermatologist. Nothing is wrong with my skin.

Amira: Oh, that's right. For some reason, I thought he was a cardiologist.

Hana: No, you're thinking of Mom's other brother, Uncle Hamad. He's the cardiologist. But I'm not having heart problems, so I don't need a cardiologist either.

Amira: Since we have no idea what the problem is, why don't you start with our regular family doctor. Dr. Lin can give you a full physical exam and help you figure out what steps to take next. Besides that, a specialist will most likely want to confer with your regular doctor. Give Dr. Lin's office a call and see if you can get an appointment this afternoon. I'll drive you over there.

Hana: OK. I guess you're right. I can start there.

Amira: Good. And stay away from those blogs and medical sites for now! They are only scaring you.

Page 183, Exercise 3B
Narrator: Number 1.

Amira: Well, since you're having vision problems, you should go to the optometrist to have your eyes evaluated.

Hana: Given that I went to the eye doctor just a few weeks ago, I'm sure nothing is wrong with my eyes. I had a complete exam, and the doctor updated the prescription for my contact lenses. Therefore, my eyes are fine. Either my eyes are totally healthy, or they're not.

Narrator: Number 2.

Amira: As I was saying, you should get Lasik surgery. Nobody wears contacts or glasses anymore. These days, everyone gets laser surgery to correct their vision.

Hana: I don't think so, Amira. I'm reluctant to have surgery on my eyes. I'm happy with my contacts, and I know plenty of people who still wear glasses or contacts.

Amira: Well, if I needed glasses, I would get Lasik surgery like everyone else I know.

Narrator: Number 3.

Hana: But it might not be my eyes. I'm also having headaches, and I feel a little dizzy. I think something is possibly wrong with my brain.

Amira: That's scary! Did you fall or hit your head recently, or do anything else that could cause a brain injury?

Hana: Well, no. But I've been reading a lot of health blogs, and I learned that blurred vision and headaches can mean you have a brain tumor.

Amira: That seems a bit extreme. Brain tumors are extremely rare.

Hana: I definitely think that's what this is. I'm worried it will spread to other parts of my brain and maybe to other organs. Tumors spread quickly. I need to get this taken care of immediately. Since it's a problem with my brain, I should probably see a neurologist. Or should I call an oncologist first, since it's probably cancerous?

Amira: You're jumping to a lot of conclusions. Blurred vision and headaches are common symptoms for a lot of conditions, aren't they? It could be high blood pressure, or diabetes, or any number of health issues. We could call Uncle Yusef and ask for advice. He's a doctor.

Page 191, Exercises 2A and 2B
Announcer: Healthcare in the United States is twice as expensive as it is in most other developed countries. Today, we'll discuss possible reasons why healthcare cost is so high in the U.S. With us today, we have Alex Ramsey, a business professor, and Linda Piper, a clinical nurse specialist. Alex, could you begin the conversation by telling us what you consider to be the main reason why healthcare is so expensive?

Alex: Well, the primary reason healthcare costs so much is high administrative costs.

Announcer: What do you mean by administrative costs?

Alex: Healthcare administration services include lots of different activities: processing patient bills and payments, working with insurance companies, finding and hiring doctors and other employees, and maintaining up-to-date technology. Hospitals must also protect patients' privacy and set up security procedures. I know a lot of people enjoy all the choices in our healthcare system, but either we cut back on these costs, or we'll always have the most expensive healthcare system in the world.

Announcer: And do you agree with that argument, Linda?

Linda: Well, I certainly agree that administrative costs are one component of our expensive healthcare system, but I'm not sure if that's the most important factor.

I think the prescription drug industry is the real problem. Have you ever noticed how much you pay when you visit the pharmacy? Most countries have government agencies that negotiate the cost of medications with pharmaceutical companies, but the U.S. does not do that. Instead, pharmaceutical companies are allowed to set the cost of medications themselves. The executives who run these companies care too much about making money.

Alex: Hmmm. I don't know whether I agree with that, Linda. It's true that medications are expensive in the U.S., but that's partly because the U.S. is a leader in developing medications. More than half of all new prescription drugs are first developed in the U.S. Drug companies have the resources to develop new medications because investors put their money into the pharmaceutical industry. If the government regulates prescription prices, it's true that it would help reduce costs, but unfortunately, it could also make investors less interested in the pharmaceutical industry, and that might lead to fewer new drugs being developed.

One area where we could cut costs is the high wages for doctors, specialists, and nurses. We should look to other countries and follow their lead. No other country in the world pays medical professionals so much. If other countries pay lower salaries, then so should we. Did you know the average American doctor receives double the pay of doctors in other countries?

Linda: I wonder if you have any idea how many years of education, training, and internships it takes to become a doctor? There are rigid requirements for getting into medical school, and all doctors in the U.S. must complete a residency program in order to practice. In addition, medical school is very expensive, which I suppose is part of the problem. In other countries, it's easier to get into medical school and many countries don't require a residency program. This is why we have excellent, highly trained doctors. If we reduce the salary, no one will want to go to medical school. We'll end up with much less qualified doctors, or we might not have any doctors at all.

Announcer: This is a fascinating conversation, but we need to take a quick break. We'll continue the discussion when we return…

Page 191, Exercise 3A
Narrator: Number 1.

Alex: Healthcare administration services include lots of different activities: processing patient bills and payments, working with insurance companies, finding and hiring doctors and other employees, and maintaining up-to-date technology. Hospitals must also protect patients' privacy and set up security procedures. I know a lot of people enjoy all the choices in our healthcare system, but either we cut back on these costs, or we'll always have the most expensive healthcare system in the world.

Narrator: Number 2.

Alex: One area where we could cut costs is the high wages for doctors, specialists, and nurses. We should look to other countries and follow their lead. No other country in the world pays medical professionals so much. If other countries pay lower salaries, then so should we. Did you know the average American doctor receives double the pay of doctors in other countries?

Narrator: Number 3.

Linda: I wonder if you have any idea how many years of education, training, and internships it takes to become a doctor? There are rigid requirements for getting into medical school, and all doctors in the U.S. must complete a residency program in order to practice. In addition, medical school is very expensive, which I suppose is part of the problem. In other countries, it's easier to get into medical school and many countries don't require a residency program. This is why we have excellent, highly trained doctors. If we reduce the salary, no one will want to go to medical school. We'll end up with much less qualified doctors, or we might not have any doctors at all.

Page 200, Exercise 1A
Supervisor: Hello?

HR Rep: Hello, this is the HR Office. Christine speaking.

Supervisor: Oh, hi!

HR Rep: Hi! I was just calling because I wasn't sure if you were aware of the upcoming changes to the benefits package.

Supervisor: What? Again?

HR Rep: Yes, I just wanted to walk you through a couple of the most significant differences so you can explain them to your staff.

Supervisor: But we just got a new benefits plan last year.

HR Rep: That's true. But, I think you'll find the changes actually make the plan better for the employees.

Supervisor: Well, that might be, but can you explain why you guys didn't get the right plan to begin with? That would have saved us all a lot of time.

HR Rep: I apologize for any frustration this is causing you.

Supervisor: I think we're all sick of these changes. You guys need to get your act together in the HR Office.

HR Rep: Well, I'm sorry you feel that way. If you'd like to make an appointment to go over the new benefits plan, please let me know.

Audio Script **289**

Audio Script

Page 200, Exercise 2C
Supervisor: Hello?
HR Rep: Hello, this is the HR Office.
Supervisor: Oh, hi!
HR Rep: Hi! I was just calling because I wasn't sure if you were aware of the upcoming changes to the benefits package.
Supervisor: In truth, my staff isn't going to be happy that there are changes.
HR Rep: Yes, I know. I'm sorry. But, I think they'll find the changes actually make the plan better. I just wanted to walk you through a couple of the most significant differences so you can explain them to your staff.
Supervisor: Oh, well, that's good to hear. I'll try to emphasize the positive changes when I share them with my staff.
HR Rep: Yes. We're really excited about the updated plan. We think it will be better for everyone.
Supervisor: Great! I do have to say, though, it's a bit frustrating to have to communicate these changes to the night staff so often. Do you have any suggestions on how I should do it?
HR Rep: We've suggested that supervisors have a meeting with all the staff before the shift starts.
Supervisor: Okay. I can certainly do that. Can I also make a suggestion?
HR Rep: Absolutely!
Supervisor: Would it be possible for your department to offer one-on-one information meetings for anyone who has questions that I can't answer?
HR Rep: That's a great idea. We can certainly do that.
Supervisor: That's perfect! I'll let my staff know they can reach out to you if they have any specific questions.
HR Rep: I really appreciate your professionalism in handling this situation.

UNIT 11 – CITIZENSHIP

Page 202 and 203, Exercises 2A, 2B, and 3A
Announcer: Hello, listeners. Today on "Around Our City," we're pleased to have our sound engineer, Hector, with us. Hector officially became a U.S. citizen yesterday afternoon. Hi, Hector. First of all, I want to say congratulations.
Hector: Thank you very much. Becoming a U.S. citizen was very important to me.
Announcer: So today, in honor of Hector's accomplishment, I'll discuss the series of steps that must be taken in order to become a citizen, and then we'll chat with Hector about the benefits of becoming a citizen.

For those seeking citizenship, the first step is to meet the eligibility requirements. Those requirements include: being at least 18 years old, having lived here as a permanent resident for at least five years, and speaking English. You also have to show good moral character by following the law and understanding and agreeing with the principles of the Constitution.

Second, applicants must download and complete the U.S. citizenship application. The application asks for information about current and past residences, employment history, education, marital status, number of children, and so on.

Next, applicants send the application and fees to the United States Citizenship and Immigration Services, or USCIS. Prior to sending the application, applicants must obtain photocopies of several important documents to verify their information. These supporting documents are submitted along with the application.

Once the application is received, the applicant will be contacted by a USCIS official. That person will give instructions for how to get a criminal background check. Then, applicants have their fingerprints taken and go through the criminal background check process.

After that, applicants take part in a naturalization interview. They answer questions about their application, background, character, and willingness to take an oath of allegiance to the U.S. During the interview, applicants are tested on their English skills and knowledge of U.S. civics.

Next, applicants have to wait patiently for USCIS to either grant or deny citizenship. If citizenship is granted, the final step is to take the Oath of Allegiance to the United States. That's the step Hector went through yesterday. After taking the Oath, the applicant is officially a U.S. citizen.

It's a lengthy process that requires commitment and determination. Let's turn to our guest now. Hector, I know you went through the long, complicated process I just described in order to become a citizen. Was it worth it?
Hector: For me, yes, it was definitely worth it.
Announcer: What do you see as the biggest benefits of U.S. citizenship?
Hector: Well, I've resided in this country for over a decade, since I was only 15 years old. I have so much respect and appreciation for this country. It's my home, and I want to become fully participating as a U.S. citizen. I plan to register to vote right away. Maybe I'll even become an elected official someday. I'd like to serve on the City Council and maybe even run for mayor. Those are the biggest benefits for me personally, but there are several other benefits to becoming a citizen, especially when interacting with other countries. Citizens can petition to bring family members to this country and travel with a U.S. passport. Citizens can also obtain citizenship for their children who were born here or abroad, and become eligible for federal jobs.
Announcer: Well, congratulations again, my fellow American. Thanks so much for speaking with us today. And when you run for public office, you'll certainly have my vote!
Hector: Thanks. I appreciate that!

Page 210, Exercises 2A and 2B
Announcer: Hello, listeners. On today's podcast, we'll speak with Professor Susan Klein from Haymond Community College. Dr. Klein will be talking to us about the process of lawmaking. Welcome, Dr. Klein.

Dr. Klein: Thank you. I'm happy to be here.
Announcer: So tell us, how is a federal law made?
Dr. Klein: First, a law starts as an idea. Anyone can think of the idea for a new law. Then they get others to sign a petition supporting the idea. If they get an adequate number of signatures, they can send it to a congressperson. If the congressperson likes the idea, he or she sponsors it by introducing it into Congress. And then the sponsor tries to gain support for the idea.
Announcer: Ok, so someone has an idea, finds people to support it, then sends it to a congressperson who sponsors it. Then what?
Dr. Klein: Next, the idea is proposed as a bill in the House of Representatives or the Senate. At that point, the bill goes to the appropriate committee. For example, if it's a bill about school reform, it goes to the Education Committee. And then the committee members vote on the bill. If the committee members vote to approve the bill, it goes back to the full House or Senate.
Announcer: And whether it goes to the House or the Senate, depends on whether the bill originally came from a senator or a representative.
Dr. Klein: Exactly. The House and the Senate are the two chambers of Congress. It goes back to the sponsor's chamber. If it passes there, it moves to the other chamber. At that point, the bill can be approved or rejected by that chamber, or it can go back to the original committee for revision. An approved bill goes to the president, who can sign or veto the bill.
Announcer: So signed bills become laws and vetoed bills are killed at the president's desk?
Dr. Klein: Yes and no. When the president signs the proposed legislation, it does indeed become a law. But as for vetoed bills, Congress has three choices. It can simply give up on the bill, or it can make changes to the bill and try again, or it can vote to override the president's veto.
Announcer: So the president's decision isn't the final word?
Dr. Klein: Not necessarily. It's a complicated process. In order to override the president's decision, the vetoed bill requires a vote of two-thirds of both chambers of Congress. That means at least 67 senators and 290 representatives must vote to override the veto. If one chamber or the other doesn't get a two-thirds majority, the president's decision stands and the bill will not become a law. But a two-thirds majority in both chambers of Congress is needed to override the president's veto.
Announcer: This is great information. This is why it's so important to contact our representatives about important legislation.
Dr. Klein: Right. Our elected officials can't represent us unless we speak up. And they are under constant pressure from big business and special-interest groups. Individual citizens need to know what bills have been proposed, and we need to let our representatives know how we feel. If we have an idea about a law that we believe should be passed, we should understand that it may remain only an idea unless we do something about it.
Announcer: Thank you, Dr. Klein, for this valuable information. We'd love to hear from our listeners. Go to our social media page where you can share your ideas for proposed legislation and post your thoughts about bills that are currently being considered in Congress.

Page 220, Exercise 1B
Employee: You asked to see me?
Personnel Manager: Uh, yes, Nadia. Come on in. So, I heard that you are having some trouble getting along with the five new line employees?
Employee: Yes, I am. Their food stinks. They take too many breaks. They don't speak English and it's impossible to work with them.
Personnel Manager: I'm surprised to hear this from you. I mean, you are an immigrant to this country, yourself.
Employee: Yes, but I'm not like them! I worked hard to become an American. They should do the same.
Personnel Manager: Well, at this company, we respect individual differences. Not everyone is in the same boat, and it is not acceptable for you to make jokes about people's culture or tell another employee to learn English or find another job. If I hear of this happening again, you will be written up.

Page 220, Exercise 2C
Narrator: Conversation between Nadia and a co-worker
Employee: It feels good to take a break, doesn't it?
Co-worker: Yeah, it's been a long day!
Employee: How are you adjusting to living and working here?
Co-worker: Oh, it's good but tough at times. I enjoy working here, but I miss my country and my family.
Employee: I understand. I remember feeling the same way when I came here… Mmm…what do you have heating up in the microwave?
Co-worker: Oh, it is a special dish from my country. Would you like to try it?
Employee: Oh, thank you… it's delicious! Thanks for sharing with me.
Narrator: Conversation between the Personnel Manager and Nadia
Personnel Manager: Nadia, do you have a minute?
Employee: Sure.
Personnel Manager: I just wanted to let you know that I really appreciate the way you are working with our new employees. You are patient and helpful. You're a great example of the company policy of showing respect for individual differences. In fact, I've even recommended you for the Employee of the Month award.
Employee: Oh my goodness! That's great! But, I really enjoy working with my coworkers. I remember how I felt when I was in their shoes - so anything I can do to help, I am happy to do.

UNIT 12 – RIGHTS AND RESPONSIBILITIES

Page 222 and 223, Exercises 2A, 2B, 3A, and 3B

Host: What is the difference between a right and a responsibility? Do citizens and non-citizens living in this country have the same rights and responsibilities? To help answer these questions, we've invited attorney Joseph Brown to our show. Thanks for joining us, Joe.

Joseph: It's my pleasure.

Host: So let's start with our first question. Could you explain the difference between a right and a responsibility?

Joseph: Of course. A right is something you may do if you want to. Everyone in this country has the right to freedom of expression and freedom of assembly. That means you're allowed to express whatever opinions you may have, and you may assemble, or gather, for any purpose, as long as it's a peaceful gathering. A responsibility, on the other hand, is an obligation, or something that you have to do. Not fulfilling your responsibilities may be punishable by law.

Host: What are some examples of civic responsibilities?

Joseph: Well, first of all, everyone must obey the law. That means you can't commit any crimes. This responsibility includes local, state, and federal laws. Following the law is required for everyone living in the United States, no exceptions.

One example of a responsibility that is reserved only for citizens, is participating in federal elections.

Host: But isn't that a right, not a responsibility? I've never looked this up, but my assumption has always been that participating in elections is completely voluntary. I don't think you can be punished for not participating.

Joseph: You make a good point. It's true that the law does not require citizens to vote. But imagine what our predecessors had to do to give us the right to vote. I believe that not bothering to exercise that right is disrespectful to the memory of those who gave their lives for us to have this privilege. Free and fair elections are the foundation of our democracy. It's a shame that not every eligible voter participates in our elections. If you're a citizen, please make it a priority to vote for your elected officials.

But I'll get off my soapbox and talk about other responsibilities. Another responsibility that is reserved only for citizens is jury duty. A jury is a group of citizens in a courtroom that listens to a trial. The jury decides the outcome of a trial. If you're a citizen and you get a jury summons, which is a court letter to serve on a jury, you must respond. It is not optional.

Another important responsibility is registering with the Selective Service. This is required for almost all men, both citizens and non-citizens, who are between 18 and 26 years old. When a man registers for the Selective Service, he tells the government that he is available to serve in the U.S. Armed Forces. Men can register at a U.S. post office or online at the Selective Service website.

The last responsibility I want to mention is paying taxes. The Constitution gives the federal government the power to collect taxes, so like it or not, we all have to pay federal income taxes every year by April 15, unless we file for an extension. The government uses that revenue to pay the nation's debts, to defend us, and to provide for the needs of the country.

Pages 230 and 231, Exercises 2A, 2B, and 3A

Podcast Host: If you watch a television crime show, you'll likely hear a police officer spell out a person's rights by citing the well-known statements: "You have the right to remain silent. Anything you say can and will be used against you in a court of law. You have the right to have an attorney present during questioning. If you cannot find an attorney, one will be appointed for you." Have you ever wondered why officers do that? Well, you're about to find out. On today's show, we're discussing one of the most famous Supreme Court cases, "Miranda v. Arizona."

First, some background information. The Constitution gives rights to people suspected of a crime. The Founding Fathers knew that governments could be unjust. They worried that government authorities could do whatever they wanted to people once they accused the people of being criminals. So when they wrote the Constitution, they added protections for people who might have been wrongly accused. The right to remain silent and the right to an attorney are two of those protections.

OK, now here's the famous case. In 1963, Ernesto Miranda, who was accused of kidnapping and raping an 18-year-old woman, was brought to the police department for questioning. Miranda admitted that he was guilty and had committed the crime. However, he had not been told that he could use or invoke his Fifth Amendment Right, which is the right to remain silent.

At the trial, his defense attorney asked the court to throw out the confession, which was the only evidence against Miranda. Miranda's confession was not thrown out, and he was found guilty.

However, Miranda's attorney took the case to the higher courts, and in 1966 the Supreme Court reversed the decision of the lower court. The Supreme Court decided that the statements Miranda made to the police could not be used as evidence, since Miranda had not known his rights.

But not knowing his rights, which made his confession illegal, did not let Miranda get away with his crime. The judicial system still worked. New evidence was found against Miranda. He was found guilty at a second trial, and he did go to prison.

The Miranda case established an important procedure for police officers. Since then, police have been required to read or tell suspects their rights before interrogating them.

Television has helped make the Miranda Rights well-known, but crime dramas have also contributed to some misconceptions. On TV shows, you often see police officers stopping someone on the street, and you hear them reading the person his or her rights. Actually, police are required to read these rights only to people whom they are about to take into custody and question. The police can arrest someone without asking questions, in which case, the police don't have to read the person any rights. Also, police don't have to read someone his or her rights to ask for personal information such as the person's name and address. So you may now be wondering if you're required to answer questions about your personal information. That depends on the state. In some states you are, in some states you're not, and in some states, you're only required to show an ID, such as a driver's license. It's best to play it safe: If you're approached by an officer, be polite and respectful, and answer basic identification questions.

But you do not need to answer any further questions, especially if the questions make you uncomfortable or you're not sure of the answer. Please note that in all states, it is illegal to provide the police with information that is false, so never give an officer a fake name or address.

Page 240, Exercise 1B

Susan: Hey, Mark! Have you seen this new memo?

Mark: Ugh! Another new memo? Not yet. Hmm.

Susan: I'm really upset about how they are taking away our longer lunch break.

Mark: Really? I mean, I guess I'd rather have one long break instead of three shorter ones, but the overall time isn't changing. At least they're not shortening our time for breaks.

Susan: Well, that's true. But, this new policy is going to be a real problem for me. I usually use my lunch break to shop for groceries and run errands. Thirty minutes just isn't long enough to do all the stuff I need to do.

Mark: Why don't you do it after work?

Susan: I have to pick up my kid from daycare right at 5:00.

Mark: That's tough.

Susan: It's just not fair. This policy is a bad policy. It makes life so much harder for working parents and for other people, too.

Mark: I think you have a good point. Why don't you give your supervisor your feedback about the policy?

Susan: Oh, I don't know. I mean, why bother? They won't listen to me anyway. The management doesn't care what I think.

Mark: Do you think so? I bet your supervisor would like to hear from you. You should tell her what you think. It's important to try to fix things that aren't working. Otherwise, how will things ever improve?

Page 240, Exercise 2C

Mark: Hi! How's it going?

Susan: Really good, actually.

Mark: Oh

Susan: Yeah, I took your advice talked to my supervisor. She said that the policy had been changed because it was difficult to manage the department when workers were taking long breaks at the same time. There were times that no one was on the floor working. She said she was open to other suggestions, but the old lunch break policy just wasn't working.

Mark: Well, that makes sense.

Susan: So, I spent some time over the weekend thinking about the problem, and I sent her an email with a suggestion.

Mark: What was your idea?

Susan: Well, I proposed that we be allowed to take longer lunch breaks two days a week on a rotating schedule. The other two days we would follow the new policy.

Mark: Wait, what? So, two days a week, I would get a long lunch break and three days a week, I'd get three shorter breaks?

Susan: Exactly! But my long breaks might be on different days than yours. That way, we're not all gone on long breaks at the same time.

Mark: That *is* a good idea. What did she say?

Susan: She thanked me for the feedback and said she appreciated that I took the initiative to let her know about the problem and suggest a solution. She said she would think about it.

Index

ACADEMIC SKILLS

Critical thinking
  comparing and contrasting
    of earning potential of
      educational levels, 54–57
    marking compare-and-
      contrast relationships in
      texts, 56
    signal words for, 43
    of two jobs, 57, 59, 248–250
  making inferences, 223
Numeracy: graphs and charts
  of advantages and
    disadvantages, 51
  bar graphs, 6, 55, 75, 94, 95,
    129, 154
  of carbon footprint, 130
  of career choice strategies, 2
  of cause-and-effect
    relationships, 111
  of climate change effects, 122
  of conflict resolution options, 70
  of cyberbullying responses, 149
  of digital age pros and cons,
    142, 143
  of earnings potential of
    educational levels, 56
  of facts vs. opinions, 171, 176
  of financial management
    strategies, 42
  of gerunds and infinitives, 4
  of goals, 8
    public health, 169
    SMART, 11
  of green jobs, 129
  of healthcare costs, 191
  of housing crash causes, 89
  of inferences, 236
  infographics, 71, 76, 177
  of interests and skills, 3
  of job interview answers, 29
  of job search strategies, 22
  line graphs, 195
  of main ideas of articles and
    paragraphs, 15, 35, 55,
    75, 95, 109, 115, 135,
    155, 175, 189, 195, 215,
    235
  of main ideas of podcasts,
    210, 222
  of main ideas of presentations,
    17
  of main ideas of speakers, 30,
    62
  of main ideas of weather and
    news reports, 102, 103,
    110
  of natural disaster effects,
    110, 111

organizational charts, 215
  process diagrams, 211
  of tips for well-being, 162
  of tone and audience, 78
  Venn diagrams, 56
  of workers' rights laws, 209
  of workplace dilemmas and
    solutions, 69
Numeracy: math skills
  budgeting, 46–47
  costs
    of climate change, 134
    of college, 54
    of health insurance plans,
      188–189
    of healthcare, 190–191, 195
    of obesity, 174
  income and salaries
    at green jobs, 129
    minimum wages, 208
    spent on housing, 47, 94–97
  medication instructions,
    186–187
  percentages
    in budgets, 46
    of carbon dioxide emissions,
      134, 138
    of computer and cell phone
      ownership, 194, 196
    of cyberbullying, 148
    of electric cars, 129
    of homeless people, 82
    of income spent on housing,
      47, 94–97
    of increase in cost of
      college, 54
    in infographics, 177
    of mortgage interest rates
      and down payments, 91
    of people achieving goals,
      9–10
    of recycling, 129
    of renting vs. buying
      homes, 89
    of unemployment, 89, 209
    of voters, 234, 238
  screen time, 154–155
  statistics, 97
Presentations
  on affordable housing, 97,
    253–254
  checklists for, 17, 57, 97, 137,
    177, 217
  on climate change, 137,
    258–259
  on comparing two jobs, 57,
    248–249
  delivery of, 57
  on famous person, 16, 243–244

keeping audience's attention in,
    137
  note-taking in preparation for,
    16, 243, 248, 253, 258,
    263, 268
  on obesity problem, 177,
    263–264
  templates for organizing, 244,
    249, 254, 259, 264, 269
  about U.S. government
    organization, 217,
    268–269
  using infographics for support
    in, 177
  using quotations for support in,
    217
  using statistics for support in,
    97
Reading
  about accessible healthcare,
    194–197
  about affordable housing, 94–97
  about Bill of Rights, 228–229
  of campaign propaganda,
    234–237
  about Cesar Cruz, 14–17
  about climate change, 134–137
  about community practices
    supporting public health,
    168–169
  of cover letters, 34–37
  about cyberbullying, 148–149
  about earning potential of
    educational levels, 54–57
  evaluating evidence for
    relevance and sufficiency
    in, 156
  evaluating problems and
    solutions in, 96
  evaluating reliability of sources
    in, 157
  evaluating soundness of
    reasoning in, 196, 197
  about excessive screen time,
    154–157
  about green jobs, 128–129
  about housing crash, 88–89
  identifying causal chain
    components in, 136
  identifying facts vs. opinions in,
    176
  identifying main ideas and
    details in, 14–17
  infographics as support in, 76
  about job interviews, 28–29
  making inferences in, 236
  of maps
    GPS, 106–107
    time zone, 206–207

marking cause-and-effect relationships in, 116
marking compare-and-contrast relationships in, 56
about obesity, 174–177
paraphrasing after, 36
about planning for big purchases, 48–49
about severe weather events, 108–109, 114–117
about SMART goals, 8–9
for steps in process, 216
summarizing of, 36
about tornadoes, 114–117
about U.S. government organization, 214–217
about workers' rights, 74–77, 208–209
about workplace dilemmas, 68–69
Writing
of arguments
about accessible healthcare, 199, 266–267
about climate change, 139, 260
identifying components of valid arguments in, 138
about limiting children's screen time, 159, 261–262
logical reasoning in, 199
recognizing hasty generalizations in, 238
relevant and sufficient evidence as support in, 158
about reliability of news articles, 239, 271–272
checklists for, 19, 39, 59, 79, 99, 119, 139, 159, 179, 199, 219, 239
commas in, with adjective clauses, 232–233
of compare-and-contrast essays, about two jobs, 59, 250
compare-and-contrast signal words in, 58
complex sentences for flow in, 118
of cover letters, 34–39
introductions to, 38
reading about, 34–37
tailored to specific job, 39, 246–247
of email to elected official, 219, 270
of essay conclusions, 98

giving examples in, 19
incorporating evidence in, 159
about interests, skills, and career goals, 19, 245
matching tone to audience and purpose in, 78
with note-taking templates, 243, 247, 248, 253, 256, 258, 261, 263, 266, 268
objective, 79
in passive voice
impact on tone, 178
using effectively, 179
of problem-solution essays
about affordable housing, 99, 253
about obesity, 179, 265
about processes, 119, 257
qualifiers to avoid hasty generalizations in, 238
revising fragment and run-on sentences in, 198
revising to be clear and concise, 218
about severe weather, 119, 256–257
of summaries and paraphrases, 36
templates for organizing, 252, 255, 257, 260, 262, 265, 267, 272
of topic sentences, 18
of workplace incident reports, 79, 251–252

CIVICS

Life skills
career goals, 1–20
describing action steps for achieving, 12–13
identifying career choice strategies, 2–3
identifying SMART goals, 8–11
using career assessment tools, 6–7
citizenship, 201–220
describing process of becoming citizen, 202–203
describing process of bill becoming law, 210–211
describing U.S. government organization, 214–217, 268–269
identifying workers' rights, 208–209
interpreting time zone maps, 206–207

civic rights and responsibilities, 221–240
evaluating campaign propaganda, 234–237
evaluating reliability of news articles, 239, 271–272
identifying responsibilities, 222–223
identifying rights in Bill of Rights, 228–229
identifying rights of people accused of crimes, 230–231
interpreting citations and law enforcement resources, 226–227
digital age, 141–160
describing cyberbullying, 148–149
describing dangers of texting and driving, 150–151
describing impact of excessive screen time, 154–157
evaluating social media for reliability, 146–147
exercising self-discipline with digital devices, 160
identifying pros and cons of, 142–143
limiting children's screen time, 159, 261–262
environmental issues, 121–140
describing climate change, 122–123
describing green jobs, 128–129
limiting carbon footprint, 130–131
promoting responsible waste disposal, 126–127
providing examples of climate change, 134–137
finances, 41–60
creating budget, 46–47
earning potential of educational levels, 54–57
evaluating strategies for big purchases, 50–51
explaining steps for managing, 42–43
green job salaries, 129
income spent on housing, 94–95
minimum wages, 208
preparing for big purchases, 48–49
health, 161–180

Index **293**

Index

describing causes and effects of obesity, 174–177, 263–265
describing community practices supporting public health, 168–169
identifying benefits of preventive healthcare, 166–167
identifying tips for well-being, 162–163
identifying ways to manage mental health, 170–171
healthcare, 181–200
contacting specialists for specific health needs, 182–183
describing factors increasing cost of, 190–191
evaluating strategies for accessible healthcare, 194–197
following medication instructions, 186–187
interpreting health insurance plans, 188–189
writing about accessible healthcare, 199, 266–267
housing, 81–100
describing affordable housing problems and solutions, 94–97, 99, 253–255
describing home loan requirements, 90–91
describing homelessness problem, 82–83
explaining causes and results of housing crash, 88–89
percentage of income spent on, 47, 94–97
using resources to explore housing options, 86–87
weather, 101–120
describing effects of natural disasters, 110–111
explaining science of tornadoes, 114–117
identifying safety measures for severe weather, 108–109
making use of reports on, 102–103
providing examples of climate change in, 134–137
using GPS to choose routes, 106–107

writing about severe weather, 119, 256–257

GRAMMAR

Adjective clauses, 84–85
punctuation of, 232–233
reducing to adjective phrases, 92–93
Adjective phrases, 92–93
Adjectives
comparative, 44–45
nouns and possessive nouns as, 204–205
participial, 212–213
superlative, 52–53
Adverbs
comparative, 44–45
superlative, 52–53
Clauses, 92
adjective, 84–85
punctuation of, 232–233
reducing to adjective phrases, 92–93
Contractions, in modals, 224
Expressions of condition, 124–125
Expressions of possibility, 24–25
Expressions of purpose, reason, and contrast, 64–65
Gerunds
describing career goals and action steps using, 12–13
sharing interests and preferences using, 4–5
Infinitives
describing career goals and action steps using, 12–13
sharing interests and preferences using, 4–5
Nouns
as adjectives, 204–205
possessive, as adjectives, 204–205
Phrases, 92
adjective, 92–93
Polite requests, with *would you mind,* 72–73
Polite suggestions, with modals, 24–25
Possessive nouns, as adjectives, 204–205
Questions
Wh-, embedded, 184–185
yes/no, embedded, 192–193
Sentences
complex, 118
compound, 118
fragment and run-on, 198
simple, 118

Verbs
active voice, 164–165
using strategically, 172–173
future continuous, making predictions with, 144–145
modals
of deduction, 224–225
for polite suggestions and expressions of possibility, 24–25
passive voice, 164–165
using strategically, 172–173
past continuous, 152–153
past participle, 212–213
past perfect, 152–153
present participle, 212–213
present perfect, 32–33
present perfect continuous, 32–33
real conditional
future, 104–105
present, 104–105
simple future, making predictions with, 144–145
simple past, 152–153
unreal conditional
future, 112–113
past, 132–133
present, 112–113

LISTENING

About carbon footprint, 130–131
About career choice strategies, 2–3
For causal chain components, 123, 131
For cause-and-effect relationships, 103, 111
About citizenship process, 202–203
About civic responsibilities, 222–223
About civic rights of people accused of crimes, 230–231
About climate change, 122–123
For comparison and contrast, 43
About conflict resolution, 70–71
About digital age pros and cons, 142–143
For evidence supporting speaker's claims, 143, 151
For evidence supporting speaker's message, 63
For facts vs. opinions, 163, 171
About financial management, 42–43
About healthcare costs, 190–191
About home loan requirements, 90–91

294 Index

About homelessness in U.S., 82–83
About job interviews, 30–31
About job promotion, 62–63
About job search strategies, 22–23
For key points that summarize messages, 23
For logical fallacies, 183
For main ideas and supporting details, 3
About making big purchases, 50–51
Making inferences in, 223
About managing mental health, 170–171
About natural disasters, 110–111
For problem-and-solution relationships, 83
About process of bills becoming laws, 210–211
About promoting well-being, 162–163
For signal words, 3
   cause-and-effect, 103
   compare-contrast, 43
   conclusion, 143
   emphasis, 123
   fact and opinion, 163
   inference, 223
   problem-and-solution, 83
   process/sequence, 203
   reasoning, 183
   summary, 23
About SMART goals, 10–11
For soundness of reasoning, 183
About specialists for specific health needs, 182–183
For steps in process, 203
About texting and driving, 150–151
About weather reports, 102–103

SPEAKING

Acknowledging contributions of others, 123
Asking for clarification, 63
About big purchases, 50–51
About carbon footprint, 130–131
About career choice strategies, 2–3
About citizenship process, 202–203
About civic responsibilities, 222–223
About civic rights of people accused of crimes, 230–231
About climate change, 122–123
Collaborating with others as team, 3

About conflict resolution, 70–71
About digital age pros and cons, 142–143
Disagreeing politely, 143
Encouraging participation, 43
Ending collaborative tasks on positive note, 223
Extending contributions of others, 103
About financial management, 42–43
About healthcare costs, 190–191
About home loan requirements, 90–91
About homelessness in U.S., 82–83
Infographics as support in, 71
About job interviews, 30–31
About job promotions, 62–63
About job search strategies, 22–23
About managing mental health, 170–171
About natural disasters, 110–111
Notes for support in, 23
Paraphrasing contributions of group, 163
Presenting evidence supporting points in, 83
About process of bills becoming laws, 210–211
About promoting well-being, 162–163
Reminding others about collaboration guidelines, 203
About SMART goals, 10–11
About specialists for specific health needs, 182–183
About texting and driving, 150–151
About weather reports, 102–103

WORK SKILLS

Career awareness
   about green jobs, 128–129
   identifying career choice strategies, 2–3
   ranking factors influencing job promotion, 62–63
   using career assessment tools, 6–7
Employability skills, 21–40
   answering interview questions, 28–29
   demonstrating willingness to learn, 20
   evaluating job interview dos and don'ts, 30–31

identifying strategies for job searches, 22–23
projecting self-confidence, 40
using online resources to find job information, 26–27
writing cover letters, 34–39, 246–247
Workplace safety, 208–209
Workplace skills, 61–80
   demonstrating professionalism, 200
   demonstrating responsibility, 100
   displaying positive attitude, 180
   emailing, 220
   evaluating conversations for conflict resolution, 70–71
   exercising leadership, 120
   exercising self-discipline with digital devices, 160
   identifying solutions to workplace dilemmas, 68–69
   identifying workers' rights, 203–209
   log of, 241–242
   negotiating for conflict resolution, 80
   protecting workers' rights, 74–77
   ranking factors influencing job promotion, 62–63
   respecting individual differences, 220
   responding to customer needs, 60
   taking initiative, 240
   using training resources to identify growth opportunities, 66–67
   working with team, 140
   writing workplace incident reports, 79, 251–252

Index **295**

Credits

Photo Credits

Front Cover: Mike Harrington/Getty Images (main image); Moof/Getty Images (top left); Thomas Barwick/Getty Images (top right).

Frontmatter: Page vi (cell phone): Tele52/Shutterstock; vi (student book cover): Mike Harrington/Stone/Getty Images, Moof/Getty Images, Thomas Barwick/Getty Images; vi (workbook cover): Mike Harrington/Stone/Getty Images, Moof/Getty Images, Thomas Barwick/Getty Images; vi (teacher's edition cover): Mike Harrington/Stone/Getty Images, Moof/Getty Images, Thomas Barwick/Getty Images; vi (p. 50): Andriy Popov/123RF; vi (man driving): Air Images/Shutterstock; vii (p. 21): Mentatdgt/Shutterstock; viii (p. 22): Rawpixel.com/Shutterstock; x (p. 26): Ollyy/Shutterstock; xi (p. 34): Andrii Yalanskyi/123RF; xiii (p. 40): Antonio Guillem/123RF; xxii (top): Courtesy of Sarah Lynn; xxii (center): Courtesy of Ronna Magy; xxii (bottom): Courtesy of Federico Salas-Isnardi.

Unit 1
Page 1: Aleksandr Davydov/123RF; 2: Maridav/Shutterstock; 8: UntitledImages/E+/Getty Images; 10: Dmitry Kalinovsky/Shutterstock; 11: Shutterstock; 14: Dr. Cesar Cruz.

Unit 2
Page 21: Mentatdgt/Shutterstock; 22: Rawpixel.com/Shutterstock; 26: Ollyy/Shutterstock; 28: MoMo Productions/DigitalVision/Getty Images; 30: Shutterstock; 31: Dean Drobot/Shutterstock; 34: Andrii Yalanskyi/123RF; 40: Antonio Guillem/123RF.

Unit 3
Page 41: Terry Vine/DigitalVision/Getty Images; 42: Shutterstock; 48: Evgeny Atamanenko/Shutterstock; 50: Andriy Popov/123RF; 52 (left): Hennadii Tantsiura/Shutterstock; 52 (right): Hennadii Tantsiura/Shutterstock; 60: Allesalltag/Alamy Stock Photo.

Unit 4
Page 61: Aleksandr Davydov/Alamy Stock Photo; 62: Luis Alvarez/DigitalVision/Getty Images; 66: Ariwasabi/Shutterstock; 68: Dean Drobot/123RF; 70:Prostock-studio/Shutterstock.

Unit 5
Page 81: Dario Earl/Alamy Stock Photo; 82: Tana888/Shutterstock; 86 (top left): New Africa/Shutterstock; 86 (top center): Roman Babakin/Shutterstock; 86 (top right): BakerJarvis/Shutterstock; 86 (bottom left): Roman Babakin/Shutterstock; 86 (bottom center): Ekkamai Chaikanta/Shutterstock; 86 (Bottom Right): Gau Meo/Shutterstock; 88: Andy Dean Photography/Shutterstock; 90: William Potter/Shutterstock; 100: Fizkes/Shutterstock.

Unit 6
Page 101: Rasica/Shutterstock; 102 (center): Dmac/Alamy Stock Photo; 108 (top left): Drew McArthur/Shutterstock; 108 (top center): Shufu Photoexperience/Shutterstock; 108 (top right): VisualCommunications/iStock Unreleased/Getty Images; 108 (bottom): New Africa/Shutterstock; 110 (left): Nevenm/Shutterstock; 110 (center): Ignazio Pier Paolo Nisi/EyeEm/Getty Images; 110 (right): Sdecoret/Shutterstock; 120 (left): Fizkes/Shutterstock; 120 (right): Weedezign/Shutterstock.

Unit 7
Page 121: Arco Images GmbH/Therin-Weise/Alamy Stock Photo; 122: 24Novembers/Shutterstock; 126: Sean Prior/123RF; 128: Zstockphotos/123RF; 130: Thodonal/123RF; 134: Satori/123RF; 140: Mangostar/Shutterstock.

Unit 8
Page 141: Antoniodiaz/Shutterstock; 142: Rawpixel.com/Shutterstock; 148: Belchonock/123RF; 150: JRP Studio/Shutterstock; 151: Mattz90/Shutterstock; 154: Jasmin Merdan/123RF; 160: CREATISTA/Shutterstock.

Unit 9
Page 161: Mosuno Media/Westend61 GmbH/Alamy Stock Photo; 162: Siam.pukkato/Shutterstock; 166: Sjenner13/123RF; 168 (top left): Ron and Joe/Shutterstock; 168 (top center): Svetla/Shutterstock; 168 (Top Right): Natianis/Shutterstock; 168 (bottom): Jason Kolenda/Alamy Stock Photo; 170: Africa Studio/Shutterstock; 171: Prostock-studio/Shutterstock; 174: Ariel Skelley/DigitalVision/Getty Images; 180: Image Source/Getty Images.

Unit 10
Page 181: SDI Productions/E+/Getty Images; 182: Kurhan/123RF; 188: Hvostik/Shutterstock; 190: Dndavis/123RF; 194: Dolgachov/123RF; 200 (left): Thevisualsyouneed/123RF; 200 (right): Mykola Kravchenko/123RF.

Unit 11
Page 201: NPS Photo / Alamy Stock Photo; 202: Jana Shea/Shutterstock; 208: Naqiuddin zakaria/Shutterstock: 210: Tonobalaguer/123RF.

Unit 12
Page 221: Hill Street Studios/DigitalVision/Getty Images; 222: Alina555/E+/Getty Images; 228: Gekaskr/123RF; 234: Artinspiring/123RF; 235: Burlingham/Shutterstock.